ARCO

Master the

MILLER

ANALOGIES TEST®

ARCO

Master the

MILLER

ANALOGIES TEST®

19th Edition

William Bader
Daniel S. Burt
David M. Killoran

THOMSON

PETERSON'S™

Australia • Canada • Mexico • Singapore • Spain • United Kingdom • United States

An ARCO Book

ARCO is a registered trademark of Thomson Learning, Inc., and is used herein under license by Thomson Peterson's.

About Thomson Peterson's

Thomson Peterson's (www.petersons.com) is a leading provider of education information and advice, with books and online resources focusing on education search, test preparation, and financial aid. Its Web site offers searchable databases and interactive tools for contacting educational institutions, online practice tests and instruction, and planning tools for securing financial aid. Thomson Peterson's serves 110 million education consumers annually.

For more information, contact Thomson Peterson's, 2000 Lenox Drive, Lawrenceville, NJ 08648; 800-338-3282; or find us on the World Wide Web at www.petersons.com/about.

Editors: Joe Krasowski and Linda Seghers; Production Editor: L. A. Wagner;
Manufacturing Manager: Ray Golaszewski; Composition Manager: Gary Rozmierski;
CD Producer: Carol Aickley; CD Online Test Preparation Associate: Halima Samad;
CD Designer: Christina Chattin; CD Web Tester: Jared A. Stein

ISSN: International Standard Serial Number information available upon request.

ISBN 10: 0-7689-2307-7
ISBN 13: 978-0-7689-2307-0

Printed in the United States of America

10 9 8 7 6 5 4 3 2 1   08 07 06

Nineteenth Edition

OTHER RECOMMENDED TITLES

ARCO Master the GRE

ARCO Master the GMAT

ARCO The Master Series LSAT

Contents

Before You Begin

HOW THIS BOOK IS ORGANIZED

Congratulations! You've just picked up a Miller Analogies Test (MAT) preparation guide that is quaranteed to help you improve your score. This book has all the answers to your questions about the MAT. It includes eight practice tests and solid test-taking advice. Use it to maximize your results and get into the graduate program of your choice.

"Top 10 Ways to Raise Your Score" lists some of the most valuable test-taking strategies to help you score high on the MAT.

Part I provides essential information about the MAT, including how to register for the test, where to take it, and how it is scored. You'll also learn what subjects are covered, what the common analogy categories are, and what traps to watch out for.

Part II is the heart of the preparation program. This section contains eight full-length practice tests followed by detailed answer explanations for each analogy.

The **Appendixes** are broken into four sections. Appendixes A–D contain lists of terms that frequently appear in MAT analogies but that could be unfamiliar to some test-takers. These lists cover Greek and Roman mythology, nations of the world, key math terms, and vocabulary. Use the appendixes as well as other resources to learn or review as much material as possible. The more you know, the less you'll have to guess. Appendix E lists the Controlled Testing Centers located throughout the United States and Canada.

SPECIAL STUDY FEATURES

ARCO Master the Miller Analogies Test is designed to be as user-friendly as it is complete. To this end, it includes several features to make your preparation easier.

Overview

Each chapter begins with a bulleted list of topics that will be covered in the chapter. You know immediately where to look to find a particular area of interest.

Summing It Up

Each chapter ends with a point-by-point summary that captures the most important topics. The summaries are a convenient way to review the content of a chapter.

In addition to the above features, be sure to look in the margins of the book for extra information and advice, including:

Note

Notes highlight critical information pertaining to the Miller Analogies Test.

Tip

Tips draw your attention to valuable concepts and advice for tackling all types of Miller Analogies Test questions.

Alert!

Alerts do just what they say—alert you to common pitfalls you might encounter while preparing for and taking the Miller Analogies Test.

ABOUT THE CD

ARCO Master the Miller Analogies Test is published with a CD. The CD contains two additional full-length computer-based practice tests that are just like the real thing. These tests will help prepare you for taking the computer-based version of the MAT.

YOU'RE WELL ON YOUR WAY TO SUCCESS

You've made a decision to apply to graduate school. *ARCO Master the Miller Analogies Test* will prepare you for the steps you'll need to take to achieve your goal—from scoring high on the MAT to being admitted to the graduate program of your choice.

GIVE US YOUR FEEDBACK

Thomson Peterson's publishes a full line of resources to help guide you through the graduate school admission process. Peterson's publications can be found at your local bookstore and library and you can access us online at www.petersons.com.

We welcome any comments or suggestions you may have about this publication and invite you to complete our online survey at www.petersons.com/booksurvey. Or you can fill out the survey at the back of this book, tear it out, and mail it to us at:

Editorial Department
Thomson Peterson's
2000 Lenox Drive
Lawrenceville, NJ 08648

Your feedback will help us to provide personalized solutions for your educational advancement.

Top 10 Ways to Raise Your Score

Learning to think past the obvious and to analyze implied meanings and relationships requires some creative thought. Because this is often what it takes to solve analogies, you may find the following strategies helpful:

1. **Determine what the analogy is all about.** That is, try to define the terms that are given.

2. **Read all the answer options carefully.** Do not select the first answer that seems to make sense. One choice may seem to fit, but a better answer choice may also be listed. Remember that you are looking for the best answer among options that may all make sense. Many of the incorrect answer options on the MAT have some relationship to the term that you are trying to match it with. However, you will correctly solve the analogy only when you determine which answer option most accurately reflects the same relationship as two given terms that form a complete pair.

3. **Consider alternative meanings of words.** If at first an analogy doesn't seem to make sense, you may need to think of one or more of the terms in a different way.

4. **Reorder the analogy.** Sometimes you can clarify the relationship in an analogy by changing the order of the terms, since the location of the terms of a valid analogy can be changed without affecting the meaning.

5. **Check the part of speech.** The answer you choose should be the same part of speech as the corresponding term in the complete pair.

6. **Make informed guesses.** If you are uncertain about the answer to an analogy, try to eliminate the answer options that do not seem to fit and then guess from among the remaining options. If you make a random guess at an answer, you have a one-in-four chance of getting it right. However, the more options you can eliminate, the better the odds are that you will guess the correct answer.

7. **Postpone difficult items.** The MAT is a timed test. Because you have 60 minutes to answer 120 questions, you have an average of 30 seconds to solve each analogy and to indicate your answer. Because each item counts the same, you may not want to spend too much time on an analogy if the relationship is not apparent to you. Your time would be more wisely used by moving on to the next analogy and returning to analogies that were unclear to you after you have completed the ones that are clear to you. Try to use the last 10 minutes or so of the testing period to go back to these items.

8. **Answer every question.** Your score is based entirely on the number of correct answers you provide, and there are no extra penalties for incorrect answers. If you have no idea what the correct answer is to a MAT item, go with a hunch or a straight guess, since an item that you leave unanswered definitely cannot contribute to your score. If you guess, at least you have a one-in-four chance of getting the item right.

9. **Mark your answers carefully.** If you are taking a paper-and-pencil version of the MAT, be sure to mark your answer to each numbered item in the corresponding number on your answer sheet. Be especially careful if you skip items. Putting the right answer in the wrong place can be extremely frustrating, and will result in an inaccurate score. Also, make sure your marks completely fill the circles. Do not mark more than one answer for each question. Questions with more than one circle marked are always scored as incorrect.

10. **If you are taking a computer-based version of the MAT, confirm that the answer you intend is the one that is displayed on the screen before you move to the next item.** You will have the opportunity to review your answer choices at the end of the test if time permits.

PART I

MAT BASICS

All About the MAT

WHAT IS THE MAT?

The MAT, officially known as the Miller Analogies Test, is a high-level test of mental ability and critical-thinking skills. The test is required by many graduate schools as part of the admissions process for a master's or a doctoral program. It also can be used as a basis for granting financial aid for graduate students. Some employers require the test when recruiting for jobs that require high levels of critical thinking and problem-solving ability.

The Miller Analogies Test won't take up your whole day. It has only 120 questions, which you're given 60 minutes to answer. These 120 questions cover a broad range of subjects. While an extensive vocabulary is essential, the questions also assume a better-than-average grasp of literature, social studies, mathematics, and science.

The MAT includes 100 core items, which count toward your score, and 20 experimental items that are being tried out for use on future test forms, which do not affect your score. Examinees may not request to take only the core items or to have only the core items scored. Because you will not know which items are experimental and which count toward your score, it is very important that you do your best on all the items on the test. There are several equivalent forms of the MAT administered in both computer-based and paper-and-pencil versions.

chapter 1

If you aren't familiar with the topic of the question, even an obvious analogy becomes difficult. It is helpful to know, though, that all questions carry equal weight and that there's no penalty for an incorrect response. So, it is definitely worth your time to work through all the questions and answer as many as you can as quickly as you can. Then you can go back and answer the questions you skipped, even if your answer is a guess. When your time is up, your answer sheet should be filled in completely.

REGISTERING FOR THE MAT

The MAT is given at more than 400 Controlled Testing Centers, which are generally located at colleges and universities. The MAT is not given on a particular date; instead, the testing centers set their own dates and fees. Controlled Testing Centers are located throughout the United States and in Puerto Rico, Canada, Great Britain, Japan, Venezuela, Saudi Arabia, and the Philippines.

The testing centers are listed in Appendix D and in the *Miller Analogies Test Candidate Information Booklet*. To obtain a copy of this booklet, contact Harcourt Assessment at the following address:

Harcourt Assessment Inc.
Miller Analogies Test
Customer Relations
19500 Bulverde Road
San Antonio, TX 78259

Phone: 800-622-3231 or 210-339-8710
Fax: 888-211-8276
Web site: www.milleranalogies.com
E-mail: MATscoring.services@harcourt.com

Test Fee

You pay the fee for taking the MAT directly to the same Controlled Testing Center where you apply to take the MAT. MAT test fees vary from Center to Center. When you apply to take the MAT, the Controlled Testing Center will tell you what its fee is and how to pay it. This fee covers one personal Score Report that will be mailed to you and up to three Official Transcripts that will be sent to schools you specify when you take the MAT.

Optional Fees

Any additional services that you would like beyond the personal Score Report and the three Official Transcripts are optional and require additional fees. You must pay any additional fees directly to Harcourt Assessment. Payment must be in the form of a money order payable to Harcourt Assessment, Inc. If you are paying from outside the United States, you must submit an international money order payable in U.S. dollars. Do not send cash or personal checks.

The following fees are required for the additional services:

- Domestic Alternative Testing Site Fee: $149

- Foreign Alternative Testing Site Fee: $149 plus additional fee for a specific site

- Replacement Retest Admission Ticket Fee: $25

- Transcript Fee: $25 per transcript

- Handscoring Fee: $35

Testing Center Guidelines and Procedures

When you report to the Controlled Testing Center (CTC), be prepared for the following:

- **You must arrive on time.** Testing will begin promptly. Those who arrive after the test begins will not be admitted.

- **If you are taking a pencil-and-paper version of the MAT, take several sharpened No. 2 pencils with erasers with you.** For accurate scoring of your Answer Booklet, only No. 2 (or HB) pencils can be used. You cannot use mechanical pencils or felt-tip, ballpoint, or other ink pens.

- **In order to be admitted for testing, whether taking a computer-based or paper-and-pencil version of the MAT, candidates must take two forms of nonexpired positive identification with them.** One form of identification must include a photograph and signature, such as a driver's license, school identification card, or a government-issued identification card or passport. A second form of positive identification may include a credit card (with or without a photograph), library card, or utility bill with your name and address appearing exactly the same as on your other form of identification.

- **You may not take calculators (including watch calculators), books, papers, notes, pagers, PDAs, cell phones, cameras, recording devices, or any other electronic devices or reference materials into the testing room.**

- **No food or beverages may be taken into the testing room.**

- **You may not wear or take a hat with a bill or brim into the testing room unless worn for a religious or medical reason, in which case you must submit an Accommodations Request Form and the appropriate documentation explaining the need for this accommodation.**

- **You may not ask any questions after the test begins, so be sure to ask any questions that you have before the test starts.**

SCORE REPORTING

After you take a paper-and-pencil version of the MAT, your Answer Booklet will be mailed to Harcourt Assessment for scoring and score reporting. It may take up to a week from the time you take the test to the time your test is scored and processed. If you take a computer-based version of the MAT, your personal information and your test answers will be transmitted and processed immediately. Regardless of which version of the MAT you take, you will receive your personal Score Report two to three weeks from the date that Harcourt Assessment receives your test.

Your personal Score Report will provide you with the scaled score and percentile ranks you received on the MAT. Your scaled score and percentile rank are derived from your raw score—the number of items you answered correctly. Because there are multiple test forms of the MAT (each with a unique set of items) and the MAT is currently given in two formats (paper-and-pencil and computer-based), there may be slight variations in the level of difficulty between the tests. For this reason, a given raw score for two different test forms, or for the same form in different formats, may not always have precisely the same meaning. To compensate for these slight variations, Harcourt Assessment converts all MAT examinees' raw scores to scores on a common scale based on the performance of the current norm group.

This reporting method makes it possible to compare the MAT scaled scores of one test form to another and from one format to another. The MAT scaled scores currently range from 200 to 600 with a mean (average) of 400. The percentile ranks on your personal Score Report indicate the percentage of examinees in the norm group who received a scaled score lower than yours. Percentile rank ranges from 1 to 99.

Specifying Score Recipients

Score recipients are those schools and other institutions that you designate to receive an Official Transcript of your MAT score. Official Transcripts will only be sent to accredited institutions of higher education and approved fellowship or scholarship organizations.

In addition to a personal Score Report, your test fee includes up to three Official Transcripts that will be sent to score recipients specified when you take the MAT. You are not required to specify any score recipient when you take the MAT. However, if you later wish to send Official

Transcripts to score recipients not specified at the time you take the MAT, you may do so by sending a written request to Harcourt Assessment with an additional Transcript Fee ($25) for each one requested.

In your Answer Booklet (for paper-and-pencil versions) or online (for computer-based versions), you will specify up to three score recipients by entering code numbers from a list that will be provided before the test begins. Failure to properly complete this section may cause your scores to be reported to the wrong school or not at all. In addition, if you indicate a school code incorrectly at the time of the test, you will later be required to pay a Transcript Fee to have an Official Transcript sent to that score recipient. Under no circumstances will you be able to change or delete a recipient school code after the examination has been completed.

If you plan to have your scores sent to an institution other than a North American post-graduate institution, or have reason to believe that your institution may not be included in the list of codes, make sure you have the complete mailing address of that score recipient with you when you report to take the MAT. You will be able to enter the mailing information for this institution in a special area on the Answer Booklet (for paper-and pencil versions) or online (for computer-based versions).

An incomplete address will cause a deletion of your request. You should keep a record of which score recipients you request your Official Transcript be reported to, in case there is a problem in the mailing or handling of your request.

The No Score Option

Should you decide while taking the MAT that you do not want the score you earn reported to anyone, you will be able to request that your test not be scored by choosing the No Score Option. How to exercise this option will be explained to you at the CTC before the test begins.

If you choose the No Score Option, your score will not be reported to any score recipients, and there will be no reportable record of your having taken the MAT. You will be sent a Retest Admission Ticket, which you must use if you wish to retake the MAT, and a blank personal Score Report.

If at the time of testing you choose the No Score Option, this request is irrevocable, and the fees you paid will not be refunded. Any later request to score your test and report your scores will not be honored.

RETAKING THE MAT

You can indeed take the test again. In fact, if you need to submit scores more than two years after taking the test, you should take the test again. If more than five years have passed since you took the MAT, you *must* take the test again. Harcourt Assessment won't report scores that are more than five years old.

When you take the MAT, your score report will include a retest admission ticket. You must present this ticket when you retake the test in order to ensure that you are not given the same test form that you took before. If you are given the same test form within twelve months of the original test, the retest score will be voided and you will have to make new arrangements to retake the test.

SUMMING IT UP

- The MAT is a test of mental ability and critical-thinking skills.

- The test consists of 120 questions that you must answer in 60 minutes.

- You can choose to take the MAT in either a pencil-and-paper or computer-based (CBT) format.

- MAT scaled scores range from 200 to 600 with a mean (average) score of 400.

All About Analogies

chapter 2

OVERVIEW

- **Solving MAT analogies**
- **The most common analogy categories**
- **The most common analogy subject areas**
- **Traps to avoid**
- **What smart test-takers know**
- **Time-cruncher study plans**
- **Summing it up**

When you get right down to it, analogies are about relationships. They test your ability to see a relationship between two words and to recognize a similar relationship between two other words. The key to analogy success is being able to express the relationship between the words in a pair.

In a MAT analogy question, you are given three capitalized words. Two of the words have a relationship. The task is to find a word among the answer choices that has the same relationship to the third capitalized word.

MAT analogies are presented in a kind of mathematical shorthand. For example, you may see:

DAY : SUN :: NIGHT : (A. ray, B. cold, C. moon, D. dark)

The : sign is read as *is to*, and the :: sign is read as *as*. So, the analogy reads "day is to sun as night is to?" The correct answer is (C), moon, because that makes a pair in which the two words are related in the same way as day and sun.

If you substitute letters for the words in this analogy, it might read, "A is to B as C is to D." However, this is not the only possible relationship in MAT analogies. In some questions, the relationship will be "A is to C as B is to D." That means that when you're solving a MAT analogy, if you can't find a relationship between the first and second words (A and B), look for a relationship between the first and third words (A and C).

11

It also helps to remember that the relationship of the words in the analogy is the same on both sides of the "equation." For example, if the pattern is A → B, and if A is a part of B, then the second relationship has to be C → D, and C is a part of D. Here's an illustration:

MINUTE : HOUR :: MONTH : (A. week, B. year, C. time, D. calendar)

The minute-to-hour relationship is a part-to-whole relationship. Looking at the answer choices, you might be tempted to select choice (A), *week*. However, that would reverse the relationship, making it month-to-week, or whole-to-part. The correct answer, (B), *year*, completes the analogy with an equal part-to-whole relationship.

SOLVING MAT ANALOGIES

With MAT analogies, your first order of business is to determine what the analogy is all about. That is, you'll want to define the terms that are given. Take a look at the words in the analogy and review what they mean. Sometimes, two of the words will help you define an unfamiliar third word; sometimes, the answer choices will clarify a mystery word. In any case, you need to know the meanings of the words so that you can figure out the relationship in the analogy.

After you've read the analogy carefully, follow these 5 steps:

❶ Find a relationship between two of the capitalized words.

❷ Make up a sentence that expresses the relationship.

❸ Try out your sentence by substituting the third capitalized word and each of the answer choices.

❹ If more than one answer seems to work, go back and make your sentence express a more specific relationship.

❺ Choose the best answer. If none of the choices works exactly, choose the one that works best.

Now, use the 5-step method to solve the following examples.

DOCTOR : SYMPTOM :: DETECTIVE : (A. mystery, B. crime, C. police, D. clue)

In this analogy, it's pretty clear that there is a strong relationship between the first two words (A and B). A symptom gives a doctor an idea about how to identify an illness. You then know that a similar relationship should exist between words three and four (C and D). So, while a detective knows that a crime has been committed, what's really needed is an idea about how to identify a solution: a clue. So, the correct answer is (D), *clue*.

DOCTOR : DETECTIVE :: SYMPTOM : (A. illness, B. mystery, C. crime, D. clue)

If the analogy were presented this way, you would not be able to establish a relationship between A and B, but you could find one instead between A and C. This tells you that the companion relationship is between B and D. The correct answer, *clue*, is the same.

TIP

What if the first two words don't seem to be related at all? A MAT question may be based on the relationship between the first and third words and the second and fourth words.

ALERT!

If none of the answer choices seems exactly right, remember that the directions tell you to choose the best answer. The correct answer won't necessarily be a perfect fit, but it will work better than the other choices.

PLAY : AUDIENCE :: BOOK : (A. writer, B. publisher, C. plot, D. reader)

There is a clear relationship between *play* and *audience:* A play entertains an audience. Now, substitute the third word and each answer choice in the same sentence.

(A) A *book* entertains a *writer*. Possible, but that's not the main purpose of a book.

(B) A *book* entertains a *publisher*. Again, possible, but not the main purpose.

(C) A *book* entertains a *plot*. This makes no sense at all, so it can be eliminated right away.

(D) A *book* entertains a *reader*. This is the answer. The sentence parallels the original sentence and also is true.

BRIM : HAT :: HAND : (A. glove, B. finger, C. foot, D. arm)

A brim is part of a hat, so you could say that this is a part-to-whole relationship. This is probably enough to complete the analogy, but if the choices don't work, you need to go back and make the relationship more specific. You might rephrase your sentence as "brim is the outside part of a hat," or "brim is not a necessary part of a hat." Once you have a solid relationship, move on to the third word and the answer choices.

TIP

Think up a simple sentence to express the relationship between the words in an analogy pair. Then, use the sentence to try out answer choices until you find one that fits.

By process of elimination, work with the answer choices to establish a relationship that's parallel to the one between *brim* and *hat*. If you can glance at the choices and eliminate one immediately, do it. In this example, though, each choice has to be considered, keeping the part-to-whole criterion in mind. The first choice, *glove*, certainly has an association with HAND, but it's not a part of *hand*. This can be eliminated.

Now take a look at *finger*. At first glance, *finger* looks pretty good; after all, it is a part of *hand*. However, the relationship you're working with is part-to-whole. Ask yourself, "Does HAND : FINGER match part-to-whole?" No! This follows a whole-to-part relationship, and you know that both sides of the analogy must have the same relationship. Therefore, *finger* is out as a possible choice.

The relationship of *hand* to *foot* is that they are both parts but not part-to-whole. As you move over to *arm*, it becomes clear why choice (D) is the best answer: A hand is indeed part of an arm. This parallels the part-to-whole BRIM : HAT relationship.

When you're solving analogies, be prepared to be flexible. Consider this example:

LETTER : WORD :: SONG : (A. story, B. music, C. note, D. orchestra)

Your first thought is that a letter is a part of a word, so this is another part-to-whole relationship. While all the choices have some logical relationship with *song*, none of the choices completes a part-to-whole relationship. Now you must go back and rethink the relationship. Ask yourself, "How else can *letter* and *word* be connected?" If *letter* is not a part of a word but rather a form of written communication, then it's clear that a word is part of a letter. Now the relationship correctly becomes whole-to-part. When you go back and review the choices, you'll find that as *song* becomes the whole, then *note* becomes the part. You now have your parallel relationship on both sides of the analogy.

If you're really having trouble finding the correct relationship, it might help to read the analogy backward. Be careful, though; if you do determine the relationship this way, remember to make the third and fourth words match the direction of the initial relationship.

The examples you've worked with so far have been A → B/C → D relationships. Let's take a look at an analogy with an A → C/B → D relationship.

HAIL : HALE :: (A. farewell, B. greet, C. hearty, D. taxi) : STRONG

Because *hail* and *hale* are homonyms (they sound alike but are spelled differently), that's probably the relationship you want to go with. However, there's no homonym for *strong*, so you have to go back and look at the relationship again. There really is no other viable relationship between *hail* and *hale*, but there certainly is one between *hale* and *strong*, your B and D words: They are synonyms. Now that you have a valid relationship, it's time to take a look at the choices.

While the phrase "hail and farewell" probably comes to mind, it does not match the synonym relationship. After looking at the others, the only synonym is choice (B), *greet*. The analogy is now balanced—there is a parallel relationship between words on both sides.

THE MOST COMMON ANALOGY CATEGORIES

Most MAT analogies fall into one of the following categories. Knowing what these categories are and looking for them as you tackle each problem will make your job much easier. Here's the list, with samples of each type:

❶ Synonyms or similar concepts

DELIVERANCE : (A. rescue, B. oration, C. liberate, D. demise) :: EXERCISE : PRACTICE

To solve this problem, note that the relationship between the C and D words is that they are synonyms. So, what you're looking for is a synonym for the A word, *deliverance*. Choice (A), *rescue*, fills the bill.

❷ Antonyms or contrasting concepts

(A. hostel, B. hostile, C. amenable, D. amoral) : AMICABLE :: CHASTE : LEWD

The relationship between *chaste* (pure or decent) and *lewd* (obscene or salacious) is that they are opposites. The opposite of *amicable* is choice (B), *hostile*.

❸ Cause and effect

HEREDITY : ENVIRONMENT :: (A. influenza, B. pneumonia, C. hemophilia, D. roseola) : RUBELLA

This is an A : C :: B : D relationship. Something present in the environment (a virus) causes rubella. To balance the analogy, look for something that is caused by heredity, which would be choice (C), *hemophilia*.

❹ Part to whole

LEAF : TREE :: KEY : (A. lock, B. door, C. computer, D. car)

It's clear that a leaf is part of a tree. While a key can be used to open a lock, it is not a part of that lock. However, a key is a part of choice (C), *computer*.

❺ Part to part

FATHER : DAUGHTER :: GILL : (A. fish, B. fin, C. lung, D. wattle)

Father and *daughter* are each part of a family. *Gill* and choice (B), *fin*, are each part of a fish. While *gill* and *fish* might seem to be a match, they represent a part-to-whole relationship.

❻ Purpose or use

GLOVE : BALL :: HOOK : (A. coat, B. line, C. fish, D. curve)

A glove catches a ball, and a hook catches choice (C), *fish*. Even though a hook could possibly catch or hold a coat, it's not as close to the initial relationship.

❼ Action to object

PITCH : FIRE :: (A. coal, B. ball, C. sound, D. slope) : GUN

At first glance, this looks like a synonym relationship between *pitch* and *fire*. The answer choices, however, don't complete the match. Instead, this becomes an A : C :: B : D relationship—you fire a gun and pitch a *ball*, choice (B).

❽ Agent to object

SPRAIN : (A. ankle, B. joint, C. twist, D. swell) :: BITE : ITCH

This one can be problematic until you figure out that *sprain* and *bite* are being used as nouns rather than verbs and that *itch* is a verb. Then, you can use choice (D), the verb *swell*, to complete the relationship of an object causing an action.

NOTE

If you can't find a pair of relationships, change your definition of one or more capitalized words.

⑨ Place

PARAGUAY : BOLIVIA :: SWITZERLAND : (A. Afghanistan, B. Poland, C. Hungary, D. Bulgaria)

Paraguay, Bolivia, and Switzerland are all landlocked countries. Because two of the answer choices, *Afghanistan* and *Hungary*, are also landlocked, you have to narrow the relationship. Paraguay and Bolivia are landlocked countries on the same continent. Only choice (C), *Hungary*, is on the same continent as Switzerland; Afghanistan is in Asia.

⑩ Association

MOZART : MUSIC :: PEI : (A. painting, B. architecture, C. sculpture, D. dance)

The composer Mozart is associated with music in the same way that Pei is associated with choice (B), *architecture*.

⑪ Sequence or time

SAIL : STEAM :: PROPELLER : (A. plane, B. engine, C. jet, D. wing)

Ships were propelled by sail, and then they were propelled by steam. The matching relationship is that planes were propelled by propeller and then by choice (C), a *jet* engine.

⑫ Characteristic or description

(A. scream, B. ear, C. shrill, D. vocal) : PIERCING :: CRY : PLAINTIVE

Just as a cry can be called plaintive, a *scream*, choice (A), can be called piercing. In this analogy, it might help to reverse the order of the pairs, placing *piercing* first, followed by the answer choices, and then by *plaintive* and *cry*. This makes it easier to find the relationship and keeps both sides balanced.

⑬ Degree

WARM : HOT :: BRIGHT : (A. dark, B. dim, C. genius, D. illuminate)

Warm is a lesser degree of temperature than hot. If you think of *bright* as a degree of intelligence rather than of light, then it is a lesser degree of intelligence than choice (C), *genius*. While *illuminate* might be tempting, it doesn't fit the relationship.

⑭ Measurement

ODOMETER : (A. speed, B. distance, C. pressure, D. temperature) :: CLOCK : TIME

There's no surprise here. A clock measures time as an odometer measures choice (B), *distance*.

⑮ **Grammatical**

BROKE : BROKEN :: (A. fled, B. flight, C. flew, D. flung) : FLOWN

In this case, *broke* and *broken* are the past tense and the past participle of the verb *break*. *Flown* is the past participle of *fly*, and the past tense is choice (C), *flew*. MAT grammar analogies can also present parts of speech and plurals.

⑯ **Mathematical**

$12\frac{1}{2}\%$: (A. $\frac{1}{4}$, B. $\frac{1}{5}$, C. $\frac{1}{8}$, D. $\frac{1}{3}$) :: $16\frac{2}{3}\%$: $\frac{1}{6}$

Mathematical MAT analogies can deal with geometrical and numerical relationships as well as equalities, which this analogy covers. Percents are really fractions with denominators of 100, so $16\frac{2}{3}\%$ equals $16\frac{2}{3}$ divided by 100, which is $\frac{1}{6}$. The matching relationship is $12\frac{1}{2}\% = 12\frac{1}{2} \div 100 =$ choice (C), $\frac{1}{8}$.

⑰ **Worker to tool**

PHYSICIAN : (A. hospital, B. patient, C. surgeon, D. X ray) :: ACTUARY : STATISTICS

An actuary is a worker who uses statistics as a tool to calculate insurance premiums. A physician is a worker who uses an X ray, choice (D), as a tool to diagnose and treat a patient.

⑱ **Nonsemantic**

Here are two types of nonsemantic analogies to work with.

HOE : ROE :: THOUGH : (A. rough, B. flood, C. flow, D. how)

This is an analogy that relies on sound rather than on meaning. The strongest relationship among all the words is that they rhyme. This leads you to choice (C), *flow*, as the best answer.

EVIL : LIVE :: STEP : (A. stand, B. stop, C. post, D. pest)

In this analogy, the arrangement and rearrangement of letters in the word create the relationship. *Evil* and *live* have the same letters in different arrangements. By rearranging the letters in *step*, you'll come up with choice (D), *pest*, as the correct answer.

THE MOST COMMON ANALOGY SUBJECT AREAS

MAT analogies are not like the analogies you may have seen on the SAT or the GRE. While those analogies tested your verbal reasoning ability, MAT analogies go beyond mere vocabulary to test your knowledge of the arts, the humanities, and the natural and social sciences. The terms used in MAT analogies can be drawn from specific college courses or general background knowledge. Because the questions cover so many subjects, there is only a handful of questions in any one area. So, even if you never took chemistry, for example, there will be enough questions in subjects you did study to enable you to do well.

Most MAT analogies are based on one of these subject areas:

General knowledge—Sports terminology; relationships between common words; frequently used abbreviations; parts of buildings; universally accepted concepts, such as the relationship between crime and punishment; common metaphors, proverbs, and sayings

Vocabulary—Words usually not used in ordinary conversation but that would be familiar through education and reading

Grammar—Singular and plural nouns, adjective and adverb endings, tenses, participles, prefixes and suffixes

Word study—Spelling, anagrams, homophones, synonyms and antonyms, rhymes, configurations

Literature—Mythology, Shakespeare, ancient and modern drama and poetry, classic and current novels

Music—Musical terms, composers and their works, instruments

Art—Artists and their works, artistic periods

Philosophy—Philosphers, their works and beliefs

History—Ancient world history, modern world history, U.S. history, documents, people, historians

Geography—Ancient and modern place names, place characteristics

Sciences—Biology, chemistry, physics, medicine, psychology, terminology, concepts, people

Mathematics—Algebra, geometry, calculus, terminology, equivalencies, simple calculations

TRAPS TO AVOID

You can raise your MAT score if you watch out for these common analogy traps:

- **Some answers may reverse the sequence of the relationship.** Part-to-whole is not the same as whole-to-part. Cause-to-effect is not the same as effect-to-cause. Smaller-to-larger is not the same as larger-to-smaller.

- **Some answers confuse the nature of the relationship.** Part-to-part [geometry : calculus] is not the same as part-to-whole [algebra : mathematics]. Cause-and-effect [fire : smoke] is not the same as association [walk : limp]. Degree [drizzle : downpour] is not the same as antonyms [dry : wet]. Association [walk : limp] is not the same as synonyms [eat : consume].

- **Some answers create a grammatical inconsistency.** The initial grammatical relationship has to be repeated when the analogy is completed. In the analogy IMPRISONED : LION :: CAGE : PARROT, the relationship is the same on both sides, but the grammatical construction is not the same. In order to be correct, the analogy should read either PRISON : LION :: CAGE : PARROT or IMPRISONED : LION :: CAGED : PARROT. In both examples, the grammatical construction is balanced on both sides of the analogy.

- **Some answers focus on the wrong relationship.** Given an analogy that begins FEATHERS : BEAK, you might think "bird" instead of "part-to-part relationship." To complete the analogy with *wing* and answer choices that include *bird* and *tail*, you might incorrectly choose *bird* rather than the best answer, *tail*.

NOTE

Know the analogy equations. Remember that there are two possible analogy equations:

A : B :: C : D or
A : C :: B : D.

WHAT SMART TEST-TAKERS KNOW

You have 60 minutes to answer 120 MAT questions. Since that means that you only have an average of 30 seconds to answer each question, it is crucial that you do not spend too much time on any one question. If an answer does not appear to you quickly, skip it and move on. If you have time at the end of the test, use that time to return to the questions that you skipped the first time through.

The analogy equation can take two forms. If you can't see a relationship between the first two terms, A and B, try to form a relationship between the first and third terms, A and C. Remember that the analogy equation can be either A is to B as C is to D, *or* A is to C as B is to D.

It's wise to read all the answer choices. Don't choose the first answer you come to that seems right—there may be a better one listed. That's why it always pays to read all the choices before selecting the one that's best.

TIP

Note that the directions ask you to choose the best answer. That's why you should always read all the answer choices before you make your final selection.

A word can have more than one meaning. If you can't see a connection between two of the capitalized terms, try to think of another meaning for one of the words. Often, a question is based on a secondary or less-common meaning of one of the words. For example, *play* may be a verb meaning "to take part in a game or sport," or it may be a noun meaning "a dramatic production." If one meaning doesn't work, try another.

The part of speech of an analogy term is an important clue. In MAT analogies, the correct answer choice will be the same part of speech as the corresponding word in the original pair. In other words, if your original word pair is NOUN : VERB and the third capitalized word is another noun, you know you must look for a verb as the correct answer choice.

Easy questions count just as much as hard ones, so it's in your best interest to answer as many as you can. Don't stop to ponder difficult questions until you've answered every question that's easy for you. Save a little time at the end of the test to go back and rethink any questions you skipped. If you still can't answer a question, remember that there's no penalty for a wrong answer, so take your best guess. If you can eliminate one or more answer choices, you can improve your chances of guessing correctly.

It's smart to keep moving. Don't spend time dissecting difficult analogies. If the answer doesn't come to you right away, guess, mark the question, and move on. If you think you're running out of time, mark all the remaining questions with the same answer choice—you just might get lucky!

Mark your answers carefully. If you are taking a paper-and-pencil version of the MAT, be sure to mark your answer to each numbered item in the corresponding number on your answer booklet. Be especially careful if you skip items. Putting the right answer in the wrong place can be extremely frustrating, and will result in an inaccurate score. Also, make sure your marks completely fill the circles. Do not mark more than one answer for each question. Questions with more than one circle marked are always scored as incorrect.

If you are taking a computer-based version of the MAT, the answer you select is shown on the screen. You will not be able to select more than one answer per item on the screen display, but it is up to you to confirm that the answer you intend is the one that is displayed on the screen before you move to the next item. You will have the opportunity to review your answer choices at the end of the test if time permits.

A watch is a must. On the MAT, time is critical. It's much faster for you to glance at your watch (especially if it has a stopwatch function) than to search around the room for a clock.

TIME-CRUNCHER STUDY PLANS

Plan A: Accelerated

Are you starting to prepare a little later than you had planned? Don't get upset—it happens. You might have to cut some corners, but you can still prepare. Follow this plan if you have at least two weeks and can give it an hour a day:

- *Skim* Chapter 1, "All About the MAT."

- *Study* Chapter 2, "All About Analogies."

- *Take* all eight practice tests and study the explanations.

- *Skim* the Appendixes.

Plan B: Top Speed

If the calendar says that your MAT is coming up in fewer than ten days, go for this superconcentrated study plan:

- *Skip* Chapter 1, "All About the MAT."

- *Study* Chapter 2, "All About Analogies."

- *Take* as many practice tests as time allows.

- *Study* explanations for the practice tests you took.

- *Skip* the rest of the book.

SUMMING IT UP

- The analogy equation can take two forms: A : B :: C : D, or A : C :: B : D.

- There's no penalty for guessing, so answer every question.

- If you don't know the answer, eliminate obviously wrong choices and make an educated guess.

- Follow these steps when solving a MAT analogy:

    1. Find a relationship between two of the capitalized words.

    2. Make up a sentence that expresses the relationship.

    3. Try out your sentence, substituting the third capitalized word and each of the answer choices.

    4. If more than one answer seems to fit, go back and make your sentence express a more specific relationship.

    5. Choose the best answer. If none of the choices fits exactly, choose the one that works best.

PART II

EIGHT PRACTICE TESTS

ANSWER SHEET PRACTICE TEST 1

1. Ⓐ Ⓑ Ⓒ Ⓓ   31. Ⓐ Ⓑ Ⓒ Ⓓ   61. Ⓐ Ⓑ Ⓒ Ⓓ   91. Ⓐ Ⓑ Ⓒ Ⓓ
2. Ⓐ Ⓑ Ⓒ Ⓓ   32. Ⓐ Ⓑ Ⓒ Ⓓ   62. Ⓐ Ⓑ Ⓒ Ⓓ   92. Ⓐ Ⓑ Ⓒ Ⓓ
3. Ⓐ Ⓑ Ⓒ Ⓓ   33. Ⓐ Ⓑ Ⓒ Ⓓ   63. Ⓐ Ⓑ Ⓒ Ⓓ   93. Ⓐ Ⓑ Ⓒ Ⓓ
4. Ⓐ Ⓑ Ⓒ Ⓓ   34. Ⓐ Ⓑ Ⓒ Ⓓ   64. Ⓐ Ⓑ Ⓒ Ⓓ   94. Ⓐ Ⓑ Ⓒ Ⓓ
5. Ⓐ Ⓑ Ⓒ Ⓓ   35. Ⓐ Ⓑ Ⓒ Ⓓ   65. Ⓐ Ⓑ Ⓒ Ⓓ   95. Ⓐ Ⓑ Ⓒ Ⓓ
6. Ⓐ Ⓑ Ⓒ Ⓓ   36. Ⓐ Ⓑ Ⓒ Ⓓ   66. Ⓐ Ⓑ Ⓒ Ⓓ   96. Ⓐ Ⓑ Ⓒ Ⓓ
7. Ⓐ Ⓑ Ⓒ Ⓓ   37. Ⓐ Ⓑ Ⓒ Ⓓ   67. Ⓐ Ⓑ Ⓒ Ⓓ   97. Ⓐ Ⓑ Ⓒ Ⓓ
8. Ⓐ Ⓑ Ⓒ Ⓓ   38. Ⓐ Ⓑ Ⓒ Ⓓ   68. Ⓐ Ⓑ Ⓒ Ⓓ   98. Ⓐ Ⓑ Ⓒ Ⓓ
9. Ⓐ Ⓑ Ⓒ Ⓓ   39. Ⓐ Ⓑ Ⓒ Ⓓ   69. Ⓐ Ⓑ Ⓒ Ⓓ   99. Ⓐ Ⓑ Ⓒ Ⓓ
10. Ⓐ Ⓑ Ⓒ Ⓓ   40. Ⓐ Ⓑ Ⓒ Ⓓ   70. Ⓐ Ⓑ Ⓒ Ⓓ   100. Ⓐ Ⓑ Ⓒ Ⓓ
11. Ⓐ Ⓑ Ⓒ Ⓓ   41. Ⓐ Ⓑ Ⓒ Ⓓ   71. Ⓐ Ⓑ Ⓒ Ⓓ   101. Ⓐ Ⓑ Ⓒ Ⓓ
12. Ⓐ Ⓑ Ⓒ Ⓓ   42. Ⓐ Ⓑ Ⓒ Ⓓ   72. Ⓐ Ⓑ Ⓒ Ⓓ   102. Ⓐ Ⓑ Ⓒ Ⓓ
13. Ⓐ Ⓑ Ⓒ Ⓓ   43. Ⓐ Ⓑ Ⓒ Ⓓ   73. Ⓐ Ⓑ Ⓒ Ⓓ   103. Ⓐ Ⓑ Ⓒ Ⓓ
14. Ⓐ Ⓑ Ⓒ Ⓓ   44. Ⓐ Ⓑ Ⓒ Ⓓ   74. Ⓐ Ⓑ Ⓒ Ⓓ   104. Ⓐ Ⓑ Ⓒ Ⓓ
15. Ⓐ Ⓑ Ⓒ Ⓓ   45. Ⓐ Ⓑ Ⓒ Ⓓ   75. Ⓐ Ⓑ Ⓒ Ⓓ   105. Ⓐ Ⓑ Ⓒ Ⓓ
16. Ⓐ Ⓑ Ⓒ Ⓓ   46. Ⓐ Ⓑ Ⓒ Ⓓ   76. Ⓐ Ⓑ Ⓒ Ⓓ   106. Ⓐ Ⓑ Ⓒ Ⓓ
17. Ⓐ Ⓑ Ⓒ Ⓓ   47. Ⓐ Ⓑ Ⓒ Ⓓ   77. Ⓐ Ⓑ Ⓒ Ⓓ   107. Ⓐ Ⓑ Ⓒ Ⓓ
18. Ⓐ Ⓑ Ⓒ Ⓓ   48. Ⓐ Ⓑ Ⓒ Ⓓ   78. Ⓐ Ⓑ Ⓒ Ⓓ   108. Ⓐ Ⓑ Ⓒ Ⓓ
19. Ⓐ Ⓑ Ⓒ Ⓓ   49. Ⓐ Ⓑ Ⓒ Ⓓ   79. Ⓐ Ⓑ Ⓒ Ⓓ   109. Ⓐ Ⓑ Ⓒ Ⓓ
20. Ⓐ Ⓑ Ⓒ Ⓓ   50. Ⓐ Ⓑ Ⓒ Ⓓ   80. Ⓐ Ⓑ Ⓒ Ⓓ   110. Ⓐ Ⓑ Ⓒ Ⓓ
21. Ⓐ Ⓑ Ⓒ Ⓓ   51. Ⓐ Ⓑ Ⓒ Ⓓ   81. Ⓐ Ⓑ Ⓒ Ⓓ   111. Ⓐ Ⓑ Ⓒ Ⓓ
22. Ⓐ Ⓑ Ⓒ Ⓓ   52. Ⓐ Ⓑ Ⓒ Ⓓ   82. Ⓐ Ⓑ Ⓒ Ⓓ   112. Ⓐ Ⓑ Ⓒ Ⓓ
23. Ⓐ Ⓑ Ⓒ Ⓓ   53. Ⓐ Ⓑ Ⓒ Ⓓ   83. Ⓐ Ⓑ Ⓒ Ⓓ   113. Ⓐ Ⓑ Ⓒ Ⓓ
24. Ⓐ Ⓑ Ⓒ Ⓓ   54. Ⓐ Ⓑ Ⓒ Ⓓ   84. Ⓐ Ⓑ Ⓒ Ⓓ   114. Ⓐ Ⓑ Ⓒ Ⓓ
25. Ⓐ Ⓑ Ⓒ Ⓓ   55. Ⓐ Ⓑ Ⓒ Ⓓ   85. Ⓐ Ⓑ Ⓒ Ⓓ   115. Ⓐ Ⓑ Ⓒ Ⓓ
26. Ⓐ Ⓑ Ⓒ Ⓓ   56. Ⓐ Ⓑ Ⓒ Ⓓ   86. Ⓐ Ⓑ Ⓒ Ⓓ   116. Ⓐ Ⓑ Ⓒ Ⓓ
27. Ⓐ Ⓑ Ⓒ Ⓓ   57. Ⓐ Ⓑ Ⓒ Ⓓ   87. Ⓐ Ⓑ Ⓒ Ⓓ   117. Ⓐ Ⓑ Ⓒ Ⓓ
28. Ⓐ Ⓑ Ⓒ Ⓓ   58. Ⓐ Ⓑ Ⓒ Ⓓ   88. Ⓐ Ⓑ Ⓒ Ⓓ   118. Ⓐ Ⓑ Ⓒ Ⓓ
29. Ⓐ Ⓑ Ⓒ Ⓓ   59. Ⓐ Ⓑ Ⓒ Ⓓ   89. Ⓐ Ⓑ Ⓒ Ⓓ   119. Ⓐ Ⓑ Ⓒ Ⓓ
30. Ⓐ Ⓑ Ⓒ Ⓓ   60. Ⓐ Ⓑ Ⓒ Ⓓ   90. Ⓐ Ⓑ Ⓒ Ⓓ   120. Ⓐ Ⓑ Ⓒ Ⓓ

answer sheet

Practice Test 1

120 QUESTIONS • 60 MINUTES

Directions: Each of these test questions consists of three capitalized words and four lettered words enclosed in parentheses. Two of the capitalized words are related in some way. Find the related words, and establish the nature of the relationship. Then study the four words lettered A, B, C, and D. Select the one lettered word that is related to the remaining capitalized word in the same way that the first two capitalized words are related. Mark the answer sheet for the letter preceding the word you select.

1. BALMY : MILD :: FAITHFUL : (A. explosive, B. docile, C. talkative, D. staunch)

2. BOLD : TIMID :: SQUANDER : (A. disperse, B. hoard, C. query, D. extinguish)

3. WATER : (A. fish, B. ocean, C. island, D. net) :: LAND : LAKE

4. GLASS : RUBBER :: BRITTLE : (A. elastic, B. scarce, C. tempered, D. spheroid)

5. DIAMETER : RADIUS :: (A. 3, B. 8, C. 2, D. 6) : 4

6. GLABROUS : FACTITIOUS :: HIRSUTE : (A. authentic, B. fictional, C. fluent, D. replete)

7. PARANOIA : SCHIZOPHRENIA :: MEGALOMANIA : (A. melancholia, B. carcinoma, C. hepatitis, D. stroke)

8. (A. sales, B. investment, C. management, D. interest) : PROFIT :: LABOR : WAGES

9. STUDENT : (A. backpack, B. briefcase, C. college, D. teacher) :: TRAVELER : SUITCASE

10. DENIGRATE : DEFAMER :: MEDIATE : (A. mathematician, B. arbitrator, C. employer, D. laborer)

11. LAKE WOBEGON : (A. Minneapolis, B. Winesburg, C. Canterbury, D. Minnesota) :: MUDVILLE : CASTERBRIDGE

12. CORNET : OBOE :: (A. cello, B. drum, C. harpsichord, D. xylophone) : GUITAR

13. JANUARY : WEDNESDAY :: JANUS : (A. Thor, B. Apollo, C. Odin, D. Diana)

14. HORSE : (A. equestrian, B. hoofed, C. cabriolet, D. herbivorous) :: TIGER : CARNIVOROUS

15. GOOD : BETTER :: (A. terrible, B. worse, C. improvement, D. bad) : WORST

16. CLAN : FEUD :: NATION : (A. war, B. politics, C. armaments, D. retaliation)

17. ABUNDANCE : ABROGATE :: DEARTH : (A. deny, B. establish, C. abstain, D. absolve)

18. ONOMATOPOEIA : METAPHOR :: SOUND : (A. hiss, B. rhyme, C. saying, D. comparison)

19. SACRAMENTO : HELENA :: ALBANY : (A. New York, B. Little Rock, C. Houston, D. San Francisco)

20. (A. scan, B. feel, C. dear, D. seen) : READ :: REAP : PEAR

21. CAUTIOUS : CIRCUMSPECT :: PRECIPITOUS : (A. premonitory, B. profound, C. stealthy, D. steep)

22. SEISMOGRAPH : GEOLOGY :: ELECTROENCEPHALOGRAPH : (A. bacteriology, B. biology, C. neurology, D. cardiology)

23. ACUTE : VENERATE :: CHRONIC : (A. revere, B. actuate, C. flout, D. repent)

24. (A. toad, B. snail, C. shark, D. alligator) : TURTLE :: TIGER : HUMAN

25. INSTINCT : PLAN :: UNCONSCIOUS : (A. involuntary, B. intentional, C. spontaneous, D. imaginary)

26. INDIA : (A. Sri Lanka, B. Greece, C. Afghanistan, D. Pakistan) :: ITALY : SWITZERLAND

27. SWIM : SWAM :: BURST : (A. busted, B. bursted, C. burst, D. bust)

28. RAISIN : GRAPE :: PRUNE : (A. apricot, B. currant, C. plum, D. berry)

29. GRAM : OUNCE :: LITER : (A. deciliter, B. quart, C. kilogram, D. pound)

30. BEAKER : CHEMIST :: STETHOSCOPE : (A. teacher, B. author, C. doctor, D. dentist)

31. LIMPID : LUCID :: TURBID : (A. torpid, B. muddy, C. truculent, D. serene)

32. MANGO : (A. coconut, B. tomato, C. cabbage, D. apple) :: PAPAYA : PASSION FRUIT

33. $.02^2$: .0004 :: $.001^2$: (A. .000001, B. .0001, C. .0002, D. .000002)

34. SADNESS : PAIN :: FAILURE : (A. medication, B. palliation, C. pleasure, D. injury)

35. AMELIA EARHART : NELLIE BLY :: AVIATION : (A. medicine, B. journalism, C. law, D. prohibition)

36. ROMAN : MANOR :: (A. cleric, B. names, C. patrimony, D. estates) : MANSE

37. LACONIC : FLACCID :: REDUNDANT : (A. succinct, B. firm, C. flimsy, D. wordy)

38. PNEUMATICS : (A. medicine, B. disease, C. physics, D. cars) :: ESKER : GEOLOGY

39. NECKLACE : MEDAL :: ADORNMENT : (A. jewel, B. metal, C. decoration, D. bronze)

40. RIVER : STREAM :: MOUNTAIN : (A. cliff, B. hill, C. canyon, D. peak)

41. HECKLE : BADGER :: (A. stock, B. deplete, C. beaver, D. stylus) : REPLENISH

42. (A. guerrilla, B. terrorist, C. quash, D. mediate) : REBELLION :: NEGOTIATE : TREATY

43. BOTANIST : PLANTS :: GEOLOGIST : (A. trees, B. rocks, C. geography, D. gems)

44. CAT : FELINE :: OX : (A. equine, B. saturnine, C. bovine, D. canine)

45. WOLF : (A. wool, B. sheep, C. ewe, D. ram) :: DOG : CAT

46. (A. $\frac{5}{16}$, B. $\frac{3}{8}$, C. $\frac{2}{6}$, D. $\frac{5}{12}$) : $\frac{9}{24}$ :: $\frac{4}{11}$: $\frac{12}{33}$

47. (A. effusiveness, B. asceticism, C. impudence, D. gullibility) : EPICURIANISM :: CONFORMITY : ICONOCLASTICISM

48. ROOM : CABIN :: HOUSE : (A. camp, B. cottage, C. hotel, D. ship)

49. BRASS : COPPER :: PEWTER : (A. lead, B. zinc, C. silver, D. bronze)

50. COWCATCHER : LOCOMOTIVE :: (A. coda, B. climax, C. epilogue, D. finale) : DENOUEMENT

51. PARIAH : OUTCAST :: ARCHON : (A. archivist, B. magistrate, C. martine, D. constable)

52. (A. cappuccino, B. shamrock, C. wine, D. palm trees) : VODKA :: DEVALERA : STALIN

53. LANCET : CUT :: CHAMOIS : (A. polish, B. pliant, C. smooth, D. sheep)

54. (A. utter, B. elapse, C. exude, D. time) : EMIT :: STEP : PETS

55. SAFE : NECKLACE :: COMBINATION : (A. torque, B. bangle, C. circlet, D. clasp)

56. EXPERIMENT : (A. science, B. elucidation, C. hypothesis, D. investigation) :: EXAMINATION : ACHIEVEMENT

57. BOY : BULLET :: MAN : (A. gun, B. artillery shell, C. holster, D. trigger)

58. ENERVATE : (A. eradicate, B. invigorate, C. disconcert, D. propagate) :: MALICE : BENEVOLENCE

59. EVIDENCE : CONVICTION :: (A. oxygen, B. carbon dioxide, C. match, D. light) : COMBUSTION

60. EDIFICATION : AWARENESS :: AGGRAVATION : (A. distress, B. excitement, C. reduction, D. deliberation)

61. NEWTON : COPERNICUS :: SHAKESPEARE : (A. Fielding, B. Jonson, C. Dickens, D. Defoe)

62. ST. AUGUSTINE : (A. Florida, B. Virginia, C. France, D. Spain) :: JAMESTOWN : ENGLAND

63. SNOW : DRIFT :: (A. hill, B. rain, C. sand, D. desert) : DUNE

64. CATAMARAN : TERMAGANT :: RAFT : (A. grisette, B. spinnaker, C. spinster, D. shrew)

65. $3^2 : 2^3 :: 9 :$ (A. 1, B. 6, C. 4, D. 8)

66. FICTION : NOVELIST :: FACTS : (A. legend, B. story, C. historian, D. research)

67. HARVARD : YALE :: BROWN : (A. Princeton, B. Purdue, C. Emory, D. Dartmouth)

68. CAT : WOLF :: (A. lion, B. dog, C. man, D. tiger) : DUCK

69. WHO : I :: WHOM : (A. we, B. me, C. whose, D. mine)

70. (A. obsequious, B. obstreperous, C. complacent, D. contumelious) : SYCOPHANT :: CONTUMACIOUS : RENEGADE

71. DOWSER : ROD :: GEOMANCER : (A. stones, B. maps, C. plants, D. configurations)

72. MINERVA : ATHENA :: (A. Jupiter, B. Juno, C. Poseidon, D. Apollo) : ZEUS

73. (A. loss, B. victory, C. game, D. team) : WIN :: MEDICINE : CURE

74. SAFARI : SWAHILI :: SALAAM : (A. Arabic, B. shalom, C. peace, D. Africa)

75. ACID : ALKALI :: 6 : (A. 1, B. 4, C. 7, D. 8)

76. PEDESTAL : (A. column, B. sculpture, C. chandelier, D. stone) :: STALAGMITE : STALACTITE

77. BONA FIDE : IN TOTO :: CARTE BLANCHE : (A. eureka, B. status quo, C. avant-garde, D. ersatz)

78. SEA : COAST :: RIVER : (A. inlet, B. delta, C. stream, D. bank)

79. AMOUNT : NUMBER :: (A. lessen, B. augment, C. less, D. enumerate) : FEWER

80. VOLUME : CUBIC METER :: (A. area, B. length, C. capacity, D. mass) : LITER

81. (A. refrain, B. precede, C. sustain, D. foray) : FORBEAR :: ADUMBRATE : FORESHADOW

82. CHAMPION : CAUSE :: (A. signature, B. introduction, C. draft, D. ink) : LETTER

83. SHADOWS : CLOUDS :: SUN : (A. water, B. dark, C. rain, D. thunder)

84. WINTER : SUMMER :: BOSTON : (A. Miami, B. Madrid, C. Sao Paulo, D. San Diego)

85. CIRCLE : SPHERE :: (A. ice, B. angle, C. oval, D. square) : CUBE

86. KINETIC : MOTION :: PISCATORIAL : (A. pizza, B. painting, C. fish, D. picturesque)

87. RESPIRATION : CO_2 :: (A. hydrolysis, B. transpiration, C. oxidation, D. photosynthesis) : O_2

88. SAND : CLAY :: GLASS : (A. stone, B. hay, C. brick, D. dirt)

89. LOUISIANA PURCHASE : (A. Mexico, B. Spain, C. Great Britain, D. France) :: ALASKA : RUSSIA

90. X : M :: (A. V, B. X, C. L, D. I) : C

91. PUCCINI : OPERA :: (A. Pavlova, B. Verdi, C. *Giselle*, D. Balanchine) : BALLET

92. POLTROON : TERROR :: PARANOIAC : (A. courage, B. shyness, C. persecution, D. paralysis)

93. DOOR : BOLT :: LETTER : (A. envelope, B. mail, C. seal, D. write)

94. AUTHOR : (A. royalties, B. charges, C. fees, D. contributions) :: AGENT : COMMISSIONS

95. OLD BAILEY : OLD VIC :: (A. Versailles, B. Bastille, C. Westminster, D. London) : LA SCALA

96. TRUDEAU : (A. Durant, B. De Toqueville, C. Malthus, D. Nast) :: ORWELL : HUXLEY

97. ORAL : AURAL :: SPEAK : (A. smell, B. see, C. sense, D. hear)

98. ACID : (A. NaHCO$_3$, B. H$_2$SO$_4$, C. NaCl, D. NaOH) :: ENZYME : AMYLASE

99. (A. sow, B. doe, C. vixen, D. bitch) : FOX :: DAM : SIRE

100. SALIVA : OIL :: MOUTH : (A. friction, B. comb, C. motor, D. cogwheel)

101. SCARCE : WARLIKE :: (A. fear, B. hardly, C. few, D. abundant) : PEACEFUL

102. ERROR : (A. recklessness, B. caution, C. indifference, D. accident) :: INEXPERIENCE : CARELESSNESS

103. MUHAMMAD ALI : CASSIUS CLAY :: (A. Matthew Henson, B. Malcolm X, C. Kareem Abdul-Jabbar, D. Adam Clayton Powell) : LEW ALCINDOR

104. FORMALDEHYDE : FREON :: (A. insulation, B. preservation, C. levitation, D. aggravation) : REFRIGERATION

105. FLAME : BURN :: INSULT : (A. inanity, B. anger, C. reparation, D. approbation)

106. TANZANIA : UNITED ARAB EMIRATES :: ESTONIA : (A. England, B. Laos, C. Brazil, D. Armenia)

107. WET SUIT : SCUBA :: TUTU : (A. church, B. Africa, C. snorkel, D. ballet)

108. *PATHÉTIQUE* : *EMPEROR* :: *EROICA* : (A. *Brandenburg*, B. *Egmont*, C. *The Nutcracker*, D. Beethoven)

109. KOESTLER : (A. Kreisler, B. Hemingway, C. Rhineland, D. Beethoven) :: DARKNESS : MOONLIGHT

110. (A. face, B. eye, C. head, D. brain) : TEAM :: EAR : PLAYER

111. TOFU : BROCCOLI :: (A. potato chips, B. liver, C. caviar, D. bread) : JELLY BEANS

112. RELIEF : BELIEVE :: RECEIVE : (A. friend, B. deceit, C. belief, D. brief)

113. LIVES : LIFE :: (A. brother-in-laws, B. brothers-in-law, C. brother-in-law's, D. brother's-in-law) : BROTHER-IN-LAW

114. (A. scientist, B. beaker, C. fume, D. chemical) : LABORATORY :: MANAGER : OFFICE

115. EYE : SHIRT :: EAR : (A. button, B. pants, C. cotton, D. clothing)

116. VIBRATION : TONE :: REFRACTION : (A. light, B. noise, C. rays, D. color)

117. GUSH : (A. torpid, B. torrid, C. lukewarm, D. comfortable) :: TRICKLE : TEPID

118. INTIMIDATE : ENCOURAGE :: (A. interdict, B. comply, C. expect, D. continue) : ALLOW

119. CLARINET : WOODWIND :: TROMBONE : (A. musician, B. percussion, C. brass, D. copper)

120. TAXATION : (A. rebellion, B. slavery, C. prohibition, D. cotton) :: REVOLUTION : CIVIL WAR

ANSWER KEY AND EXPLANATIONS

1. **D**	25. **B**	49. **A**	73. **C**	97. **D**
2. **B**	26. **D**	50. **B**	74. **A**	98. **B**
3. **C**	27. **C**	51. **B**	75. **D**	99. **C**
4. **A**	28. **C**	52. **B**	76. **C**	100. **C**
5. **B**	29. **B**	53. **A**	77. **C**	101. **D**
6. **A**	30. **C**	54. **D**	78. **D**	102. **D**
7. **A**	31. **B**	55. **D**	79. **C**	103. **C**
8. **C**	32. **A**	56. **C**	80. **C**	104. **B**
9. **A**	33. **A**	57. **B**	81. **A**	105. **B**
10. **B**	34. **D**	58. **B**	82. **C**	106. **D**
11. **B**	35. **B**	59. **A**	83. **A**	107. **D**
12. **A**	36. **B**	60. **A**	84. **C**	108. **A**
13. **C**	37. **B**	61. **B**	85. **D**	109. **D**
14. **D**	38. **C**	62. **D**	86. **C**	110. **C**
15. **B**	39. **C**	63. **C**	87. **D**	111. **A**
16. **A**	40. **B**	64. **D**	88. **C**	112. **B**
17. **B**	41. **A**	65. **D**	89. **D**	113. **B**
18. **D**	42. **C**	66. **C**	90. **D**	114. **A**
19. **B**	43. **B**	67. **D**	91. **D**	115. **B**
20. **C**	44. **C**	68. **C**	92. **C**	116. **D**
21. **D**	45. **B**	69. **B**	93. **C**	117. **B**
22. **C**	46. **B**	70. **A**	94. **A**	118. **A**
23. **C**	47. **B**	71. **D**	95. **B**	119. **C**
24. **D**	48. **D**	72. **A**	96. **D**	120. **B**

1. BALMY : MILD :: FAITHFUL : (A. explosive, B. docile, C. talkative, D. staunch)

   The correct answer is (D). Balmy and mild are synonyms; therefore, the task is to look for a synonym for faithful, which in this case is staunch.

2. BOLD : TIMID :: SQUANDER : (A. disperse, B. hoard, C. query, D. extinguish)

   The correct answer is (B). Bold and timid are related as antonyms. Squander, meaning to spend extravagantly, is the opposite of hoard, meaning to gather or accumulate.

3. WATER : (A. fish. B. ocean, C. island, D. net) :: LAND : LAKE

   The correct answer is (C). Land and lake are related geographically in the same way as water and island; as land surrounds a lake, so does water surround an island.

4. GLASS : RUBBER :: BRITTLE : (A. elastic, B. scarce, C. tempered, D. spheroid)

   The correct answer is (A). A specific characteristic of glass is that it is brittle. Similarly, a specific characteristic of rubber is that it is elastic.

5. DIAMETER : RADIUS :: (A. 3, B. 8, C. 2, D. 6) : 4

    The correct answer is (B). This is a mathematical relationship. A diameter is twice the length of a radius in a given circle; therefore, the missing term must be a number that is twice as great as 4. That, of course, is 8. In your own mind, you might say simply, "2 : 1 :: 2 : 1."

6. GLABROUS : FACTITIOUS :: HIRSUTE : (A. authentic, B. fictional, C. fluent, D. replete)

    The correct answer is (A). Glabrous (hairless) and hirsute (hairy) are antonyms. The only antonym for factitious (artificial) is authentic.

7. PARANOIA : SCHIZOPHRENIA :: MEGALOMANIA : (A. melancholia, B. carcinoma, C. hepatitis, D. stroke)

    The correct answer is (A). Every term in this analogy is a form of mental illness. Paranoia, a psychosis characterized by delusions of persecution, and schizophrenia, a psychosis characterized by disintegration of the personality, are related by the fact that each is a form of mental illness. Megalomania, a psychosis characterized by infantile feelings of personal omnipotence, is also a form of mental illness. Therefore, the missing term must be melancholia, a psychosis characterized by extreme depression. All other choices name physical illnesses.

8. (A. sales, B. investment, C. management, D. interest) : PROFIT :: LABOR : WAGES

    The correct answer is (C). Labor is associated with wages in the same way that management is associated with profit. In both cases, the association is of people working for a reward. Sales, investment, and interest may each be said to yield a profit, but these do not parallel the relationship of people to their reward as established by the given word pair. In solving this analogy, you must have the mental flexibility to think of labor and management as groups of people rather than as activities. If you think of labor as an activity, there are too many possible correct answers.

9. STUDENT : (A. backpack, B. briefcase, C. college, D. teacher) :: TRAVELER : SUITCASE

    The correct answer is (A). This is an analogy of purpose and association. A traveler uses a suitcase; similarly, a student uses a backpack.

10. DENIGRATE : DEFAMER :: MEDIATE : (A. mathematician, B. arbitrator, C. employer, D. laborer)

    The correct answer is (B). The relationship is one of action to agent. Denigrate (to belittle or to malign) is the action taken by the defamer (one who injures by giving misleading or false reports) in the same way that mediate (to act as an intermediary agent) is the action taken by the arbitrator (one chosen to settle differences between parties in dispute).

11. LAKE WOBEGON : (A. Minneapolis, B. Winesburg, C. Canterbury, D. Minnesota) :: MUDVILLE : CASTERBRIDGE

    The correct answer is (B). Mudville, the town in the poem "Casey at the Bat," and Casterbridge, the town in the Hardy novel *The Mayor of Casterbridge*, are fictional places. Likewise, Lake Wobegon, of Keillor's book *Lake Wobegon Days*, and Winesburg, of Anderson's *Winesburg, Ohio*, are fictional places.

12. CORNET : OBOE :: (A. cello, B. drum, C. harpsichord, D. xylophone) : GUITAR

The correct answer is (A). This is a part-to-part analogy. A cornet and an oboe are each part of the larger category of wind instruments in the same way that a guitar and a cello are each part of the larger category of string instruments. A harpsichord, too, belongs to the category of string instruments; however, because it has internal rather than external strings, it is not as closely related to guitar as is cello.

13. JANUARY : WEDNESDAY :: JANUS : (A. Thor, B. Apollo, C. Odin, D. Diana)

The correct answer is (C). January was named for Janus, the guardian deity of gates in Roman mythology, as Wednesday was named for Odin, chief of the Scandinavian gods. The Anglo-Saxon version of Odin was Woden; hence, Woden's Day became Wednesday.

14. HORSE : (A. equestrian, B. hoofed, C. cabriolet, D. herbivorous) :: TIGER : CARNIVOROUS

The correct answer is (D). This is a characteristic relationship. A specific characteristic of a tiger is that it is carnivorous (meat eating), as a specific characteristic of a horse is that it is herbivorous (plant eating).

15. GOOD : BETTER :: (A. terrible, B. worse, C. improvement, D. bad) : WORST

The correct answer is (B). This is an analogy of degree. Adjectives such as good and bad have three degrees of comparison: positive, comparative, and superlative. In this question, good, which is the positive degree, is less good than better, the comparative degree, to the same extent that worse, the comparative, is less bad than worst, the superlative degree.

16. CLAN : FEUD :: NATION : (A. war, B. politics, C. armaments, D. retaliation)

The correct answer is (A). The relationship is one of object to action. Just as a clan may become involved in a feud, so may a nation become involved in a war. If you solve this analogy via an A : C :: B : D model, the relationship becomes one of degree. A clan is smaller than a nation; thus, its conflict, a feud, is smaller than a war.

17. ABUNDANCE : ABROGATE :: DEARTH : (A. deny, B. establish, C. abstain, D. absolve)

The correct answer is (B). Abundance and dearth are antonyms. The opposite of abrogate (to nullify or cancel) is establish.

18. ONOMATOPOEIA : METAPHOR :: SOUND : (A. hiss, B. rhyme, C. saying, D. comparison)

The correct answer is (D). Onomatopoeia (a word whose sound suggests its sense) is a figure of speech that makes a sound relationship. Metaphor (an implied comparison between unlike things) is a figure of speech that makes a comparison.

19. SACRAMENTO : HELENA :: ALBANY : (A. New York, B. Little Rock, C. Houston, D. San Francisco)

The correct answer is (B). Sacramento and Helena are related because each is a capital city: Sacramento is the capital of California, and Helena is the capital of Montana. Because Albany is also a state capital, it must be paired with Little Rock, the capital of Arkansas, to complete the analogy.

20. (A. scan, B. feel, C. dear, D. seen) : READ :: REAP : PEAR

The correct answer is (C). This is a nonsemantic analogy. Transposing the first and last letters of reap forms the word pear, just as transposing the first and last letters of read forms the word dear.

21. CAUTIOUS : CIRCUMSPECT :: PRECIPITOUS : (A. premonitory, B. profound, C. stealthy, D. steep)

The correct answer is (D). Cautious and circumspect are related as synonyms. The only synonym offered for precipitous is steep.

22. SEISMOGRAPH : GEOLOGY :: ELECTROENCEPHALOGRAPH : (A. bacteriology, B. biology, C. neurology, D. cardiology)

The correct answer is (C). This is an analogy of purpose. A seismograph, an instrument for recording vibrations within the earth, is used in geology (the study of the earth), just as an electroencephalograph, an instrument for recording brain waves, is used in neurology (the scientific study of the nervous system).

23. ACUTE : VENERATE :: CHRONIC : (A. revere, B. actuate, C. flout, D. repent)

The correct answer is (C). Acute and chronic are related as antonyms. Acute means having a sudden onset, a sharp rise, and a short course; chronic means marked by long duration or frequent recurrence. Venerate, which means to honor, must therefore be paired with its opposite, flout, meaning to scoff or to treat with contemptuous disregard.

24. (A. toad, B. snail, C. shark, D. alligator) : TURTLE :: TIGER : HUMAN

The correct answer is (D). This is a part-to-part analogy. Tiger and human are each part of the larger category of mammals. Turtle, which is part of the larger category of reptiles, must therefore be paired with alligator, the only reptile among the answer choices. A toad is an amphibian.

25. INSTINCT : PLAN :: UNCONSCIOUS : (A. involuntary, B. intentional, C. spontaneous, D. imaginary)

The correct answer is (B). An instinct is an unreasoned or unconscious response to a stimulus. A plan is a reasoned or intentional response to a stimulus.

26. INDIA : (A. Sri Lanka, B. Greece, C. Afghanistan, D. Pakistan) :: ITALY : SWITZERLAND

The correct answer is (D). The relationship between Italy and Switzerland is that they share a common border, as do India and Pakistan.

27. SWIM : SWAM :: BURST : (A. busted, B. bursted, C. burst, D. bust)

The correct answer is (C). The grammatical relationship between swim and swam is one of present tense to past tense; therefore, the task is to find the past tense of burst, which is also burst.

28. RAISIN : GRAPE :: PRUNE : (A. apricot, B. currant, C. plum, D. berry)

The correct answer is (C). The relationship is one of origin or sequence. A raisin is a dried grape, just as a prune is a dried plum.

29. GRAM : OUNCE :: LITER : (A. deciliter, B. quart, C. kilogram, D. pound)

The correct answer is (B). A gram is a metric measure of weight. It is paired with an ounce, which is an American measure of weight. A liter is a metric measure of volume that must be paired with its near equivalent, an American quart. In the American system of weights and measures, an ounce may also be a measure of volume, but it would be impossible to create an analogy with the necessary parallels with any interpretation other than that ounce is a measure of weight.

30. BEAKER : CHEMIST :: STETHOSCOPE : (A. teacher, B. author, C. doctor, D. dentist)

The correct answer is (C). This is an analogy of tool to its user or object to agent. A beaker is used by a chemist in the course of his or her work, as a stethoscope is used by a doctor in the performance of his or her work.

31. LIMPID : LUCID :: TURBID : (A. torpid, B. muddy, C. truculent, D. serene)

The correct answer is (B). Limpid and lucid are synonyms meaning clear. A synonym for turbid is muddy.

32. MANGO : (A. coconut, B. tomato, C. cabbage, D. apple) :: PAPAYA : PASSION FRUIT

The correct answer is (A). The mango, coconut, papaya, and passion fruit are all juicy fruits that are grown primarily in tropical climates.

33. $.02^2$: .0004 :: $.001^2$: (A. .000001, B. .0001, C. .0002, D. .000002)

The correct answer is (A). $(.02)^2 = .0004$; $(.001)^2 = .000001$.

34. SADNESS : PAIN :: FAILURE : (A. medication, B. palliation, C. pleasure, D. injury)

The correct answer is (D). The relationship of the given word pair is one of cause and effect. Sadness may be caused by failure in the same way that pain may be caused by an injury.

35. AMELIA EARHART : NELLIE BLY :: AVIATION : (A. medicine, B. journalism, C. law, D. prohibition)

The correct answer is (B). This is an analogy of the association of famous women to the field in which they pioneered. Amelia Earhart achieved fame as one of the first women in aviation; Nellie Bly was one of the first women in journalism.

36. ROMAN : MANOR :: (A. cleric, B. names, C. patrimony, D. estates) : MANSE

The correct answer is (B). Roman and manor are anagrams. So, too, are names and manse.

37. LACONIC : FLACCID :: REDUNDANT : (A. succinct, B. firm, C. flimsy, D. wordy)

The correct answer is (B). Laconic (concise) and redundant (excessively wordy) are antonyms. Among the answer choices, the only antonym for flaccid (flabby or limp) is firm.

38. PNEUMATICS : (A. medicine, B. disease, C. physics, D. cars) :: ESKER : GEOLOGY

The correct answer is (C). An esker (a ridge formed by a glacial stream) is part of the field of geology, as pneumatics (the use of gas or air pressure) is part of the field of physics.

39. NECKLACE : MEDAL :: ADORNMENT : (A. jewel, B. metal, C. decoration, D. bronze)

The correct answer is (C). A necklace is used for adornment as a medal is used for decoration.

40. RIVER : STREAM :: MOUNTAIN : (A. cliff, B. hill, C. canyon, D. peak)

The correct answer is (B). This is an analogy of degree. A river is larger than a stream, as a mountain is larger than a hill.

41. HECKLE : BADGER :: (A. stock, B. deplete, C. beaver, D. stylus) : REPLENISH

The correct answer is (A). Heckle and needle are synonyms meaning to harass. The only synonym offered for replenish is stock.

42. (A. guerrilla, B. terrorist, C. quash, D. mediate) : REBELLION :: NEGOTIATE : TREATY

The correct answer is (C). The relationship of the given word pair is action to object. One may negotiate (bring about by mutual agreement) a treaty just as one may quash (crush) a rebellion.

43. BOTANIST : PLANTS :: GEOLOGIST : (A. trees, B. rocks, C. geography, D. gems)

The correct answer is (B). The first word pair is related by the association of a scientist to the object of study. Of the choices offered, only the study of rocks is related to the geologist as the study of plants is related to the botanist. To the extent that gemstones occur naturally among the rocks, the geologist will study them as well, but the primary concern of a geologist is rocks, their composition, and their history.

44. CAT : FELINE :: OX : (A. equine, B. saturnine, C. bovine, D. canine)

The correct answer is (C). Feline means of or relating to the cat family, as bovine means of or relating to the ox or cow family.

45. WOLF : (A. wool, B. sheep, C. ewe, D. ram) :: DOG : CAT

The correct answer is (B). A dog and cat are simply two different kinds of animal. A wolf and sheep are likewise two different kinds of animal. Sex is not a factor in the relationship of dog to cat, so it must not enter the analogy in relationship to the wolf.

46. (A. $\frac{5}{16}$, B. $\frac{3}{8}$, C. $\frac{2}{6}$, D. $\frac{5}{12}$): $\frac{9}{24}$ :: $\frac{4}{11}$: $\frac{12}{33}$

The correct answer is (B). Dividing the numerator and denominator by 3, $\frac{12}{33}$ can be reduced to $\frac{4}{11}$. Similarly, dividing the numerator and denominator by 3, $\frac{9}{24}$ can be reduced to $\frac{3}{8}$.

47. (A. effusiveness, B. asceticism, C. impudence, D. gullibility) : EPICURIANISM :: CONFORMITY : ICONOCLASTICISM

The correct answer is (B). The relationship is one of opposition. An ascetic person denies his or her desires, while an epicure shows no restraint (particularly with respect to food consumption). Similarly, a conformist is a follower of conventional ideals, whereas an iconoclast rebels against traditional principles.

48. ROOM : CABIN :: HOUSE : (A. camp, B. cottage, C. hotel, D. ship)

The correct answer is (D). A room is a division of a house—specifically, a living unit of a house. A cabin is a living unit of a ship.

49. BRASS : COPPER :: PEWTER : (A. lead, B. zinc, C. silver, D. bronze)

The correct answer is (A). Brass is an alloy consisting essentially of copper and zinc. Pewter is an alloy consisting of tin and lead.

50. COWCATCHER : LOCOMOTIVE :: (A. coda, B. climax, C. epilogue, D. finale) : DENOUEMENT

The correct answer is (B). A cowcatcher immediately precedes a locomotive as a climax (the point of highest dramatic tension) immediately precedes the denouement (the unraveling or outcome of a sequence of events) in a story or a play.

51. PARIAH : OUTCAST :: ARCHON : (A. archivist, B. magistrate, C. martine, D. constable)

The correct answer is (B). Pariah and outcast are synonyms. The only synonym offered for archon is magistrate.

52. (A. cappuccino, B. shamrock, C. wine, D. palm trees) : VODKA :: DEVALERA : STALIN

The correct answer is (B). Joseph Stalin was the leader of the Soviet Union, which is intimately associated with vodka. Eamon Devalera was the leader of Ireland, which is intimately associated with the shamrock.

53. LANCET : CUT :: CHAMOIS : (A. polish, B. pliant, C. smooth, D. sheep)

The correct answer is (A). This is an analogy of purpose. A lancet is a sharp surgical instrument used to cut; a chamois is a soft, pliant leather prepared from the skin of the chamois or from sheepskin used to polish.

54. (A. utter, B. elapse, C. exude, D. time) : EMIT :: STEP : PETS

The correct answer is (D). This is a nonsemantic analogy. Time spelled backward is emit, as step spelled backward is pets.

55. SAFE : NECKLACE :: COMBINATION : (A. torque, B. bangle, C. circlet, D. clasp)

The correct answer is (D). A safe is opened by a combination; a necklace is opened by a clasp.

56. EXPERIMENT : (A. science, B. elucidation, C. hypothesis, D. investigation) :: EXAMINATION : ACHIEVEMENT

The correct answer is (C). An experiment tests a hypothesis as an examination tests achievement.

57. BOY : BULLET :: MAN : (A. gun, B. artillery shell, C. holster, D. trigger)

The correct answer is (B). The relationship is one of degree. A man is larger than a boy; an artillery shell is larger and more effective than a bullet.

58. ENERVATE : (A. eradicate, B. invigorate, C. disconcert, D. propagate) :: MALICE : BENEVOLENCE

The correct answer is (B). Malice and benevolence are antonyms. The only antonym offered for enervate (to drain of strength) is invigorate.

59. EVIDENCE : CONVICTION :: (A. oxygen, B. carbon dioxide, C. match, D. light) : COMBUSTION

The correct answer is (A). Evidence is necessary for conviction in the judicial process, just as oxygen is necessary for the chemical process of combustion. Heat is also necessary for combustion, but the source of heat may be other than a match.

60. EDIFICATION : AWARENESS :: AGGRAVATION : (A. distress, B. excitement, C. reduction, D. deliberation)

The correct answer is (A). The relationship of the given word pair is one of cause and effect because edification (enlightenment) results in awareness. Similarly, aggravation results in distress.

61. NEWTON : COPERNICUS :: SHAKESPEARE : (A. Fielding, B. Jonson, C. Dickens, D. Defoe)

The correct answer is (B). Newton and Copernicus are noted for their contributions to the field of science. Both Shakespeare and Jonson are well known for both drama and poetry. Notice that each of the alternatives names a figure from the field of literature; therefore, it is necessary to narrow the relationship to a particular area or areas of literature in order to answer this question correctly.

62. ST. AUGUSTINE : (A. Florida, B. Virginia, C. France, D. Spain) :: JAMESTOWN : ENGLAND

The correct answer is (D). Jamestown was England's first permanent settlement in the New World, just as St. Augustine was Spain's first permanent settlement.

63. SNOW : DRIFT :: (A. hill, B. rain, C. sand, D. desert) : DUNE

The correct answer is (C). When blown by the wind, snow forms a drift, and sand forms a dune.

64. CATAMARAN : TERMAGANT :: RAFT : (A. grisette, B. spinnaker, C. spinster, D. shrew)

The correct answer is (D). Catamaran and raft are synonyms, as are termagant and shrew.

65. $3^2 : 2^3 :: 9 :$ (A. 1, B. 6, C. 4, D. 8)

The correct answer is (D).

$3^2 = 3 \times 3 = 9$

$2^3 = 2 \times 2 \times 2 = 8$

66. FICTION : NOVELIST :: FACTS : (A. legend, B. story, C. historian, D. research)

The correct answer is (C). Fiction is the province of the novelist, as facts are the province of the historian.

67. HARVARD : YALE :: BROWN : (A. Princeton, B. Purdue, C. Emory, D. Dartmouth)

The correct answer is (D). The relationship between the terms of the given word pair is one of place. Harvard and Yale are both located in New England, as are Brown and Dartmouth.

68. CAT : WOLF :: (A. lion, B. dog, C. man, D. tiger) : DUCK

The correct answer is (C). A cat and wolf are related in that they are each members of the larger category of four-legged creatures. A duck, which is a two-legged creature, must therefore be paired with the only other two-legged creature, which is man.

69. WHO : I :: WHOM : (A. we, B. me, C. whose, D. mine)

The correct answer is (B). This is a grammatical analogy. *Who* is nominative, and *whom* is objective. Likewise, *I* is nominative, and *me* is objective.

70. (A. obsequious, B. obstreperous, C. complacent, D. contumelious) : SYCOPHANT :: CONTUMACIOUS : RENEGADE

The correct answer is (A). The relationship between the words of the given pair is one of characteristic. Contumacious (an adjective meaning rebellious) describes a renegade (a noun meaning one who rejects lawful or conventional behavior). Similarly, obsequious (an adjective meaning subservient) describes a sycophant (a noun meaning servile flatterer or parasite).

71. DOWSER : ROD :: GEOMANCER : (A. stones, B. maps, C. plants, D. configurations)

The correct answer is (D). A dowser divines the presence of water or minerals by means of a rod, as a geomancer divines by means of geographical features or configurations.

72. MINERVA : ATHENA :: (A. Jupiter, B. Juno, C. Poseidon, D. Apollo) : ZEUS

The correct answer is (A). The relationship is that of father to daughter, as well as of Roman to Greek names for the primary deity and his daughter. Athena was the daughter of Zeus in Greek mythology; Minerva was the daughter of Jupiter in Roman mythology.

73. (A. loss, B. victory, C. game, D. team) : WIN :: MEDICINE : CURE

The correct answer is (C). The objective of a game is to win, as the objective of medicine is to cure. The relationship is that of objective to action.

74. SAFARI : SWAHILI :: SALAAM : (A. Arabic, B. shalom, C. peace, D. Africa)

The correct answer is (A). Safari means journey in the Swahili language. Salaam is an Arabic greeting. This is an answer you should be able to get by elimination. Swahili is a language, and Arabic is the only language offered among the choices.

75. ACID : ALKALI :: 6 : (A. 1, B. 4, C. 7, D. 8)

The correct answer is (D). Acidity and alkalinity are expressed on a pH scale whose values run from 0 to 14, with 7 representing neutrality. Numbers less than 7 indicate increasing acidity, and numbers greater than 7 represent increasing alkalinity. Therefore, ACID : ALKALI :: 6 (a pH indicating mild acidity) : 8 (a pH indicating mild alkalinity).

76. PEDESTAL : (A. column, B. sculpture, C. chandelier, D. stone) :: STALAGMITE : STALACTITE

The correct answer is (C). Stalagmites and stalactites are deposits of calcium carbonate formed by the dripping of calcareous water in a cave. A stalagmite grows up from the floor of the cave, while a stalactite hangs down from the ceiling of the cave. Similarly, a pedestal is an architectural support or base that raises something up from the ground, and a chandelier is a lighting fixture that hangs down from the ceiling.

77. BONA FIDE : IN TOTO :: CARTE BLANCHE : (A. eureka, B. status quo, C. avant-garde, D. ersatz)

The correct answer is (C). Bona fide (meaning in good faith) and in toto (meaning in full) are Latin words that have been borrowed intact for use in English. Avant-garde (meaning pioneer) and carte blanche (meaning blanket permission) are French words that have been borrowed intact for use in English. Eureka is borrowed from the Greek; status quo comes from Latin; and ersatz comes from German.

78. SEA : COAST :: RIVER : (A. inlet, B. delta, C. stream, D. bank)

The correct answer is (D). This is an analogy of place or of whole to part. The land bordering the sea is the coast, as the land bordering a river is a bank.

79. AMOUNT : NUMBER :: (A. lessen, B. augment, C. less, D. enumerate) : FEWER

The correct answer is (C). In this grammatical analogy, amount refers to quantity or bulk, while number refers to items that can be counted one by one. Similarly, less refers to quantity, and fewer refers to items that can be counted.

80. VOLUME : CUBIC METER :: (A. area, B. length, C. capacity, D. mass) : LITER

The correct answer is (C). The relationship expressed by the given word pair is one of measurement. Volume may be measured in cubic meters, as capacity may be measured in liters.

81. (A. refrain, B. precede, C. sustain, D. foray) : FORBEAR :: ADUMBRATE : FORESHADOW

The correct answer is (A). Adumbrate and foreshadow are synonyms. The only synonym offered for forbear (meaning to hold back or abstain) is refrain.

82. CHAMPION : CAUSE :: (A. signature, B. introduction, C. draft, D. ink) : LETTER

The correct answer is (C). This is an analogy of action to object. One may champion a cause, as one may draft a letter. This is another of those analogy questions that requires mental flexibility. If you insist upon thinking of champion as a noun—for indeed a champion may have a cause—you cannot find a parallel noun on the other side of the analogy. Once you switch your thinking and recognize that champion is being used as a verb, it is easy to find a parallel activity the object of which is a letter.

83. SHADOWS : CLOUDS :: SUN : (A. water, B. dark, C. rain, D. thunder)

The correct answer is (A). Sun is necessary to the formation of shadows, as water is necessary to the formation of clouds. C : A :: D : B.

84. WINTER : SUMMER :: BOSTON : (A. Miami, B. Madrid, C. Sao Paulo, D. San Diego)

The correct answer is (C). When it is winter in Boston, it is summer in Sao Paulo because the seasons are reversed in the northern and southern hemispheres.

85. CIRCLE : SPHERE :: (A. ice, B. angle, C. oval, D. square) : CUBE

The correct answer is (D). A circle is a plane figure; a sphere is the corresponding solid figure. A square is a plane figure, and a cube is the corresponding solid figure.

86. KINETIC : MOTION :: PISCATORIAL : (A. pizza, B. painting, C. fish, D. picturesque)

The correct answer is (C). Kinetic is an adjective meaning of or relating to motion, as piscatorial is an adjective meaning of or relating to fish.

87. RESPIRATION : CO_2 :: (A. hydrolysis, B. transpiration, C. oxidation, D. photosynthesis) : O_2

   The correct answer is (D). During the process of respiration, living things take in oxygen and give off CO_2 and water. During the process of photosynthesis, green plants take in carbon dioxide and water and give off O_2.

88. SAND : CLAY :: GLASS : (A. stone, B. hay, C. brick, D. dirt)

   The correct answer is (C). The relationship existing between the terms of the given word pair is one of purpose because sand is used to make glass. Similarly, clay is used to make brick.

89. LOUISIANA PURCHASE : (A. Mexico, B. Spain, C. Great Britain, D. France) :: ALASKA : RUSSIA

   The correct answer is (D). Alaska was purchased from Russia (in 1867), as the area known as the Louisiana Purchase was purchased from France (in 1803).

90. X : M :: (A. V, B. X, C. L, D. I) : C

   The correct answer is (D). The relationship between Roman numerals X (10) and M (1,000) is 1 to 100. The same relationship exists between the Roman numerals I (1) and C (100).

91. PUCCINI : OPERA :: (A. Pavlova, B. Verdi, C. *Giselle*, D. Balanchine) : BALLET

   The correct answer is (D). Puccini created operas, as Balanchine created ballets. Although Pavlova was a famous ballerina and *Giselle* is the name of a well-known ballet, only Balanchine (as a choreographer) stands in the same relationship to the ballet as Puccini (as a composer) stands in relationship to opera.

92. POLTROON : TERROR :: PARANOIAC : (A. courage, B. shyness, C. persecution, D. paralysis)

   The correct answer is (C). A characteristic of a poltroon (coward) is a feeling of terror, as a characteristic of a paranoiac is a feeling of persecution.

93. DOOR : BOLT :: LETTER : (A. envelope, B. mail, C. seal, D. write)

   The correct answer is (C). The relationship between the terms of the given word pair is one of object to action. However, three of the choices offered are actions one may take on the object letter. Therefore, it is necessary to narrow the relationship to the specific action of closing or securing. A door is secured by a bolt, and a letter is secured by a seal.

94. AUTHOR : (A. royalties, B. charges, C. fees, D. contributions) :: AGENT : COMMISSIONS

   The correct answer is (A). The relationship is one of an individual to his or her means of payment. An agent receives commissions (a percentage of the total fees paid) for his or her part in a business transaction. An author receives royalties (a percentage of the total payment made for a work) for his or her part in creating the work sold.

95. OLD BAILEY : OLD VIC :: (A. Versailles, B. Bastille, C. Westminster, D. London) : LA SCALA

   The correct answer is (B). The Old Vic is a theater is London; La Scala is the Milan opera house. Both are houses in which performances take place. Old Bailey is a London court with prison attached; the Bastille was a Paris prison.

96. TRUDEAU : (A. Durant, B. De Toqueville, C. Malthus, D. Nast) :: ORWELL : HUXLEY

The correct answer is (D). Both George Orwell and Aldous Huxley wrote novels with heavy political content set in the future. Both Garry Trudeau and Thomas Nast gained fame as political cartoonists.

97. ORAL : AURAL :: SPEAK : (A. smell, B. see, C. sense, D. hear)

The correct answer is (D). Oral means uttered by the mouth or spoken. Aural means of or relating to the ear or to the sense of hearing. Therefore, oral describes speak as aural describes hear.

98. ACID : (A. NaHCO$_3$, B. H$_2$SO$_4$, C. NaCl, D. NaOH) :: ENZYME : AMYLASE

The correct answer is (B). The formula for a specific acid is H$_2$SO$_4$ (sulfuric acid). The name for a specific enzyme is amylase.

99. (A. sow, B. doe, C. vixen, D. bitch) : FOX :: DAM : SIRE

The correct answer is (C). This analogy is one of female to male. A vixen is a female animal, and a fox is her male counterpart. A dam is a female animal parent, and a sire is her male counterpart.

100. SALIVA : OIL :: MOUTH : (A. friction, B. comb, C. motor, D. cogwheel)

The correct answer is (C). A characteristic of saliva is that it lubricates the mouth. A characteristic of oil is that it lubricates a motor.

101. SCARCE : WARLIKE :: (A. fear, B. hardly, C. few, D. abundant) : PEACEFUL

The correct answer is (D). Warlike is the opposite of peaceful; scarce is the opposite of abundant.

102. ERROR : (A. recklessness, B. caution, C. indifference, D. accident) :: INEXPERIENCE : CARELESSNESS

The correct answer is (D). In this case, either cause may have either effect, but maintaining the analogy, inexperience may lead to an error, while carelessness may lead to an accident.

103. MUHAMMAD ALI : CASSIUS CLAY :: (A. Matthew Henson, B. Malcolm X, C. Kareem Abdul-Jabbar, D. Adam Clayton Powell) : LEW ALCINDOR

The correct answer is (C). You would have to call this an analogy based on identity or perhaps sequence. Muhammad Ali is Cassius Clay. Cassius Clay became Muhammad Ali when he converted to the Black Muslim faith. Kareem Abdul-Jabbar is Lew Alcindor. Lew Alcindor became Kareem Abdul-Jabbar when he converted to the Black Muslim faith.

104. FORMALDEHYDE : FREON :: (A. insulation, B. preservation, C. levitation, D. aggravation) : REFRIGERATION

The correct answer is (B). Freon is used in refrigeration; formaldehyde is used for preservation, often for biological specimens.

105. FLAME : BURN :: INSULT : (A. inanity, B. anger, C. reparation, D. approbation)

The correct answer is (B). A flame may burn you; an insult may anger you.

106. TANZANIA : UNITED ARAB EMIRATES :: ESTONIA : (A. England, B. Laos, C. Brazil, D. Armenia)

The correct answer is (D). The first two countries, Tanzania and the United Arab Emirates, have in common that they came into being through the voluntary alliance of two or more independent countries. Estonia and Armenia also have histories in common. Both were once independent nations that were subsumed by the Soviet Union. Upon dissolution of the Soviet Union, they became independent nations again.

107. WET SUIT : SCUBA :: TUTU : (A. church, B. Africa, C. snorkel, D. ballet)

The correct answer is (D). A wet suit is the garb associated with scuba diving; a tutu is clothing associated with ballet.

108. *PATHÉTIQUE* : *EMPEROR* :: *EROICA* : (A. *Brandenburg*, B. *Egmont*, C. *The Nutcracker*, D. Beethoven)

The correct answer is (A). The *Pathétique* and *Eroica* are both symphonies (the first by Tchaikovsky and the second by Beethoven), although composers are irrelevant to this analogy. The *Emperor* and the *Brandenburg* are concerti, the first by Beethoven and the second by Bach. You could legitimately categorize this as a part-to-part analogy. The *Egmont* is an overture, and *The Nutcracker* is a suite.

109. KOESTLER : (A. Kreisler, B. Hemingway, C. Rhineland, D. Beethoven) :: DARKNESS : MOONLIGHT

The correct answer is (D). Koestler wrote *Darkness at Noon*; Beethoven wrote the *Moonlight Sonata*. The analogy moves from literature into music, but the relationship is clear.

110. (A. face, B. eye, C. head, D. brain) : TEAM :: EAR : PLAYER

The correct answer is (C). A player is part of a team; an ear is part of a head. Be careful: The ear usually is behind the face.

111. TOFU : BROCCOLI :: (A. potato chips, B. liver, C. caviar, D. bread) : JELLY BEANS

The correct answer is (A). Tofu and broccoli are considered to be among the most nutritious and healthful foods; potato chips and jelly beans fall into the category of junk foods.

112. RELIEF : BELIEVE :: RECEIVE : (A. friend, B. deceit, C. belief, D. brief)

The correct answer is (B). RELIEF : BELIEVE :: RECEIVE : DECEIT :: ie : ie : ei : ei. All seven terms correctly follow the rule, "I before E except after C," so this interpretation is the only one possible.

113. LIVES : LIFE :: (A. brother-in-laws, B. brothers-in-law, C. brother-in-law's, D. brother's-in-law) : BROTHER-IN-LAW

The correct answer is (B). LIVES : LIFE :: BROTHERS-IN-LAW : BROTHER-IN-LAW :: plural : singular.

114. (A. scientist, B. beaker, C. fume, D. chemical) : LABORATORY :: MANAGER : OFFICE

The correct answer is (A). A manager works in an office; a scientist works in a laboratory.

115. EYE : SHIRT :: EAR : (A. button, B. pants, C. cotton, D. clothing)

The correct answer is (B). Eye and ear are both sensory organs; shirt and pants are both articles of clothing.

116. VIBRATION : TONE :: REFRACTION : (A. light, B. noise, C. rays, D. color)

The correct answer is (D). Vibration of sound waves creates tone; refraction of light rays creates color.

117. GUSH : (A. torpid, B. torrid, C. lukewarm, D. comfortable) :: TRICKLE : TEPID

The correct answer is (B). A gush is a much heavier, quicker flow than a trickle; torrid is much hotter than tepid.

118. INTIMIDATE : ENCOURAGE :: (A. interdict, B. comply, C. expect, D. continue) : ALLOW

The correct answer is (A). To intimidate is to discourage, which is the opposite of encourage; to interdict is to prohibit, which is the opposite of to allow.

119. CLARINET : WOODWIND :: TROMBONE : (A. musician, B. percussion, C. brass, D. copper)

The correct answer is (C). A clarinet is part of the woodwind instruments; a trombone is part of the brass instruments.

120. TAXATION : (A. rebellion, B. slavery, C. prohibition, D. cotton) :: REVOLUTION : CIVIL WAR

The correct answer is (B). Taxation without representation was one of the causes of the American Revolution; disagreement over slavery was one of the causes of the Civil War.

ANSWER SHEET PRACTICE TEST 2

1. Ⓐ Ⓑ Ⓒ Ⓓ	31. Ⓐ Ⓑ Ⓒ Ⓓ	61. Ⓐ Ⓑ Ⓒ Ⓓ	91. Ⓐ Ⓑ Ⓒ Ⓓ
2. Ⓐ Ⓑ Ⓒ Ⓓ	32. Ⓐ Ⓑ Ⓒ Ⓓ	62. Ⓐ Ⓑ Ⓒ Ⓓ	92. Ⓐ Ⓑ Ⓒ Ⓓ
3. Ⓐ Ⓑ Ⓒ Ⓓ	33. Ⓐ Ⓑ Ⓒ Ⓓ	63. Ⓐ Ⓑ Ⓒ Ⓓ	93. Ⓐ Ⓑ Ⓒ Ⓓ
4. Ⓐ Ⓑ Ⓒ Ⓓ	34. Ⓐ Ⓑ Ⓒ Ⓓ	64. Ⓐ Ⓑ Ⓒ Ⓓ	94. Ⓐ Ⓑ Ⓒ Ⓓ
5. Ⓐ Ⓑ Ⓒ Ⓓ	35. Ⓐ Ⓑ Ⓒ Ⓓ	65. Ⓐ Ⓑ Ⓒ Ⓓ	95. Ⓐ Ⓑ Ⓒ Ⓓ
6. Ⓐ Ⓑ Ⓒ Ⓓ	36. Ⓐ Ⓑ Ⓒ Ⓓ	66. Ⓐ Ⓑ Ⓒ Ⓓ	96. Ⓐ Ⓑ Ⓒ Ⓓ
7. Ⓐ Ⓑ Ⓒ Ⓓ	37. Ⓐ Ⓑ Ⓒ Ⓓ	67. Ⓐ Ⓑ Ⓒ Ⓓ	97. Ⓐ Ⓑ Ⓒ Ⓓ
8. Ⓐ Ⓑ Ⓒ Ⓓ	38. Ⓐ Ⓑ Ⓒ Ⓓ	68. Ⓐ Ⓑ Ⓒ Ⓓ	98. Ⓐ Ⓑ Ⓒ Ⓓ
9. Ⓐ Ⓑ Ⓒ Ⓓ	39. Ⓐ Ⓑ Ⓒ Ⓓ	69. Ⓐ Ⓑ Ⓒ Ⓓ	99. Ⓐ Ⓑ Ⓒ Ⓓ
10. Ⓐ Ⓑ Ⓒ Ⓓ	40. Ⓐ Ⓑ Ⓒ Ⓓ	70. Ⓐ Ⓑ Ⓒ Ⓓ	100. Ⓐ Ⓑ Ⓒ Ⓓ
11. Ⓐ Ⓑ Ⓒ Ⓓ	41. Ⓐ Ⓑ Ⓒ Ⓓ	71. Ⓐ Ⓑ Ⓒ Ⓓ	101. Ⓐ Ⓑ Ⓒ Ⓓ
12. Ⓐ Ⓑ Ⓒ Ⓓ	42. Ⓐ Ⓑ Ⓒ Ⓓ	72. Ⓐ Ⓑ Ⓒ Ⓓ	102. Ⓐ Ⓑ Ⓒ Ⓓ
13. Ⓐ Ⓑ Ⓒ Ⓓ	43. Ⓐ Ⓑ Ⓒ Ⓓ	73. Ⓐ Ⓑ Ⓒ Ⓓ	103. Ⓐ Ⓑ Ⓒ Ⓓ
14. Ⓐ Ⓑ Ⓒ Ⓓ	44. Ⓐ Ⓑ Ⓒ Ⓓ	74. Ⓐ Ⓑ Ⓒ Ⓓ	104. Ⓐ Ⓑ Ⓒ Ⓓ
15. Ⓐ Ⓑ Ⓒ Ⓓ	45. Ⓐ Ⓑ Ⓒ Ⓓ	75. Ⓐ Ⓑ Ⓒ Ⓓ	105. Ⓐ Ⓑ Ⓒ Ⓓ
16. Ⓐ Ⓑ Ⓒ Ⓓ	46. Ⓐ Ⓑ Ⓒ Ⓓ	76. Ⓐ Ⓑ Ⓒ Ⓓ	106. Ⓐ Ⓑ Ⓒ Ⓓ
17. Ⓐ Ⓑ Ⓒ Ⓓ	47. Ⓐ Ⓑ Ⓒ Ⓓ	77. Ⓐ Ⓑ Ⓒ Ⓓ	107. Ⓐ Ⓑ Ⓒ Ⓓ
18. Ⓐ Ⓑ Ⓒ Ⓓ	48. Ⓐ Ⓑ Ⓒ Ⓓ	78. Ⓐ Ⓑ Ⓒ Ⓓ	108. Ⓐ Ⓑ Ⓒ Ⓓ
19. Ⓐ Ⓑ Ⓒ Ⓓ	49. Ⓐ Ⓑ Ⓒ Ⓓ	79. Ⓐ Ⓑ Ⓒ Ⓓ	109. Ⓐ Ⓑ Ⓒ Ⓓ
20. Ⓐ Ⓑ Ⓒ Ⓓ	50. Ⓐ Ⓑ Ⓒ Ⓓ	80. Ⓐ Ⓑ Ⓒ Ⓓ	110. Ⓐ Ⓑ Ⓒ Ⓓ
21. Ⓐ Ⓑ Ⓒ Ⓓ	51. Ⓐ Ⓑ Ⓒ Ⓓ	81. Ⓐ Ⓑ Ⓒ Ⓓ	111. Ⓐ Ⓑ Ⓒ Ⓓ
22. Ⓐ Ⓑ Ⓒ Ⓓ	52. Ⓐ Ⓑ Ⓒ Ⓓ	82. Ⓐ Ⓑ Ⓒ Ⓓ	112. Ⓐ Ⓑ Ⓒ Ⓓ
23. Ⓐ Ⓑ Ⓒ Ⓓ	53. Ⓐ Ⓑ Ⓒ Ⓓ	83. Ⓐ Ⓑ Ⓒ Ⓓ	113. Ⓐ Ⓑ Ⓒ Ⓓ
24. Ⓐ Ⓑ Ⓒ Ⓓ	54. Ⓐ Ⓑ Ⓒ Ⓓ	84. Ⓐ Ⓑ Ⓒ Ⓓ	114. Ⓐ Ⓑ Ⓒ Ⓓ
25. Ⓐ Ⓑ Ⓒ Ⓓ	55. Ⓐ Ⓑ Ⓒ Ⓓ	85. Ⓐ Ⓑ Ⓒ Ⓓ	115. Ⓐ Ⓑ Ⓒ Ⓓ
26. Ⓐ Ⓑ Ⓒ Ⓓ	56. Ⓐ Ⓑ Ⓒ Ⓓ	86. Ⓐ Ⓑ Ⓒ Ⓓ	116. Ⓐ Ⓑ Ⓒ Ⓓ
27. Ⓐ Ⓑ Ⓒ Ⓓ	57. Ⓐ Ⓑ Ⓒ Ⓓ	87. Ⓐ Ⓑ Ⓒ Ⓓ	117. Ⓐ Ⓑ Ⓒ Ⓓ
28. Ⓐ Ⓑ Ⓒ Ⓓ	58. Ⓐ Ⓑ Ⓒ Ⓓ	88. Ⓐ Ⓑ Ⓒ Ⓓ	118. Ⓐ Ⓑ Ⓒ Ⓓ
29. Ⓐ Ⓑ Ⓒ Ⓓ	59. Ⓐ Ⓑ Ⓒ Ⓓ	89. Ⓐ Ⓑ Ⓒ Ⓓ	119. Ⓐ Ⓑ Ⓒ Ⓓ
30. Ⓐ Ⓑ Ⓒ Ⓓ	60. Ⓐ Ⓑ Ⓒ Ⓓ	90. Ⓐ Ⓑ Ⓒ Ⓓ	120. Ⓐ Ⓑ Ⓒ Ⓓ

answer sheet

Practice Test 2

120 QUESTIONS • 60 MINUTES

Directions: Each of these test questions consists of three capitalized words and four lettered words enclosed in parentheses. Two of the capitalized words are related in some way. Find the two related words, and establish the nature of the relationship. Then study the four words lettered A, B, C, and D. Select the one lettered word that is related to the remaining capitalized words in the same way that the first two capitalized words are related. Mark the answer sheet for the letter preceding the word you select.

1. SURFEIT : (A. collect, B. empty, C. glut, D. spoil) :: ARROGATE : USURP

2. ROBBERY : INCARCERATION :: (A. marking, B. singing, C. sleeping, D. embezzlement) : APPLAUSE

3. ICHTHYOLOGY : (A. insects, B. mammals, C. fish, D. invertebrates) :: ORNITHOLOGY : BIRDS

4. FIRST : PENULTIMATE :: JANUARY : (A. December, B. November, C. February, D. June)

5. HOPE : PLEASURE :: DESPONDENCY : (A. frolic, B. gratification, C. joy, D. anguish)

6. DICHOTOMY : DISSEMBLE :: DIVISION : (A. feign, B. assemble, C. resemble, D. return)

7. LONGFELLOW : WHITMAN :: (A. Tagore, B. Keats, C. Heine, D. Dickens) : TENNYSON

8. MITER : BISHOP :: (A. stole, B. cleric, C. robe, D. biretta) : PRIEST

9. OK : PA :: KS : (A. CT, B. AZ, C. WV, D. NY)

10. SEED : BREED :: (A. origin, B. specimen, C. need, D. act) : DEED

11. (A. influence, B. compose, C. touch, D. infect) : RESULT :: AFFECT : EFFECT

12. SAUTÉING : COOKERY :: PAINTING : (A. juggling, B. forestry, C. art, D. medicine)

49

13. CAMPHOR : AROMATIC :: LILAC : (A. lavender, B. leaf, C. fragrant, D. rose)

14. (A. skiers, B. winter, C. athletes, D. blades) : SKATES :: RUNNERS : SLEDS

15. LOCARNO : SWITZERLAND :: ARGONNE : (A. France, B. Quebec, C. Germany, D. Belgium)

16. ARMY : FOOD :: DEFENSE : (A. digestion, B. vegetation, C. nutrition, D. supply)

17. TAN : (A. Fitzgerald, B. Woolf, C. Orwell, D. Wolfe) :: JONG : WALKER

18. BENEFICENT : INIMICAL :: DELETERIOUS : (A. amicable, B. hostile, C. matchless, D. ordinary)

19. ANEMOMETER : (A. smell, B. texture, C. wind, D. pressure) :: ODOMETER : DISTANCE

20. WHIP : HORN :: CRACK : (A. blow, B. break, C. tattoo, D. march)

21. HILL : MOUNTAIN :: (A. depression, B. discomfort, C. headache, D. fear) : PAIN

22. (A. *The Merry Widow*, B. *Naughty Marietta*, C. *Iolanthe*, D. *Carmen*) : *MIKADO* :: *H.M.S. PINAFORE* : *GONDOLIERS*

23. BELL : HOLMES :: (A. Watson, B. Edison, C. Graham, D. Doyle) : WATSON

24. WHEEL : SPOKE :: (A. heaven, B. ribbon, C. rim, D. bulb) : FILAMENT

25. POLICE OFFICER : (A. convict, B. justice, C. conduct, D. crime) :: FIREFIGHTER : FIRE

26. ROUND : CHUCK :: (A. circle, B. flank, C. chipped, D. throw) : RIB

27. FRACTIOUS : SYSTEMATIC :: DEBILITATE : (A. invigorate, B. undermine, C. diverge, D. annul)

28. FOUR : TWENTY :: (A. two, B. five, C. three, D. seven) : FIFTEEN

29. GROUND CREW : SEMAPHORE :: PILOT : (A. radio, B. airplane, C. stewardess, D. copilot)

30. GLAND : ENDOCRINE :: MUSCLE : (A. hard, B. strong, C. desiccated, D. striated)

31. PROHIBITED : BANNED :: CANONICAL : (A. reputable, B. authoritative, C. referred, D. considered)

32. INTERMINABLE : ENDLESS :: APPARENT : (A. concise, B. ostensible, C. transparent, D. improbable)

33. ICE : STEAM :: BRICK : (A. straw, B. mortar, C. pole, D. stone)

34. BREATHING : (A. oxygen, B. lungs, C. carbon dioxide, D. nose) :: CRYING : TEARS

35. EXERTION : EXHAUSTION :: CRUELTY : (A. cozen, B. annoy, C. suffering, D. competition)

36. JAMES I : (A. James II, B. George I, C. Elizabeth I, D. Charles I) :: GEORGE V : EDWARD VIII

37. PLANS : ARCHITECT :: TREACHERY : (A. thief, B. traitor, C. cheater, D. killer)

38. 4! : 24 :: (A. 5!, B. 6!, C. 20!, D. 40!) : 120

39. ANCHOR : KEY :: (A. dock, B. boat, C. prow, D. keel) : CHAIN

40. (A. Scopes, B. Darrow, C. Darwin, D. Jennings) : BRYAN :: SACCO : VANZETTI

41. (A. subterranean, B. subconscious, C. superb, D. advertised) : SUBLIMINAL :: PLETHORIC : SUPERFLUOUS

42. VICTORY : PYRRHIC :: FRUIT : (A. ripe, B. bitter, C. pie, D. tree)

43. TOUCH : DOWN :: (A. walk, B. river, C. home, D. stocking) : RUN

44. MITOSIS : DIVISION :: OSMOSIS : (A. diffusion, B. concentration, C. digestion, D. metamorphosis)

45. SUN : (A. summer, B. tan, C. sunscreen, D. beach) :: COLD : OVERCOAT

46. PHOEBUS : (A. Helius, B. Eos, C. Diana, D. Perseus) :: SUN : MOON

47. (A. equality, B. generous, C. wantonness, D. goodness) : LIBERTINE :: ADVOCACY : LAWYER

48. POUND : KILOGRAM :: WEIGHT : (A. mass, B. area, C. volume, D. capacity)

49. PRECARIOUS : ZEALOUS :: CERTAIN : (A. apathetic, B. ardent, C. indigent, D. sensitive)

50. PONDER : THOUGHT :: ARBITRATE : (A. endorsement, B. plan, C. fine, D. dispute)

51. OBSTRUCT : IMPENETRABLE :: IMPEDE : (A. forbearing, B. hidden, C. impervious, D. merciful)

52. OCTAVE : SESTET :: (A. scale, B. ending, C. quatrain, D. symphony) : COUPLET

53. NOVEL : (A. epic, B. drama, C. volume, D. story) :: *TOM SAWYER* : *AENEID*

54. PURSER : (A. bank, B. ship, C. race track, D. highway) :: BRAKEMAN : TRAIN

55. DRINK : SECURITY :: THIRST : (A. assuredness, B. stocks, C. fear, D. money)

56. CIRCLE : OVAL :: (A. figure, B. octagon, C. starfish, D. semicircle) : PARALLELOGRAM

57. RESILIENCY : RUBBER :: LAMBENCY : (A. oil, B. sheep, C. candlelight, D. lawn)

58. VIRTUOSO : (A. orchestra, B. home, C. prison, D. college) :: TEACHER : CLASSROOM

59. KEYBOARD : (A. small, B. office, C. mouse, D. radio) :: LIPSTICK : COMPACT

60. (A. 4, B. 7, C. 9, D. 14) : 28 :: 11 : 44

61. CAPE : ARROYO :: PROMONTORY : (A. gully, B. waterfall, C. meadow, D. fen)

62. BINDING : BOOK :: WELDING : (A. box, B. tank, C. chair, D. wire)

63. SERFDOM : FEUDALISM :: ENTREPRENEURSHIP : (A. laissez-faire, B. captain, C. radical, D. capitalism)

64. (A. bassos, B. dynamos, C. heroes, D. solos) : EMBARGOES :: VOLCANOES : TOMATOES

65. FOAL : HORSE :: CYGNET : (A. ring, B. fish, C. swan, D. constellation)

66. WARFARE : (A. ingenuity, B. commerce, C. separate, D. destruction) :: TYRANNY : DISSENT

67. HOUSE : BUILD :: TRENCH : (A. dig, B. trap, C. obliterate, D. dry)

68. CELL : WORKER :: ORGANISM : (A. occupation, B. proletariat, C. product, D. nation)

69. ANGLO-SAXON : ENGLISH :: LATIN : (A. Roman, B. Greek, C. Italian, D. Mediterranean)

70. SHERMAN : GEORGIA :: KITCHENER : (A. South Africa, B. Rome, C. Australia, D. Quebec)

71. CHARM : TALISMAN :: FEALTY : (A. allegiance, B. faith, C. payment, D. real estate)

72. ACCELERATOR : (A. cylinder, B. inertia, C. motion, D. exhaust) :: CATALYST : CHANGE

73. INTELLIGENCE : UNDERSTANDING :: CONFUSION : (A. frustration, B. pleasure, C. school, D. comprehension)

74. TALKING : YELLING :: GIGGLING : (A. rejoicing, B. laughing, C. chuckling, D. sneering)

75. 49 : 7 :: (A. 98, B. 103, C. 94, D. 144) : 12

76. (A. Chrysler, B. mink, C. chauffeur, D. Boeing) : CADILLAC :: BEAVER : CHEVROLET

77. BREAK : BROKEN :: FLY : (A. flied, B. flew, C. flown, D. flying)

78. DEFALCATE : EXCULPATE :: EMBEZZLEMENT : (A. blame, B. uncover, C. exoneration, D. divulge)

79. SAW : (A. teeth, B. knife, C. board, D. blade) :: SCISSORS : CLOTH

80. PEDAL : PIANO :: BRIDGE : (A. case, B. tune, C. rosin, D. violin)

81. BUCOLIC : CIMMERIAN :: PEACEFUL : (A. warlike, B. tenebrous, C. doubtful, D. smirking)

82. FLATTERY : (A. unity, B. self-interest, C. honesty, D. openness) :: FLIGHT : SAFETY

83. PRAYER : (A. church, B. Bible, C. religion, D. fulfillment) :: RESEARCH : DISCOVERY

84. PAYMENT : PREMIUM :: DEBT : (A. cracker, B. prize, C. insurance, D. scarcity)

85. SACRIFICE : HIT :: STEAL : (A. leave, B. slay, C. walk, D. rob)

86. (A. clap, B. play, C. doom, D. fork) : MOOD :: SLEEK : KEELS

87. DEMOLISH : BUILDING :: (A. sail, B. raze, C. dock, D. scuttle) : SHIP

88. LOGGIA : JALOUSIE :: GALLERY : (A. lintel, B. dowel, C. jamb, D. shutter)

89. PAGE : CUB :: (A. book, B. paper, C. herald, D. knight) : REPORTER

90. VIRGO : TAURUS :: SEPTEMBER : (A. May, B. January, C. June, D. November)

91. FELICITY : CONGENIAL :: BLISS : (A. clever, B. cordial, C. fierce, D. unfriendly)

92. WHEEL : FENDER :: (A. dashboard, B. bow, C. caboose, D. pedal) : RUDDER

93. REQUEST : VISIT :: DEMAND : (A. return, B. welcome, C. invasion, D. house)

94. DENOUEMENT : (A. climax, B. outcome, C. complication, D. untying) :: DEBIT : CREDIT

95. STRAIGHT : POKER :: SMASH : (A. hit, B. tennis, C. ruin, D. bat)

96. (A. small, B. sandwich, C. surprise, D. tight) : SCROOGE :: LYNCH : GUILLOTINE

97. VALLEY : GORGE :: MOUNTAIN : (A. hill, B. cliff, C. acme, D. high)

98. ALPHA : OMEGA :: MERCURY : (A. Saturn, B. planet, C. Pluto, D. Venus)

99. CHIFFON : TWEED :: (A. synthetic, B. sheer, C. dark, D. textured) : ROUGH

100. SIDEREAL : (A. side, B. part, C. stars, D. planets) :: LUNAR : MOON

101. GRIND : (A. wear, B. tear, C. see, D. darn) :: KNIFE : STOCKING

102. (A. Jacob, B. Benjamin, C. Isaac, D. David) : JOSEPH :: GEORGE V : ELIZABETH II

103. FIRE : SMOKE :: PROFLIGACY : (A. debt, B. prodigality, C. profit, D. deceit)

104. HERO : VALOR :: HERETIC : (A. dissent, B. bravado, C. reverence, D. discretion)

105. IRON : (A. bread, B. penicillin, C. virus, D. disease) :: RUST : MOLD

106. HALF-MAST : ELEGY :: UPSIDE DOWN : (A. excitement, B. error, C. confusion, D. distress)

107. WING : BEAK :: PAW : (A. tail, B. foot, C. cat, D. dog)

108. SINKS : ROCK :: FLOATS : (A. feather, B. light, C. flies, D. drowns)

109. LAUGH : (A. bathe, B. lather, C. water, D. dry) :: SMILE : WASH

110. LAY : LIES :: ATE : (A. eater, B. eats, C. eating, D. eat)

111. (A. loud, B. resounding, C. response, D. echo) : BALL :: RESONANT : RESILIENT

112. PRAISE : (A. exhort, B. exclaim, C. extort, D. extol) :: DRONE : DECLAIM

113. BUOYANT : CORK :: (A. jewel, B. watch, C. brilliant, D. extravagant) : DIAMOND

114. (A. wardrobes, B. tears, C. silverware, D. fall) : CLOTHING :: BREAK : DISHES

115. HANDPLOW : (A. building, B. skyscraper, C. stairs, D. feet) :: TRACTOR : ELEVATOR

116. (A. steel, B. head, C. combat, D. football) : FACE :: HELMET : MASK

117. REFEREE : RULES :: CONSCIENCE : (A. thought, B. regulations, C. morals, D. Freud)

118. TUNDRA : DESERT :: (A. exotic, B. dry, C. salty, D. frozen) : DRY

119. HISTORY : (A. fact, B. war, C. peace, D. geography) :: FABLE : FICTION

120. CORPORATION : (A. mayor, B. state, C. nation, D. government) :: PRESIDENT : GOVERNOR

ANSWER KEY AND EXPLANATIONS

1. C	25. D	49. A	73. A	97. B
2. B	26. B	50. D	74. B	98. C
3. C	27. A	51. C	75. D	99. B
4. B	28. C	52. C	76. B	100. C
5. D	29. A	53. A	77. C	101. D
6. A	30. D	54. B	78. C	102. C
7. B	31. B	55. C	79. C	103. A
8. D	32. B	56. B	80. D	104. A
9. D	33. A	57. C	81. B	105. A
10. C	34. C	58. A	82. B	106. D
11. A	35. C	59. C	83. D	107. A
12. C	36. D	60. B	84. C	108. A
13. C	37. B	61. A	85. C	109. A
14. D	38. A	62. B	86. C	110. B
15. A	39. B	63. D	87. D	111. D
16. C	40. B	64. C	88. D	112. D
17. B	41. B	65. C	89. D	113. C
18. A	42. B	66. D	90. A	114. B
19. C	43. C	67. A	91. B	115. C
20. A	44. A	68. B	92. B	116. B
21. B	45. C	69. C	93. C	117. C
22. C	46. C	70. A	94. C	118. D
23. A	47. C	71. A	95. B	119. A
24. D	48. A	72. C	96. B	120. B

1. SURFEIT : (A. collect, B. empty, C. glut, D, spoil) :: ARROGATE : USURP

   The correct answer is (C). Arrogate and usurp, which both mean to seize without justification, are related as synonyms; the only synonym for surfeit, meaning to satiate, is glut.

2. ROBBERY : INCARCERATION :: (A. marking, B. singing, C. sleeping, D. embezzlement) : APPLAUSE

   The correct answer is (B). This is a cause-and-effect analogy. Robbery can result in incarceration, and singing can result in applause.

3. ICHTHYOLOGY : (A. insects, B. mammals, C. fish, D. invertebrates) :: ORNITHOLOGY : BIRDS

   The correct answer is (C). The relationship is one of classification. Ichthyology is the study of fish, and ornithology is the study of birds.

4. IIRST : PENULTIMATE :: JANUARY : (A. December, B. November, C. February, D. June)

   The correct answer is (B). This is a sequence relationship. January is the first month of a year, and November is the penultimate, or next to last, month of a year.

5. HOPE : PLEASURE :: DESPONDENCY : (A. frolic, B. gratification, C. joy, D. anguish)

   The correct answer is (D). Hope and despondency are contrasting concepts. The concept that contrasts with pleasure is anguish.

6. DICHOTOMY : DISSEMBLE :: DIVISION : (A. feign, B. assemble, C. resemble, D. return)

   The correct answer is (A). Dichotomy and division are synonyms; a synonym for dissemble (meaning to disguise) is feign.

7. LONGFELLOW : WHITMAN :: (A. Tagore, B. Keats, C. Heine, D. Dickens) : TENNYSON

   The correct answer is (B). The relationship between Longfellow and Whitman is that both of them were American poets. Because Tennyson was an English poet, the task is to determine who is another English poet. Keats is the only choice. Dickens was an English novelist, Heine was a German poet and philosopher, and Tagore was a Hindu poet.

8. MITER : BISHOP :: (A. stole, B. cleric, C. robe, D. biretta) : PRIEST

   The correct answer is (D). The analogy is one of association. A miter is a head ornament usually worn by a bishop; a biretta is a cap characteristically worn by a priest. A stole and a robe are also worn by a priest, but biretta more specifically completes the correspondence with miter as headgear.

9. OK : PA :: KS : (A. CT, B. AZ, C. WV, D. NY)

   The correct answer is (D). OK and KS are both proper post office abbreviations for states (Oklahoma and Kansas). Oklahoma is also on the southern border of Kansas; PA (Pennsylvania in post office abbreviation) is on the southern border of NY (New York). WV (West Virginia) also borders upon PA, but its geographic relationship to PA is the reverse of that of KS to OK. KS is to the north of OK; WV is to the south of PA.

10. SEED : BREED :: (A. origin, B. specimen, C. need, D. act) : DEED

    The correct answer is (C). This is a nonsemantic analogy. Seed, breed, deed, and need all rhyme.

11. (A. influence, B. compose, C. touch, D. infect) : RESULT :: AFFECT : EFFECT

    The correct answer is (A). This is an analogy of synonyms. Affect is a verb meaning to influence. Effect as a noun means result. (The verb effect means to bring about.)

12. SAUTÉING : COOKERY :: PAINTING : (A. juggling, B. forestry, C. art, D. medicine)

    The correct answer is (C). The relationship is one of action to object. Sautéing is one act or form of cookery; painting is one act or form of art.

13. CAMPHOR : AROMATIC :: LILAC : (A. lavender, B. leaf, C. fragrant, D. rose)

    The correct answer is (C). Aromatic is a characteristic of camphor; a characteristic of lilac is fragrant.

14. (A. skiers, B. winter, C. athletes, D. blades) : SKATES :: RUNNERS : SLEDS

    The correct answer is (D). This is a part-to-whole analogy. Blades are parts of skates; runners are parts of sleds.

15. LOCARNO : SWITZERLAND :: ARGONNE : (A. France, B. Quebec, C. Germany, D. Belgium)

The correct answer is (A). The relationship is one of place. Locarno is located in Switzerland; the Argonne, a region that saw fierce fighting during the First World War, is in France near the Belgian border.

16. ARMY : FOOD :: DEFENSE : (A. digestion, B. vegetation, C. nutrition, D. supply)

The correct answer is (C). This is a purpose analogy. A purpose of an army is to provide defense; a purpose of food is to provide nutrition.

17. TAN : (A. Fitzgerald, B. Woolf, C. Orwell, D. Wolfe) :: JONG : WALKER

The correct answer is (B). Tan, Woolf, Jong, and Walker are all female authors. All other answer choices refer to male authors.

18. BENEFICENT : INIMICAL :: DELETERIOUS : (A. amicable, B. hostile, C. matchless, D. ordinary)

The correct answer is (A). Beneficent (beneficial) and deleterious (harmful) are antonyms. The only available antonym for inimical (hostile) is amicable (friendly).

19. ANEMOMETER : (A. smell, B. texture, C. wind, D. pressure) :: ODOMETER : DISTANCE

The correct answer is (C). The analogy is one of function. An odometer measures distance; an anemometer measures the velocity of the wind.

20. WHIP : HORN :: CRACK : (A. blow, B. break, C. tattoo, D. march)

The correct answer is (A). The relationship is one of object to action. One may crack a whip; one may blow a horn.

21. HILL : MOUNTAIN :: (A. depression, B. discomfort, C. headache, D. fear) : PAIN

The correct answer is (B). In this analogy of degree, a hill is a smaller version of a mountain; discomfort is a lesser version of pain. Note that a headache and depression are specific types of pain or discomfort, not degrees.

22. (A. *The Merry Widow*, B. *Naughty Marietta*, C. *Iolanthe*, D. *Carmen*) : *MIKADO* :: *H.M.S. PINAFORE* : *GONDOLIERS*

The correct answer is (C). The relationship is one of classification or part to part. The *Mikado*, *H.M.S. Pinafore*, and *Gondoliers* are all operettas written by Gilbert and Sullivan. *Iolanthe* is the only other Gilbert and Sullivan operetta offered among the choices.

23. BELL : HOLMES :: (A. Watson, B. Edison, C. Graham, D. Doyle) : WATSON

The correct answer is (A). This analogy is based upon the relationship of an individual to his assistant. Sherlock Holmes's name is often paired with that of his loyal and admiring assistant, Watson. The first person to hear a message over the newly invented telephone was Alexander Graham Bell's assistant, Watson.

24. WHEEL : SPOKE :: (A. heaven, B. ribbon, C. rim, D. bulb) : FILAMENT

The correct answer is (D). This is a part-to-whole relationship. A spoke is part of a wheel, just as a filament is part of a light bulb.

25. POLICE OFFICER : (A. convict, B. justice, C. conduct, D. crime) :: FIREFIGHTER : FIRE

The correct answer is (D). One characteristic of a firefighter is that he or she fights a fire. Similarly, a characteristic of a police officer is that he or she fights crime.

26. ROUND : CHUCK :: (A. circle, B. flank, C. chipped, D. throw) : RIB

The correct answer is (B). Every term in this analogy—round, chuck, and rib—is a cut of beefsteak. Therefore, the missing term must be flank.

27. FRACTIOUS : SYSTEMATIC :: DEBILITATE : (A. invigorate, B. undermine, C. diverge, D. annul)

The correct answer is (A). The given pair is related as antonyms because fractious means wild or unruly, the opposite of systematic. Debilitate, which means to weaken, must be paired with its opposite, invigorate, which means to strengthen.

28. FOUR : TWENTY :: (A. two, B. five, C. three, D. seven) : FIFTEEN

The correct answer is (C). In this numerical analogy, the relationship between four and twenty is a one-to-five ratio; the number with the same ratio to fifteen is three. The sentence by which you solve this analogy question is: "Twenty divided by five equals four; fifteen divided by five equals three."

29. GROUND CREW : SEMAPHORE :: PILOT : (A. radio, B. airplane, C. stewardess, D. copilot)

The correct answer is (A). The analogy is based upon agent and object or, better still, worker and tool. The ground crew gives messages to the cockpit crew by way of semaphore flags or lights; the pilot transmits messages by way of radio.

30. GLAND : ENDOCRINE :: MUSCLE : (A. hard, B. strong, C. desiccated, D. striated)

The correct answer is (D). Endocrine is one type of gland; one type of muscle is striated.

31. PROHIBITED : BANNED :: CANONICAL : (A. reputable, B. authoritative, C. referred, D. considered)

The correct answer is (B). Prohibited and banned are related as synonyms; a synonym for canonical is authoritative.

32. INTERMINABLE : ENDLESS :: APPARENT : (A. concise, B. ostensible, C. transparent, D. improbable)

The correct answer is (B). Interminable and endless are synonyms, as are apparent and ostensible.

33. ICE : STEAM :: BRICK : (A. straw, B. mortar, C. pole, D. stone)

The correct answer is (A). This analogy has to do with characteristics. Ice is solid; steam has little substance. Brick is solid; by comparison with brick, straw has little substance.

34. BREATHING : (A. oxygen, B. lungs, C. carbon dioxide, D. nose) :: CRYING : TEARS

The correct answer is (C). The relationship is action to object because crying releases tears. The task, then, is to determine what breathing releases. The process of respiration involves the intake of oxygen and the release of carbon dioxide.

35. EXERTION : EXHAUSTION :: CRUELTY : (A. cozen, B. annoy, C. suffering, D. competition)

   The correct answer is (C). Exertion causes exhaustion; cruelty causes suffering.

36. JAMES I : (A. James II, B. George I, C. Elizabeth I, D. Charles I) :: GEORGE V : EDWARD VIII

   The correct answer is (D). The relationship is one of sequence. The English king Edward VIII followed George V. To complete the analogy, you must choose Charles I, successor to James I.

37. PLANS : ARCHITECT :: TREACHERY : (A. thief, B. traitor, C. cheater, D. killer)

   The correct answer is (B). The analogy is based upon association. Plans are associated with an architect, as treachery is associated with a traitor.

38. 4! : 24 :: (A. 5!, B. 6!, C. 20!, D. 40!) : 120

   The correct answer is (A). $4! = 4 \times 3 \times 2 \times 1 = 24$, as $5! = 5 \times 4 \times 3 \times 2 \times 1 = 120$.

39. ANCHOR : KEY :: (A. dock, B. boat, C. prow, D. keel) : CHAIN

   The correct answer is (B). A key hangs from a chain; an anchor hangs from a boat.

40. (A. Scopes, B. Darrow, C. Darwin, D. Jennings) : BRYAN :: SACCO : VANZETTI

   The correct answer is (B). Sacco and Vanzetti are associated as codefendants in a famous trial. Bryan and Darrow are associated as opposing counsel in the famous trial of John Scopes, who was tried for teaching the theory of evolution in defiance of Tennessee law.

41. (A. subterranean, B. subconscious, C. superb, D. advertised) : SUBLIMINAL :: PLETHORIC : SUPERFLUOUS

   The correct answer is (B). Plethoric and superfluous are synonyms for excess; a synonym for subliminal is subconscious, meaning outside the area of conscious awareness.

42. VICTORY : PYRRHIC :: FRUIT : (A. ripe, B. bitter, C. pie, D. tree)

   The correct answer is (B). A Pyrrhic victory is a bitter one because it means a victory gained at ruinous loss; therefore, Pyrrhic is an undesirable characteristic of victory. A similar undesirable characteristic of fruit is bitterness.

43. TOUCH : DOWN :: (A. walk, B. river, C. home, D. stocking) : RUN

   The correct answer is (C). The relationship between touch and down is grammatical because these words can be used by themselves and also as a common sports-oriented compound word; therefore, the task is to determine which word can be used by itself and also as part of a common sports-oriented compound word with run. Home is the correct choice.

44. MITOSIS : DIVISION :: OSMOSIS : (A. diffusion, B. concentration, C. digestion, D. metamorphosis)

The correct answer is (A). The relationship is one of part to whole. Mitosis is one kind of division—specifically, the series of processes that takes place in the nucleus of a dividing cell, which results in the formation of two new nuclei, each having the same number of chromosomes as the parent nucleus. Osmosis is one kind of diffusion—specifically, diffusion through a semipermeable membrane separating a solution of lesser solute concentration from one of greater concentration to equalize the concentration of the two solutions.

45. SUN : (A. summer, B. tan, C. sunscreen, D. beach) :: COLD : OVERCOAT

The correct answer is (C). The purpose or function of an overcoat is to protect one from the cold; sunscreen protects one from the sun.

46. PHOEBUS : (A. Helius, B. Eos, C. Diana, D. Perseus) :: SUN : MOON

The correct answer is (C). This is a mythological analogy. Phoebus is the god of the sun; Diana is the goddess of the moon.

47. (A. equality, B. generous, C. wantonness, D. goodness) : LIBERTINE :: ADVOCACY : LAWYER

The correct answer is (C). The relationship is one of characteristic. One characteristic of a lawyer is his or her advocacy or support of his or her client; a characteristic of a libertine, or one who leads a dissolute life, is wantonness.

48. POUND : KILOGRAM :: WEIGHT : (A. mass, B. area, C. volume, D. capacity)

The correct answer is (A). This is a descriptive analogy. A pound is a measurement of weight; likewise, a kilogram is sometimes considered a measure of weight but is also a measure of mass.

49. PRECARIOUS : ZEALOUS :: CERTAIN : (A. apathetic, B. ardent, C. indigent, D. sensitive)

The correct answer is (A). Precarious and certain are antonyms; an antonym for zealous is apathetic.

50. PONDER : THOUGHT :: ARBITRATE : (A. endorsement, B. plan, C. fine, D. dispute)

The correct answer is (D). The correspondence is one of action to object. To ponder aids thought; to arbitrate aids a dispute.

51. OBSTRUCT : IMPENETRABLE :: IMPEDE : (A. forbearing, B. hidden, C. impervious, D. merciful)

The correct answer is (C). Obstruct and impede are synonyms; a synonym for impenetrable is impervious.

52. OCTAVE : SESTET :: (A. scale, B. ending, C. quatrain, D. symphony) : COUPLET

The correct answer is (C). This is an analogy of parts. Octave, sestet, and couplet are all parts of a sonnet. Only quatrain among the choices is also a part of a sonnet. If you know nothing about sonnets, you might notice that the three capitalized terms all have something to do with numbers—octave, 8; sestet, 6; couplet, 2—and so choose as the fourth term quatrain, 4.

53. NOVEL : (A. epic, B. drama, C. volume, D. story) :: *TOM SAWYER* : *AENEID*

   The correct answer is (A). The relationship between *Tom Sawyer* and the *Aeneid* is one of classification. *Tom Sawyer* is a novel, and the *Aeneid* is an epic.

54. PURSER : (A. bank, B. ship, C. race track, D. highway) :: BRAKEMAN : TRAIN

   The correct answer is (B). The correspondence is one of association or place. A brakeman is associated with a train; a purser is associated with a ship.

55. DRINK : SECURITY :: THIRST : (A. assuredness, B. stocks, C. fear, D. money)

   The correct answer is (C). Drink serves the function of relieving thirst; security serves the function of relieving fear.

56. CIRCLE : OVAL :: (A. figure, B. octagon, C. starfish, D. semicircle) : PARALLELOGRAM

   The correct answer is (B). A circle and an oval are both figures enclosed with one continuous curved side. Because a parallelogram is a figure enclosed with straight sides, the task is to find another straight-sided figure. Octagon is the only available choice.

57. RESILIENCY : RUBBER :: LAMBENCY : (A. oil, B. sheep, C. candlelight, D. lawn)

   The correct answer is (C). Resiliency is a characteristic of rubber; lambency, which means brightness or flickering, is a characteristic of candlelight.

58. VIRTUOSO : (A. orchestra, B. home, C. prison, D. college) :: TEACHER : CLASSROOM

   The correct answer is (A). A teacher works in a classroom; therefore, the task is to determine where a virtuoso works. Among the choices, an orchestra is the most likely place.

59. KEYBOARD : (A. small, B. office, C. mouse, D. radio) :: LIPSTICK : COMPACT

   The correct answer is (C). In this part-to-part analogy, lipstick and a compact are usually parts of the contents of a purse; a keyboard and a mouse are usually parts of a computer.

60. (A. 4, B. 7, C. 9, D. 14) : 28 :: 11 : 44

   The correct answer is (B). The numerical relationship between 11 and 44 is a ratio of 1 to 4; therefore, the task is to determine what number when paired with 28 is also in the ratio of 1 to 4. The answer is 7. The sentence is: "$44 \div 11 = 4$, just as $28 \div 7 = 4$."

61. CAPE : ARROYO :: PROMONTORY : (A. gully, B. waterfall, C. meadow, D. fen)

   The correct answer is (A). Cape and promontory are synonyms meaning a point of land jutting into the sea; a synonym for arroyo is gully.

62. BINDING : BOOK :: WELDING : (A. box, B. tank, C. chair, D. wire)

   The correct answer is (B). Binding secures or holds together a book; welding secures or holds together a tank.

63. SERFDOM : FEUDALISM :: ENTREPRENEURSHIP : (A. laissez-faire, B. captain, C. radical, D. capitalism)

   The correct answer is (D). Serfdom is a characteristic of feudalism; entrepreneurship is a characteristic of capitalism. Laissez-faire may be an aspect of both entrepreneurship and of capitalism, but in creating an analogy, capitalism forms a much better parallel with feudalism.

64. (A. bassos, B. dynamos, C. heroes, D. solos) : EMBARGOES :: VOLCANOES : TOMATOES

   The correct answer is (C). The relationship between volcanoes and tomatoes is grammatical. Each is a plural formed by adding "es." Because embargoes is also a plural formed by adding "es," the task is to find another word that also forms its plural this way. Heroes is the correct choice.

65. FOAL : HORSE :: CYGNET : (A. ring, B. fish, C. swan, D. constellation)

   The correct answer is (C). A foal is a young horse; a cygnet is a young swan. The relationship is one of young to old, or sequence.

66. WARFARE : (A. ingenuity, B. commerce, C. separate, D. destruction) :: TYRANNY : DISSENT

   The correct answer is (D). This analogy is one of cause and effect. Tyranny often leads to dissent; warfare often leads to destruction.

67. HOUSE : BUILD :: TRENCH : (A. dig, B. trap, C. obliterate, D. dry)

   The correct answer is (A). The relationship is object to action. A house is something to build; a trench is something to dig.

68. CELL : WORKER :: ORGANISM : (A. occupation, B. proletariat, C. product, D. nation)

   The correct answer is (B). The correspondence is one of part to whole. A cell is part of an organism; a worker is part of the proletariat. A worker may also be part of a nation, but proletariat is more specifically related to a worker.

69. ANGLO-SAXON : ENGLISH :: LATIN : (A. Roman, B. Greek, C. Italian, D. Mediterranean)

   The correct answer is (C). This is a sequence relationship. Anglo-Saxon is an early form of English; Latin is an early form of Italian.

70. SHERMAN : GEORGIA :: KITCHENER : (A. South Africa, B. Rome, C. Australia, D. Quebec)

   The correct answer is (A). General Sherman is remembered for his march through Georgia during the Civil War. He burned everything in his path as part of the Union's "scorched earth" policy. General Kitchener followed an identical policy in his conquest of South Africa during the Boer War.

71. CHARM : TALISMAN :: FEALTY : (A. allegiance, B. faith, C. payment, D. real estate)

   The correct answer is (A). Charm and talisman are synonyms; a synonym for fealty is allegiance.

72. ACCELERATOR : (A. cylinder, B. inertia, C. motion, D. exhaust) :: CATALYST : CHANGE

   The correct answer is (C). The relationship is that of cause and effect. A catalyst causes change, and an accelerator causes motion.

73. INTELLIGENCE : UNDERSTANDING :: CONFUSION : (A. frustration, B. pleasure, C. school, D. comprehension)

   The correct answer is (A). Understanding is a characteristic of intelligence; a characteristic of confusion is frustration.

74. TALKING : YELLING :: GIGGLING : (A. rejoicing, B. laughing, C. chuckling, D. sneering)

The correct answer is (B). Yelling is a greater degree of talking; a greater degree of giggling is laughing. Chuckling, while not exactly a synonym for giggling, is of the same degree. Rejoicing is more inclusive than laughing; it adds a dimension not called for in an analogy that begins "talking : yelling" and that offers a more specific choice.

75. 49 : 7 :: (A. 98, B. 103, C. 94, D. 144) : 12

The correct answer is (D). The number 7 squared is 49; the number 12 squared is 144.

76. (A. Chrysler, B. mink, C. chauffeur, D. Boeing) : CADILLAC :: BEAVER : CHEVROLET

The correct answer is (B). The correspondence is one of part to part. Chevrolet and Cadillac are both types of automobiles. Because a beaver is a type of animal, to complete the analogy, another type of animal must be selected. Mink is the only available choice.

77. BREAK : BROKEN :: FLY : (A. flied, B. flew, C. flown, D. flying)

The correct answer is (C). In this grammatical analogy, the past participle of break is broken; the past participle of fly is flown.

78. DEFALCATE : EXCULPATE :: EMBEZZLEMENT : (A. blame, B. uncover, C. exoneration, D. divulge)

The correct answer is (C). This is an action-to-object analogy. To defalcate is an act of embezzlement; to exculpate is an act of exoneration.

79. SAW : (A. teeth, B. knife, C. board, D. blade) :: SCISSORS : CLOTH

The correct answer is (C). The relationship is one of purpose because the purpose of scissors is to cut cloth, just as the purpose of a saw is to cut a board.

80. PEDAL : PIANO :: BRIDGE : (A. case, B. tune, C. rosin, D. violin)

The correct answer is (D). A pedal is part of a piano; a bridge is part of a violin.

81. BUCOLIC : CIMMERIAN :: PEACEFUL : (A. warlike, B. tenebrous, C. doubtful, D. smirking)

The correct answer is (B). Bucolic and peaceful are synonyms because bucolic refers to pastoral and peaceful scenes; a synonym of cimmerian, meaning shrouded in gloom and darkness, is tenebrous.

82. FLATTERY : (A. unity, B. self-interest, C. honesty, D. openness) :: FLIGHT : SAFETY

The correct answer is (B). A purpose of flight is safety; a purpose of flattery is self-interest.

83. PRAYER : (A. church, B. Bible, C. religion, D. fulfillment) :: RESEARCH : DISCOVERY

The correct answer is (D). The relationship is one of purpose. The aim of research is discovery; the aim of prayer is fulfillment.

84. PAYMENT : PREMIUM :: DEBT : (A. cracker, B. prize, C. insurance, D. scarcity)

The correct answer is (C). The correspondence is one of association. Payment is the term applied to money expended to reduce a debt, just as premium is the term applied to money expended to obtain insurance.

85. SACRIFICE : HIT :: STEAL : (A. leave, B. slay, C. walk, D. rob)

The correct answer is (C). Sacrifice, hit, and steal are all plays in baseball games. Among the choices, only walk is another type of baseball play.

86. (A. clap, B. play, C. doom, D. fork) : MOOD :: SLEEK : KEELS

The correct answer is (C). The relationship is nonsemantic. Sleek spelled backward is keels; mood spelled backward is doom. Actually, once you have ascertained that there is no meaningful or grammatical relationship among the three capitalized terms, you need only note that all three contain double letters and that only one choice has double letters.

87. DEMOLISH : BUILDING :: (A. sail, B. raze, C. dock, D. scuttle) : SHIP

The correct answer is (D). The relationship is action to object. To destroy a building, you can demolish it; to destroy a ship, you can scuttle it.

88. LOGGIA : JALOUSIE :: GALLERY : (A. lintel, B. dowel, C. jamb, D. shutter)

The correct answer is (D). Loggia and gallery are both types of porches; because jalousie is a type of blind, the task is to find another type of blind, and shutter is the correct choice.

89. PAGE : CUB :: (A. book, B. paper, C. herald, D. knight) : REPORTER

The correct answer is (D). The relationship is one of degree. A cub is a young reporter; a page is a young knight.

90. VIRGO : TAURUS :: SEPTEMBER : (A. May, B. January, C. June, D. November)

The correct answer is (A). The zodiac sign Virgo is associated with the month of September; Taurus is associated with May.

91. FELICITY : CONGENIAL :: BLISS : (A. clever, B. cordial, C. fierce, D. unfriendly)

The correct answer is (B). Felicity and bliss are synonyms; a synonym for congenial is cordial.

92. WHEEL : FENDER :: (A. dashboard, B. bow, C. caboose, D. pedal) : RUDDER

The correct answer is (B). Both a wheel and a fender are parts of a larger automotive unit; a rudder and a bow are both parts of a ship.

93. REQUEST : VISIT :: DEMAND : (A. return, B. welcome, C. invasion, D. house)

The correct answer is (C). The relationship is one of degree. Request is a polite term, and a demand can be an unpleasant request. Visit is a polite term, so the task is to find a word that denotes an unpleasant visit. Invasion is the correct choice.

94. DENOUEMENT : (A. climax, B. outcome, C. complication, D. untying) :: DEBIT : CREDIT

The correct answer is (C). Debit and credit are antonyms; an antonym for denouement is complication.

95. STRAIGHT : POKER :: SMASH : (A. hit, B. tennis, C. ruin, D. bat)

The correct answer is (B). A straight is a characteristic of a poker game; a smash is a characteristic stroke in a game of tennis.

96. (A. small, B. sandwich, C. surprise, D. tight) : SCROOGE :: LYNCH : GUILLOTINE

The correct answer is (B). Every term in this analogy is a word derived from a person's name. Scrooge comes from Dickens's Ebenezer Scrooge in *A Christmas Carol*; lynch, to put to death by mob action, comes from Judge Lynch; and a guillotine takes its name from Dr. Joseph Guillotin. Among the choices, only sandwich describes both a thing and a person from which it takes its name. The Earl of Sandwich is said to have been the first to put meat between slices of bread.

97. VALLEY : GORGE :: MOUNTAIN : (A. hill, B. cliff, C. acme, D. high)

The correct answer is (B). A gorge is a steep part of a valley; a cliff is a steep part of a mountain.

98. ALPHA : OMEGA :: MERCURY : (A. Saturn, B. planet, C. Pluto, D. Venus)

The correct answer is (C). The relationship is one of sequence. Just as Alpha and Omega are the first and last letters in the Greek alphabet, Mercury and Pluto, respectively, are the planets closest to and farthest from the sun.

99. CHIFFON : TWEED :: (A. synthetic, B. sheer, C. dark. D. textured) : ROUGH

The correct answer is (B). This analogy is one of characteristic. A characteristic of tweed is that it is rough; a characteristic of chiffon is that it is sheer.

100. SIDEREAL : (A. side, B. part, C. stars, D. planets) :: LUNAR : MOON

The correct answer is (C). The relationship is one of association. Lunar is associated with the moon; sidereal is related to the stars.

101. GRIND : (A. wear, B. tear, C. see, D. darn) :: KNIFE : STOCKING

The correct answer is (D). By way of repairing, you grind a knife and darn a stocking.

102. (A. Jacob, B. Benjamin, C. Isaac, D. David) : JOSEPH :: GEORGE V : ELIZABETH II

The correct answer is (C). The relationship hinges upon the relationship between grandparent and grandchild. George V was Elizabeth II's grandfather; Isaac was the grandfather of Joseph. The Biblical family progression is Abraham : Isaac :: Jacob : Joseph.

103. FIRE : SMOKE :: PROFLIGACY : (A. debt, B. prodigality, C. profit, D. deceit)

The correct answer is (A). A fire very often causes smoke; profligacy, extravagant spending, very often leads one into debt. Prodigality is a synonym for profligacy.

104. HERO : VALOR :: HERETIC : (A. dissent, B. bravado, C. reverence, D. discretion)

The correct answer is (A). The hero's stock in trade is valor; the heretic makes a mark by dissent or nonconformity.

105. IRON : (A. bread, B. penicillin, C. virus, D. disease) :: RUST : MOLD

The correct answer is (A). Iron rusts; bread gets moldy.

106. HALF-MAST : ELEGY :: UPSIDE DOWN : (A. excitement, B. error, C. confusion, D. distress)

The correct answer is (D). The flag at half-mast is a symbol of mourning; an elegy is a funeral dirge. The flag being flown upside down is a signal of distress and a call for help.

107. WING : BEAK :: PAW : (A. tail, B. foot, C. cat, D. dog)

   The correct answer is (A). Wing and beak are both parts of a bird; paw and tail are both parts of an animal. Foot is not the correct answer because paw and foot are two names for the same part.

108. SINKS : ROCK :: FLOATS : (A. feather, B. light, C. flies, D. drowns)

   The correct answer is (A). A rock sinks; a feather floats.

109. LAUGH : (A. bathe, B. lather, C. water, D. dry) :: SMILE : WASH

   The correct answer is (A). To laugh is more intensive than to smile; to bathe is more intensive than merely to wash.

110. LAY : LIES :: ATE : (A. eater, B. eats, C. eating, D. eat)

   The correct answer is (B). LAY : ATE :: LIES : EATS :: past : present. In order to determine the tense of the word lay, it is imperative to look at it in conjunction with the term in the choice (C) position.

111. (A. loud, B. resounding, C. response, D. echo) : BALL :: RESONANT : RESILIENT

   The correct answer is (D). A ball is resilient; an echo is resonant. Both bounce.

112. PRAISE : (A. exhort, B. exclaim, C. extort, D. extol) :: DRONE : DECLAIM

   The correct answer is (D). To drone is to speak languidly in a monotone; to declaim is to make a fiery oration. To praise is to say something nice; to extol is to glorify.

113. BUOYANT : CORK :: (A. jewel, B. watch, C. brilliant, D. extravagant) : DIAMOND

   The correct answer is (C). A cork is buoyant; a diamond is brilliant.

114. (A. wardrobes, B. tears, C. silverware, D. fall) : CLOTHING :: BREAK : DISHES

   The correct answer is (B). Dishes break; clothing tears; accidents happen.

115. HANDPLOW : (A. building, B. skyscraper, C. stairs, D. feet) :: TRACTOR : ELEVATOR

   The correct answer is (C). The handplow preceded the tractor as the implement for preparing the fields for planting; the stairs preceded the elevator as a means for reaching higher floors of a building. The analogy is based upon sequence of technological development. This is a commonly used analogy form.

116. (A. steel, B. head, C. combat, D. football) : FACE :: HELMET : MASK

   The correct answer is (B). A mask serves as protection for the face; a helmet serves as protection for the head.

117. REFEREE : RULES :: CONSCIENCE : (A. thought, B. regulations, C. morals, D. Freud)

   The correct answer is (C). The referee enforces the rules; one's conscience enforces one's morals.

118. TUNDRA : DESERT :: (A. exotic, B. dry, C. salty, D. frozen) : DRY

   The correct answer is (D). The desert is dry; the tundra is frozen.

119. HISTORY : (A. fact, B. war, C. peace, D. geography) :: FABLE : FICTION

   The correct answer is (A). History is fact; a fable is fiction.

120. CORPORATION : (A. mayor, B. state, C. nation, D. government) :: PRESIDENT : GOVERNOR

   The correct answer is (B). A president is part of a corporation—in fact, its head. The governor is part of the state government—in fact, he or she is its head.

ANSWER SHEET PRACTICE TEST 3

1. Ⓐ Ⓑ Ⓒ Ⓓ	31. Ⓐ Ⓑ Ⓒ Ⓓ	61. Ⓐ Ⓑ Ⓒ Ⓓ	91. Ⓐ Ⓑ Ⓒ Ⓓ
2. Ⓐ Ⓑ Ⓒ Ⓓ	32. Ⓐ Ⓑ Ⓒ Ⓓ	62. Ⓐ Ⓑ Ⓒ Ⓓ	92. Ⓐ Ⓑ Ⓒ Ⓓ
3. Ⓐ Ⓑ Ⓒ Ⓓ	33. Ⓐ Ⓑ Ⓒ Ⓓ	63. Ⓐ Ⓑ Ⓒ Ⓓ	93. Ⓐ Ⓑ Ⓒ Ⓓ
4. Ⓐ Ⓑ Ⓒ Ⓓ	34. Ⓐ Ⓑ Ⓒ Ⓓ	64. Ⓐ Ⓑ Ⓒ Ⓓ	94. Ⓐ Ⓑ Ⓒ Ⓓ
5. Ⓐ Ⓑ Ⓒ Ⓓ	35. Ⓐ Ⓑ Ⓒ Ⓓ	65. Ⓐ Ⓑ Ⓒ Ⓓ	95. Ⓐ Ⓑ Ⓒ Ⓓ
6. Ⓐ Ⓑ Ⓒ Ⓓ	36. Ⓐ Ⓑ Ⓒ Ⓓ	66. Ⓐ Ⓑ Ⓒ Ⓓ	96. Ⓐ Ⓑ Ⓒ Ⓓ
7. Ⓐ Ⓑ Ⓒ Ⓓ	37. Ⓐ Ⓑ Ⓒ Ⓓ	67. Ⓐ Ⓑ Ⓒ Ⓓ	97. Ⓐ Ⓑ Ⓒ Ⓓ
8. Ⓐ Ⓑ Ⓒ Ⓓ	38. Ⓐ Ⓑ Ⓒ Ⓓ	68. Ⓐ Ⓑ Ⓒ Ⓓ	98. Ⓐ Ⓑ Ⓒ Ⓓ
9. Ⓐ Ⓑ Ⓒ Ⓓ	39. Ⓐ Ⓑ Ⓒ Ⓓ	69. Ⓐ Ⓑ Ⓒ Ⓓ	99. Ⓐ Ⓑ Ⓒ Ⓓ
10. Ⓐ Ⓑ Ⓒ Ⓓ	40. Ⓐ Ⓑ Ⓒ Ⓓ	70. Ⓐ Ⓑ Ⓒ Ⓓ	100. Ⓐ Ⓑ Ⓒ Ⓓ
11. Ⓐ Ⓑ Ⓒ Ⓓ	41. Ⓐ Ⓑ Ⓒ Ⓓ	71. Ⓐ Ⓑ Ⓒ Ⓓ	101. Ⓐ Ⓑ Ⓒ Ⓓ
12. Ⓐ Ⓑ Ⓒ Ⓓ	42. Ⓐ Ⓑ Ⓒ Ⓓ	72. Ⓐ Ⓑ Ⓒ Ⓓ	102. Ⓐ Ⓑ Ⓒ Ⓓ
13. Ⓐ Ⓑ Ⓒ Ⓓ	43. Ⓐ Ⓑ Ⓒ Ⓓ	73. Ⓐ Ⓑ Ⓒ Ⓓ	103. Ⓐ Ⓑ Ⓒ Ⓓ
14. Ⓐ Ⓑ Ⓒ Ⓓ	44. Ⓐ Ⓑ Ⓒ Ⓓ	74. Ⓐ Ⓑ Ⓒ Ⓓ	104. Ⓐ Ⓑ Ⓒ Ⓓ
15. Ⓐ Ⓑ Ⓒ Ⓓ	45. Ⓐ Ⓑ Ⓒ Ⓓ	75. Ⓐ Ⓑ Ⓒ Ⓓ	105. Ⓐ Ⓑ Ⓒ Ⓓ
16. Ⓐ Ⓑ Ⓒ Ⓓ	46. Ⓐ Ⓑ Ⓒ Ⓓ	76. Ⓐ Ⓑ Ⓒ Ⓓ	106. Ⓐ Ⓑ Ⓒ Ⓓ
17. Ⓐ Ⓑ Ⓒ Ⓓ	47. Ⓐ Ⓑ Ⓒ Ⓓ	77. Ⓐ Ⓑ Ⓒ Ⓓ	107. Ⓐ Ⓑ Ⓒ Ⓓ
18. Ⓐ Ⓑ Ⓒ Ⓓ	48. Ⓐ Ⓑ Ⓒ Ⓓ	78. Ⓐ Ⓑ Ⓒ Ⓓ	108. Ⓐ Ⓑ Ⓒ Ⓓ
19. Ⓐ Ⓑ Ⓒ Ⓓ	49. Ⓐ Ⓑ Ⓒ Ⓓ	79. Ⓐ Ⓑ Ⓒ Ⓓ	109. Ⓐ Ⓑ Ⓒ Ⓓ
20. Ⓐ Ⓑ Ⓒ Ⓓ	50. Ⓐ Ⓑ Ⓒ Ⓓ	80. Ⓐ Ⓑ Ⓒ Ⓓ	110. Ⓐ Ⓑ Ⓒ Ⓓ
21. Ⓐ Ⓑ Ⓒ Ⓓ	51. Ⓐ Ⓑ Ⓒ Ⓓ	81. Ⓐ Ⓑ Ⓒ Ⓓ	111. Ⓐ Ⓑ Ⓒ Ⓓ
22. Ⓐ Ⓑ Ⓒ Ⓓ	52. Ⓐ Ⓑ Ⓒ Ⓓ	82. Ⓐ Ⓑ Ⓒ Ⓓ	112. Ⓐ Ⓑ Ⓒ Ⓓ
23. Ⓐ Ⓑ Ⓒ Ⓓ	53. Ⓐ Ⓑ Ⓒ Ⓓ	83. Ⓐ Ⓑ Ⓒ Ⓓ	113. Ⓐ Ⓑ Ⓒ Ⓓ
24. Ⓐ Ⓑ Ⓒ Ⓓ	54. Ⓐ Ⓑ Ⓒ Ⓓ	84. Ⓐ Ⓑ Ⓒ Ⓓ	114. Ⓐ Ⓑ Ⓒ Ⓓ
25. Ⓐ Ⓑ Ⓒ Ⓓ	55. Ⓐ Ⓑ Ⓒ Ⓓ	85. Ⓐ Ⓑ Ⓒ Ⓓ	115. Ⓐ Ⓑ Ⓒ Ⓓ
26. Ⓐ Ⓑ Ⓒ Ⓓ	56. Ⓐ Ⓑ Ⓒ Ⓓ	86. Ⓐ Ⓑ Ⓒ Ⓓ	116. Ⓐ Ⓑ Ⓒ Ⓓ
27. Ⓐ Ⓑ Ⓒ Ⓓ	57. Ⓐ Ⓑ Ⓒ Ⓓ	87. Ⓐ Ⓑ Ⓒ Ⓓ	117. Ⓐ Ⓑ Ⓒ Ⓓ
28. Ⓐ Ⓑ Ⓒ Ⓓ	58. Ⓐ Ⓑ Ⓒ Ⓓ	88. Ⓐ Ⓑ Ⓒ Ⓓ	118. Ⓐ Ⓑ Ⓒ Ⓓ
29. Ⓐ Ⓑ Ⓒ Ⓓ	59. Ⓐ Ⓑ Ⓒ Ⓓ	89. Ⓐ Ⓑ Ⓒ Ⓓ	119. Ⓐ Ⓑ Ⓒ Ⓓ
30. Ⓐ Ⓑ Ⓒ Ⓓ	60. Ⓐ Ⓑ Ⓒ Ⓓ	90. Ⓐ Ⓑ Ⓒ Ⓓ	120. Ⓐ Ⓑ Ⓒ Ⓓ

answer sheet

Practice Test 3

Directions: Each of these test questions consists of three capitalized words and four lettered words enclosed in parentheses. Two of the capitalized words are related in some way. Find the two related words, and establish the nature of the relationship. Then study the four words lettered A, B, C, and D. Select the one lettered word that is related to the remaining capitalized word in the same way that the first two capitalized words are related. Mark the answer sheet for the letter preceding the word you select.

1. SCEPTER : AUTHORITY :: SCALES : (A. weight, B. justice, C. commerce, D. greed)

2. STONEHENGE : EASTER ISLAND :: (A. yeti, B. dodo, C. nene, D. rhea) : LOCH NESS MONSTER

3. WORM : MOUSE :: BIRD : (A. man, B. snake, C. rodent, D. cheese)

4. (A. artist, B. description, C. narration, D. personality) : CHARACTERIZATION :: PICTURE : PORTRAIT

5. (A. orate, B. sing, C. mumble, D. speak) : TALK :: SCRAWL : WRITE

6. LYNDON JOHNSON : JOHN F. KENNEDY :: ANDREW JOHNSON : (A. Ulysses S. Grant, B. Abraham Lincoln, C. Martin Van Buren, D. William Pierce)

7. 46 : 39 :: (A. 61, B. 42, C. 76, D. 39) : 54

8. STEAM : WATER :: (A. lake, B. cloud, C. salt, D. tide) : OCEAN

9. SODIUM : SALT :: OXYGEN : (A. acetylene, B. carbon tetrachloride, C. water, D. ammonia)

10. (A. theft, B. notoriety, C. police, D. jail) : CRIME :: CEMETERY : DEATH

11. GRASS : (A. cow, B. onion, C. lettuce, D. earth) :: SNOW : MILK

12. HAND : (A. girth, B. fingers, C. horse, D. glove) :: LIGHT-YEAR : SPACE

13. QUISLING : CHAMBERLAIN :: COLLABORATION : (A. appeasement, B. negotiation, C. rejection, D. diplomacy)

14. PICCOLO : (A. trumpet, B. trombone, C. horn, D. baritone saxophone) :: VIOLIN : BASS

15. DIVULGE : DISCLOSE :: APPRAISAL : (A. revision, B. respite, C. continuation, D. estimate)

16. WEALTH : TANGIBLE :: (A. price, B. gold, C. success, D. gifts) : INTANGIBLE

17. HEMOGLOBIN : COACHES :: BLOOD : (A. train, B. whip, C. fuel, D. road)

18. SHELTER : (A. refuge, B. cave, C. mansion, D. protection) :: BREAD : CAKE

19. AFFLUENT : (A. charity, B. diligence, C. misfortune, D. indifference) :: IMPOVERISHED : LAZINESS

20. INNING : BASEBALL :: (A. time, B. midnight, C. era, D. chronology) : HISTORY

21. E.M. : (A. A.C., B. L.G., C. P.D., D. P.G.) :: FORSTER : WODEHOUSE

22. (A. stifle, B. tell, C. joke, D. offer) : LAUGH :: THROW : JAVELIN

23. CHARLESTON : (A. Tucson, B. Jackson, C. Williamsburg, D. Chicago) :: BOSTON : PHILADELPHIA

24. VINTNER : MINER :: (A. vines, B. wine, C. liquid, D. bottle) : ORE

25. (A. jaguar, B. mink, C. lion, D. chinchilla) : GIRAFFE :: TIGER : ZEBRA

26. (A. Athena, B. Artemis, C. Hera, D. Medea) : FRIGGA :: ZEUS : ODIN

27. 5 : 8 :: 25 : (A. 29, B. 40, C. 60, D. 108)

28. LIMP : CANE :: (A. cell, B. muscle, C. heat, D. cold) : TISSUE

29. CONFESSOR : KINGMAKER :: EDWARD : (A. Warwick, B. Alfred, C. George, D. Gloucester)

30. (A. parchment, B. concrete, C. cardboard, D. timber) : ADOBE :: PAPER : PAPYRUS

31. HANDS : ARMS :: (A. Roman, B. crack, C. Diana, D. destiny) : MORPHEUS

32. HYMN : THEIR :: CELL : (A. score, B. peal, C. tree, D. mile)

33. DOG : SWAN :: (A. bark, B. noise, C. days, D. collie) : SONG

34. EINSTEIN : MALTHUS :: RELATIVITY : (A. population, B. religion, C. economy, D. democracy)

35. GALLEY : ROOKERY :: MEAL : (A. ship, B. seal, C. peal, D. chess)

36. PEACH : (A. apple, B. beet, C. grape, D. tomato) :: CHERRY : RADISH

37. LASSITUDE : (A. longitude, B. languor, C. purity, D. alacrity) :: PARSIMONY : BENEFACTION

38. THERMOSTAT : REGULATE :: (A. draft, B. windows, C. insulation, D. thermometer) : CONSERVE

39. MONGREL : PEDIGREE :: BOOR : (A. thoroughbred, B. manners, C. ancestry, D. lineage)

40. (A. Earth, B. Venus, C. Sputnik, D. berry) : PLANET :: CANAL : RIVER

41. PIRAEUS : OSTIA :: (A. Athens, B. Florence, C. Milan, D. Crete) : ROME

42. (A. psychology, B. philology, C. philosophy, D. philately) : PHRENOLOGY :: ASTRONOMY : ASTROLOGY

43. ORACLE : LOGICIAN :: INTUITION : (A. guess, B. syllogism, C. faith, D. Venn)

44. PELEE : (A. France, B. soccer, C. Martinique, D. Brazil) :: ETNA : SICILY

45. GERONTOLOGY : GENEALOGY :: (A. families, B. aging, C. gerunds, D. birth) : LINEAGE

46. ROMAN : (A. Caesar, B. backward, C. gladiator, D. handlebar) :: NOSE : MUSTACHE

47. HYDROGEN : 1 :: (A. carbon, B. oxygen, C. nitrogen, D. potassium) : 16

48. (A. protein, B. nucleus, C. neutron, D. vacuole) : PROTON :: ARCH : HEEL

49. 19 : 23 :: (A. 7, B. 11, C. 13, D. 17) : 13

50. BOND : STOCK :: DEBT : (A. preferred, B. option, C. equality, D. equity)

51. (A. Laos, B. Indonesia, C. Afghanistan, D. Japan) : INDIA :: NEVADA : COLORADO

52. CONCISE : (A. refined, B. expanded, C. convex, D. blunt) :: REMOVE : OBLITERATE

53. TRAINING : ACUMEN :: (A. stupidity, B. experience, C. hunger, D. restlessness) : INANITION

54. BANTAM : (A. fly, B. chicken, C. fowl, D. small) :: WELTER : LIGHT

55. JACKET : (A. lapel, B. button, C. vest, D. dinner) :: PANTS : CUFF

56. (A. grave, B. aggravated, C. theft, D. first degree) : GRAND :: ASSAULT : LARCENY

57. (A. Athena, B. Ceres, C. Artemis, D. Aphrodite) : ZEUS :: EVE : ADAM

58. SERAPHIC : (A. Napoleonic, B. Mephistophelean, C. Alexandrine, D. euphoric) :: IMPROVIDENT : PRESCIENT

59. STRIPES : (A. bars, B. oak leaf, C. stars, D. general) :: SERGEANT : MAJOR

60. (A. precarious, B. deleterious, C. deterred, D. immortal) : CELEBRATED :: DEADLY : LIONIZED

61. MANET : REMBRANDT :: (A. Picasso, B. Dali, C. Pollock, D. Cézanne) : VAN GOGH

62. (A. glove, B. stocking, C. weakness, D. clothing) : GAUNTLET :: HAT : HELMET

63. STAPES : COCHLEA :: BRIM : (A. hat, B. derby, C. crown, D. head)

64. (A. rococo, B. severe, C. Etruscan, D. stylish) : ORNAMENTED :: SOGGY : MOIST

65. BURSAR : (A. funds, B. semester, C. accounts, D. purse) :: SEMINAR : IVY

66. NEW YORK : RHODES :: LIBERTY : (A. Colossus, B. London, C. tyranny, D. freedom)

67. RUBY : EMERALD :: TOMATO : (A. rose, B. radish, C. pasta, D. lettuce)

68. SOLID : MELTING :: SOLUTION : (A. saturation, B. liquefaction, C. heating, D. mixing)

69. (A. royal, B. kingly, C. regal, D. princely) : LAGER :: TIME : EMIT

70. HENRY FIELDING : (A. Victorian, B. Romantic, C. Restoration, D. Augustan) :: BEN JONSON : ELIZABETHAN

71. ARKANSAS : FLORIDA :: NEW MEXICO : (A. Tennessee, B. Ohio, C. California, D. Illinois)

72. SIN : ATONEMENT :: (A. clemency, B. peace, C. war, D. virtue) : REPARATION

73. (A. solo, B. duet, C. trio, D. quartet) : QUINTET :: BOXING : BASKETBALL

74. JULIAN : GREGORIAN :: (A. pope, B. Mayan, C. American, D. Canadian) : AZTEC

75. (A. echo, B. elephant, C. page, D. blue) : MEMORY :: DENIM : BLOSSOM

76. (A. Jupiter, B. Hippocrates, C. Cadmus, D. Ptolemy) : HANNIBAL :: CADUCEUS : SWORD

77. STYX : RUBICON :: ANATHEMA : (A. curse, B. pariah, C. parsee, D. song)

78. EPISTEMOLOGY : (A. letters, B. weapons, C. knowledge, D. roots) :: PALEONTOLOGY : FOSSILS

79. (A. ear, B. foundry, C. corps, D. fife) : FLINT :: DRUM : STEEL

80. JAVELIN : (A. run, B. pass, C. mount, D. toss) :: EYE : BLINK

81. PLATO : (A. Socrates, B. Sophocles, C. Aristophanes, D. Aristotle) :: FREUD : JUNG

82. (A. law, B. book, C. band, D. wagon) : WAINWRIGHT :: DICTIONARY : LEXICOGRAPHER

83. 15 : 6 :: 23 : (A. 8, B. 7, C. 6, D. 5)

84. CONCERT : (A. andante, B. a cappella, C. opera, D. artistry) :: PERFORMANCE : PANTOMIME

85. (A. uniform, B. commander, C. platoon, D. sentry) : DOG :: GARRISON : FLOCK

86. PORTUGAL : IBERIA :: TOOTH : (A. dentist, B. cavity, C. nail, D. comb)

87. RADIUS : (A. circle, B. arc, C. chord, D. diameter) :: YARD : FATHOM

88. EMINENT : LOWLY :: FREQUENT : (A. often, B. frivolous, C. rare, D. soon)

89. FILIGREE : METAL :: (A. lace, B. linen, C. cotton, D. silk) : THREAD

90. INTAGLIO : (A. cameo, B. caviar, C. Machiavellian, D. harem) :: CONCAVE : CONVEX

91. MEZZANINE : (A. orchestra, B. stage, C. proscenium, D. second balcony) ::
     ABDOMEN : THORAX

92. ROTUND : GAUNT :: (A. unruly, B. onerous, C. tractable, D. strong) :
     CONTUMACIOUS

93. GLACIER : MOLASSES :: (A. dirge, B. moth, C. spring, D. mountain) : TORTOISE

94. FOLD : (A. fell, B. hand, C. falls, D. boat) :: FORD : STREAM

95. VERDI : (A. *La Traviata*, B. *Fidelio*, C. *Aida*, D. *Rigoletto*) :: CHOPIN : *PARSIFAL*

96. SUBSTITUTE : TEAM :: UNDERSTUDY : (A. school, B. congregation, C. actor,
     D. cast)

97. PORT : (A. vintage, B. harbor, C. starboard, D. left) :: HEADLIGHTS : TRUNK

98. YORKTOWN : VICKSBURG :: CONCORD : (A. Philadelphia, B. Providence,
     C. Antietam, D. Valley Forge)

99. (A. border, B. score, C. quart, D. quatrain) : LINE :: SQUARE : CORNER

100. ROOSTER : (A. crow, B. coop, C. egg, D. owl) :: EFFERVESCENT : EFFETE

101. GELDING : CAPON :: (A. stallion, B. waterfowl, C. steer, D. mongrel) : EUNUCH

102. SIMPLEST : (A. fewest, B. myriad, C. more, D. most) :: SIMPLE : MANY

103. WEEK : DAY :: DAY : (A. month, B. second, C. hour, D. night)

104. FINIAL : PEDIMENT :: PINNACLE : (A. basement, B. lineage, C. gable,
     D. obstruction)

105. (A. their, B. your, C. we're, D. one's) : THEY'RE :: NE'ER : E'ER

106. HAIR : (A. grass, B. fish, C. scales, D. orangutan) :: FEATHER : OSTRICH

107. DIAPASON : (A. diaphragm, B. clef, C. chord, D. organ) :: KEYNOTE : TONIC

108. TOMORROW : YESTERDAY :: FUTURE : (A. present, B. unknown, C. year, D. past)

109. SEER : (A. auctioneer, B. dissembler, C. mendicant, D. philanthropist) ::
     PRESCIENCE : CHARITY

110. TONE : HEARING :: COLOR : (A. pigment, B. sight, C. melody, D. picture)

111. HANG : (A. gallows, B. nail, C. murderer, D. picture) :: BEHEAD : GUILLOTINE

112. SAMSON : ACHILLES :: (A. lion, B. hair, C. Delilah, D. pillars) : HEEL

113. MUTE : CUSHION :: HORN : (A. chair, B. padding, C. soften, D. pillow)

114. PLAY : REHEARSE :: GAME : (A. football, B. practice, C. coach, D. players)

115. COVET : (A. acquire, B. want, C. possess, D. pretext) :: GRIEF : DISTRESS

116. CELL : (A. mitosis, B. organism, C. phone, D. prisoner) :: CORRAL : LIVESTOCK

117. CARTON : DARNAY :: DAMON : (A. Runyan, B. Heloise, C. Romeo, D. Pythias)

118. MARBLE : (A. palace, B. engraving, C. agate, D. quarry) :: SALT : MINE

119. QUART : PINT :: GALLON : (A. inch, B. gram, C. liter, D. quart)

120. (A. radii, B. radial, C. radices, D. radiums) : ANALYSES :: RADIUS : ANALYSIS

ANSWER KEY AND EXPLANATIONS

1. **B**	25. **A**	49. **B**	73. **A**	97. **C**
2. **A**	26. **C**	50. **D**	74. **B**	98. **C**
3. **B**	27. **B**	51. **C**	75. **A**	99. **D**
4. **B**	28. **D**	52. **D**	76. **B**	100. **D**
5. **C**	29. **A**	53. **C**	77. **A**	101. **C**
6. **B**	30. **B**	54. **A**	78. **C**	102. **D**
7. **A**	31. **D**	55. **A**	79. **D**	103. **C**
8. **B**	32. **B**	56. **B**	80. **D**	104. **C**
9. **C**	33. **C**	57. **A**	81. **D**	105. **C**
10. **D**	34. **A**	58. **B**	82. **D**	106. **D**
11. **C**	35. **B**	59. **B**	83. **D**	107. **C**
12. **C**	36. **B**	60. **B**	84. **B**	108. **D**
13. **A**	37. **D**	61. **D**	85. **D**	109. **D**
14. **D**	38. **C**	62. **A**	86. **D**	110. **B**
15. **D**	39. **B**	63. **C**	87. **D**	111. **A**
16. **C**	40. **C**	64. **A**	88. **C**	112. **B**
17. **A**	41. **A**	65. **B**	89. **A**	113. **A**
18. **C**	42. **A**	66. **A**	90. **A**	114. **B**
19. **B**	43. **B**	67. **D**	91. **D**	115. **B**
20. **C**	44. **C**	68. **A**	92. **C**	116. **D**
21. **D**	45. **B**	69. **C**	93. **A**	117. **D**
22. **A**	46. **D**	70. **D**	94. **B**	118. **D**
23. **C**	47. **B**	71. **C**	95. **B**	119. **D**
24. **B**	48. **C**	72. **C**	96. **D**	120. **A**

1. SCEPTER : AUTHORITY :: SCALES : (A. weight, B. justice, C. commerce, D. greed)

   The correct answer is (B). A scepter is a symbol of authority; scales are a symbol of justice.

2. STONEHENGE : EASTER ISLAND :: (A. yeti, B. dodo, C. nene, D. rhea) : LOCH NESS MONSTER

   The correct answer is (A). The factor that all terms of this analogy have in common is that all concern mysteries. Stonehenge and the statues at Easter Island present mysteries as to their origin and purpose. The yeti, otherwise known as the Abominable Snowman, and the Loch Ness Monster present mysteries as to their existence and nature. The dodo is an extinct bird presenting no mystery. The nene is a Hawaiian goose, and the rhea is a South American bird somewhat akin to an ostrich.

3. WORM : MOUSE :: BIRD : (A. man, B. snake, C. rodent, D. cheese)

   The correct answer is (B). The relationship is that of object to actor or eaten to eater. A bird eats a worm; a snake eats a mouse.

4. (A. artist, B. description, C. narration, D. personality) : CHARACTERIZATION ::
PICTURE : PORTRAIT

The correct answer is (B). A portrait is a picture of a person; a characterization is a
description of the qualities or traits of a person.

5. (A. orate, B. sing, C. mumble, D. speak) : TALK :: SCRAWL : WRITE

The correct answer is (C). To mumble is to talk carelessly, thus making it difficult to
be understood; to scrawl is to write carelessly, thus making it difficult to be understood.

6. LYNDON JOHNSON : JOHN F. KENNEDY :: ANDREW JOHNSON : (A. Ulysses S.
Grant, B. Abraham Lincoln, C. Martin Van Buren, D. William Pierce)

The correct answer is (B). Lyndon Johnson was the vice president who succeeded
John F. Kennedy following Kennedy's assassination. Andrew Johnson was the vice
president under Abraham Lincoln who became president after Lincoln's assassination.

7. 46 : 39 :: (A. 61, B. 42, C. 76, D. 39) : 54

The correct answer is (A). In a mathematical analogy, always look first for the
simplest relationship between two terms. The difference between 46 and 39 is 7.
Because the number in choice (A) is 7 greater than the fourth term, your analogy is all
set. $46 - 39 = 7$; $61 - 54 = 7$. Choice (D) is incorrect because it reverses the order of the
relationship.

8. STEAM : WATER :: (A. lake, B. cloud, C. salt, D. tide) : OCEAN

The correct answer is (B). This is an analogy of the gaseous to the liquid state of a
substance. Steam is the vapor form into which water is converted by heat. A cloud is the
vapor form into which ocean water is converted by condensation.

9. SODIUM : SALT :: OXYGEN : (A. acetylene, B. carbon tetrachloride, C. water,
D. ammonia)

The correct answer is (C). Sodium is one of the elements of salt; oxygen is one of the
elements of water.

10. (A. theft, B. notoriety, C. police, D. jail) : CRIME :: CEMETERY : DEATH

The correct answer is (D). In this analogy of cause and effect, a crime usually results
in time spent in jail; death usually results in burial in a cemetery.

11. GRASS : (A. cow, B. onion, C. lettuce, D. earth) :: SNOW : MILK

The correct answer is (C). Snow and milk are related because they are both white;
grass and lettuce are both green.

12. HAND : (A. girth, B. fingers, C. horse, D. glove) :: LIGHT-YEAR : SPACE

The correct answer is (C). This analogy is one of measurement. A light-year is a unit
of measurement in space. A hand is a unit of measurement (equal to 4 inches) used to
determine the height of a horse.

13. QUISLING : CHAMBERLAIN :: COLLABORATION : (A. appeasement, B. negotiation,
C. rejection, D. diplomacy)

The correct answer is (A). This analogy comes straight out of World War II. Quisling
was the Norwegian leader who quickly made common cause with the Nazis and became
infamous for his collaboration. Chamberlain was the British Prime Minister who
thought that appeasement, giving Czechoslovakia to Hitler, would satisfy the Nazi
hunger for conquest and would avert the war.

14. PICCOLO : (A. trumpet, B. trombone, C. horn, D. baritone saxophone) :: VIOLIN : BASS

The correct answer is (D). A violin is a small, high-pitched string instrument; a bass is a large, low-pitched string instrument. Because a piccolo is a small, high-pitched woodwind instrument, then a large, low-pitched woodwind instrument must be selected to complete the analogy. A baritone saxophone is the correct choice. Trumpet and trombone are brass, not woodwind, instruments. An English horn is classified as a woodwind, but an unspecified horn is considered brass.

15. DIVULGE : DISCLOSE :: APPRAISAL : (A. revision, B. respite, C. continuation, D. estimate)

The correct answer is (D). Divulge and disclose are synonyms; a synonym for appraisal is estimate.

16. WEALTH : TANGIBLE :: (A. price, B. gold, C. success, D. gifts) : INTANGIBLE

The correct answer is (C). The correspondence is one of characteristic. Wealth is usually measured in tangible units; success is often measured in intangible units.

17. HEMOGLOBIN : COACHES :: BLOOD : (A. train, B. whip, C. fuel, D. road)

The correct answer is (A). In this analogy of a part to a whole, hemoglobin is part of blood; coaches constitute parts of a train.

18. SHELTER : (A. refuge, B. cave, C. mansion, D. protection) :: BREAD : CAKE

The correct answer is (C). Bread and cake are related because the former is a necessity and the latter is a luxury; similarly, a shelter is a necessity, and a mansion is a luxury. It's a matter of degree.

19. AFFLUENT : (A. charity, B. diligence, C. misfortune, D. indifference) :: IMPOVERISHED : LAZINESS

The correct answer is (B). In this cause-and-effect analogy, diligence may contribute to making one affluent; laziness may contribute to making one impoverished.

20. INNING : BASEBALL :: (A. time, B. midnight, C. era, D. chronology) : HISTORY

The correct answer is (C). The relationship is one of measurement. A division of a baseball game is an inning; a phase of history is called an era.

21. E.M. : (A. A.C., B. L.G., C. P.D., D. P.G.) :: FORSTER : WODEHOUSE

The correct answer is (D). The analogy depends upon matching the initials to the last names of two British authors: E.M. Forster and P.G. Wodehouse.

22. (A. stifle, B. tell, C. joke, D. offer) : LAUGH :: THROW : JAVELIN

The correct answer is (A). This is an action-to-object analogy. One may throw a javelin, and one may stifle, or repress, a laugh. This question may prove puzzling because there is absolutely no meaningful relationship between throwing a javelin and stifling a laugh. However, the action-to-object relationship is real and legitimate.

23. CHARLESTON : (A. Tucson, B. Jackson, C. Williamsburg, D. Chicago) :: BOSTON : PHILADELPHIA

The correct answer is (C). In this place analogy, Charleston, Boston, and Philadelphia are related because they were important colonial cities. Among the available choices, only Williamsburg was another colonial city.

24. VINTNER : MINER :: (A. vines, B. wine, C. liquid, D. bottle) : ORE

The correct answer is (B). The relationship here is that of agent to the object of his or her actions. The miner works to extract ore from the earth; the vintner works to produce and to sell wine.

25. (A. jaguar, B. mink, C. lion, D, chinchilla) : GIRAFFE :: TIGER : ZEBRA

The correct answer is (A). A jaguar and a giraffe are related because both have spots; a tiger and a zebra are both striped.

26. (A. Athena, B. Artemis, C. Hera, D. Medea) : FRIGGA :: ZEUS : ODIN

The correct answer is (C). Zeus was king of the gods in Greek mythology; Hera was his wife. Odin was the supreme god in Norse mythology; Frigga was his wife.

27. 5 : 8 :: 25 : (A. 29, B. 40, C. 60, D. 108)

The correct answer is (B). 25 is the square of 5, but 64, the square of 8, is not offered as a choice, so you must rethink, $5 \times 5 = 25$; $5 \times 8 = 40$.

28. LIMP : CANE :: (A. cell, B. muscle, C. heat, D. cold) : TISSUE

The correct answer is (D). A person with a limp is likely to use a cane; a person with a cold is likely to use a tissue.

29. CONFESSOR : KINGMAKER :: EDWARD : (A. Warwick, B. Alfred, C. George, D. Gloucester)

The correct answer is (A). The correspondence is one of association. Edward was known as the Confessor; Warwick was known as the Kingmaker.

30. (A. parchment, B. concrete, C. cardboard, D. timber) : ADOBE :: PAPER : PAPYRUS

The correct answer is (B). This is an analogy of sequence. Adobe was used before concrete as a building material; papyrus was used before paper as a writing material.

31. HANDS : ARMS :: (A. Roman, B. crack, C. Diana, D. destiny) : MORPHEUS

The correct answer is (D). Truly this is an analogy based upon association. In commonly used expressions, the linkage is "in the arms of Morpheus" and "in the hands of destiny."

32. HYMN : THEIR :: CELL : (A. score, B. peal, C. tree, D. mile)

The correct answer is (B). Each of the given terms in this analogy has a homophone, a word pronounced the same but spelled differently: hymn (him); their (there); and cell (sell). Among the choices, only peal has a homophone (peel).

33. DOG : SWAN :: (A. bark, B. noise, C. days, D. collie) : SONG

The correct answer is (C). The relationship is one of association. We speak of a swan song—that is, a farewell appearance or final act—and dog days, a period of hot, sultry weather or stagnation and inactivity. Swans do not sing; therefore, for purposes of this analogy, the barking of dogs is irrelevant.

34. EINSTEIN : MALTHUS :: RELATIVITY : (A. population, B. religion, C. economy, D. democracy)

The correct answer is (A). The correspondence is between a thinker and the theory with which he is associated. Einstein developed the theory of relativity; Malthus is famous for his theory of population. Although Malthus was an economist, it is not his field but his theory that successfully completes this analogy. The relationship of Malthus to the economy would be analogous to the relationship of Einstein to physics.

35. GALLEY : ROOKERY :: MEAL : (A. ship, B. seal, C. peal, D. chess)

The correct answer is (B). In this analogy of place, a galley is where a meal is produced, usually on board a ship; a rookery is the nesting place of a colony of seals, usually a rocky promontory or an isolated rock. It serves as the place where seals live and breed.

36. PEACH : (A. apple, B. beet, C. grape, D. tomato) :: CHERRY : RADISH

The correct answer is (B). A peach and a cherry are fruits that grow on trees; a radish and a beet are root vegetables.

37. LASSITUDE : (A. longitude, B. languor, C. purity, D. alacrity) :: PARSIMONY : BENEFACTION

The correct answer is (D). The opposite of parsimony, or stinginess, is benefaction, which means charitable donation; an antonym for lassitude, meaning listlessness, is alacrity, which means promptness of response.

38. THERMOSTAT : REGULATE :: (A. draft, B. windows, C. insulation, D. thermometer) : CONSERVE

The correct answer is (C). The purpose of a thermostat is to regulate room temperature; the purpose of insulation is to conserve energy.

39. MONGREL : PEDIGREE :: BOOR : (A. thoroughbred, B. manners, C. ancestry, D. lineage)

The correct answer is (B). A mongrel has no pedigree, just as a boor has no manners.

40. (A. Earth, B. Venus, C. Sputnik, D. berry) : PLANET :: CANAL : RIVER

The correct answer is (C). The correspondence is between man-made and natural objects. Sputnik is a man-made object that orbits; a planet is a natural object that orbits. Similarly, a canal is a man-made waterway, and a river is a natural waterway.

41. PIRAEUS : OSTIA :: (A. Athens, B. Florence, C. Milan, D. Crete) : ROME

The correct answer is (A). In this place analogy, Piraeus is a port city near Athens; Ostia was a port city near Rome.

42. (A. psychology, B. philology, C. philosophy, D. philately) : PHRENOLOGY :: ASTRONOMY : ASTROLOGY

The correct answer is (A). Because astronomy and astrology both deal with the stars (with astronomy being the accepted science and astrology a disputed or questionable science), the task is to find an accepted science similar to the disputed science of phrenology (which deals with the head). Psychology is accepted and is the correct choice.

43. ORACLE : LOGICIAN :: INTUITION : (A. guess, B. syllogism, C. faith, D. Venn)

The correct answer is (B). The correspondence is one of thinker to tool. An oracle's prophecies can be based on intuition; a logician may reason by means of a syllogism, a formal scheme of deductive thinking.

44. PELEE : (A. France, B. soccer, C. Martinique, D. Brazil) :: ETNA : SICILY

The correct answer is (C). In this analogy of place or location, Etna is a volcano located on the island of Sicily. Pelee is a volcano located on the island of Martinique.

45. GERONTOLOGY : GENEALOGY :: (A. families, B. aging, C. gerunds, D. birth) : LINEAGE

The correct answer is (B). The relationship is one of classification. Gerontology is the study of aging; genealogy is the study of lineage.

46. ROMAN : (A. Caesar, B. backward, C. gladiator, D. handlebar) :: NOSE : MUSTACHE

The correct answer is (D). We speak of a Roman nose and a handlebar mustache. The correspondence is one of association.

47. HYDROGEN : 1 :: (A. carbon, B. oxygen, C. nitrogen, D. potassium) : 16

The correct answer is (B). Hydrogen, the lightest element, has an atomic weight of 1. Oxygen, with eight protons and eight neutrons in its nucleus, has an atomic weight of 16. Knowledge of chemistry is essential to this answer. Without such knowledge, you must guess.

48. (A. protein, B. nucleus, C. neutron, D. vacuole) : PROTON :: ARCH : HEEL

The correct answer is (C). The relationship is one of part to part. An arch and a heel are parts of a foot; protons and neutrons are parts of the nucleus of an atom.

49. 19 : 23 :: (A. 7, B. 11, C. 13, D. 17) : 13

The correct answer is (B). A prime number is a number that is divisible by no other numbers except 1 and itself. All the terms in question 49, the given terms and the choices, are prime numbers, so you must base your answer on another relationship. Numbers 19 and 23 are prime numbers in sequence. Completing the analogy, 11 and 13 are prime numbers in sequence.

50. BOND : STOCK :: DEBT : (A. preferred, B. option, C. equality, D. equity)

The correct answer is (D). A bond is a certificate of debt issued by an institution. Stock is a certificate of equity, also issued by an institution.

51. (A. Laos, B. Indonesia, C. Afghanistan, D. Japan) : INDIA :: NEVADA : COLORADO

The correct answer is (C). In this analogy of place, Nevada and Colorado are states separated by another state, Utah. India and Afghanistan are countries separated by another country, Pakistan.

52. CONCISE : (A. refined, B. expanded, C. convex, D. blunt) :: REMOVE : OBLITERATE

The correct answer is (D). Remove and obliterate are synonyms, both resulting in elimination but varying in intensity. Therefore, you must find another word for concise that has the same result yet varies in intensity. Concise means succinct or pithy; blunt is a synonym but has the stronger connotation of brusqueness or rudeness.

53. TRAINING : ACUMEN :: (A. stupidity, B. experience, C. hunger, D. restlessness) : INANITION

The correct answer is (C). In this cause-and-effect analogy, training results in acumen or keenness of perception or discernment. Similarly, hunger results in inanition, a loss of vitality from absence of food and water.

54. BANTAM : (A. fly, B. chicken, C. fowl, D. small) :: WELTER : LIGHT

The correct answer is (A). Bantam, welter, light, and fly are all weight divisions in boxing.

55. JACKET : (A. lapel, B. button, C. vest, D. dinner) :: PANTS : CUFF

The correct answer is (A). A lapel is a folded-over part of a jacket; a cuff is a folded-over part of a pair of pants.

56. (A. grave, B. aggravated, C. theft, D. first degree) : GRAND :: ASSAULT : LARCENY

The correct answer is (B). Assault and larceny are both legal terms for crimes. Grand corresponds to larceny, describing the degree of the crime. The term that indicates the degree of assault is aggravated.

57. (A. Athena, B. Ceres, C. Artemis, D. Aphrodite) : ZEUS :: EVE : ADAM

The correct answer is (A). In this analogy of association of object to agent, Athena is said to have sprung from the head of Zeus; Eve is said to have been made from the rib of Adam.

58. SERAPHIC : (A. Napoleonic, B. Mephistophelean, C. Alexandrine, D. euphoric) :: IMPROVIDENT : PRESCIENT

The correct answer is (B). Improvident and prescient are related as antonyms. The former relates to the inability and the latter to the ability to foresee the future. Similarly, the opposite of seraphic, which means angelic, is Mephistophelean, which means devilish.

59. STRIPES : (A. bars, B. oak leaf, C. stars, D. general) :: SERGEANT : MAJOR

The correct answer is (B). In the army, stripes are associated with the rank of sergeant; an oak leaf is associated with the rank of major.

60. (A. precarious, B. deleterious, C. deterred, D. immortal) : CELEBRATED :: DEADLY : LIONIZED

The correct answer is (B). In this cause-and-effect analogy, something that is deleterious (exceedingly harmful) may prove deadly; a person who is celebrated (widely known) may be lionized.

61. MANET : REMBRANDT :: (A. Picasso, B. Dali, C. Pollock, D. Cézanne) : VAN GOGH

The correct answer is (D). Rembrandt and Van Gogh, the initial B : D related pair, were both Dutch painters. Manet and Cézanne were both French painters. The painter paired with the French Manet must be a French painter because the painter paired with the Dutch Rembrandt is a Dutch painter. Although Picasso spent most of his artistic life in France, he was Spanish.

62. (A. glove, B. stocking, C. weakness, D. clothing) : GAUNTLET :: HAT : HELMET

The correct answer is (A). A hat is an ordinary head covering. A helmet is a head covering worn in war. Because a gauntlet is a hand covering worn in war, you must look for an ordinary hand covering: a glove.

63. STAPES : COCHLEA :: BRIM : (A. hat, B. derby, C. crown, D. head)

   The correct answer is (C). The stapes and the cochlea are parts of an ear; a brim and a crown are parts of a hat. This is a part-to-part analogy. Avoid the part-to-whole temptation.

64. (A. rococo, B. severe, C. Etruscan, D. stylish) : ORNAMENTED :: SOGGY : MOIST

   The correct answer is (A). The relationship is one of degree. Rococo means excessively ornamented; soggy means excessively moist.

65. BURSAR : (A. funds, B. semester, C. accounts, D. purse) :: SEMINAR : IVY

   The correct answer is (B). A bursar, a seminar, and ivy are all things associated with college. To complete the analogy, another term associated with college must be selected; that term is semester.

66. NEW YORK : RHODES :: LIBERTY : (A. Colossus, B. London, C. tyranny, D. freedom)

   The correct answer is (A). The Statue of Liberty is set at the entrance to the harbor of New York; a bronze statue of Apollo, known as the Colossus, was set at the entrance to the harbor of ancient Rhodes. The analogy is one of place or location, but you do need some knowledge of ancient history in order to answer it.

67. RUBY : EMERALD :: TOMATO : (A. rose, B. radish, C. pasta, D. lettuce)

   The correct answer is (D). A ruby is a red gem, and an emerald is a green gem; a tomato is red, and lettuce is green.

68. SOLID : MELTING :: SOLUTION : (A. saturation, B. liquefaction, C. heating, D. mixing)

   The correct answer is (A). In this measurement analogy, the melting point is an important measure of a solid; the saturation point is an important measurement of a solution.

69. (A. royal, B. kingly, C. regal, D. princely) : LAGER :: TIME : EMIT

   The correct answer is (C). In this nonsemantic analogy, regal spelled backward is lager; time spelled backward is emit.

70. HENRY FIELDING : (A. Victorian, B. Romantic, C. Restoration, D. Augustan) :: BEN JONSON : ELIZABETHAN

   The correct answer is (D). The correspondence is one of association. Ben Jonson is associated with the Elizabethan period, the last part of the sixteenth century. Similarly, the novelist and playwright Henry Fielding is associated with the Augustan, or eighteenth-century, period.

71. ARKANSAS : FLORIDA :: NEW MEXICO : (A. Tennessee, B. Ohio, C. California, D. Illinois)

   The correct answer is (C). In this place analogy, Arkansas and New Mexico are interior states; Florida and California are related because they are coastal states.

72. SIN : ATONEMENT :: (A. clemency, B. peace, C. war, D. virtue) : REPARATION

   The correct answer is (C). Atonement is compensation made for an offense against moral or religious law (a sin). Reparation is compensation made by a defeated nation for losses sustained by another nation as a result of war between the two nations.

73. (A. solo, B. duet, C. trio, D. quartet) : QUINTET :: BOXING : BASKETBALL

The correct answer is (A). A boxing match is fought by solo contestants, with one on each side; a basketball team is a quintet, with five players on each side.

74. JULIAN : GREGORIAN :: (A. pope, B. Mayan, C. American, D. Canadian) : AZTEC

The correct answer is (B). In this analogy, Julian, Gregorian, and Aztec are all types of calendars that were used at one time in the past. Among the available choices, only Mayan was another type of calendar.

75. (A. echo, B. elephant, C. page, D. blue) : MEMORY :: DENIM : BLOSSOM

The correct answer is (A). Memory, denim, and blossom are all related because of a common characteristic: They all tend to fade. An echo also fades.

76. (A. Jupiter, B. Hippocrates, C. Cadmus, D. Ptolemy) : HANNIBAL :: CADUCEUS : SWORD

The correct answer is (B). In this association analogy, a sword is a symbol of warfare, associated with Hannibal, a great soldier; a caduceus is a symbol for medicine and should be related to Hippocrates, a famous physician.

77. STYX : RUBICON :: ANATHEMA : (A. curse, B. pariah, C. parsee, D. song)

The correct answer is (A). This analogy is based on synonyms. Both the Styx and the Rubicon represent points of no return. The Styx is the river that the dead cross into Hades; the Rubicon is a line, which, once crossed, represents total commitment. An anathema is a curse.

78. EPISTEMOLOGY : (A. letters, B. weapons, C. knowledge, D. roots) :: PALEONTOLOGY : FOSSILS

The correct answer is (C). Paleontology is concerned with the study of fossils; epistemology is concerned with the study of knowledge.

79. (A. ear, B. foundry, C. corps, D. fife) : FLINT :: DRUM : STEEL

The correct answer is (D). In this part-to-part analogy, a fife is used with a drum to make up a marching corps; a flint is used with steel to produce a fire.

80. JAVELIN : (A. run, B. pass, C. mount, D. throw) :: EYE : BLINK

The correct answer is (D). The correspondence is one of object to action. One can blink an eye, and one can throw a javelin, a metal spear.

81. PLATO : (A. Socrates, B. Sophocles, C. Aristophanes, D. Aristotle) :: FREUD : JUNG

The correct answer is (D). Aristotle was a follower, albeit with modifications, of Plato; Jung was a follower, again with modifications, of Freud.

82. (A. law, B. book, C. band, D. wagon) : WAINWRIGHT :: DICTIONARY : LEXICOGRAPHER

The correct answer is (D). This analogy is one of worker to the article created. A lexicographer compiles a dictionary; a wainwright makes a wagon.

83. 15 : 6 :: 23 : (A. 8, B. 7, C. 6, D. 5)

The correct answer is (D). Think of this as a nonsemantic or configurational analogy utilizing numbers instead of words. $1 + 5 = 6$; $2 + 3 = 5$. In other words, the two digits of the first number added together create the next number.

84. CONCERT : (A. andante, B. a cappella, C. opera, D. artistry) :: PERFORMANCE : PANTOMIME

The correct answer is (B). A concert in which there is singing without musical accompaniment is a cappella; a dramatic performance in which there is no dialogue is a pantomime.

85. (A. uniform, B. commander, C. platoon, D. sentry) : DOG :: GARRISON : FLOCK

The correct answer is (D). A sentry guards a garrison; a sheep dog guards a flock.

86. PORTUGAL : IBERIA :: TOOTH : (A. dentist, B. cavity, C. nail, D. comb)

The correct answer is (D). Portugal is part of the peninsula of Iberia; a tooth is part of a comb. You must shift your thinking away from the mouth to arrive at the answer.

87. RADIUS : (A. circle, B. arc, C. chord, D. diameter) :: YARD : FATHOM

The correct answer is (D). A yard (3 feet) is half as long as a fathom (6 feet). In a given circle, the radius is half as long as the diameter.

88. EMINENT : LOWLY :: FREQUENT : (A. often, B. frivolous, C. rare, D. soon)

The correct answer is (C). Eminent and lowly are antonyms; an antonym for frequent is rare.

89. FILIGREE : METAL :: (A. lace, B. linen, C. cotton, D. silk) : THREAD

The correct answer is (A). In this definition analogy, filigree is delicate ornamental openwork made of metal; lace is delicate openwork fabric made from thread.

90. INTAGLIO : (A. cameo, B. caviar, C. Machiavellian, D. harem) :: CONCAVE : CONVEX

The correct answer is (A). Concave means curving inward, whereas convex means curving outward. Intaglio is incised carving. It relates, therefore, to concave. A cameo, which is carved in relief, corresponds to convex.

91. MEZZANINE : (A. orchestra, B. stage, C. proscenium, D. second balcony) :: ABDOMEN : THORAX

The correct answer is (D). The mezzanine is located directly below the second balcony, just as the abdomen is located below the thorax.

92. ROTUND : GAUNT :: (A. unruly, B. onerous, C. tractable, D. strong) : CONTUMACIOUS

The correct answer is (C). Rotund, which refers to something rounded in figure or plump, is the opposite of gaunt, which means thin. An antonym for contumacious, meaning disobedient or rebellious, is tractable, meaning docile or yielding.

93. GLACIER : MOLASSES :: (A. dirge, B. moth, C. spring, D. mountain) : TORTOISE

The correct answer is (A). A glacier, molasses, and a tortoise are all related because they move slowly. Among the choices given, only a dirge is also slow moving.

94. FOLD : (A. fell, B. hand, C. falls, D. boat) :: FORD : STREAM

The correct answer is (B). In this action-to-object analogy, one may ford a stream, and one can fold a hand in cards. Mental flexibility is a must in answering Miller Analogy questions.

95. VERDI : (A. *La Traviata*, B. *Fidelio*, C. *Aida*, D. *Rigoletto*) :: CHOPIN : *PARSIFAL*

The correct answer is (B). Chopin did not compose *Parsifal*. To complete the analogy, you must select what Verdi did not compose. The correct choice is *Fidelio*, which was composed by Beethoven.

96. SUBSTITUTE : TEAM :: UNDERSTUDY : (A. school, B. congregation, C. actor, D. cast)

The correct answer is (D). A substitute is used to replace someone on a team; an understudy is used to replace someone in a cast.

97. PORT : (A. vintage, B. harbor, C. starboard, D. left) :: HEADLIGHTS : TRUNK

The correct answer is (C). Port and starboard are opposite sides of a ship; the headlights and the trunk are at opposite ends of an automobile.

98. YORKTOWN : VICKSBURG :: CONCORD : (A. Philadelphia, B. Providence, C. Antietam, D. Valley Forge)

The correct answer is (C). In this place analogy, Yorktown was the site of a major battle in the Revolutionary War; Vicksburg was the site of a major battle in the Civil War. Because Concord was also a site of a Revolutionary War battle, another Civil War battle site must be found to complete the analogy. Antietam is the correct choice.

99. (A. border, B. score, C. quart, D. quatrain) : LINE :: SQUARE : CORNER

The correct answer is (D). This analogy is based upon a four-in-one ratio. There are four lines in a quatrain and four corners to a square.

100. ROOSTER : (A. crow, B. coop, C. egg, D. owl) :: EFFERVESCENT : EFFETE

The correct answer is (D). Because *effervescent*, meaning *exuberant*, and *effete*, meaning *exhausted*, are opposites, the task is to find a contrast for *rooster*. A rooster is associated with morning, whereas an owl is a night bird.

101. GELDING : CAPON :: (A. stallion, B. waterfowl, C. steer, D. mongrel) : EUNUCH

The correct answer is (C). All four terms of this analogy represent parts of the same class. A gelding is a castrated horse; a capon is a castrated chicken; a steer is a castrated bull; a eunuch is a castrated human male.

102. SIMPLEST : (A. fewest, B. myriad, C. more, D. most) :: SIMPLE : MANY

The correct answer is (D). SIMPLEST : MOST :: SIMPLE : MANY :: superlative : positive.

103. WEEK : DAY :: DAY : (A. month, B. second, C. hour, D. night)

The correct answer is (C). A week is longer than a day; a day is longer than an hour.

104. FINIAL : PEDIMENT :: PINNACLE : (A. basement, B. lineage, C. gable, D. obstruction)

The correct answer is (C). Actually, all four terms in this analogy are synonyms or near synonyms. A finial is a top ornament. A pediment is the triangular space that forms a gable. A pinnacle is a lofty peak or a church spire. A gable is the triangular end at the top of a building. The other three choices do not refer to the uppermost portions of a structure.

105. (A. their, B. your, C. we're, D. one's) : THEY'RE :: NE'ER : E'ER

The correct answer is (C). WE'RE : THEY'RE :: NE'ER : E'ER :: we are : they are :: never : ever. On each side of the analogy, there are parallel contractions.

106. HAIR : (A. grass, B. fish, C. scales, D. orangutan) :: FEATHER : OSTRICH

The correct answer is (D). Feathers serve as the outside covering of an ostrich; hair serves as the outside covering of an orangutan.

107. DIAPASON : (A. diaphragm, B. clef, C. chord, D. organ) :: KEYNOTE : TONIC

The correct answer is (C). Diapason is the full range of harmonic sound, hence a chord played on an organ. The tonic, also known as a keynote, is the first note of a diatonic scale.

108. TOMORROW : YESTERDAY :: FUTURE : (A. present, B. unknown, C. year, D. past)

The correct answer is (D). TOMORROW (today) YESTERDAY :: FUTURE (present) PAST.

109. SEER : (A. auctioneer, B. dissembler, C. mendicant, D. philanthropist) :: PRESCIENCE : CHARITY

The correct answer is (D). The seer is known for prescience; the philanthropist is known for charity.

110. TONE : HEARING :: COLOR : (A. pigment, B. sight, C. melody, D. picture)

The correct answer is (B). The object of hearing is a tone; the object of sight is color.

111. HANG : (A. gallows, B. nail, C. murderer, D. picture) :: BEHEAD : GUILLOTINE

The correct answer is (A). On both sides of the analogy, we have effective manners of execution. The gallows is used to hang the victim; the guillotine is used to behead.

112. SAMSON : ACHILLES :: (A. lion, B. hair, C. Delilah, D. pillars) : HEEL

The correct answer is (B). Achilles' downfall was the arrow that entered the unprotected area of his heel; Samson's downfall was the cutting of his hair. Delilah betrayed Samson by telling of his weakness, but Samson's hair, as a body part, is analogous to Achilles' heel.

113. MUTE : CUSHION :: HORN : (A. chair, B. padding, C. soften, D. pillow)

The correct answer is (A). A mute softens the sound of a horn; a cushion softens the seat of a chair.

114. PLAY : REHEARSE :: GAME : (A. football, B. practice, C. coach, D. players)

The correct answer is (B). In a quest for perfection, the cast will rehearse the play; the team will practice the game.

115. COVET : (A. acquire, B. want, C. possess, D. pretext) :: GRIEF : DISTRESS

The correct answer is (B). Grief is intensive and all-encompassing distress; to covet is to want inordinately.

116. CELL : (A. mitosis, B. organism, C. phone, D. prisoner) :: CORRAL : LIVESTOCK

The correct answer is (D). A corral holds livestock; a cell holds prisoners.

117. CARTON : DARNAY :: DAMON : (A. Runyan, B. Heloise, C. Romeo, D. Pythias)

The correct answer is (D). This analogy is based upon unselfish sacrifice. In Dickens's novel *A Tale of Two Cities*, Sidney Carton goes to the guillotine in place of Charles Darnay. According to legend, in ancient Syracuse, Pythias was sentenced to die, but his friend Damon volunteered to serve as hostage so that Pythias could return home to say goodbye. Theoretically, if Pythias had not returned, Damon would have died in his place, so the analogy is complete and accurate. Actually, Pythias did return, and the king, Dionysus, was so impressed that he pardoned him rather than proceeding with the execution.

118. MARBLE : (A. palace, B. engraving, C. agate, D. quarry) :: SALT : MINE

The correct answer is (D). One mines salt; one quarries marble. This might just as well be an analogy of place. Salt comes from a mine; marble comes from a quarry.

119. QUART : PINT :: GALLON : (A. inch, B. gram, C. liter, D. quart)

The correct answer is (D). A quart is more than a pint; a gallon is more than a quart. A gallon is also more than a liter, but because the initial pair represents nonmetric measures, it is best to maintain the analogy in nonmetric terms.

120. (A. radii, B. radial, C. radices, D. radiums) : ANALYSES :: RADIUS : ANALYSIS

The correct answer is (A). RADII : ANALYSES :: RADIUS : ANALYSIS :: plural : singular.

answers practice test 3

Practice Test 4

89

ANSWER SHEET PRACTICE TEST 4

1. Ⓐ Ⓑ Ⓒ Ⓓ	31. Ⓐ Ⓑ Ⓒ Ⓓ	61. Ⓐ Ⓑ Ⓒ Ⓓ	91. Ⓐ Ⓑ Ⓒ Ⓓ
2. Ⓐ Ⓑ Ⓒ Ⓓ	32. Ⓐ Ⓑ Ⓒ Ⓓ	62. Ⓐ Ⓑ Ⓒ Ⓓ	92. Ⓐ Ⓑ Ⓒ Ⓓ
3. Ⓐ Ⓑ Ⓒ Ⓓ	33. Ⓐ Ⓑ Ⓒ Ⓓ	63. Ⓐ Ⓑ Ⓒ Ⓓ	93. Ⓐ Ⓑ Ⓒ Ⓓ
4. Ⓐ Ⓑ Ⓒ Ⓓ	34. Ⓐ Ⓑ Ⓒ Ⓓ	64. Ⓐ Ⓑ Ⓒ Ⓓ	94. Ⓐ Ⓑ Ⓒ Ⓓ
5. Ⓐ Ⓑ Ⓒ Ⓓ	35. Ⓐ Ⓑ Ⓒ Ⓓ	65. Ⓐ Ⓑ Ⓒ Ⓓ	95. Ⓐ Ⓑ Ⓒ Ⓓ
6. Ⓐ Ⓑ Ⓒ Ⓓ	36. Ⓐ Ⓑ Ⓒ Ⓓ	66. Ⓐ Ⓑ Ⓒ Ⓓ	96. Ⓐ Ⓑ Ⓒ Ⓓ
7. Ⓐ Ⓑ Ⓒ Ⓓ	37. Ⓐ Ⓑ Ⓒ Ⓓ	67. Ⓐ Ⓑ Ⓒ Ⓓ	97. Ⓐ Ⓑ Ⓒ Ⓓ
8. Ⓐ Ⓑ Ⓒ Ⓓ	38. Ⓐ Ⓑ Ⓒ Ⓓ	68. Ⓐ Ⓑ Ⓒ Ⓓ	98. Ⓐ Ⓑ Ⓒ Ⓓ
9. Ⓐ Ⓑ Ⓒ Ⓓ	39. Ⓐ Ⓑ Ⓒ Ⓓ	69. Ⓐ Ⓑ Ⓒ Ⓓ	99. Ⓐ Ⓑ Ⓒ Ⓓ
10. Ⓐ Ⓑ Ⓒ Ⓓ	40. Ⓐ Ⓑ Ⓒ Ⓓ	70. Ⓐ Ⓑ Ⓒ Ⓓ	100. Ⓐ Ⓑ Ⓒ Ⓓ
11. Ⓐ Ⓑ Ⓒ Ⓓ	41. Ⓐ Ⓑ Ⓒ Ⓓ	71. Ⓐ Ⓑ Ⓒ Ⓓ	101. Ⓐ Ⓑ Ⓒ Ⓓ
12. Ⓐ Ⓑ Ⓒ Ⓓ	42. Ⓐ Ⓑ Ⓒ Ⓓ	72. Ⓐ Ⓑ Ⓒ Ⓓ	102. Ⓐ Ⓑ Ⓒ Ⓓ
13. Ⓐ Ⓑ Ⓒ Ⓓ	43. Ⓐ Ⓑ Ⓒ Ⓓ	73. Ⓐ Ⓑ Ⓒ Ⓓ	103. Ⓐ Ⓑ Ⓒ Ⓓ
14. Ⓐ Ⓑ Ⓒ Ⓓ	44. Ⓐ Ⓑ Ⓒ Ⓓ	74. Ⓐ Ⓑ Ⓒ Ⓓ	104. Ⓐ Ⓑ Ⓒ Ⓓ
15. Ⓐ Ⓑ Ⓒ Ⓓ	45. Ⓐ Ⓑ Ⓒ Ⓓ	75. Ⓐ Ⓑ Ⓒ Ⓓ	105. Ⓐ Ⓑ Ⓒ Ⓓ
16. Ⓐ Ⓑ Ⓒ Ⓓ	46. Ⓐ Ⓑ Ⓒ Ⓓ	76. Ⓐ Ⓑ Ⓒ Ⓓ	106. Ⓐ Ⓑ Ⓒ Ⓓ
17. Ⓐ Ⓑ Ⓒ Ⓓ	47. Ⓐ Ⓑ Ⓒ Ⓓ	77. Ⓐ Ⓑ Ⓒ Ⓓ	107. Ⓐ Ⓑ Ⓒ Ⓓ
18. Ⓐ Ⓑ Ⓒ Ⓓ	48. Ⓐ Ⓑ Ⓒ Ⓓ	78. Ⓐ Ⓑ Ⓒ Ⓓ	108. Ⓐ Ⓑ Ⓒ Ⓓ
19. Ⓐ Ⓑ Ⓒ Ⓓ	49. Ⓐ Ⓑ Ⓒ Ⓓ	79. Ⓐ Ⓑ Ⓒ Ⓓ	109. Ⓐ Ⓑ Ⓒ Ⓓ
20. Ⓐ Ⓑ Ⓒ Ⓓ	50. Ⓐ Ⓑ Ⓒ Ⓓ	80. Ⓐ Ⓑ Ⓒ Ⓓ	110. Ⓐ Ⓑ Ⓒ Ⓓ
21. Ⓐ Ⓑ Ⓒ Ⓓ	51. Ⓐ Ⓑ Ⓒ Ⓓ	81. Ⓐ Ⓑ Ⓒ Ⓓ	111. Ⓐ Ⓑ Ⓒ Ⓓ
22. Ⓐ Ⓑ Ⓒ Ⓓ	52. Ⓐ Ⓑ Ⓒ Ⓓ	82. Ⓐ Ⓑ Ⓒ Ⓓ	112. Ⓐ Ⓑ Ⓒ Ⓓ
23. Ⓐ Ⓑ Ⓒ Ⓓ	53. Ⓐ Ⓑ Ⓒ Ⓓ	83. Ⓐ Ⓑ Ⓒ Ⓓ	113. Ⓐ Ⓑ Ⓒ Ⓓ
24. Ⓐ Ⓑ Ⓒ Ⓓ	54. Ⓐ Ⓑ Ⓒ Ⓓ	84. Ⓐ Ⓑ Ⓒ Ⓓ	114. Ⓐ Ⓑ Ⓒ Ⓓ
25. Ⓐ Ⓑ Ⓒ Ⓓ	55. Ⓐ Ⓑ Ⓒ Ⓓ	85. Ⓐ Ⓑ Ⓒ Ⓓ	115. Ⓐ Ⓑ Ⓒ Ⓓ
26. Ⓐ Ⓑ Ⓒ Ⓓ	56. Ⓐ Ⓑ Ⓒ Ⓓ	86. Ⓐ Ⓑ Ⓒ Ⓓ	116. Ⓐ Ⓑ Ⓒ Ⓓ
27. Ⓐ Ⓑ Ⓒ Ⓓ	57. Ⓐ Ⓑ Ⓒ Ⓓ	87. Ⓐ Ⓑ Ⓒ Ⓓ	117. Ⓐ Ⓑ Ⓒ Ⓓ
28. Ⓐ Ⓑ Ⓒ Ⓓ	58. Ⓐ Ⓑ Ⓒ Ⓓ	88. Ⓐ Ⓑ Ⓒ Ⓓ	118. Ⓐ Ⓑ Ⓒ Ⓓ
29. Ⓐ Ⓑ Ⓒ Ⓓ	59. Ⓐ Ⓑ Ⓒ Ⓓ	89. Ⓐ Ⓑ Ⓒ Ⓓ	119. Ⓐ Ⓑ Ⓒ Ⓓ
30. Ⓐ Ⓑ Ⓒ Ⓓ	60. Ⓐ Ⓑ Ⓒ Ⓓ	90. Ⓐ Ⓑ Ⓒ Ⓓ	120. Ⓐ Ⓑ Ⓒ Ⓓ

answer sheet

Practice Test 4

120 QUESTIONS • 60 MINUTES

Directions: Each of these test questions consists of three capitalized words and four lettered words enclosed in parentheses. Two of the capitalized words are related in some way. Find the two related words, and establish the nature of the relationship. Then study the four words lettered A, B, C, and D. Select the one lettered word that is related to the remaining capitalized word in the same way that the first two capitalized words are related. Mark the answer sheet for the letter preceding the word you select.

1. NEEDLE : (A. thread, B. pen, C. eye, D. hole) :: GLOBE : ORANGE

2. ARCHIPELAGO : ISLAND :: GALAXY : (A. universe, B. space, C. star, D. Milky Way)

3. DUCTILE : (A. malleable, B. adamant, C. regal, D. channel) :: LATENT : COVERT

4. NEWSPRINT : (A. paper, B. linotype, C. newsstand, D. tree) :: STEEL : ORE

5. EXPERIMENTATION : MATRICULATION :: DISCOVERY : (A. mothering, B. molding, C. learning, D. wedding)

6. BUTTER : GUNS :: (A. plowshares, B. margarine, C. fig trees, D. pruning hooks) : SWORDS

7. *MAINE* : (A. Miami, B. Cuba, C. Puerto Rico, D. Quebec) :: *ARIZONA* : HAWAII

8. (A. *Plaza Suite*, B. *Manhattan*, C. *Brighton Beach Memoirs*, D. *Auntie Mame*) : *BILOXI BLUES* :: *ANNIE HALL* : *RADIO DAYS*

9. MANTISSA : LOGARITHM :: SINE : (A. cosine, B. ratio, C. exponent, D. trigonometry)

10. BOXER : BOER :: (A. England, B. China, C. India, D. Empress) : SOUTH AFRICA

11. (A. Bartók, B. Mozart, C. Fauré, D. Beethoven) : WAGNER :: TCHAIKOVSKY : PROKOFIEV

12. (A. grind, B. thresh, C. harvest, D. grow) : WHEAT :: DISTILL : WATER

13. BRAGGADOCIO : RETICENCE :: MISERLINESS : (A. profligacy, B. ecstasy, C. obloquy, D. falsity)

14. 625 : (A. 5^5, B. 6^4, C. 7^4, D. 12^3) :: 5^4 : 2,401

15. SANDHURST : ENGLAND :: (A. Harvard, B. Pittsburgh, C. West Point, D. MIT) : UNITED STATES

16. AURICLE : VENTRICLE :: (A. sinus, B. epiglottis, C. thalamus, D. esophagus) : CEREBELLUM

17. (A. trees, B. circus, C. merry-go-round, D. skateboard) : STILTS :: BUS : AUDITORIUM

18. PARIS : (A. London, B. Priam, C. Achilles, D. Helen) :: ACHILLES : HECTOR

19. GENEROUS : LAVISH :: TIMOROUS : (A. tumid, B. craven, C. courageous, D. foolhardy)

20. MECCA : VARANASI :: MOSLEM : (A. Islam, B. India, C. Hindu, D. Buddhist)

21. POLO : MALLET :: (A. hockey, B. football, C. baseball, D. basketball) : STICK

22. (A. barber, B. bristle, C. comb, D. stroke) : BRUSH :: CRUISER : FLEET

23. HUDSON : BUICK :: PACKARD : (A. Stutz, B. Locomobile, C. Maxwell, D. Oldsmobile)

24. IRREGULAR : SYMMETRY :: (A. dentures, B. savory, C. distasteful, D. cavernous) : TOOTHSOME

25. (A. Jenner, B. Magyar, C. Bede, D. Pericles) : KOOP :: SCHWEITZER : SALK

26. ASSAYER : ORE :: SPECTROMETER : (A. lens, B. refraction, C. mirror, D. eye)

27. BRAZIL : (A. Portugal, B. Spain, C. Venezuela, D. Suriname) :: GUYANA : FRENCH GUIANA

28. (A. lunch, B. meal, C. breakfast, D. brunch) : SUPPER :: SMOG : HAZE

29. APPRAISAL : REVENUE :: (A. defrosting, B. clear, C. hiding, D. sun) : VISIBILITY

30. F : X :: 1 : (A. 4, B. 8, C. 2, D. 6)

31. RUPEE : (A. shah, B. euro, C. rial, D. krone) :: INDIA : NETHERLANDS

32. (A. servile, B. kowtow, C. unruly, D. inhibited) : OBSEQUIOUS :: IMPRECATORY : EULOGISTIC

33. BLUE : ORANGE :: (A. indigo, B. yellow, C. purple, D. red) : GREEN

34. CHEETAH : SPEED :: (A. blade, B. dullness, C. bird, D. incision) : KEENNESS

35. (A. hock, B. jockey, C. stable, D. hand) : HORSE :: TONGUE : BELL

36. EPILOGUE : NOVEL :: (A. cheers, B. curtain call, C. performance, D. introduction) : APPLAUSE

37. (A. Nantucket, B. Puerto Rico, C. Hawaii, D. Long Island) : UNITED STATES :: TASMANIA : AUSTRALIA

38. ANCHISES : (A. Troilus, B. Achilles, C. Ajax, D. Aeneas) :: JOCASTA : OEDIPUS

39. LEES : DREGS :: SYBARITIC : (A. sensual, B. moderate, C. cultish, D. servile)

40. ISRAEL : VIETNAM :: JORDAN : (A. Cambodia, B. Korea, C. Nepal, D. France)

41. MAP : (A. explorer, B. geography, C. legend, D. atlas) :: TEXT : FOOTNOTE

42. (A. clock, B. watch, C. time, D. hour) : TELL :: GUM : CHEW

43. BERET : DERBY :: PILLBOX : (A. fedora, B. shawl, C. cravat, D. stole)

44. COOPER : (A. lithographer, B. cartographer, C. photographer, D. biographer) :: BARREL : MAP

45. PUPA : (A. tadpole, B. larva, C. cocoon, D. insect) :: FETUS : CHILD

46. DEALING : STOCK EXCHANGE :: (A. preserving, B. selling, C. buying, D. copying) : LANDMARK

47. UPRISING : (A. revolution, B. settlement, C. quarrel, D. disquiet) :: FIB : LIE

48. (A. Crete, B. Malta, C. Sicily, D. Corsica) : SARDINIA :: BOLIVIA : ARGENTINA

49. EVIL : EXORCISE :: BREAD : (A. carbohydrate, B. break, C. sandwich, D. shred)

50. COWARD : (A. loser, B. lily-livered, C. hero, D. villain) :: YOLK : ALBUMEN

51. (A. humid, B. speedy, C. piquant, D. moist) : VAPID :: OBDURATE : COMPASSIONATE

52. CUCUMBER : WATERMELON :: CANTALOUPE : (A. squash, B. radish, C. cherry, D. plum)

53. (A. stick, B. percussion, C. cymbal, D. head) : DRUM :: STRINGS : VIOLIN

54. ILLNESS : (A. debility, B. hospital, C. doctor, D. panacea) :: VIBRATION : SOUND

55. VERDUN : DUNKIRK :: YPRES : (A. Belleau Woods, B. El Alamein, C. San Juan Hill, D. Marne)

56. (A. gain, B. reward, C. loot, D. profit) : ROBBERY :: REVENGE : VENDETTA

57. ANALYSIS : FREUD :: (A. manipulation, B. illness, C. sex, D. stimulation) : OSTEOPATHY

58. CLAUSTROPHOBIA : CLOSETS :: AGORAPHOBIA : (A. ships, B. sheep, C. plants, D. plains)

59. SEARCH : FIND :: FIGHT : (A. win, B. lose, C. seek, D. contend)

60. (A. affection, B. encouragement, C. blasphemy, D. oblivion) : FRACAS :: APHRODITE : MARS

61. H : S :: (A. M, B. L, C. I, D. P) : W

62. HASTILY : DESPONDENTLY :: CIRCUMSPECTLY : (A. quick, B. circuit, C. rate, D. slowly)

63. BOXER : TABBY :: LABRADOR : (A. fighter, B. poodle, C. calico, D. nanny)

64. CROESUS : (A. boat, B. wealth, C. pleats, D. loyalty) :: ODYSSEUS : CRAFT

65. LUCERNE : MICHIGAN :: GENEVA : (A. United States, B. Victoria, C. Okeechobee, D. Switzerland)

66. (A. tally, B. game, C. concert, D. run) : SCORE :: PLAY : SCRIPT

67. FLAUBERT : (A. madame, B. field, C. knife, D. writer) :: JOYCE : PORTRAIT

68. DOG : INTRUDER :: (A. burglar, B. cat, C. knight, D. maiden) : DRAGON

69. MENDACIOUS : DECEITFUL :: AUSPICIOUS : (A. indifferent, B. submerged, C. propitious, D. bereft)

70. PARTRIDGE : RABBIT :: (A. quail, B. pen, C. birds, D. covey) : WARREN

71. LAPIDARY : (A. ruby, B. wood, C. lick, D. food) :: SCULPTOR : ALABASTER

72. BEES : FILE :: BIRDS : (A. grade, B. rank, C. fold, D. twist)

73. MANY : MUCH :: FEW : (A. minus, B. more, C. small, D. little)

74. FORSOOK : DRANK :: FROZEN : (A. swum, B. wrote, C. sang, D. chose)

75. SANDAL : BOOT :: (A. hammer, B. hatchet, C. shoemaker, D. blade) : AX

76. HORSE : (A. man, B. goat, C. archer, D. bull) :: CENTAUR : SATYR

77. (A. anode, B. bird, C. purchase, D. battery) : CELL :: ARROW : SHAFT

78. FELONY : MISDEMEANOR :: SIN : (A. piccalilli, B. picayune, C. peccadillo, D. picador)

79. NOVEMBER : APRIL :: (A. May, B. June, C. July, D. August) : SEPTEMBER

80. ALBANIA : POLAND :: CHINA : (A. Czechoslovakia, B. Russia, C. Sumatra, D. India)

81. WASTEFUL : (A. parsimonious, B. neglectful, C. vast, D. prodigal) :: DISINTERESTED : IMPARTIAL

82. SCHOONER : ZIGGURAT :: CRUISER : (A. cutter, B. campanile, C. viking, D. tug)

83. (A. pine, B. cedar, C. ash, D. willow) : OAK :: MOURNFUL : STURDY

84. ADVISE : EXHORT :: (A. force, B. tempt, C. prohibit, D. prevent) : ENTICE

85. STEEL : WELD :: LIPS : (A. frown, B. purse, C. fold, D. smirk)

86. TESTIMONY : (A. confession, B. judge, C. witness, D. trial) :: BIOGRAPHY : AUTOBIOGRAPHY

87. STRATUM : SYLLABUS :: (A. strati, B. stratums, C. stratus, D. strata) : SYLLABI

88. LAMB : DEER :: (A. rabbit, B. peacock, C. horse, D. pig) : LION

89. VELOCITY : (A. wind, B. earth, C. vibration, D. destruction) :: BEAUFORT : RICHTER

90. (A. distance, B. program, C. station, D. tube) : TELEVISION :: LEADER : ANARCHY

91. TAPS : VESPERS :: (A. painting, B. needle, C. revelry, D. reveille) : MATINS

92. PROSTRATE : (A. dazzling, B. stealing, C. submission, D. dehydrated) :: SUPINE : SLEEPING

93. MAHATMA GANDHI : WAR :: CARRY NATION : (A. suffrage, B. alcohol, C. temperance, D. employment)

94. $\frac{2}{7}$: (A. $\frac{1}{16}$, B. $\frac{3}{28}$, C. $\frac{3}{21}$, D. $\frac{1}{14}$) :: $\frac{4}{7}$: $\frac{1}{7}$

95. (A. roc, B. canary, C. albatross, D. condor) : VULTURE :: PHOENIX : EAGLE

96. TINE : FORK :: (A. car, B. gearshift, C. flange, D. wheelwright) : WHEEL

97. (A. tie, B. appearance, C. shoes, D. decoration) : ATTIRE :: WIT : COMMUNICATION

98. HUSK : (A. fish, B. chops, C. gristle, D. filet) :: GRAIN : MEAT

99. SURPRISED : (A. interested, B. astounded, C. expected, D. unknown) :: WORK : TOIL

100. INEBRIOUS : (A. intoxicated, B. dull, C. sincere, D. abstemious) :: SPARTAN : GARRULOUS

101. CLUB : (A. prehistoric, B. cave, C. cannon, D. rampage) :: GUN : HOUSE

102. (A. proboscis, B. smell, C. olfactory, D. redolent) : TACTILE :: NOSE : FINGER

103. BARREL : SILO :: WINE : (A. horses, B. toss, C. grain, D. refuse)

104. LONDON : (A. Florence, B. Madrid, C. Milan, D. Rome) :: GLOBE THEATER : LA SCALA

105. TWIG : (A. thorn, B. branch, C. leaf, D. rose) :: BUD : FLOWER

106. (A. October, B. autumn, C. season, D. sadness) : SPRING :: LEAVES : FEVER

107. CARROT : COW :: PLANT : (A. meat, B. herd, C. animal, D. stockyard)

108. INGENUE : KNAVE :: NAIVETÉ : (A. chivalry, B. chicanery, C. morality, D. subtlety)

109. RUN : WALK :: (A. number, B. total, C. multiply, D. subtract) : ADD

110. (A. teacher, B. player, C. actor, D. surgeon) : TEAM :: OSCAR® : PENNANT

111. JABBER : GIBBERISH :: QUIDNUNC : (A. quisling, B. busybody, C. theorist, D. testator)

112. ENGLAND : DENMARK :: (A. Sweden, B. China, C. France, D. Thailand) : ISRAEL

113. GESUNDHEIT : AL DENTE :: CAVEAT EMPTOR : (A. buyer beware, B. amicus curiae, C. savoir faire, D. thank goodness)

114. HIS : (A. its, B. it's, C. her's, D. their's) :: MINE : YOURS

115. TRAIN : (A. steamer, B. pier, C. water, D. track) :: STATION : WHARF

116. BRACES : (A. suspenders, B. belt, C. band, D. tram) :: LORRY : TRUCK

117. HORSE : (A. telephone, B. letter, C. communication, D. transportation) :: AUTOMOBILE : TELEGRAM

118. CREPUSCULAR : CURSORY :: DIM : (A. profane, B. egregious, C. superficial, D. unique)

119. REPUGN : COMPROMISE :: RESCIND : (A. refuse, B. rest, C. decipher, D. validate)

120. UKRAINE : STEPPES :: ARGENTINA : (A. mountains, B. pampas, C. tundra, D. valleys)

ANSWER KEY AND EXPLANATIONS

1. **B**	25. **A**	49. **B**	73. **D**	97. **D**
2. **C**	26. **B**	50. **C**	74. **A**	98. **C**
3. **A**	27. **D**	51. **C**	75. **B**	99. **B**
4. **D**	28. **D**	52. **A**	76. **B**	100. **D**
5. **C**	29. **A**	53. **D**	77. **D**	101. **B**
6. **A**	30. **A**	54. **A**	78. **C**	102. **C**
7. **B**	31. **B**	55. **B**	79. **B**	103. **C**
8. **C**	32. **C**	56. **C**	80. **A**	104. **C**
9. **D**	33. **D**	57. **A**	81. **D**	105. **B**
10. **B**	34. **A**	58. **D**	82. **B**	106. **B**
11. **D**	35. **A**	59. **A**	83. **D**	107. **C**
12. **B**	36. **B**	60. **A**	84. **B**	108. **B**
13. **A**	37. **C**	61. **B**	85. **B**	109. **C**
14. **C**	38. **D**	62. **D**	86. **A**	110. **C**
15. **C**	39. **A**	63. **C**	87. **D**	111. **B**
16. **C**	40. **A**	64. **B**	88. **B**	112. **C**
17. **D**	41. **C**	65. **C**	89. **C**	113. **C**
18. **C**	42. **C**	66. **C**	90. **A**	114. **A**
19. **B**	43. **A**	67. **A**	91. **D**	115. **A**
20. **C**	44. **B**	68. **C**	92. **C**	116. **A**
21. **A**	45. **D**	69. **C**	93. **B**	117. **B**
22. **B**	46. **A**	70. **D**	94. **D**	118. **C**
23. **D**	47. **A**	71. **A**	95. **A**	119. **D**
24. **C**	48. **D**	72. **B**	96. **C**	120. **B**

1. NEEDLE : (A. thread, B. pen, C. eye, D. hole) :: GLOBE : ORANGE

   The correct answer is (B). A globe and an orange are related because they are both round; a needle and a pen are both pointed.

2. ARCHIPELAGO : ISLAND :: GALAXY : (A. universe, B. space, C. star, D. Milky Way)

   The correct answer is (C). This is a whole-to-part analogy. An archipelago is made up of islands; a galaxy is made up of stars. A galaxy is part of the universe; the order of the relationship is the reverse of that between archipelago and island. The Milky Way is a galaxy.

3. DUCTILE : (A. malleable, B. adamant, C. regal, D. channel) :: LATENT : COVERT

   The correct answer is (A). Latent and covert are synonyms meaning hidden or concealed. A synonym for ductile, which means something easily influenced or altered, is malleable.

4. NEWSPRINT : (A. paper, B. linotype, C. newsstand, D. tree) :: STEEL : ORE

   The correct answer is (D). In this analogy, the relationship is one of source to product. An original source of steel is ore; an original source of newsprint is a tree.

5. EXPERIMENTATION : MATRICULATION :: DISCOVERY : (A. mothering, B. molding, C. learning, D. wedding)

The correct answer is (C). In this purpose analogy, a purpose of experimentation is discovery; a purpose of matriculation is learning.

6. BUTTER : GUNS :: (A. plowshares, B. margarine, C. fig trees, D. pruning hooks) : SWORDS

The correct answer is (A). The implication of the saying "Butter is better than guns" is that peace is better than war. The passage from Isaiah, "They shall bend their swords into plowshares . . ." has the same implication. Pruning hooks are paired with spears.

7. *MAINE* : (A. Miami, B. Cuba, C. Puerto Rico, D. Quebec) :: *ARIZONA* : HAWAII

The correct answer is (B). The opening blow of Japan's involvement in the Second World War was the sinking of the battleship *Arizona* in Honolulu harbor in Hawaii. The Spanish-American War began with the sinking of the battleship *Maine* in Havana harbor, Cuba.

8. (A. *Plaza Suite,* B. *Manhattan,* C. *Brighton Beach Memoirs,* D. *Auntie Mame*) : *BILOXI BLUES* :: *ANNIE HALL* : *RADIO DAYS*

The correct answer is (C). *Annie Hall* and *Radio Days* are movies by Woody Allen in which he draws heavily upon his childhood experiences. *Brighton Beach Memoirs* and *Biloxi Blues* are autobiographical Neil Simon plays.

9. MANTISSA : LOGARITHM :: SINE : (A. cosine, B. ratio, C. exponent, D. trigonometry)

The correct answer is (D). This analogy from the language of mathematics is based on a part-to-whole relationship. A mantissa is the decimal part of a logarithm. Sine is a function in trigonometry.

10. BOXER : BOER :: (A. England, B. China, C. India, D. Empress) : SOUTH AFRICA

The correct answer is (B). This is an analogy involving history and place. The Boer War took place in South Africa; the Boxer Rebellion occurred in China.

11. (A. Bartók, B. Mozart, C. Fauré, D. Beethoven) : WAGNER :: TCHAIKOVSKY : PROKOFIEV

The correct answer is (D). Tchaikovsky and Prokofiev are related because they both are composers from Russia; therefore, to complete the analogy, Wagner, a composer from Germany, must be paired with Beethoven, another German composer.

12. (A. grind, B. thresh, C. harvest, D. grow) : WHEAT :: DISTILL : WATER

The correct answer is (B). In this action-to-object analogy, you distill water to remove unwanted substances from the refined water; similarly, you thresh wheat to separate the grains from the unwanted chaff.

13. BRAGGADOCIO : RETICENCE :: MISERLINESS : (A. profligacy, B. ecstasy, C. obloquy, D. falsity)

The correct answer is (A). Braggadocio, which means boastfulness, is opposite to reticence; an antonym for miserliness, which means stinginess, is profligacy, meaning reckless wastefulness.

14. 625 : (A. 5^5, B. 6^4, C. 7^4, D. 12^3) :: 5^4 : 2,401

The correct answer is (C). The nature of the relationship should be clear: synonyms. If need be, a bit of trial and error will yield the answer. 5^4 = 625 :: 7^4 = 2,401.

15. SANDHURST : ENGLAND :: (A. Harvard, B. Pittsburgh, C. West Point, D. MIT) : UNITED STATES

The correct answer is (C). Sandhurst is a school in England that trains future military officers; West Point has the same function in the United States.

16. AURICLE : VENTRICLE :: (A. sinus, B. epiglottis, C. thalamus, D. esophagus) : CEREBELLUM

The correct answer is (C). In this part-to-part analogy, the auricle and ventricle are both parts of the heart; the cerebellum and thalamus are parts of the brain.

17. (A. trees, B. circus, C. merry-go-round, D. skateboard) : STILTS :: BUS : AUDITORIUM

The correct answer is (D). A bus and an auditorium are related because they are intended to serve more than one person; stilts and a skateboard are usually intended for one person alone.

18. PARIS : (A. London, B. Priam, C. Achilles, D. Helen) :: ACHILLES : HECTOR

The correct answer is (C). In Homer's *Iliad,* Achilles slew Hector, and later Paris slew Achilles.

19. GENEROUS : LAVISH :: TIMOROUS : (A. tumid, B. craven, C. courageous, D. foolhardy)

The correct answer is (B). A person who is extremely generous is lavish; a person who is extremely timorous is craven, or cowardly.

20. MECCA : VARANASI :: MOSLEM : (A. Islam, B. India, C. Hindu, D. Buddhist)

The correct answer is (C). In this place analogy, Mecca is the sacred city of the Moslems; Varanasi is the sacred city of the Hindus.

21. POLO : MALLET :: (A. hockey, B. football, C. baseball, D. basketball) : STICK

The correct answer is (A). A mallet is a piece of equipment used by polo players. Similarly, a stick is a piece of equipment used by hockey players.

22. (A. barber, B. bristle, C. comb, D. stroke) : BRUSH :: CRUISER : FLEET

The correct answer is (B). In this analogy of a part to a whole, a bristle is part of a brush; a cruiser is part of a fleet.

23. HUDSON : BUICK :: PACKARD : (A. Stutz, B. Locomobile, C. Maxwell, D. Oldsmobile)

The correct answer is (D). Hudson and Packard are names of cars that are no longer made; Buick and Oldsmobile are names of currently produced cars.

24. IRREGULAR : SYMMETRY :: (A. dentures, B. savory, C. distasteful, D. cavernous) : TOOTHSOME

The correct answer is (C). Irregular is opposite in meaning to symmetry. An antonym for toothsome, which means delicious, is distasteful.

25. (A. Jenner, B. Magyar, C. Bede, D. Pericles) : KOOP :: SCHWEITZER : SALK

The correct answer is (A). Jenner, Koop, Schweitzer, and Salk are all related as physicians.

26. ASSAYER : ORE :: SPECTROMETER : (A. lens, B. refraction, C. mirror, D. eye)

The correct answer is (B). In this analogy of association, an assayer's job is to measure and analyze ore; a spectrometer measures and analyzes refraction.

27. BRAZIL : (A. Portugal, B. Spain, C. Venezuela, D. Suriname) :: GUYANA : FRENCH GUIANA

The correct answer is (D). Guyana, French Guiana, Brazil, and Suriname are all related in that they are the four South American countries in which Spanish is not the major language. Respectively, the languages spoken are English, French, Portuguese, and Dutch.

28. (A. lunch, B. meal, C. breakfast, D. brunch) : SUPPER :: SMOG : HAZE

The correct answer is (D). There is a two-to-one relationship in this analogy because smog is a combination of two atmospheric conditions, smoke and fog, while haze is one atmospheric condition. Similarly, brunch combines two meals, breakfast and lunch, while supper is just one meal.

29. APPRAISAL : REVENUE :: (A. defrosting, B. clear, C. hiding, D. sun) : VISIBILITY

The correct answer is (A). This is a purpose analogy. The purpose of the appraisal of a house is to gain tax revenue; the purpose of defrosting a windshield is to increase visibility. Note that the sun is a cause of visibility, not the purpose of it.

30. F : X :: 1 : (A. 4, B. 8, C. 2, D. 6)

The correct answer is (A). The correspondence is mathematical. F is the 6th letter of the alphabet, and X is the 24th. Their ratio is 1 : 4. Upon seeing the "X," you might have expected this analogy to be based upon Roman numerals, but you should have shifted gears very quickly upon the realization that "F" is not a Roman numeral.

31. RUPEE : (A. shah, B. euro, C. rial, D. krone) :: INDIA : NETHERLANDS

The correct answer is (B). The rupee is the basic unit of currency in India. The basic unit of currency in the Netherlands is the euro.

32. (A. servile, B. kowtow, C. unruly, D. inhibited) : OBSEQUIOUS :: IMPRECATORY : EULOGISTIC

The correct answer is (C). Imprecatory, which means damning, is opposite to eulogistic, meaning full of praise. Similarly, an antonym of obsequious, meaning compliant, is unruly, meaning difficult to discipline.

33. BLUE : ORANGE :: (A. indigo, B. yellow, C. purple, D. red) : GREEN

The correct answer is (D). Blue and orange are related as complementary colors; red and green are also complementary colors.

34. CHEETAH : SPEED :: (A. blade, B. dullness, C. bird, D. incision) : KEENNESS

The correct answer is (A). In this characteristic analogy, a cheetah is known for its speed; a blade is proverbially known for its keenness.

35. (A. hock, B. jockey, C. stable, D. hand) : HORSE :: TONGUE : BELL

The correct answer is (A). The correspondence is one of part to whole. A hock is part of a horse, the joint of the hind leg; a tongue is part of a bell.

36. EPILOGUE : NOVEL :: (A. cheers, B. curtain call, C. performance, D. introduction) : APPLAUSE

The correct answer is (B). In this sequence analogy, an epilogue follows the main action of a novel. A curtain call follows applause in a performance.

37. (A. Nantucket, B. Puerto Rico, C. Hawaii, D. Long Island) : UNITED STATES :: TASMANIA : AUSTRALIA

The correct answer is (C). Tasmania is an island state of Australia; Hawaii is an island state of the United States.

38. ANCHISES : (A. Troilus, B. Achilles, C. Ajax, D. Aeneas) :: JOCASTA : OEDIPUS

The correct answer is (D). Jocasta was the mother of Oedipus; Anchises was the father of Aeneas.

39. LEES : DREGS :: SYBARITIC : (A. sensual, B. moderate, C. cultish, D. servile)

The correct answer is (A). Lees is a synonym for dregs. Similarly, a synonym for sybaritic, devoted to pleasure or luxury, is sensual.

40. ISRAEL : VIETNAM :: JORDAN : (A. Cambodia, B. Korea, C. Nepal, D. France)

The correct answer is (A). Israel and Jordan are countries that were both once part of the land of Palestine. Vietnam and Cambodia were both once parts of French Indochina.

41. MAP : (A. explorer, B. geography, C. legend, D. atlas) :: TEXT : FOOTNOTE

The correct answer is (C). A footnote is an explanatory reference in a text; a legend is an explanatory list of symbols used on a map.

42. (A. clock, B. watch, C. time, D. hour) : TELL :: GUM : CHEW

The correct answer is (C). In this action-to-object analogy, one can tell time and one can chew gum.

43. BERET : DERBY :: PILLBOX : (A. fedora, B. shawl, C. cravat, D. stole)

The correct answer is (A). Beret, derby, pillbox, and fedora are types of hats.

44. COOPER : (A. lithographer, B. cartographer, C. photographer, D. biographer) :: BARREL : MAP

The correct answer is (B). The correspondence is one of worker to the thing created. A cooper makes a barrel; a cartographer makes a map.

45. PUPA : (A. tadpole, B. larva, C. cocoon, D. insect) :: FETUS : CHILD

The correct answer is (D). In this sequence analogy, the pupa is the last stage of development before the birth of an insect, just as the fetus is the last stage of development before the birth of a child.

46. DEALING : STOCK EXCHANGE :: (A. preserving, B. selling, C. buying, D. copying) : LANDMARK

The correct answer is (A). The correspondence is one of action to situation. Dealing is an activity related to the stock exchange. Preserving is a typical activity associated with a landmark.

47. UPRISING : (A. revolution, B. settlement, C. quarrel, D. disquiet) :: FIB : LIE

The correct answer is (A). In this analogy of degree, a fib is not quite telling a lie; an uprising may not quite be a revolution.

48. (A. Crete, B. Malta, C. Sicily, D. Corsica) : SARDINIA :: BOLIVIA : ARGENTINA

The correct answer is (D). The relationship is one of geographical location. Bolivia is a country directly north of Argentina. Corsica is an island located directly north of the island of Sardinia.

49. EVIL : EXORCISE : BREAD : (A. carbohydrate, B. break, C. sandwich, D. shred)

The correct answer is (B). The correspondence is one of object to action. One may exorcise evil; one may break bread.

50. COWARD : (A. loser, B. lily-livered, C. hero, D. villain) :: YOLK : ALBUMEN

The correct answer is (C). The yolk is the yellow part of an egg, and the albumen is part of the egg white. A coward is associated with the color yellow; a hero is associated with the color white.

51. (A. humid, B. speedy, C. piquant, D. moist) : VAPID :: OBDURATE : COMPASSIONATE

The correct answer is (C). Obdurate, meaning hardened in feelings, and compassionate, meaning sympathetic to the distress of others, are antonyms. Piquant, meaning pungent or savory, and vapid, meaning insipid or flat, are also antonyms.

52. CUCUMBER : WATERMELON :: CANTALOUPE : (A. squash, B. radish, C. cherry, D. plum)

The correct answer is (A). Cucumber, watermelon, cantaloupe, and squash are all related because they have many seeds and grow on vines.

53. (A. stick, B. percussion, C. cymbal, D. head) : DRUM :: STRINGS : VIOLIN

The correct answer is (D). In this part-to-whole analogy, a violin has strings and a drum has a head.

54. ILLNESS : (A. debility, B. hospital, C. doctor, D. panacea) :: VIBRATION : SOUND

The correct answer is (A). The correspondence is one of cause and effect. Vibration causes sound; illness causes debility.

55. VERDUN : DUNKIRK :: YPRES : (A. Belleau Woods, B. El Alamein, C. San Juan Hill, D. Marne)

The correct answer is (B). Verdun and Ypres were battles fought in World War I; Dunkirk and El Alamein were famous battles of World War II.

56. (A. gain, B. reward, C. loot, D. profit) : ROBBERY :: REVENGE : VENDETTA

The correct answer is (C). Revenge is the object of a vendetta; loot is the object of a robbery. Gain or profit might also be objects of robbery, but loot is a more specific and characteristic object.

57. ANALYSIS : FREUD :: (A. manipulation, B. illness, C. sex, D. stimulation) : OSTEOPATHY

The correct answer is (A). Freud attempted to relieve mental disorders through analysis; osteopathy attempts to relieve physical disorders through manipulation of affected parts.

58. CLAUSTROPHOBIA : CLOSETS :: AGORAPHOBIA : (A. ships, B. sheep, C. plants, D. plains)

The correct answer is (D). A person suffering from claustrophobia (a fear of closed spaces) would fear closets; a person suffering from agoraphobia (fear of open spaces) would fear plains.

59. SEARCH : FIND :: FIGHT : (A. win, B. lose, C. seek, D. contend)

The correct answer is (A). A positive result of a search is to find what you are looking for; a positive result of a fight is to win.

60. (A. affection, B. encouragement, C. blasphemy, D. oblivion) : FRACAS :: APHRODITE : MARS

The correct answer is (A). In mythology, Mars, as the god of war, would encourage a fracas; as the goddess of love, Aphrodite would encourage affection.

61. H : S :: (A. M, B. L, C. I, D. P) : W

The correct answer is (B). In this sequence analogy, the difference between H, the eighth letter in the alphabet, and S, the nineteenth, is 11. The letter with the same relation to W, the 23rd letter, is L, the 12th letter in the alphabet.

62. HASTILY : DESPONDENTLY :: CIRCUMSPECTLY : (A. quick, B. circuit, C. rate, D. slowly)

The correct answer is (D). The correspondence here is grammatical. Hastily, despondently, and circumspectly are all related as adverbs. Among the choices given, only slowly is also an adverb.

63. BOXER : TABBY :: LABRADOR : (A. fighter, B. poodle, C. calico, D. nanny)

The correct answer is (C). Boxer and Labrador are both breeds of dog; tabby and calico are both descriptive terms applied to cat markings.

64. CROESUS : (A. boat, B. wealth, C. pleats, D. loyalty) :: ODYSSEUS : CRAFT

The correct answer is (B). In this characteristic analogy, Croesus was known for his great wealth; Odysseus was known for his great craft.

65. LUCERNE : MICHIGAN :: GENEVA : (A. United States, B. Victoria, C. Okeechobee, D. Switzerland)

The correct answer is (C). In this place analogy, Lake Lucerne and Lake Geneva are in Switzerland; Lake Michigan and Lake Okeechobee are in the United States.

66. (A. tally, B. game, C. concert, D. run) : SCORE :: PLAY : SCRIPT

The correct answer is (C). The script is the written text of a play; the score is the written version of the music to be played at a concert.

67. FLAUBERT : (A. madame, B. field, C. knife, D. writer) :: JOYCE : PORTRAIT

The correct answer is (A). James Joyce wrote a famous book with the word portrait in the title: *Portrait of the Artist as a Young Man.* Gustave Flaubert wrote a famous book with the word madame in the title: *Madame Bovary.*

68. DOG : INTRUDER :: (A. burglar, B. cat, C. knight, D. maiden) : DRAGON

The correct answer is (C). Call this one agent to object. The dog attacks the intruder; the knight attacks the dragon.

69. MENDACIOUS : DECEITFUL :: AUSPICIOUS : (A. indifferent, B. submerged, C. propitious, D. bereft)

The correct answer is (C). Mendacious and deceitful are synonyms, as are auspicious and propitious.

70. PARTRIDGE : RABBIT :: (A. quail, B. pen, C. birds, D. covey) : WARREN

The correct answer is (D). Rabbits congregate in a warren; partridges congregate in a covey.

71. LAPIDARY : (A. ruby, B. wood, C. lick, D. food) :: SCULPTOR : ALABASTER

The correct answer is (A). The relationship is one of worker to his or her material. A lapidary (an engraver of precious stones) may work with a ruby; a sculptor may work with alabaster.

72. BEES : FILE :: BIRDS : (A. grade, B. rank, C. fold, D. twist)

The correct answer is (B). The correspondence is one of association of words. We speak of birds and bees and also of rank and file.

73. MANY : MUCH :: FEW : (A. minus, B. more, C. small, D. little)

The correct answer is (D). The analogy is based upon the grammatical distinction between number and amount. Make up a parallel sentence to choose the best answer. "Many (in number) raindrops make much (in amount) water; few (in number) raindrops make little (in amount) water."

74. FORSOOK : DRANK :: FROZEN : (A. swum, B. wrote, C. sang, D. chose)

The correct answer is (A). In this grammatical analogy, forsook and drank are simple past tenses; frozen and swum are past participles.

75. SANDAL : BOOT :: (A. hammer, B. hatchet, C. shoemaker, D. blade) : AX

The correct answer is (B). This relationship is one of degree. A sandal is a lighter version of footwear than a boot; a hatchet is a smaller version of a sharp-edged instrument than an ax.

76. HORSE : (A. man, B. goat, C. archer, D. bull) :: CENTAUR : SATYR

The correct answer is (B). In this mythological analogy, a centaur is half horse, half man; a satyr is half goat, half man.

77. (A. anode, B. bird, C. purchase, D. battery) : CELL :: ARROW : SHAFT

The correct answer is (D). The correspondence is one of whole to part. A cell is part of a battery; a shaft is part of an arrow.

78. FELONY : MISDEMEANOR :: SIN : (A. piccalilli, B. picayune, C. peccadillo, D. picador)

    The correct answer is (C). In this degree analogy, a felony is a more serious offense than a misdemeanor; similarly, a sin is a more serious offense than a peccadillo (a slight offense).

79. NOVEMBER : APRIL :: (A. May, B. June, C. July, D. August) : SEPTEMBER

    The correct answer is (B). In the words of the well-known mnemonic rhyme, "Thirty days hath September, April, June, and November."

80. ALBANIA : POLAND :: CHINA : (A. Czechoslovakia, B. Russia, C. Sumatra, D. India)

    The correct answer is (A). This analogy has to do with political alignments in the Communist world right up to the dissolution of the USSR. Albania and China had Communist governments that were entirely outside the sphere of influence of the Soviet Union. Poland and Czechoslovakia were very much under Soviet domination until their rebellions spurred the breakup of the union.

81. WASTEFUL : (A. parsimonious, B. neglectful, C. vast, D. prodigal) :: DISINTERESTED : IMPARTIAL

    The correct answer is (D). Disinterested is a synonym for impartial; a synonym for wasteful is prodigal.

82. SCHOONER : ZIGGURAT :: CRUISER : (A. cutter, B. campanile, C. viking, D. tug)

    The correct answer is (B). A schooner and a cruiser are both types of ships. A ziggurat and a campanile are both types of towers.

83. (A. pine, B. cedar, C. ash, D. willow) : OAK :: MOURNFUL : STURDY

    The correct answer is (D). In this analogy of characteristics, we speak of the mighty (sturdy) oak and the weeping (mournful) willow.

84. ADVISE : EXHORT :: (A. force, B. tempt, C. prohibit, D. prevent) : ENTICE

    The correct answer is (B). The relationship is one of degree. Exhort means to urge on, which is a stronger degree of advise; entice is a stronger degree of tempt.

85. STEEL : WELD :: LIPS : (A. frown, B. purse, C. fold, D. smirk)

    The correct answer is (B). In this action-to-object analogy, you weld two pieces of steel to join or hold them together; you purse your lips by holding or pressing them together.

86. TESTIMONY : (A. confession, B. judge, C. witness, D. trial) :: BIOGRAPHY : AUTOBIOGRAPHY

    The correct answer is (A). Testimony is a statement about someone else; a confession is a statement about oneself. A biography is the written history of another person's life; an autobiography is the written history of one's own life.

87. STRATUM : SYLLABUS :: (A. strati, B. stratums, C. stratus, D. strata) : SYLLABI

    The correct answer is (D). The relationship in this analogy is grammatical. The plural of syllabus is syllabi; the plural of stratum is strata.

88. LAMB : DEER :: (A. rabbit, B. peacock, C. horse, D. pig) : LION

    The correct answer is (B). A lamb and a deer are related because they are both considered mild-mannered; a peacock and a lion are related because they are both considered proud.

89. VELOCITY : (A. wind, B. earth, C. vibration, D. destruction) :: BEAUFORT : RICHTER

The correct answer is (C). The Beaufort Scale (invented by Sir Francis Beaufort) indicates velocity of the wind in numbers from 0 to 17. The Richter Scale (named after Charles Richter) indicates the magnitude of a seismic vibration or earthquake.

90. (A. distance, B. program, C. station, D. tube) : TELEVISION :: LEADER : ANARCHY

The correct answer is (A). The Greek root *tele* in television means distance; the Greek root *arch* in anarchy means leader.

91. TAPS : VESPERS :: (A. painting, B. needle, C. revelry, D. reveille) : MATINS

The correct answer is (D). Taps is an evening military signal, and vespers are evening prayers; reveille is a morning military signal, and matins are morning prayers.

92. PROSTRATE : (A. dazzling, B. stealing, C. submission, D. dehydrated) :: SUPINE : SLEEPING

The correct answer is (C). In this situation-to-action analogy, a person who is prostrate is in a position for submission; a person who is supine is in a position for sleeping.

93. MAHATMA GANDHI : WAR :: CARRY NATION : (A. suffrage, B. alcohol, C. temperance, D. employment)

The correct answer is (B). Mahatma Gandhi was opposed to all forms of violence, including war, as Carry Nation was opposed to the use of any kind of alcohol.

94. $\frac{2}{7}$: (A. $\frac{1}{16}$, B. $\frac{3}{28}$, C. $\frac{3}{21}$, D. $\frac{1}{14}$) :: $\frac{4}{7}$: $\frac{1}{7}$

The correct answer is (D). In this mathematical analogy, $\frac{1}{4}$ of $\frac{4}{7}$ is $\frac{1}{7}$; $\frac{1}{4}$ of $\frac{2}{7}$ is $\frac{1}{14}$.

95. (A. roc, B. canary, C. albatross, D. condor) : VULTURE :: PHOENIX : EAGLE

The correct answer is (A). The relationship is one of real to imaginary. A phoenix is an imaginary bird, and an eagle is an actual bird. Similarly, a roc is imaginary and a vulture is real.

96. TINE : FORK :: (A. car, B. gearshift, C. flange, D. wheelwright) : WHEEL

The correct answer is (C). A tine is part of a fork; a flange is part of a wheel.

97. (A. tie, B. appearance, C. shoes, D. decoration) : ATTIRE :: WIT : COMMUNICATION

The correct answer is (D). One's attire is brightened with some decoration; one's communication is brightened with wit.

98. HUSK : (A. fish, B. chops, C. gristle, D. filet) :: GRAIN : MEAT

The correct answer is (C). In this analogy, the relationship is one of discardable to usable. The husk is the discardable part of grain; gristle is the discardable part of meat.

99. SURPRISED : (A. interested, B. astounded, C. expected, D. unknown) :: WORK : TOIL

The correct answer is (B). The correspondence is one of degree. Work is a milder form of toil; surprised is a milder form of astounded.

100. INEBRIOUS : (A. intoxicated, B. dull, C. sincere, D. abstemious) :: SPARTAN : GARRULOUS

    The correct answer is (D). Spartan, meaning terse in speech, is the opposite of garrulous. Inebrious, which means drunken, is the opposite of abstemious, or temperate.

101. CLUB : (A. prehistoric, B. cave, C. cannon, D. rampage) :: GUN : HOUSE

    The correct answer is (B). A club, as a weapon, long preceded the gun. In fact, the club is from the same prehistoric era as the cave, which preceded the house.

102. (A. proboscis, B. smell, C. olfactory, D. redolent) : TACTILE :: NOSE : FINGER

    The correct answer is (C). The tactile sense is to the finger as the olfactory sense is to the nose.

103. BARREL : SILO :: WINE : (A. horses, B. toss, C. grain, D. refuse)

    The correct answer is (C). A barrel serves to store wine; a silo serves to store grain.

104. LONDON : (A. Florence, B. Madrid, C. Milan, D. Rome) :: GLOBE THEATER : LA SCALA

    The correct answer is (C). The Globe Theater is in London; La Scala opera house is in Milan.

105. TWIG : (A. thorn, B. branch, C. leaf, D. rose) :: BUD : FLOWER

    The correct answer is (B). A bud develops and becomes a flower; a twig develops and becomes a branch.

106. (A. October, B. autumn, C. season, D. sadness) : SPRING :: LEAVES : FEVER

    The correct answer is (B). This analogy is based on words that often appear in conjunction. Spring fever and autumn leaves simply go together.

107. CARROT : COW :: PLANT : (A. meat, B. herd, C. animal, D. stockyard)

    The correct answer is (C). A carrot is a plant; a cow is an animal. In order for meat to be the correct answer, the analogy would have to read "carrot : cow :: vegetable : meat."

108. INGENUE : KNAVE :: NAIVETÉ : (A. chivalry, B. chicanery, C. morality, D. subtlety)

    The correct answer is (B). A characteristic of the ingenue is her naiveté; a characteristic of the knave is chicanery, trickery, or artful deception.

109. RUN : WALK :: (A. number, B. total, C. multiply, D. subtract) : ADD

    The correct answer is (C). Run is greater than walk; to multiply makes the total grow much more quickly than to add.

110. (A. teacher, B. player, C. actor, D. surgeon) : TEAM :: OSCAR® : PENNANT

    The correct answer is (C). A team wins a pennant; an actor wins an Oscar®.

111. JABBER : GIBBERISH :: QUIDNUNC : (A. quisling, B. busybody, C. theorist, D. testator)

    The correct answer is (B). Jabber and gibberish are both nonsense; quidnunc is a busybody.

answers practice test 4

112. ENGLAND : DENMARK :: (A. Sweden, B. China, C. France, D. Thailand) : ISRAEL

The correct answer is (C). England and Denmark are both constitutional monarchies; France and Israel both have republican forms of government. The like forms of government on each side of the equation create this analogy. Sweden and Thailand are both constitutional monarchies; China is a Communist dictatorship.

113. GESUNDHEIT : AL DENTE :: CAVEAT EMPTOR : (A. buyer beware, B. amicus curiae, C. savoir faire, D. thank goodness)

The correct answer is (C). Look for relationships without considering meanings whenever you encounter foreign words. You can always focus on meanings later if you find no simpler relationship. In this analogy, the first two terms are totally unrelated except that each comes from a different foreign language and that each has been incorporated into the English language without translation. On the other side of the analogy, it is possible to choose two more such words that come from two additional foreign languages and that have been incorporated into English. Gesundheit is German and means "good health"; al dente is Italian and means chewy, literally, "to the teeth"; caveat emptor is Latin and means "buyer beware"; savoir faire is French and means "social polish." Amicus curiae is also Latin, so it does not suit the requirement of the analogy.

114. HIS : (A. its, B. it's, C. her's, D. their's) :: MINE : YOURS

The correct answer is (A). HIS : ITS :: MINE : YOURS. All four terms are possessives. A pronoun does not take an apostrophe in the possessive.

115. TRAIN : (A. steamer, B. pier, C. water, D. track) :: STATION : WHARF

The correct answer is (A). The train pulls into the station; the steamer pulls in at the wharf. Resist the temptation to choose pier, the synonym of wharf.

116. BRACES : (A. suspenders, B. belt, C. band, D. tram) :: LORRY : TRUCK

The correct answer is (A). This is an analogy of identity. In Britain, a lorry is a truck, and braces are suspenders.

117. HORSE : (A. telephone, B. letter, C. communication, D. transportation) :: AUTOMOBILE : TELEGRAM

The correct answer is (B). Technology again: The horse is a less sophisticated means of transportation than the automobile; the letter is a less technologically sophisticated means of communication than the telegram.

118. CREPUSCULAR : CURSORY :: DIM : (A. profane, B. egregious, C. superficial, D. unique)

The correct answer is (C). Crepuscular means dim; cursory means superficial. The analogy reads A : C :: B : D.

119. REPUGN : COMPROMISE :: RESCIND : (A. refuse, B. rest, C. decipher, D. validate)

The correct answer is (D). Repugn, meaning oppose, is the opposite of compromise; rescind, meaning take back, is the opposite of validate, meaning confirm.

120. UKRAINE : STEPPES :: ARGENTINA : (A. mountains, B. pampas, C. tundra, D. valleys)

The correct answer is (B). Steppes are large, level, treeless plains of the Ukraine; pampas are large, level, grass-covered plains of Argentina.

ANSWER SHEET PRACTICE TEST 5

1. Ⓐ Ⓑ Ⓒ Ⓓ	31. Ⓐ Ⓑ Ⓒ Ⓓ	61. Ⓐ Ⓑ Ⓒ Ⓓ	91. Ⓐ Ⓑ Ⓒ Ⓓ
2. Ⓐ Ⓑ Ⓒ Ⓓ	32. Ⓐ Ⓑ Ⓒ Ⓓ	62. Ⓐ Ⓑ Ⓒ Ⓓ	92. Ⓐ Ⓑ Ⓒ Ⓓ
3. Ⓐ Ⓑ Ⓒ Ⓓ	33. Ⓐ Ⓑ Ⓒ Ⓓ	63. Ⓐ Ⓑ Ⓒ Ⓓ	93. Ⓐ Ⓑ Ⓒ Ⓓ
4. Ⓐ Ⓑ Ⓒ Ⓓ	34. Ⓐ Ⓑ Ⓒ Ⓓ	64. Ⓐ Ⓑ Ⓒ Ⓓ	94. Ⓐ Ⓑ Ⓒ Ⓓ
5. Ⓐ Ⓑ Ⓒ Ⓓ	35. Ⓐ Ⓑ Ⓒ Ⓓ	65. Ⓐ Ⓑ Ⓒ Ⓓ	95. Ⓐ Ⓑ Ⓒ Ⓓ
6. Ⓐ Ⓑ Ⓒ Ⓓ	36. Ⓐ Ⓑ Ⓒ Ⓓ	66. Ⓐ Ⓑ Ⓒ Ⓓ	96. Ⓐ Ⓑ Ⓒ Ⓓ
7. Ⓐ Ⓑ Ⓒ Ⓓ	37. Ⓐ Ⓑ Ⓒ Ⓓ	67. Ⓐ Ⓑ Ⓒ Ⓓ	97. Ⓐ Ⓑ Ⓒ Ⓓ
8. Ⓐ Ⓑ Ⓒ Ⓓ	38. Ⓐ Ⓑ Ⓒ Ⓓ	68. Ⓐ Ⓑ Ⓒ Ⓓ	98. Ⓐ Ⓑ Ⓒ Ⓓ
9. Ⓐ Ⓑ Ⓒ Ⓓ	39. Ⓐ Ⓑ Ⓒ Ⓓ	69. Ⓐ Ⓑ Ⓒ Ⓓ	99. Ⓐ Ⓑ Ⓒ Ⓓ
10. Ⓐ Ⓑ Ⓒ Ⓓ	40. Ⓐ Ⓑ Ⓒ Ⓓ	70. Ⓐ Ⓑ Ⓒ Ⓓ	100. Ⓐ Ⓑ Ⓒ Ⓓ
11. Ⓐ Ⓑ Ⓒ Ⓓ	41. Ⓐ Ⓑ Ⓒ Ⓓ	71. Ⓐ Ⓑ Ⓒ Ⓓ	101. Ⓐ Ⓑ Ⓒ Ⓓ
12. Ⓐ Ⓑ Ⓒ Ⓓ	42. Ⓐ Ⓑ Ⓒ Ⓓ	72. Ⓐ Ⓑ Ⓒ Ⓓ	102. Ⓐ Ⓑ Ⓒ Ⓓ
13. Ⓐ Ⓑ Ⓒ Ⓓ	43. Ⓐ Ⓑ Ⓒ Ⓓ	73. Ⓐ Ⓑ Ⓒ Ⓓ	103. Ⓐ Ⓑ Ⓒ Ⓓ
14. Ⓐ Ⓑ Ⓒ Ⓓ	44. Ⓐ Ⓑ Ⓒ Ⓓ	74. Ⓐ Ⓑ Ⓒ Ⓓ	104. Ⓐ Ⓑ Ⓒ Ⓓ
15. Ⓐ Ⓑ Ⓒ Ⓓ	45. Ⓐ Ⓑ Ⓒ Ⓓ	75. Ⓐ Ⓑ Ⓒ Ⓓ	105. Ⓐ Ⓑ Ⓒ Ⓓ
16. Ⓐ Ⓑ Ⓒ Ⓓ	46. Ⓐ Ⓑ Ⓒ Ⓓ	76. Ⓐ Ⓑ Ⓒ Ⓓ	106. Ⓐ Ⓑ Ⓒ Ⓓ
17. Ⓐ Ⓑ Ⓒ Ⓓ	47. Ⓐ Ⓑ Ⓒ Ⓓ	77. Ⓐ Ⓑ Ⓒ Ⓓ	107. Ⓐ Ⓑ Ⓒ Ⓓ
18. Ⓐ Ⓑ Ⓒ Ⓓ	48. Ⓐ Ⓑ Ⓒ Ⓓ	78. Ⓐ Ⓑ Ⓒ Ⓓ	108. Ⓐ Ⓑ Ⓒ Ⓓ
19. Ⓐ Ⓑ Ⓒ Ⓓ	49. Ⓐ Ⓑ Ⓒ Ⓓ	79. Ⓐ Ⓑ Ⓒ Ⓓ	109. Ⓐ Ⓑ Ⓒ Ⓓ
20. Ⓐ Ⓑ Ⓒ Ⓓ	50. Ⓐ Ⓑ Ⓒ Ⓓ	80. Ⓐ Ⓑ Ⓒ Ⓓ	110. Ⓐ Ⓑ Ⓒ Ⓓ
21. Ⓐ Ⓑ Ⓒ Ⓓ	51. Ⓐ Ⓑ Ⓒ Ⓓ	81. Ⓐ Ⓑ Ⓒ Ⓓ	111. Ⓐ Ⓑ Ⓒ Ⓓ
22. Ⓐ Ⓑ Ⓒ Ⓓ	52. Ⓐ Ⓑ Ⓒ Ⓓ	82. Ⓐ Ⓑ Ⓒ Ⓓ	112. Ⓐ Ⓑ Ⓒ Ⓓ
23. Ⓐ Ⓑ Ⓒ Ⓓ	53. Ⓐ Ⓑ Ⓒ Ⓓ	83. Ⓐ Ⓑ Ⓒ Ⓓ	113. Ⓐ Ⓑ Ⓒ Ⓓ
24. Ⓐ Ⓑ Ⓒ Ⓓ	54. Ⓐ Ⓑ Ⓒ Ⓓ	84. Ⓐ Ⓑ Ⓒ Ⓓ	114. Ⓐ Ⓑ Ⓒ Ⓓ
25. Ⓐ Ⓑ Ⓒ Ⓓ	55. Ⓐ Ⓑ Ⓒ Ⓓ	85. Ⓐ Ⓑ Ⓒ Ⓓ	115. Ⓐ Ⓑ Ⓒ Ⓓ
26. Ⓐ Ⓑ Ⓒ Ⓓ	56. Ⓐ Ⓑ Ⓒ Ⓓ	86. Ⓐ Ⓑ Ⓒ Ⓓ	116. Ⓐ Ⓑ Ⓒ Ⓓ
27. Ⓐ Ⓑ Ⓒ Ⓓ	57. Ⓐ Ⓑ Ⓒ Ⓓ	87. Ⓐ Ⓑ Ⓒ Ⓓ	117. Ⓐ Ⓑ Ⓒ Ⓓ
28. Ⓐ Ⓑ Ⓒ Ⓓ	58. Ⓐ Ⓑ Ⓒ Ⓓ	88. Ⓐ Ⓑ Ⓒ Ⓓ	118. Ⓐ Ⓑ Ⓒ Ⓓ
29. Ⓐ Ⓑ Ⓒ Ⓓ	59. Ⓐ Ⓑ Ⓒ Ⓓ	89. Ⓐ Ⓑ Ⓒ Ⓓ	119. Ⓐ Ⓑ Ⓒ Ⓓ
30. Ⓐ Ⓑ Ⓒ Ⓓ	60. Ⓐ Ⓑ Ⓒ Ⓓ	90. Ⓐ Ⓑ Ⓒ Ⓓ	120. Ⓐ Ⓑ Ⓒ Ⓓ

answer sheet

Practice Test 5

Directions: Each of these test questions consists of three capitalized words and four lettered words enclosed in parentheses. Two of the capitalized words are related in some way. Find the two related words, and establish the nature of the relationship. Then study the four words lettered A, B, C, and D. Select the one lettered word that is related to the remaining capitalized word in the same way that the first two capitalized words are related. Mark the answer sheet for the letter preceding the word you select.

1. FEAST : MEAL :: VELLUM : (A. paper, B. fur, C. cotton, D. forest)

2. (A. leave, B. audition, C. divide, D. correct) : APPLY :: PART : POSITION

3. OXEN : STRENGTH :: (A. furnace, B. animal, C. cattle, D. ants) : INDUSTRY

4. ASSIDUOUS : EGREGIOUS :: (A. jubilant, B. desultory, C. diligent, D. bitter) : FLAGRANT

5. SHIP : (A. crow's nest, B. deck, C. prow, D. mast) :: COLUMN : CAPITAL

6. DAVID COPPERFIELD : TINY TIM :: (A. Joseph Andrews, B. Ahab, C. Becky Sharp, D. Little Nell) : OLIVER TWIST

7. CLEOPATRA : (A. Caesar, B. snake, C. knife, D. beauty) :: MARIE ANTIONETTE : GUILLOTINE

8. (A. circle, B. heart, C. dissemination, D. artery) : CIRCULATE :: DITCH : IRRIGATE

9. BRIGHT : GAUDY :: (A. urged, B. implied, C. prevented, D. acquiesced) : COMPELLED

10. (A. dissidence, B. deficiency, C. irreverence, D. deference) : DISRESPECT :: IMBUE : EXTRACT

11. EGO : ID :: SELF : (A. desire, B. society, C. conscience, D. morality)

12. ACCELERATOR : (A. automobile, B. driver, C. speed, D. brake) :: PROGRESS : RECESSION

13. (A. gem, B. spore, C. illegitimacy, D. superficiality) : SPURIOUS :: MONEY : COUNTERFEIT

14. AMIN : (A. Elizabeth II, B. Waldheim, C. Qaddafi, D. Adenauer) :: KING : BUNCHE

15. 225 : AREA :: (A. 2,744, B. 3,375, C. 38,416, D. 50,625) : VOLUME

16. QUEUE : (A. borough, B. pool, C. line, D. broom) :: CUE : BROUGHAM

17. COLONEL : REGIMENT :: (A. major, B. captain, C. private, D. general) : BATTALION

18. DILETTANTE : (A. thorough, B. painstaking, C. diplomatic, D. superficial) :: BOISTEROUS : LOUD

19. HANDLEBARS : SPOKE :: KEYBOARD : (A. basket, B. chip, C. music, D. retort)

20. (A. rectify, B. error, C. find, D. realize) : MISTAKE :: REGAIN : LOSS

21. INDEX : FRONTISPIECE :: MATURITY : (A. adolescence, B. infancy, C. contents, D. adulthood)

22. TAUTOLOGICAL : REDUNDANT :: (A. mature, B. incipient, C. obnoxious, D. late) : INCHOATE

23. SQUARE : (A. triangle, B. triplet, C. poem, D. duet) :: QUADRUPLET : COUPLET

24. MAY : (A. horn, B. charity, C. tempest, D. despair) :: FEAR : COD

25. (A. m, B. p, C. l, D. t) : H :: W : S

26. CHOLERIC : AMIABLE :: (A. timid, B. scared, C. mute, D. temerarious) : CIRCUMSPECT

27. IRON : (A. hard, B. strong, C. steel, D. pig) :: OIL : CRUDE

28. (A. astronomy, B. play, C. symphony, D. clouds) : STAR :: CONCERT : SOLOIST

29. SALUTE : (A. motto, B. reveille, C. mess, D. orders) :: TROOP : EAGLE

30. PROVISIONS : QUARTERMASTER :: (A. screwdriver, B. knife, C. saddle, D. manuscript) : SCRIVENER

31. ATLANTIS : (A. Pompeii, B. Xanadu, C. Byzantium, D. Zanzibar) :: SHANGRI-LA : EL DORADO

32. WIND : DEFICIT :: EROSION : (A. spending, B. appreciation, C. borrowing, D. employment)

33. (A. slot, B. note, C. band, D. harmony) : VALVE :: HARMONICA : TRUMPET

34. FLAUNT : (A. destructively, B. stupidly, C. willingly, D. boastfully) :: BETRAY : DECEPTIVELY

35. HOUYHNHNM : YAHOO :: REASON : (A. learning, B. intelligence, C. ignorance, D. genius)

36. DEFIED : ASTRIDE :: EARTH : (A. geography, B. zoology, C. birth, D. life)

37. ST. PETERSBURG : LENINGRAD :: (A. Stalingrad, B. Leningrad, C. Moscow, D. Odessa) : ST. PETERSBURG

38. (A. 1999, B. 1900, C. 1901, D. 1902) : 1910 :: 1950 : 1959

39. ADVOCATE : (A. impute, B. allude, C. pursue, D. impugn) :: AMELIORATE : IMPAIR

40. HENRY MOORE : (A. Rodin, B. Pavlov, C. Van Gogh, D. Gertrude Stein) :: DONATELLO : BERNINI

41. HO CHI MINH : GANDHI :: FRANCE : (A. Indochina, B. Great Britain, C. Vietnam, D. India)

42. HEDGER : SHRUBBERY :: (A. snuffer, B. gardener, C. whittler, D. stickler) : STICK

43. MAN : (A. bird, B. centipede, C. elephant, D. automobile) :: WHEELBARROW : BICYCLE

44. (A. velocity, B. viscosity, C. temperature, D. density) : FLUID :: FRICTION : SOLID

45. CANTON : COUNTY :: (A. Ohio, B. Japan, C. Switzerland, D. China) : IRELAND

46. PECK : PINT :: 1 : (A. 4, B. 16, C. 8, D. 2)

47. TWEEZERS : BLEACH :: (A. steel, B. light, C. adding machine, D. eraser) : PICKPOCKET

48. HARANGUING : (A. persuade, B. filet, C. cleaning, D. arbitrate) :: FILIBUSTERING : OBSTRUCT

49. SHERRY : BEER :: PORT : (A. champagne, B. sauterne, C. claret, D. muscatel)

50. HONOR : GOVERNOR :: (A. Excellency, B. Majesty, C. Highness, D. Grace) : DUKE

51. ANDIRON : PEDESTAL :: (A. log, B. bucket, C. anvil, D. skillet) : STATUE

52. GENERAL : STARS :: COLONEL : (A. oak, B. silver, C. gold, D. eagle)

53. (A. insist, B. reply, C. demur, D. demand) : REFUSE :: LAZY : INERT

54. HEART : HEAD :: VENERY : (A. ribaldry, B. flesh, C. mortality, D. restraint)

55. CALORIE : (A. energy, B. weight, C. metabolism, D. food) :: CENTURY : TIME

56. FLORIDA : SAUDI ARABIA :: (A. Louisiana, B. Georgia, C. Arkansas, D. Iraq) : IRAN

57. *KING LEAR* : *DIE FLEDERMAUS* :: *MACBETH* : (A. *Tosca*, B. *Othello*, C. *Ruddigore*, D. *Les Misérables*)

58. BOARDWALK : (A. Park Place, B. Atlantic City, C. display, D. escalator) :: STRAND : STORE

59. (A. Parliament, B. Congress, C. Great Britain, D. Senate) : LORDS :: HOUSE : COMMONS

60. 1789 : (A. Germany, B. France, C. England, D. Russia) :: 1776 : UNITED STATES

61. MALLARD : CANVASBACK :: (A. snow, B. north, C. drake, D. gander) : CANADIAN

62. WELL-FED : (A. penurious, B. healthy, C. wealthy, D. miserly) :: HUNGRY :
IMPECUNIOUS

63. LAERTES : (A. Odysseus, B. Polonius, C. Claudius, D. Ophelia) :: ICARUS :
DAEDALUS

64. SYRACUSE : (A. Oneonta, B. Geneva, C. Raleigh, D. Sparta) :: CARTHAGE :
ALEXANDRIA

65. DISPIRITED : DEPRESSED :: (A. obligato, B. innuendo, C. declaration,
D. crescendo) : INSINUATION

66. ORGANISM : (A. plant, B. animal, C. bacteria, D. cell) :: LIGHT : WAVE

67. KÖLN : WIEN :: COLOGNE : (A. Vienna, B. Prague, C. Warsaw, D. Hamburg)

68. DCX : MDCCCXXX :: (A. CLX, B. XLI, C. LCD, D. LXVII) : CXXIII

69. WISDOM : (A. lion, B. owl, C. fox, D. deer) :: SPRING : ROBIN

70. BUTTERFLY : (A. insect, B. silkworm, C. wings, D. summer) :: CHRYSALIS :
COCOON

71. ICELAND : NORWAY :: (A. winter, B. queen, C. president, D. sovereign) : KING

72. ROME : (A. NATO, B. SEATO, C. SALT II, D. EEC) :: VERSAILLES : LEAGUE OF
NATIONS

73. CYLINDER : LOCK :: MOTOR : (A. shaft, B. canal, C. tackle, D. escape)

74. BANANA : (A. sapphire, B. saltcellar, C. stone, D. tree) :: BUTTER : SKY

75. GNASH : TEETH :: (A. fold, B. clasp, C. gnarl, D. wring) : HANDS

76. (A. opossum, B. fox, C. beaver, D. lady) : KANGAROO :: CHICKEN : COCKROACH

77. APHRODITE : VENUS :: ARES : (A. Mercury, B. Mars, C. Apollo, D. Hermes)

78. METAPHYSICS : (A. humanities, B. medicine, C. logic, D. art) :: EPISTEMOLOGY :
ETHICS

79. CLARINET : PIANO :: WIND : (A. reed, B. wood, C, percussion, D. pianist)

80. ELEVATOR : SKYSCRAPER :: (A. gangplank, B. companionway, C. bulkhead,
D. bridge) : SHIP

81. PROPENSITY : (A. riches, B. weight, C. bias, D. thought) :: CLUB : MACE

82. SALZBURG : STRATFORD :: (A. Goethe, B. Avon, C. Mozart, D. Brahms) :
SHAKESPEARE

83. FLAMMABLE : INFLAMMABLE :: PERTINENT : (A. impertinent, B. inopportune,
C. incoherent, D. relevant)

84. (A. revolution, B. dance, C. torque, D. axis) : ROTATE :: FRICTION : RESIST

85. PRISM : (A. spectrum, B. reflection, C. light, D. binoculars) :: FAMINE : WANT

86. LOOP : HUB :: BEEF : (A. corn, B. beans, C. tobacco, D. cotton)

87. JANUARY : (A. Cleveland, B. June, C. Washington, D. Hermes) :: SUNDAY : MERCURY

88. LIFT : ELEVATOR :: (A. oil, B. grease, C. gas, D. petrol) : GASOLINE

89. (A. $\frac{1}{6}$, B. $\frac{4}{5}$, C. $\frac{2}{5}$, D. $\frac{2}{10}$) : $\frac{1}{10}$ :: $\frac{3}{4}$: $\frac{3}{16}$

90. TORT : LITIGATION :: CONTRACT : (A. signature, B. obligation, C. clause, D. equity)

91. BULL : (A. wolf, B. turtle, C. fish, D. snail) :: CRAB : LION

92. EQUINOX : SOLSTICE :: SEPTEMBER : (A. November, B. January, C. June, D. March)

93. (A. hand, B. brow, C. rose, D. soon) : KNIT :: DICTATION : TAKE

94. GARROTING : DEATH :: CANVASSING : (A. painting, B. shelter, C. votes, D. fight)

95. PUSILLANIMOUS : INVIDIOUS :: (A. paronomasia, B. slather, C. melodramatically, D. perfunctory) : SANCTIMONIOUS

96. SUN : JAPAN :: (A. scythe, B. crescent, C. Caspian, D. hammer) : TURKEY

97. CICERO : DEMOSTHENES :: ROOSEVELT : (A. MacArthur, B. Hemingway, C. Shaw, D. Churchill)

98. TYRO : (A. tyrant, B. master, C. amateur, D. dabbler) :: TURPITUDE : PROBITY

99. COKE : COAL :: (A. oil, B. planks, C. saw, D. lumberjack) : TIMBER

100. SHOE : (A. belt, B. cobbler, C. pair, D. bell) :: SAW : GEAR

101. DEGRADE : MARTIAL :: LAUD : (A. military, B. noisy, C. worried, D. halcyon)

102. MAN : BREAD :: HORSE : (A. stable, B. duck, C. barn, D. hay)

103. AIRPLANE : (A. kite, B. ship, C. bird, D. helicopter) :: BUS : TRAIN

104. FACULTY : STAFF :: UNIVERSITY : (A. intern, B. patient, C. workers, D. hospital)

105. HEW : (A. hewn, B. mow, C. toe, D. hue) :: BLEW : BLUE

106. WORK : (A. employment, B. entertainment, C. office, D. income) :: FOOD : GROWTH

107. IMMATURITY : (A. anger, B. childhood, C. adulthood, D. incompatibility) :: COMPETITION : MONOPOLY

108. SHIVER : COLD :: TREMBLE : (A. hot, B. happiness, C. fear, D. intelligence)

109. AK : MN :: (A. AS, B. AZ, C. NB, D. IO) : PA

110. (A. Apollo, B. Janus, C. Eros, D. Jupiter) : JUNO :: ZEUS : HERA

111. CULINARY : (A. bedroom, B. closet, C. knife, D. kitchen) :: ECUMENICAL : CHURCH

112. LEAF : (A. leafs, B. leave, C. left, D. leaves) :: MEDIUM : MEDIA

113. FINGER : PALM :: (A. shoe, B. foot, C. sole, D. limb) : HEEL

114. PINE : (A. Christmas, B. tree, C. fir, D. loss) :: POINSETTIA : FLOWER

115. (A. throne, B. prince, C. kingdom, D. majesty) : FILLY :: KING : MARE

116. (A. individual, B. baby, C. adult, D. male) : OAK :: INFANT : ACORN

117. INFANT : TODDLER :: ADOLESCENT : (A. tyke, B. adult, C. youngster, D. masculine)

118. (A. men, B. his, C. man's, D. mine) : MINE :: MAN : I

119. RAGE : (A. irk, B. annoy, C. anger, D. mischief) :: DEMONIC : NAUGHTY

120. HOUR : MINUTE :: MINUTE : (A. time, B. day, C. second, D. moment)

ANSWER KEY AND EXPLANATIONS

1. **A**	25. **C**	49. **A**	73. **B**	97. **D**
2. **B**	26. **D**	50. **D**	74. **A**	98. **B**
3. **D**	27. **D**	51. **A**	75. **D**	99. **B**
4. **C**	28. **B**	52. **D**	76. **A**	100. **D**
5. **A**	29. **A**	53. **C**	77. **B**	101. **D**
6. **D**	30. **D**	54. **D**	78. **C**	102. **D**
7. **B**	31. **B**	55. **A**	79. **C**	103. **D**
8. **D**	32. **C**	56. **A**	80. **B**	104. **D**
9. **A**	33. **A**	57. **C**	81. **C**	105. **D**
10. **D**	34. **D**	58. **D**	82. **C**	106. **D**
11. **A**	35. **C**	59. **D**	83. **D**	107. **C**
12. **D**	36. **C**	60. **B**	84. **C**	108. **C**
13. **A**	37. **B**	61. **A**	85. **A**	109. **B**
14. **C**	38. **C**	62. **C**	86. **B**	110. **D**
15. **B**	39. **D**	63. **B**	87. **C**	111. **D**
16. **D**	40. **A**	64. **D**	88. **D**	112. **D**
17. **A**	41. **B**	65. **B**	89. **C**	113. **C**
18. **D**	42. **C**	66. **D**	90. **B**	114. **B**
19. **B**	43. **C**	67. **A**	91. **C**	115. **B**
20. **A**	44. **B**	68. **B**	92. **C**	116. **C**
21. **B**	45. **C**	69. **B**	93. **B**	117. **B**
22. **B**	46. **B**	70. **B**	94. **C**	118. **C**
23. **D**	47. **D**	71. **C**	95. **D**	119. **C**
24. **A**	48. **A**	72. **D**	96. **B**	120. **C**

1. FEAST : MEAL :: VELLUM : (A. paper, B. fur, C. cotton, D. forest)

   The correct answer is (A). In this analogy of degree, a feast is a rich and expensive meal; vellum is a rich and expensive kind of paper.

2. (A. leave, B. audition, C. divide, D. correct) : APPLY :: PART : POSITION

   The correct answer is (B). The correspondence is one of action to object. You apply for a position of employment; you audition for a part in a play.

3. OXEN : STRENGTH :: (A. furnace, B. animal, C. cattle, D. ants) : INDUSTRY

   The correct answer is (D). In this association analogy, oxen are associated with strength; ants are associated with industry.

4. ASSIDUOUS : EGREGIOUS :: (A. jubilant, B. desultory, C. diligent, D. bitter) : FLAGRANT

   The correct answer is (C). In this synonym analogy, another word for egregious is flagrant. A synonym for assiduous is diligent.

5. SHIP : (A. crow's nest, B. deck, C. prow, D. mast) :: COLUMN : CAPITAL

    The correct answer is (A). A crow's nest is a small observation platform near the top of the mast of a ship; a capital is the uppermost part of a column.

6. DAVID COPPERFIELD : TINY TIM :: (A. Joseph Andrews, B. Ahab, C. Becky Sharp, D. Little Nell) : OLIVER TWIST

    The correct answer is (D). The relationship among David Copperfield, Tiny Tim, and Oliver Twist is that they are all fictional characters created by Charles Dickens. To complete the analogy, another Dickens character must be selected, and Little Nell is the correct choice.

7. CLEOPATRA : (A. Caesar, B. snake, C. knife, D. beauty) :: MARIE ANTIONETTE : GUILLOTINE

    The correct answer is (B). Marie Antionette was killed by a guillotine; Cleopatra was killed by a snake by which she was bitten.

8. (A. circle, B. heart, C. dissemination, D. artery) : CIRCULATE :: DITCH : IRRIGATE

    The correct answer is (D). In this object-to-action analogy, a ditch is the channel through which water flows to irrigate; an artery is the vessel or channel through which blood may circulate.

9. BRIGHT : GAUDY :: (A. urged, B. implied, C. prevented, D. acquiesced) : COMPELLED

    The correct answer is (A). The relationship is one of degree because something that is gaudy is excessively bright; compelled is excessively urged.

10. (A. dissidence, B. deficiency, C. irreverence, D. deference) : DISRESPECT :: IMBUE : EXTRACT

    The correct answer is (D). Imbue, meaning to permeate, is the opposite of extract, meaning to draw out. The opposite of disrespect is deference.

11. EGO : ID :: SELF : (A. desire, B. society, C. conscience, D. morality)

    The correct answer is (A). Ego is a psychological term for self; id is a psychological term for desire. The psychological term for conscience is superego.

12. ACCELERATOR : (A. automobile, B. driver, C. speed, D. brake) :: PROGRESS : RECESSION

    The correct answer is (D). An accelerator and a brake have opposite functions; similarly, progress and recession are opposite in meaning.

13. (A. gem, B. spore, C. illegitimacy, D. superficiality) : SPURIOUS :: MONEY : COUNTERFEIT

    The correct answer is (A). A gem is worthless when it is spurious—that is, false; money is worthless when it is counterfeit.

14. AMIN : (A. Elizabeth II, B. Waldheim, C. Qaddafi, D. Adenauer) :: KING : BUNCHE

    The correct answer is (C). Martin Luther King and Ralph Bunche were both very reliable men working for peace. Idi Amin and Muammar el-Qaddafi were known for tyranny, ruthlessness, and erratic behavior. While Kurt Waldheim's behavior has also been questioned, his reputation does not fall into the same league as those of Amin and Qaddafi.

15. 225 : AREA :: (A. 2,744, B. 3,375, C. 38,416, D. 50,625) : VOLUME

The correct answer is (B). The area of a figure is 225 square units. With no additional given information, one must assume that the figure is a square. One side of the figure is 15 units long because the square root of 225 is 15. The analogy asks for the volume of the cube based upon the figure related to its area. 15 × 15 × 15 = 3,375 cubic units.

16. QUEUE : (A. borough, B. pool, C. line, D. broom) :: CUE : BROUGHAM

The correct answer is (D). Queue and cue are homophones, different in meaning but pronounced the same; broom and brougham are also pronounced the same.

17. COLONEL : REGIMENT :: (A. major, B. captain, C. private, D. general) : BATTALION

The correct answer is (A). A colonel leads a regiment; a major leads a battalion.

18. DILETTANTE : (A. thorough, B. painstaking, C. diplomatic, D. superficial) :: BOISTEROUS : LOUD

The correct answer is (D). A boisterous person tends to be loud; a dilettante, a dabbler, tends to be superficial.

19. HANDLEBARS : SPOKE :: KEYBOARD : (A. basket, B. chip, C. music, D. retort)

The correct answer is (B). This is a part-to-part analogy. Handlebars and a spoke are parts of a bicycle; a keyboard and a chip are parts of a computer.

20. (A. rectify, B. error, C. find, D. realize) : MISTAKE :: REGAIN : LOSS

The correct answer is (A). The relationship is one of action to object. To improve a poor or unfortunate condition, one may rectify a mistake, and one may regain a loss.

21. INDEX : FRONTISPIECE :: MATURITY : (A. adolescence, B. infancy, C. contents, D. adulthood)

The correct answer is (B). In this sequence analogy, the index comes at the end of a book, and the frontispiece comes at the beginning; maturity comes in the latter part of life, and infancy comes in the beginning.

22. TAUTOLOGICAL : REDUNDANT :: (A. mature, B. incipient, C. obnoxious, D. late) : INCHOATE

The correct answer is (B). Tautological is a synonym for redundant; inchoate, which means at an early state of development, is a synonym for incipient.

23. SQUARE : (A. triangle, B. triplet, C. poem, D. duet) :: QUADRUPLET : COUPLET

The correct answer is (D). Quadruplet refers to a group of four; a couplet consists of two successive rhyming lines of verse. Because a square has four sides, a term involving a pair must be chosen to complete the analogy. A duet, a composition for two performers, is the only possible choice.

24. MAY : (A. horn, B. charity, C. tempest, D. despair) :: FEAR : COD

The correct answer is (A). In this place analogy, May, Fear, and Cod are all names of capes. To complete the analogy, another cape must be selected, and Cape Horn is the correct choice.

25. (A. m, B. p, C. l, D. t) : H :: W : S

The correct answer is (C). In the alphabet, W is the fourth letter after S; L is the fourth letter after H.

26. CHOLERIC : AMIABLE :: (A. timid, B. scared, C. mute, D. temerarious) : CIRCUMSPECT

The correct answer is (D). Choleric, which means bad-tempered, and amiable, meaning agreeable, are opposites; temerarious, which means rash and reckless, and circumspect, meaning careful, are opposites.

27. IRON : (A. hard, B. strong, C. steel, D. pig) :: OIL : CRUDE

The correct answer is (D). In this product-to-source analogy, oil in its rough state is called crude oil; iron in its rough state is called pig iron.

28. (A. astronomy, B. play, C. symphony, D. clouds) : STAR :: CONCERT : SOLOIST

The correct answer is (B). A star takes the leading role in a play; a soloist takes the leading role in a concert.

29. SALUTE : (A. motto, B. reveille, C. mess, D. orders) :: TROOP : EAGLE

The correct answer is (A). Salute, troop, and eagle are all things associated with the Boy Scouts. To complete the analogy, another element of scouting should be selected, and motto is the correct choice. Reveille and mess are associated with Boy Scout camping, but it is not necessary to extend to camping to complete this analogy.

30. PROVISIONS : QUARTERMASTER :: (A. screwdriver, B. knife, C. saddle, D. manuscript) : SCRIVENER

The correct answer is (D). In this worker-to-job analogy, a quartermaster's job is to secure provisions for an army; a scrivener's job is to copy a manuscript.

31. ATLANTIS : (A. Pompeii, B. Xanadu, C. Byzantium, D. Zanzibar) :: SHANGRI-LA : EL DORADO

The correct answer is (B). Atlantis, Shangri-La, and El Dorado are related because each is an undocumented place. Xanadu, the only undocumented place among the answer choices, correctly completes this analogy.

32. WIND : DEFICIT :: EROSION : (A. spending, B. appreciation, C. borrowing, D. employment)

The correct answer is (C). In this cause-and-effect analogy, one effect of excessive wind is soil erosion; an effect of an excessive deficit is borrowing to make up for expenditures. Excessive spending is a cause of a deficit, not an effect.

33. (A. slot, B. note, C. band, D. harmony) : VALVE :: HARMONICA : TRUMPET

The correct answer is (A). The correspondence is one of part to whole. A valve is part of a trumpet; a slot is part of a harmonica.

34. FLAUNT : (A. destructively, B. stupidly, C. willingly, D. boastfully) :: BETRAY : DECEPTIVELY

The correct answer is (D). To flaunt is to act boastfully; to betray is to act deceptively.

35. HOUYHNHNM : YAHOO :: REASON : (A. learning, B. intelligence, C. ignorance, D. genius)

The correct answer is (C). In *Gulliver's Travels,* by Jonathan Swift, a houyhnhnm symbolizes intelligence and reason, whereas a yahoo symbolizes the opposite, stupidity or ignorance.

36. DEFIED : ASTRIDE :: EARTH : (A. geography, B. zoology, C. birth, D. life)

The correct answer is (C). In this nonsemantic rhyming analogy, defied rhymes with astride; earth rhymes with birth.

37. ST. PETERSBURG : LENINGRAD :: (A. Stalingrad, B. Leningrad, C. Moscow, D. Odessa) : ST. PETERSBURG

The correct answer is (B). The analogy is based on identity. The soviet name for the city was Leningrad. Before the Revolution and after the dissolution of the Soviet Union, the name for the city was and now is St. Petersburg.

38. (A. 1999, B. 1900, C. 1901, D. 1902) : 1910 :: 1950 : 1959

The correct answer is (C). In this sequence analogy, the difference between 1901 and 1910 is nine years; the difference between 1950 and 1959 is nine years. The mathematics of this problem is simple, but the use of dates is deceptive. When dates appear to be meaningless, you must look for a relationship along another dimension, just as when words appear unrelated you must seek a grammatical or nonsemantic relationship.

39. ADVOCATE : (A. impute, B. allude, C. pursue, D. impugn) :: AMELIORATE : IMPAIR

The correct answer is (D). Ameliorate, meaning to improve or to make better, is the opposite of impair, meaning to make worse. The opposite of advocate, meaning to support or to plead in favor of, is impugn, meaning to deny or to attack as false.

40. HENRY MOORE : (A. Rodin, B. Pavlov, C. Van Gogh, D. Gertrude Stein) :: DONATELLO : BERNINI

The correct answer is (A). The connection among Henry Moore, Donatello, and Bernini is that they are all sculptors. To complete the analogy, another sculptor must be chosen, and Rodin is the correct choice.

41. HO CHI MINH : GANDHI :: FRANCE : (A. Indochina, B. Great Britain, C. Vietnam, D. India)

The correct answer is (B). Ho Chi Minh and Gandhi were both leaders of independence movements in countries colonized by European nations. Ho Chi Minh, a leftist revolutionary, fought to expel France from Indochina. Gandhi, an advocate of nonviolence and passive resistance, led the movement to expel Great Britain from India.

42. HEDGER : SHRUBBERY :: (A. snuffer, B. gardener, C. whittler, D. stickler) : STICK

The correct answer is (C). A hedger trims shrubbery; a whittler trims a stick.

43. MAN : (A. bird, B. centipede, C. elephant, D. automobile) :: WHEELBARROW : BICYCLE

The correct answer is (C). The relationship is a numerical ratio of one to two. A wheelbarrow has one wheel; a bicycle has two. Similarly, a man has two legs, and an elephant has four. Approach this analogy by looking first at the two adjacent capitalized words. You will instantly recognize that a wheelbarrow has one wheel and a bicycle has two. Man uses both a wheelbarrow and a bicycle, and none of the choices logically uses either, so you should begin to suspect a numerical analogy. A centipede with its 100 legs is a distracter that also serves as a clue. Because the wheel ratio is one to two, you must be careful not to choose the bird, which has the same number of legs as the man.

44. (A. velocity, B. viscosity, C. temperature, D. density) : FLUID :: FRICTION : SOLID

    The correct answer is (B). Viscosity is the resistance of a fluid to flow, just as friction is the resistance to relative motion between two solids.

45. CANTON : COUNTY :: (A. Ohio, B. Japan, C. Switzerland, D. China) : IRELAND

    The correct answer is (C). A canton is a territorial division in Switzerland; a county is a territorial division in Ireland.

46. PECK : PINT :: 1 : (A. 4, B. 16, C. 8, D. 2)

    The correct answer is (B). In this measurement analogy, a peck is equal to 8 quarts. A pint is half of a quart; therefore, 1 peck is equal to 16 pints.

47. TWEEZERS : BLEACH :: (A. steel, B. light, C. adding machine, D. eraser) : PICKPOCKET

    The correct answer is (D). The relationship among tweezers, bleach, and a pickpocket is that they all remove something. Among the choices, an eraser also removes something, a written mistake.

48. HARANGUING : (A. persuade, B. filet, C. cleaning, D. arbitrate) :: FILIBUSTERING : OBSTRUCT

    The correct answer is (A). In this purpose analogy, a purpose of filibustering is to obstruct passage of legislation. The purpose of haranguing is to persuade or coax another party to accept your position.

49. SHERRY : BEER :: PORT : (A. champagne, B. sauterne, C. claret, D. muscatel)

    The correct answer is (A). Sherry has no carbonation; beer has carbonation. Port has no carbonation; champagne has carbonation.

50. HONOR : GOVERNOR :: (A. Excellency, B. Majesty, C. Highness, D. Grace) : DUKE

    The correct answer is (D). The proper way to refer to people in certain positions or ranks is to say his honor, the governor, and his grace, the duke.

51. ANDIRON : PEDESTAL :: (A. log, B. bucket, C. anvil, D. skillet) : STATUE

    The correct answer is (A). An andiron holds a log; a pedestal holds a statue.

52. GENERAL : STARS :: COLONEL : (A. oak, B. silver, C. gold, D. eagle)

    The correct answer is (D). In this association analogy, stars symbolize the rank of general; an eagle symbolizes the rank of colonel.

53. (A. insist, B. reply, C. demur, D. demand) : REFUSE :: LAZY : INERT

    The correct answer is (C). The relationship is one of degree. Lazy, meaning sluggish, is a lesser degree of immobility than inert. To demur, meaning to hesitate, delay, or object, is a lesser degree of protestation than to refuse.

54. HEART : HEAD :: VENERY : (A. ribaldry, B. flesh, C. mortality, D. restraint)

    The correct answer is (D). It is often said that the ways of the heart are the opposite to the ways of the head; the opposite of venery, the gratification of desires, is restraint.

55. CALORIE : (A. energy, B. weight, C. metabolism, D. food) :: CENTURY : TIME

    The correct answer is (A). A calorie is a measure of the heat-producing or energy-producing value of food. A century is a measure of time.

56. FLORIDA : SAUDI ARABIA :: (A. Louisiana, B. Georgia, C. Arkansas, D. Iraq) : IRAN

The correct answer is (A). In this place analogy, Saudi Arabia and Iran are both countries bordering on the Persian Gulf; Florida and Louisiana are states that border on the Gulf of Mexico. And, just as Saudi Arabia and Iran do not border on each other, so also Florida and Louisiana do not have a common border.

57. *KING LEAR : DIE FLEDERMAUS :: MACBETH :* (A. *Tosca,* B. *Othello,* C. *Ruddigore,* D. *Les Misérables)*

The correct answer is (C). *King Lear* and *Macbeth* are both Shakespearean tragedies. *Die Fledermaus* and *Ruddigore* are both comic operas. The writer of the two comedies is irrelevant because no other choice is a comedy.

58. BOARDWALK : (A. Park Place, B. Atlantic City, C. display, D. escalator) :: STRAND : STORE

The correct answer is (D). A boardwalk is a kind of walkway along a strand or beach; an escalator is a kind of walkway in a department store.

59. (A. Parliament, B. Congress, C. Great Britain, D. Senate) : LORDS :: HOUSE : COMMONS

The correct answer is (D). The Senate and the House of Lords are the upper houses of the U.S. Congress and the British Parliament, respectively; the House of Representatives and House of Commons are the lower houses.

60. 1789 : (A. Germany, B. France, C. England, D. Russia) :: 1776 : UNITED STATES

The correct answer is (B). The dates mark the beginnings of two highly significant revolutions. 1776 was the beginning of the revolution in what was to become the United States; 1789 was the beginning year of the revolution in France.

61. MALLARD : CANVASBACK :: (A. snow, B. north, C. drake, D. gander) : CANADIAN

The correct answer is (A). This is a part-to-part relationship. Mallard and canvasback both belong to the group "ducks." Canadian and snow both belong to the group "geese."

62. WELL-FED : (A. penurious, B. healthy, C. wealthy, D. miserly) :: HUNGRY : IMPECUNIOUS

The correct answer is (C). The relationship is that of opposites. A well-fed person is not hungry; a wealthy person is not impecunious, or lacking money.

63. LAERTES : (A. Odysseus, B. Polonius, C. Claudius, D. Ophelia) :: ICARUS : DAEDALUS

The correct answer is (B). In Greek mythology, Icarus is the son of Daedalus; in Shakespeare's play *Hamlet,* Laertes is the son of Polonius.

64. SYRACUSE : (A. Oneonta, B. Geneva, C. Raleigh, D. Sparta) :: CARTHAGE : ALEXANDRIA

The correct answer is (D). Syracuse, Sparta, Carthage, and Alexandria are all names of ancient historical communities.

65. DISPIRITED : DEPRESSED :: (A. obligato, B. innuendo, C. declaration, D. crescendo) : INSINUATION

The correct answer is (B). Dispirited and depressed are synonyms; innuendo and insinuation are also synonyms.

66. ORGANISM : (A. plant, B. animal, C. bacteria, D. cell) :: LIGHT : WAVE

The correct answer is (D). In this whole-to-part analogy, an organism is made up of cells; light consists physically of waves.

67. KÖLN : WIEN :: COLOGNE : (A. Vienna, B. Prague, C. Warsaw, D. Hamburg)

The correct answer is (A). The German name for Cologne is Köln; the German name for Vienna is Wien.

68. DCX : MDCCCXXX :: (A. CLX, B. XLI, C. LCD, D. LXVII) : CXXIII

The correct answer is (B). If you are required to perform mathematical calculations with large Roman numerals, you may be pretty certain that the calculations will be very simple ones. Begin by translating into Arabic numerals. DCX = 610. MDCCCXXX = 1,830. By inspection you can see that 610 × 3 = 1,830. Now translate the third Roman numeral. CXXIII = 123. The fourth term must be one third of 123 or 4l, which is XLI.

69. WISDOM : (A. lion, B. owl, C. fox, D. deer) :: SPRING : ROBIN

The correct answer is (B). The relationship is one of association. A robin is associated with the coming of spring; an owl is associated with great wisdom.

70. BUTTERFLY : (A. insect, B. silkworm, C. wings, D. summer) :: CHRYSALIS : COCOON

The correct answer is (B). An early stage in the development of the butterfly is the chrysalis; an early stage in the development of the silkworm is the cocoon. Chrysalis and cocoon are synonyms. Butterfly and silkworm are not synonyms, but they do bear the same sequential relationship to the enveloped stage of development.

71. ICELAND : NORWAY :: (A. winter, B. queen, C. president, D. sovereign) : KING

The correct answer is (C). Norway is a constitutional monarchy headed by a king; Iceland is a republic headed by a president.

72. ROME : (A. NATO, B. SEATO, C. SALT II, D. EEC) :: VERSAILLES : LEAGUE OF NATIONS

The correct answer is (D). The groundwork for the League of Nations was laid out in the Treaty of Versailles in 1919. The initial planning for the EEC (European Economic Community) was drafted in the Treaty of Rome in 1957. The NATO (North Atlantic Treaty Organization) alliance was forged in Washington, D.C., in 1949: SEATO (Southeast Asia Treaty Organization) in Manila in 1954; and SALT II (Strategic Arms Limitation Treaty II) in Vienna in 1979.

73. CYLINDER : LOCK :: MOTOR : (A. shaft, B. canal, C. tackle, D. escape)

The correct answer is (B). A cylinder is part of a motor; a lock is part of a canal. This is a difficult analogy because a cylinder is also part of a lock. However, if you begin and stick with this relationship, you can then choose only that a shaft is part of a motor, which is a reverse relationship and creates an incorrect analogy.

74. BANANA : (A. sapphire, B. saltcellar, C. stone, D. tree) :: BUTTER : SKY

The correct answer is (A). Butter is yellow, and sky is blue; because a banana is yellow, the task is to find the choice that is blue: a sapphire.

75. GNASH : TEETH :: (A. fold, B. clasp, C. gnarl, D. wring) : HANDS

The correct answer is (D). In this action-to-object analogy, you may gnash your teeth or wring your hands in anger or dismay. All of the other choices are also activities that can be done with your hands, but they are not characteristically a sign of anger or dismay.

76. (A. opossum, B. fox, C. beaver, D. lady) : KANGAROO :: CHICKEN : COCKROACH

The correct answer is (A). A chicken and a cockroach are both related as oviparous or egg bearing. An opossum and a kangaroo are both classified as marsupials, pouched mammals.

77. APHRODITE : VENUS :: ARES : (A. Mercury, B. Mars, C. Apollo, D. Hermes)

The correct answer is (B). Aphrodite is the Greek goddess of love and beauty; Venus is her Roman counterpart. Ares is the Greek god of war; Mars is his Roman counterpart.

78. METAPHYSICS : (A. humanities, B. medicine, C. logic, D. art) :: EPISTEMOLOGY : ETHICS

The correct answer is (C). The four terms of this analogy are all related in that epistemology, ethics, metaphysics, and logic constitute four of the five branches of philosophy. The fifth is aesthetics.

79. CLARINET : PIANO :: WIND : (A. reed, B. wood, C. string, D. pianist)

The correct answer is (C). A clarinet is a wind instrument; a piano is a string instrument.

80. ELEVATOR : SKYSCRAPER :: (A. gangplank, B. companionway, C. bulkhead, D. bridge) : SHIP

The correct answer is (B). An elevator is used to ascend and descend once inside a skyscraper; a companionway, a ship's staircase, is used for the same purpose in a ship.

81. PROPENSITY : (A. riches, B. weight, C. bias, D. thought) :: CLUB : MACE

The correct answer is (C). In this degree analogy, a propensity is a lesser degree of opinion than is a bias; a club is a less ominous weapon than a mace, which is a spiked club.

82. SALZBURG : STRATFORD :: (A. Goethe, B. Avon, C. Mozart, D. Brahms) : SHAKESPEARE

The correct answer is (C). Stratford is the birthplace of Shakespeare; Salzburg is the birthplace of Mozart.

83. FLAMMABLE : INFLAMMABLE :: PERTINENT : (A. impertinent, B. inopportune, C. incoherent, D. relevant)

The correct answer is (D). Flammable and inflammable are synonyms; pertinent and relevant are also synonyms.

84. (A. revolution, B. dance, C. torque, D. axis) : ROTATE :: FRICTION : RESIST

The correct answer is (C). In this cause-and-effect analogy, friction causes something to resist moving; torque causes something to rotate. The effects are opposite, but the cause-to-effect relationship is the same.

85. PRISM : (A. spectrum, B. reflection, C. light, D. binoculars) :: FAMINE : WANT

The correct answer is (A). In this product-source analogy, a spectrum is created by a prism; want is produced by a famine, which is a scarcity.

86. LOOP : HUB :: BEEF : (A. corn, B. beans, C. tobacco, D. cotton)

The correct answer is (B). The loop and the hub are nicknames for the downtown business districts of Chicago and Boston, respectively; Chicago is known for its beef, and Boston is known for its beans.

87. JANUARY : (A. Cleveland, B. June, C. Washington, D. Hermes) :: SUNDAY : MERCURY

The correct answer is (C). We have a number of firsts here: January is the first month; Sunday is the first day of the week; Mercury is the first planet in distance from the sun; and Washington was the first U.S. president.

88. LIFT : ELEVATOR :: (A. oil, B. grease, C. gas, D. petrol) : GASOLINE

The correct answer is (D). Lift is the British word for an elevator; petrol is the British word for gasoline.

89. (A. $\frac{1}{6}$, B. $\frac{4}{5}$, C. $\frac{2}{5}$, D. $\frac{2}{10}$) : $\frac{1}{10}$ :: $\frac{3}{4}$: $\frac{3}{16}$

The correct answer is (C). In this numerical analogy, $\frac{1}{4}$ of $\frac{3}{4}$ is $\frac{3}{16}$; $\frac{1}{4}$ of $\frac{2}{5}$ is $\frac{1}{10}$.

90. TORT : LITIGATION :: CONTRACT : (A. signature, B. obligation, C. clause, D. equity)

The correct answer is (B). A tort is a wrong that entails litigation; a contract is an agreement that entails obligation.

91. BULL : (A. wolf, B. turtle, C. fish, D. snail) :: CRAB : LION

The correct answer is (C). The bull (Taurus), fish (Pisces), crab (Cancer), and lion (Leo) are all signs of the zodiac.

92. EQUINOX : SOLSTICE :: SEPTEMBER : (A. November, B. January, C. June, D. March)

The correct answer is (C). Equinox refers to either of the two times each year when the sun crosses the equator and day and night are everywhere of equal length, occurring about March 21 and September 23. Solstice refers to one of the two points at which the sun's apparent position on the celestial sphere reaches its greatest distance above or below the celestial equator, occurring about June 22 and December 22.

93. (A. hand, B. brow, C. rose, D. soon) : KNIT :: DICTATION : TAKE

The correct answer is (B). In this action-to-object analogy, one may knit a brow, and one may take dictation.

94. GARROTING : DEATH :: CANVASSING : (A. painting, B. shelter, C. votes, D. fight)

The correct answer is (C). The correspondence is one of cause and effect. Garroting (strangling) commonly causes death; canvassing (soliciting for support) commonly results in votes.

95. PUSILLANIMOUS : INVIDIOUS :: (A. paronomasia, B. slather, C. melodramatically, D. perfunctory) : SANCTIMONIOUS

The correct answer is (D). The Miller Analogies Test tends to get into some esoteric vocabulary but not much. If the words seem excessively long or obscure, look for another relationship before trying to define and determine meaningful relationships. In this analogy based upon grammar, pusillanimous, invidious, and sanctimonious are all adjectives. The only choice that is an adjective is perfunctory. With paronomasia, you should know by its ending that it is a noun; slather is a verb or a noun; and melodramatically is an adverb.

96. SUN : JAPAN :: (A. scythe, B. crescent, C. Caspian, D. hammer) : TURKEY

The correct answer is (B). The crescent is a symbol associated with Turkey, just as the rising sun is a symbol associated with Japan.

97. CICERO : DEMOSTHENES :: ROOSEVELT : (A. MacArthur, B. Hemingway, C. Shaw, D. Churchill)

The correct answer is (D). Cicero and Demosthenes are related as orators; Roosevelt and Churchill are related as statesmen.

98. TYRO : (A. tyrant, B. master, C. amateur, D. dabbler) :: TURPITUDE : PROBITY

The correct answer is (B). The opposite of turpitude, which means baseness, is probity, meaning uprightness. An antonym for tyro, a beginner, is master. If you are unfamiliar with the meaning of a particular word, such as tyro, but understand the relationship between the remaining pair of words, closely examine the relationship between the four answer choices. In most analogy problems, if two answer choices are synonymous, neither is likely to be correct. In this case, amateur and dabbler are synonyms, and both can be eliminated from consideration.

99. COKE : COAL :: (A. oil, B. planks, C. saw, D. lumberjack) : TIMBER

The correct answer is (B). In this product-source analogy, coke is obtained by heating coal; planks are formed by cutting timber.

100. SHOE : (A. belt, B. cobbler, C. pair, D. bell) :: SAW : GEAR

The correct answer is (D). A saw and a gear both have teeth; a shoe and a bell both have a tongue.

101. DEGRADE : MARTIAL :: LAUD : (A. military, B. noisy, C. worried, D. halcyon)

The correct answer is (D). To degrade is the opposite of to laud; martial, meaning military, is the opposite of halcyon, meaning peaceful.

102. MAN : BREAD :: HORSE : (A. stable, B. duck, C. barn, D. hay)

The correct answer is (D). The purpose of bread is to sustain man; the purpose of hay is to sustain a horse.

103. AIRPLANE : (A. kite, B. ship, C. bird, D. helicopter) :: BUS : TRAIN

The correct answer is (D). Bus and train are both forms of ground transportation; airplane and helicopter are both forms of air transportation.

104. FACULTY : STAFF :: UNIVERSITY : (A. intern, B. patient, C. workers, D. hospital)

The correct answer is (D). The faculty is a major functional unit of the university; the staff serves the same function in the hospital. An intern is a member of the staff.

105. HEW : (A. hewn, B. mow, C. toe, D. hue) :: BLEW : BLUE

The correct answer is (D). This analogy is based on the homophonic relationship between each pair. Blew and blue are pronounced the same yet have different meanings and spellings. The same is also true for hew and hue.

106. WORK : (A. employment, B. entertainment, C. office, D. income) :: FOOD : GROWTH

The correct answer is (D). Work creates income; food promotes growth.

107. IMMATURITY : (A. anger, B. childhood, C. adulthood, D. incompatibility) :: COMPETITION : MONOPOLY

The correct answer is (C). Immaturity is a trait associated with childhood, which makes it a near opposite of adulthood; competition is a trait associated with open trade and hence is a near opposite of a monopoly. If the terms of the initial pair are not exact opposites, the second pair need not be exact opposites either, but their relationship must parallel the relationship of the first pair.

108. SHIVER : COLD :: TREMBLE : (A. hot, B. happiness, C. fear, D. intelligence)

The correct answer is (C). You shiver with cold; you tremble with fear. With happiness, you quiver.

109. AK : MN :: (A. AS, B. AZ, C. NB, D. IO) : PA

The correct answer is (B). AK and MN are correct postal service abbreviations for Alaska and Minnesota; AZ and PA are correct postal service abbreviations for Arizona and Pennsylvania. The other choices are not correct postal service abbreviations.

110. (A. Apollo, B. Janus, C. Eros, D. Jupiter) : JUNO :: ZEUS : HERA

The correct answer is (D). Zeus and Hera are husband and wife, king and queen of the Greek gods; Jupiter and Juno are husband and wife, the Roman counterparts of Zeus and Hera.

111. CULINARY : (A. bedroom, B. closet, C. knife, D. kitchen) :: ECUMENICAL : CHURCH

The correct answer is (D). Ecumenical has to do with the church; culinary has to do with the kitchen or with cooking.

112. LEAF : (A. leafs, B. leave, C. left, D. leaves) :: MEDIUM : MEDIA

The correct answer is (D). LEAF : LEAVES :: MEDIUM : MEDIA :: singular : plural.

113. FINGER : PALM :: (A. shoe, B. foot, C. sole, D. limb) : HEEL

The correct answer is (C). Finger and palm are both parts of the hand; sole and heel are both parts of the foot. The relationship of the parts from one side of the equation to the other is not analogous, but because no other part-to-part choices are offered, a more precise relationship is not required.

114. PINE : (A. Christmas, B. tree, C. fir, D. loss) :: POINSETTIA : FLOWER

The correct answer is (B). Pine is a kind of tree; poinsettia is a kind of flower. Beware of associations that do not constitute true analogies.

115. (A. throne, B. prince, C. kingdom, D. majesty) : FILLY :: KING : MARE

The correct answer is (B). A filly grows up to become a mare; a prince grows up to become a king.

116. (A. individual, B. baby, C. adult, D. male) : OAK :: INFANT : ACORN

The correct answer is (C). Great oaks grow from little acorns; an infant grows into an adult.

117. INFANT : TODDLER :: ADOLESCENT : (A. tyke, B. adult, C. youngster, D. masculine)

The correct answer is (B). The infant proceeds to the very next stage and becomes a toddler; an adolescent proceeds to the very next stage and becomes an adult. Proximity of stages as well as sequence enters into your correct choice.

118. (A. men, B. his, C. man's, D. mine) : MINE :: MAN : I

The correct answer is (C). MAN'S : MINE :: MAN : I :: possessive : subjective.

119. RAGE : (A. irk, B. annoy, C. anger, D. mischief) :: DEMONIC : NAUGHTY

The correct answer is (C). One who is demonic is fiendish, much worse than naughty; rage is much more intense than simple anger.

120. HOUR : MINUTE :: MINUTE : (A. time, B. day, C. second, D. moment)

The correct answer is (C). An hour is longer than a minute; a minute is longer than a second. The fact that there are 60 minutes in an hour and 60 seconds in a minute is irrelevant to this analogy.

ANSWER SHEET PRACTICE TEST 6

1. Ⓐ Ⓑ Ⓒ Ⓓ
2. Ⓐ Ⓑ Ⓒ Ⓓ
3. Ⓐ Ⓑ Ⓒ Ⓓ
4. Ⓐ Ⓑ Ⓒ Ⓓ
5. Ⓐ Ⓑ Ⓒ Ⓓ
6. Ⓐ Ⓑ Ⓒ Ⓓ
7. Ⓐ Ⓑ Ⓒ Ⓓ
8. Ⓐ Ⓑ Ⓒ Ⓓ
9. Ⓐ Ⓑ Ⓒ Ⓓ
10. Ⓐ Ⓑ Ⓒ Ⓓ
11. Ⓐ Ⓑ Ⓒ Ⓓ
12. Ⓐ Ⓑ Ⓒ Ⓓ
13. Ⓐ Ⓑ Ⓒ Ⓓ
14. Ⓐ Ⓑ Ⓒ Ⓓ
15. Ⓐ Ⓑ Ⓒ Ⓓ
16. Ⓐ Ⓑ Ⓒ Ⓓ
17. Ⓐ Ⓑ Ⓒ Ⓓ
18. Ⓐ Ⓑ Ⓒ Ⓓ
19. Ⓐ Ⓑ Ⓒ Ⓓ
20. Ⓐ Ⓑ Ⓒ Ⓓ
21. Ⓐ Ⓑ Ⓒ Ⓓ
22. Ⓐ Ⓑ Ⓒ Ⓓ
23. Ⓐ Ⓑ Ⓒ Ⓓ
24. Ⓐ Ⓑ Ⓒ Ⓓ
25. Ⓐ Ⓑ Ⓒ Ⓓ
26. Ⓐ Ⓑ Ⓒ Ⓓ
27. Ⓐ Ⓑ Ⓒ Ⓓ
28. Ⓐ Ⓑ Ⓒ Ⓓ
29. Ⓐ Ⓑ Ⓒ Ⓓ
30. Ⓐ Ⓑ Ⓒ Ⓓ

31. Ⓐ Ⓑ Ⓒ Ⓓ
32. Ⓐ Ⓑ Ⓒ Ⓓ
33. Ⓐ Ⓑ Ⓒ Ⓓ
34. Ⓐ Ⓑ Ⓒ Ⓓ
35. Ⓐ Ⓑ Ⓒ Ⓓ
36. Ⓐ Ⓑ Ⓒ Ⓓ
37. Ⓐ Ⓑ Ⓒ Ⓓ
38. Ⓐ Ⓑ Ⓒ Ⓓ
39. Ⓐ Ⓑ Ⓒ Ⓓ
40. Ⓐ Ⓑ Ⓒ Ⓓ
41. Ⓐ Ⓑ Ⓒ Ⓓ
42. Ⓐ Ⓑ Ⓒ Ⓓ
43. Ⓐ Ⓑ Ⓒ Ⓓ
44. Ⓐ Ⓑ Ⓒ Ⓓ
45. Ⓐ Ⓑ Ⓒ Ⓓ
46. Ⓐ Ⓑ Ⓒ Ⓓ
47. Ⓐ Ⓑ Ⓒ Ⓓ
48. Ⓐ Ⓑ Ⓒ Ⓓ
49. Ⓐ Ⓑ Ⓒ Ⓓ
50. Ⓐ Ⓑ Ⓒ Ⓓ
51. Ⓐ Ⓑ Ⓒ Ⓓ
52. Ⓐ Ⓑ Ⓒ Ⓓ
53. Ⓐ Ⓑ Ⓒ Ⓓ
54. Ⓐ Ⓑ Ⓒ Ⓓ
55. Ⓐ Ⓑ Ⓒ Ⓓ
56. Ⓐ Ⓑ Ⓒ Ⓓ
57. Ⓐ Ⓑ Ⓒ Ⓓ
58. Ⓐ Ⓑ Ⓒ Ⓓ
59. Ⓐ Ⓑ Ⓒ Ⓓ
60. Ⓐ Ⓑ Ⓒ Ⓓ

61. Ⓐ Ⓑ Ⓒ Ⓓ
62. Ⓐ Ⓑ Ⓒ Ⓓ
63. Ⓐ Ⓑ Ⓒ Ⓓ
64. Ⓐ Ⓑ Ⓒ Ⓓ
65. Ⓐ Ⓑ Ⓒ Ⓓ
66. Ⓐ Ⓑ Ⓒ Ⓓ
67. Ⓐ Ⓑ Ⓒ Ⓓ
68. Ⓐ Ⓑ Ⓒ Ⓓ
69. Ⓐ Ⓑ Ⓒ Ⓓ
70. Ⓐ Ⓑ Ⓒ Ⓓ
71. Ⓐ Ⓑ Ⓒ Ⓓ
72. Ⓐ Ⓑ Ⓒ Ⓓ
73. Ⓐ Ⓑ Ⓒ Ⓓ
74. Ⓐ Ⓑ Ⓒ Ⓓ
75. Ⓐ Ⓑ Ⓒ Ⓓ
76. Ⓐ Ⓑ Ⓒ Ⓓ
77. Ⓐ Ⓑ Ⓒ Ⓓ
78. Ⓐ Ⓑ Ⓒ Ⓓ
79. Ⓐ Ⓑ Ⓒ Ⓓ
80. Ⓐ Ⓑ Ⓒ Ⓓ
81. Ⓐ Ⓑ Ⓒ Ⓓ
82. Ⓐ Ⓑ Ⓒ Ⓓ
83. Ⓐ Ⓑ Ⓒ Ⓓ
84. Ⓐ Ⓑ Ⓒ Ⓓ
85. Ⓐ Ⓑ Ⓒ Ⓓ
86. Ⓐ Ⓑ Ⓒ Ⓓ
87. Ⓐ Ⓑ Ⓒ Ⓓ
88. Ⓐ Ⓑ Ⓒ Ⓓ
89. Ⓐ Ⓑ Ⓒ Ⓓ
90. Ⓐ Ⓑ Ⓒ Ⓓ

91. Ⓐ Ⓑ Ⓒ Ⓓ
92. Ⓐ Ⓑ Ⓒ Ⓓ
93. Ⓐ Ⓑ Ⓒ Ⓓ
94. Ⓐ Ⓑ Ⓒ Ⓓ
95. Ⓐ Ⓑ Ⓒ Ⓓ
96. Ⓐ Ⓑ Ⓒ Ⓓ
97. Ⓐ Ⓑ Ⓒ Ⓓ
98. Ⓐ Ⓑ Ⓒ Ⓓ
99. Ⓐ Ⓑ Ⓒ Ⓓ
100. Ⓐ Ⓑ Ⓒ Ⓓ
101. Ⓐ Ⓑ Ⓒ Ⓓ
102. Ⓐ Ⓑ Ⓒ Ⓓ
103. Ⓐ Ⓑ Ⓒ Ⓓ
104. Ⓐ Ⓑ Ⓒ Ⓓ
105. Ⓐ Ⓑ Ⓒ Ⓓ
106. Ⓐ Ⓑ Ⓒ Ⓓ
107. Ⓐ Ⓑ Ⓒ Ⓓ
108. Ⓐ Ⓑ Ⓒ Ⓓ
109. Ⓐ Ⓑ Ⓒ Ⓓ
110. Ⓐ Ⓑ Ⓒ Ⓓ
111. Ⓐ Ⓑ Ⓒ Ⓓ
112. Ⓐ Ⓑ Ⓒ Ⓓ
113. Ⓐ Ⓑ Ⓒ Ⓓ
114. Ⓐ Ⓑ Ⓒ Ⓓ
115. Ⓐ Ⓑ Ⓒ Ⓓ
116. Ⓐ Ⓑ Ⓒ Ⓓ
117. Ⓐ Ⓑ Ⓒ Ⓓ
118. Ⓐ Ⓑ Ⓒ Ⓓ
119. Ⓐ Ⓑ Ⓒ Ⓓ
120. Ⓐ Ⓑ Ⓒ Ⓓ

answer sheet

Practice Test 6

120 QUESTIONS • 60 MINUTES

Directions: Each of these test questions consists of three capitalized words and four lettered words enclosed in parentheses. Two of the capitalized words are related in some way. Find the two related words, and establish the nature of the relationship. Then study the four words lettered A, B, C, and D. Select the one lettered word that is related to the remaining capitalized word in the same way that the first two capitalized words are related. Mark the answer sheet for the letter preceding the word you select.

1. SHINGLE : (A. siding, B. granite, C. thatch, D. roof) :: TILE : SLATE

2. SCRUB : SHINE :: (A. turn, B. top, C. spiral, D. dance) : SPIN

3. (A. larva, B. embryo, C. caduceus, D. tadpole) : FROG :: CATERPILLAR : BUTTERFLY

4. LEAP : STRIDE :: JUMP : (A. fall, B. step, C. skip, D. bound)

5. CAT : MOUSE :: (A. polar bear, B. wolf, C. orca, D. rat) : RABBIT

6. MERCURY : MICA :: QUICKSILVER : (A. Formica, B. saltpeter, C. isinglass, D. hydroxide)

7. ROMEO : JULIET :: (A. Pyramus, B. Hercules, C. Endymion, D. Philemon) : THISBE

8. QUEENSLAND : (A. New Zealand, B. Brisbane, C. Victoria, D. Melbourne) :: ALBERTA : ONTARIO

9. BOUILLABAISSE : L'ORANGE :: (A. paella, B. a la mode, C. custard, D. chowder) : PEKING

10. (A. Annapolis, B. Williams, C. Baltimore, D. McHenry) : MARYLAND :: PENN : PENNSYLVANIA

11. $\frac{1}{2}$: .5 :: $\frac{5}{20}$: (A. $\frac{1}{5}$, B. .02, C. $\frac{1}{4}$, D. .25)

12. HYDE PARK : ROOSEVELT :: OYSTER BAY : (A. Kennedy, B. Tyler, C. Coolidge, D. Roosevelt)

13. PEPSIN : PTYALIN :: PROTEIN : (A. meat, B. starch, C. saliva, D. vitamins)

14. RAPHAEL : MICHELANGELO :: (A. Monet, B. Hockney, C. Braque, D. Veronese) : PICASSO

15. GOBI : (A. Mojave, B. Swahili, C. Masai, D. Africa) :: TIGRIS : EUPHRATES

16. CAPON : (A. rooster, B. turkey, C. chicken, D. steer) :: MULE : TANGELO

17. 12 : 3 :: 44 : (A. 33, B. 3, C. 11, D. 22)

18. GO : WENT :: READ : (A. wrote, B. learned, C. scan, D. read)

19. (A. "Lycidas," B. "Thanatopsis," C. "Adonais," D. "Astrophel") : "ELEGY" :: BRYANT : GRAY

20. *MAINE* : (A. Spanish-American War, B. Pearl Harbor, C. War of 1812, D. *Lusitania*) :: ALAMO : TEXAS WAR OF INDEPENDENCE

21. VENUS : URANUS :: (A. Ursa, B. Mercury, C. Haley, D. Sirius) :: POLARIS

22. TRUMAN : (A. reconstruction, B. policy, C. containment, D. rearmament) :: CHAMBERLAIN : APPEASEMENT

23. JOHN : IRVING :: (A. Toni, B. Jack, C. Stephen, D. Mary) : MORRISON

24. SAMISEN : (A. plasma, B. sampan, C. teapot, D. banjo) :: AMOEBA : PARAMECIUM

25. BIENNIAL : BIANNUAL :: TWO : (A. one, B. one half, C. two, D. fifty)

26. *PYGMALION* : *MY FAIR LADY* :: (A. *Fiddler on the Roof,* B. *The Pawnbroker,* C. *The Matchmaker,* D. *A House Is Not a Home*) : *HELLO, DOLLY!*

27. JACKSON : VAN BUREN :: WILSON : (A. Buchanan, B. Tyler, C. Taft, D. Ford)

28. (A. Algeria, B. Zimbabwe, C. Rwanda, D. Liberia) : SIERRA LEONE :: ANGOLA : MOZAMBIQUE

29. FISSION : ENERGY :: (A. fusion, B. inertia, C. mass, D. entropy) : ENERGY

30. CHRISTIE : (A. Queen, B. Holmes, C. Seaman, D. Gardner) :: POIROT : MASON

31. BACH : HANDEL :: MONET : (A. Brontë, B. Kant, C. Cassatt, D. Sibelius)

32. 9 : 27 :: 4 : (A. 9, B. 8, C. 18, D. 3)

33. (A. C.S.A., B. O.S.S., C. A.C.W., D. O.P.A.) : CIA :: I.W.W. : CIO

34. SUNNITE : SHIITE :: (A. Presbyterian, B. Hindu, C. Catholic, D. Protestant) : EPISCOPALIAN

35. *ANIMAL FARM* : (A. Eric Blair, B. William Blair, C. William Porter, D. Thomas Wolfe) :: *PUDD'NHEAD WILSON* : SAMUEL LANGHORNE CLEMENS

36. STRIKE : LOCKOUT :: CONTRADICT : (A. appeal, B. repeat, C. agree, D. annul)

37. COLLIER : MINER :: (A. diamond, B. remission, C. bracelet, D. talisman) : AMULET

38. LOBSTER : SPIDER :: (A. arthropod, B. crayfish, C. phylum, D. crustacean) : ARACHNID

39. HOMER : (A. Pindar, B. Ovid, C. Heraclitus, D. Aeneas) :: HERODOTUS : THUCYDIDES

40. HAIL : HALE :: (A. glare, B. pair, C. pear, D. fair) : PARE

41. MANET : *PROUST* :: GAINSBOROUGH : (A. Goya, B. *La Maja*, C. *Blue Boy*, D. Addison)

42. INFLAMMABLE : COMBUSTIBLE :: INVALUABLE : (A. priceless, B. worthless, C. untrue, D. deteriorating)

43. 3,280.8 ft. : (A. mile, B. kilometer, C. fathom, D. league) :: 946 ml. : QUART

44. OIL : (A. sun, B. gasoline, C. petroleum, D. olive) :: COAL : WIND

45. (A. Brahms, B. Beethoven, C. Debussy, D. Haydn) : TCHAIKOVSKY :: *PASTORALE* : *PATHETIQUE*

46. ESTONIA : RUSSIA :: (A. Georgia, B. China, C. Cuba, D. Monaco) : LATVIA

47. FLAMINGO : (A. horned owl, B. flicker, C. catbird, D. heron) :: CHICKEN : TURKEY

48. 1^2 : 1 :: 5^2 : (A. 3, B. 25, C. l, D. 10)

49. SCOTLAND : UNITED KINGDOM :: HOLLAND : (A. The Netherlands, B. Flanders, C. Europe, D. Belgium)

50. (A. griffin, B. giraffe, C. zebra, D. dinosaur) : DODO :: UNICORN : MASTODON

51. ANOPHELES : MALARIA :: AEDES : (A. cholera, B. dengue, C. bubonic plague, D. typhus)

52. OVOLO : CAVETTO :: (A. fertile, B. soprano, C. convex, D. poetic) : CONCAVE

53. CANTERBURY : (A. Chaucer, B. Hemingway, C. Updike, D. Forster) :: CASTERBRIDGE : HARDY

54. (A. laugh, B. weep, C. squirrels, D. geese) : QUAIL :: GAGGLE : COVEY

55. MANY : RAINDROPS :: MUCH : (A. lightning, B. snowflakes, C. puddle, D. water)

56. HEART : STOMACH :: (A. ear, B. arteries, C. intestines, D. capillaries) : DUODENUM

57. BRISTLES : (A. razor, B. toothbrush, C. monkey, D. flower) :: FEATHERS : DUSTER

58. CHEETAH : LEOPARD :: WOLF : (A. feline, B. canine, C. hyena, D. lupus)

59. TILES : (A. checkers, B. faucet, C. badminton, D. mah-jongg) :: DICE : BACKGAMMON

60. (A. statehouse, B. battlement, C. church, D. fortress) : CHURCH :: CITADEL : CATHEDRAL

61. 5 : $\sqrt{36}$ :: 8 : (A. 9, B. $\sqrt{81}$, C. $\sqrt{9}$, D. $\sqrt{64}$)

62. (A. crime, B. punishment, C. jury, D. verdict) : SENTENCE :: ANTEPENULT : PENULT

63. PANDA : (A. condor, B. bear, C. goldfish, D. ostrich) :: RACCOON : CROW

64. *LUSITANIA* : BRITAIN :: 007 : (A. Japan, B. Korea, C. USSR, D. James Bond)

65. YARD : FATHOM :: (A. eclipse, B. new, C. half, D. moon) : FULL

66. LANGSTON HUGHES : DOUGHTRY LONG :: (A. Marianne Moore, B. Gwendolyn Brooks, C. Gertrude Stein, D. Emily Dickinson) : MAYA ANGELOU

67. SAT : (A. PEP, B. ACT, C. TAT, D. NTE) :: GRE : MAT

68. TULIP : ASTER :: SPRING : (A. chicken, B. jump, C. fall, D. well)

69. BOLL WEEVIL : GYPSY MOTH :: (A. bee, B. termite, C. cockroach, D. louse) : PRAYING MANTIS

70. GHENT : (A. American Revolution, B. World War I, C. War of 1812, D. Hundred Years' War) :: P'ANMUNJOM : KOREAN WAR

71. (A. Nymph, B. Syrinx, C. Naiad, D. Chaos) : PAN :: ECHO : NARCISSUS

72. (A. terrapin, B. terrestrial, C. teuton, D. termagant) : SYCOPHANT :: VIRAGO : TOADY

73. KNESSET : ISRAEL :: DIET : (A. Kashrut, B. Luther, C. Japan, D. Congress)

74. *LES MISÉRABLES* : VICTOR HUGO :: (A. *Le Rouge et le Noir,* B. *Notre Dame de Paris,* C. *Les Trois Mousquetaires,* D. *Madame Bovary*) : ALEXANDRE DUMAS

75. ITS : IT'S :: (A. their, B. their's, C. there, D. there's) : THEY'RE

76. NICTATE : WINK :: (A. oscillate, B. osculate, C. ossify, D. oscultate) : KISS

77. INFLUENZA : VIRUS :: HODGKIN'S DISEASE : (A. schizophrenia, B. pulmonary disease, C. leprosy, D. cancer)

78. 28 : 82 :: 56 : (A. 54, B. 30, C. 65, D. 136)

79. *MAMA LUCIA* : (A. *Lucia de Lamermoor,* B. *Cavalleria Rusticana,* C. *Marriage of Figaro,* D. *Tosca*) :: *FIGARO* : *BARBER OF SEVILLE*

80. MINNEAPOLIS : NEW ORLEANS :: ALBANY : (A. Boston, B. Cleveland, C. New York City, D. Louisiana)

81. STAG : BILLY :: DOE : (A. William, B. Hinny, C. Kid, D. Nanny)

82. ROGET : (A. bridge, B. synonyms, C. thesaurus, D. quiz shows) :: WEBSTER : DEFINITIONS

83. OCULIST : OPHTHALMOLOGIST :: CHIROPODIST : (A. chiropractor, B. cardiologist, C. osteopath, D. podiatrist)

84. GNU : GNAT :: (A. koala, B. knight, C. kestrell, D. kangaroo) : KNAVE

85. ALLAH : (A. Islam, B. Mohammed, C. Christianity, D. God) :: HORUS : NEPTUNE

86. 15 : 5 :: 23 : (A. 1, B. 2, C. 5, D. 6)

87. CYRILLIC : RUSSIAN :: ROMAN : (A. Gypsy, B. English, C. numerals, D. Arabic)

88. PASTERN : (A. flank, B. rural, C. horse, D. church) :: PISTIL : STAMEN

89. @ : & :: 2 : (A. #, B. 5, C. 7, D. $\frac{1}{2}$)

90. SADAT : JERUSALEM :: (A. Mao Tse-tung, B. Nixon, C. Ho Chi Minh, D. Sun Yat Sen) : CHINA

91. (A. Alice, B. Medusa, C. Narcissus, D. Minerva) : ADONIS :: QUASIMODO : SNOW WHITE

92. ANTHROPOLOGY : MARGARET MEAD :: (A. archaeology, B. history, C. philosophy, D. psychology) : HOWARD CARTER

93. AMBITION : MACBETH :: JEALOUSY : (A. Caesar, B. Brutus, C. Othello, D. Shylock)

94. "FAUST" : (A. Mephistopheles, B. Goethe, C. folklore, D. Faulkner) :: "WASTELAND" : ELIOT

95. (A. ibid., B. etc., C. asst., D. dz.) : ET AL. :: OP. CIT. : CF.

96. YALTA : ROOSEVELT :: (A. Munich, B. Potsdam, C. Bastogne, D. Corregidor) : TRUMAN

97. *THE MAGIC FLUTE* : (A. *Iolanthe*, B. *Turandot*, C. *Il Trovatore*, D. *Don Giovanni*) :: *AIDA : DON CARLOS*

98. OXYGEN : (A. air, B. hydrogen, C. carbon dioxide, D. carbon monoxide) :: FAUNA : FLORA

99. (A. Sleeping Beauty, B. Cinderella, C. Rapunzel, D. Goldilocks) : PRINCE CHARMING :: FROG : PRINCESS

100. 9 : 104 :: BEETHOVEN : (A. Mozart, B. Sibelius, C. Haydn, D. Casals)

101. RUDDER : SHIP :: WHEEL : (A. car, B. truck, C. boat, D. string)

102. KARATE : FOOT :: FENCING : (A. chop, B. hand, C. foil, D. glove)

103. LEECH : PARASITE :: MUSHROOM : (A. host, B. butcher, C. turner, D. saprophyte)

104. LEAVENING : FERMENTATION :: ARGUMENT : (A. fight, B. precipitation, C. condensation, D. hail)

105. AMUSING : HILARIOUS :: SMART : (A. melancholy, B. genius, C. odd, D. happy)

106. LIST : ITEM :: CONSTITUTION : (A. person, B. article, C. disk, D. motion)

107. READ : BOOK :: LISTEN : (A. salty, B. movie, C. nose, D. music)

108. PREMIERE : MOVIE :: UNVEILING : (A. statue, B. president, C. teenager, D. subject)

109. PARROT : TROPICS :: ROADRUNNER : (A. house, B. India, C. desert, D. zoo)

110. MEDIAN : MIDDLE :: MEAN : (A. radius, B. measurement, C. designer, D. average)

111. BONES : LIGAMENT :: MUSCLE : (A. elasticity, B. tendon, C. cell, D. finger)

112. DOWN : FLUFFY :: SATIN : (A. fast, B. fluent, C. smooth, D. warm)

113. BURL : TREE :: PEARL : (A. oyster, B. copper, C. wood, D. sand)

114. YEAST : LEAVEN :: IODINE : (A. bubble, B. antiseptic, C. medicine, D. dough)

115. LIST : CAPSIZE :: CAREEN : (A. rise, B. crash, C. irk, D. discover)

116. PERIMETER : POLYGON :: CIRCUMFERENCE : (A. circle, B. triangle, C. square, D. angle)

117. OMEGA : ENDING :: ALPHA : (A. sorority, B. femur, C. beginning, D. ray)

118. EXPURGATE : PASSAGES :: DEFOLIATE : (A. leaves, B. checks, C. ideas, D. privacy)

119. GERM : DISEASE :: WAR : (A. treacherous, B. women, C. medicine, D. destruction)

120. QUASH : MOTION :: QUELL : (A. squeeze, B. destroy, C. riots, D. impel)

ANSWER KEY AND EXPLANATIONS

1. **C**	25. **B**	49. **A**	73. **C**	97. **D**
2. **A**	26. **C**	50. **A**	74. **C**	98. **C**
3. **D**	27. **B**	51. **B**	75. **A**	99. **A**
4. **B**	28. **B**	52. **C**	76. **B**	100. **C**
5. **B**	29. **A**	53. **A**	77. **D**	101. **A**
6. **C**	30. **D**	54. **D**	78. **C**	102. **C**
7. **A**	31. **C**	55. **D**	79. **B**	103. **D**
8. **C**	32. **B**	56. **B**	80. **C**	104. **A**
9. **D**	33. **B**	57. **B**	81. **D**	105. **B**
10. **C**	34. **A**	58. **C**	82. **B**	106. **B**
11. **D**	35. **A**	59. **D**	83. **D**	107. **D**
12. **D**	36. **C**	60. **D**	84. **B**	108. **A**
13. **B**	37. **D**	61. **B**	85. **D**	109. **C**
14. **C**	38. **D**	62. **D**	86. **D**	110. **D**
15. **A**	39. **A**	63. **A**	87. **B**	111. **B**
16. **D**	40. **B**	64. **B**	88. **A**	112. **C**
17. **C**	41. **C**	65. **C**	89. **C**	113. **A**
18. **D**	42. **A**	66. **B**	90. **B**	114. **B**
19. **B**	43. **B**	67. **B**	91. **B**	115. **B**
20. **A**	44. **A**	68. **C**	92. **A**	116. **A**
21. **D**	45. **B**	69. **A**	93. **C**	117. **C**
22. **C**	46. **A**	70. **C**	94. **B**	118. **A**
23. **A**	47. **D**	71. **B**	95. **A**	119. **D**
24. **D**	48. **B**	72. **D**	96. **B**	120. **C**

1. SHINGLE : (A. siding, B. granite, C. thatch, D. roof) :: TILE : SLATE

   The correct answer is (C). The analogy is one of part to part. Tile and slate are both roofing materials; shingle and thatch are roofing materials as well.

2. SCRUB : SHINE :: (A. turn, B. top, C. spiral, D. dance) : SPIN

   The correct answer is (A). In this cause-and-effect analogy, to scrub something causes it to shine, and to turn something causes it to spin.

3. (A. larva, B. embryo, C. caduceus, D. tadpole) : FROG :: CATERPILLAR : BUTTERFLY

   The correct answer is (D). This is a sequential analogy; the tadpole stage precedes the frog, and a caterpillar precedes a butterfly.

4. LEAP : STRIDE :: JUMP : (A. fall, B. step, C. skip, D. bound)

   The correct answer is (B). The relationship is one of degree. A leap is a very large jump; a stride is a very large step.

5. CAT : MOUSE :: (A. polar bear, B. wolf, C. orca, D. rat) : RABBIT

   The correct answer is (B). The relationship of cat to mouse is that of predator to prey. A rabbit is preyed upon by wolves.

6. MERCURY : MICA :: QUICKSILVER : (A. Formica, B. saltpeter, C. isinglass, D. hydroxide)

The correct answer is (C). The relationship is that of synonyms. Mercury is often known as quicksilver; mica is often called isinglass.

7. ROMEO : JULIET :: (A. Pyramus, B. Hercules, C. Endymion, D. Philemon) : THISBE

The correct answer is (A). Romeo and Juliet were tragic lovers whose parents forbade their marriage. This story closely parallels that of the mythological Pyramus and Thisbe, whose love was also thwarted by their parents.

8. QUEENSLAND : (A. New Zealand, B. Brisbane, C. Victoria, D. Melbourne) :: ALBERTA : ONTARIO

The correct answer is (C). The relationship is that of part to part. Alberta and Ontario are both Canadian provinces; Queensland and Victoria are both Australian provinces.

9. BOUILLABAISSE : L'ORANGE :: (A. paella, B. a la mode, C. custard, D. chowder) : PEKING

The correct answer is (D). L'orange and Peking are ways of preparing duck; bouillabaisse and chowder are different kinds of fish stews.

10. (A. Annapolis, B. Williams, C. Baltimore, D. McHenry) : MARYLAND :: PENN : PENNSYLVANIA

The correct answer is (C). William Penn established the colony that later became the state of Pennsylvania; Lord Baltimore established the colony that became the state of Maryland.

11. $\frac{1}{2}$: .5 :: $\frac{5}{20}$: (A. $\frac{1}{5}$, B. .02, C. $\frac{1}{4}$, D. .25)

The correct answer is (D). The relationship is that of a fraction to its decimal equivalent. $\frac{1}{2}$ = .5; $\frac{5}{20}$ = .25.

12. HYDE PARK : ROOSEVELT :: OYSTER BAY : (A. Kennedy, B. Tyler, C. Coolidge, D. Roosevelt)

The correct answer is (D). Hyde Park was the family home of Franklin D. Roosevelt; Oyster Bay was the family home of Theodore Roosevelt.

13. PEPSIN : PTYALIN :: PROTEIN : (A. meat, B. starch, C. saliva, D. vitamins)

The correct answer is (B). Pepsin is an enzyme that breaks down protein into amino acids; ptyalin is the enzyme that decomposes starch. The analogy is one of function.

14. RAPHAEL : MICHELANGELO :: (A. Monet, B. Hockney, C. Braque, D. Veronese) : PICASSO

The correct answer is (C). Raphael and Michelangelo are both artists from the Renaissance Era. Braque and Picasso are both Cubist artists from the early twentieth century.

15. GOBI : (A. Mojave, B. Swahili, C. Masai, D. Africa) :: TIGRIS : EUPHRATES

The correct answer is (A). Gobi and Mojave are both deserts; Tigris and Euphrates are both rivers.

16. CAPON : (A. rooster, B. turkey, C. chicken, D. steer) :: MULE : TANGELO

    The correct answer is (D). The analogy is one of shared characteristic. Mule and tangelo share the characteristic that both are man-made hybrids. Capon and steer also share a characteristic: Both are castrated males of their species that are raised specially for their meat.

17. 12 : 3 :: 44 : (A. 33, B. 3, C. 11, D. 22)

    The correct answer is (C). The analogy stems from the divisibility of the first number by the second and the answer yielded by the division. $12 \div 3 = 4$; $44 \div 11 = 4$. The sign "::" does not necessarily mean "equals."

18. GO : WENT :: READ : (A. wrote, B. learned, C. scan, D. read)

    The correct answer is (D). This is a grammatical analogy. *Went* is the past tense of *go; read* is the past tense of *read*.

19. (A. "Lycidas," B. "Thanatopsis," C. "Adonais," D. "Astrophel") : "ELEGY" :: BRYANT : GRAY

    The correct answer is (B). Thomas Gray wrote "Elegy Written in a Country Churchyard," commonly known as Gray's "Elegy"; William Cullen Bryant wrote "Thanatopsis."

20. *MAINE* : (A. Spanish-American War, B. Pearl Harbor, C. War of 1812, D. *Lusitania*) :: ALAMO : TEXAS WAR OF INDEPENDENCE

    The correct answer is (A). The battle of the Alamo, a mission in Texas at which all defenders were killed, was the turning point of the Texas War of Independence. The rallying cry of the Texans was "Remember the Alamo." The sinking of the battleship *Maine* in Havana Harbor brought the United States into the Spanish-American War. The American call to battle was "Remember the *Maine*."

21. VENUS : URANUS :: (A. Ursa, B. Mercury, C. Haley, D. Sirius) : POLARIS

    The correct answer is (D). Venus and Uranus are both planets; Sirius (the Dog Star) and Polaris (the North Star) are both stars.

22. TRUMAN : (A. reconstruction, B. policy, C. containment, D. rearmament) :: CHAMBERLAIN : APPEASEMENT

    The correct answer is (C). In this analogy of association, just as British Prime Minister Neville Chamberlain is associated with the policy of appeasement, so President Harry Truman is associated with the policy of Soviet containment.

23. JOHN : IRVING :: (A. Toni, B. Jack, C. Stephen, D. Mary) : MORRISON

    The correct answer is (A). The relationship is between the first and last name of a well-known contemporary author. John Irving is the author of *The World According to Garp* and *The Cider House Rules*. Toni Morrison is the author of *Beloved* and *Tar Baby*.

24. SAMISEN : (A. plasma, B. sampan, C. teapot, D. banjo) :: AMOEBA : PARAMECIUM

    The correct answer is (D). An amoeba and a paramecium are both simple water organisms; a samisen and a banjo are both simple stringed instruments.

25. BIENNIAL : BIANNUAL :: TWO : (A. one, B. one half, C. two, D. fifty)

    The correct answer is (B). A biennial event happens once every two years; a biannual event occurs twice a year or every one-half year.

26. *PYGMALION : MY FAIR LADY* :: (A. *Fiddler on the Roof*, B. *The Pawnbroker*, C. *The Matchmaker*, D. *A House Is Not a Home*) : *HELLO, DOLLY!*

The correct answer is (C). *Pygmalion* is the George Bernard Shaw play upon which the musical *My Fair Lady* was based; *The Matchmaker* is the Thornton Wilder play upon which the musical *Hello, Dolly!* was based.

27. JACKSON : VAN BUREN :: WILSON : (A. Buchanan, B. Tyler, C. Taft, D. Ford)

The correct answer is (B). Jackson and Van Buren both entered the White House as widowers and remained single throughout their tenure; both Wilson and Tyler married second wives while in the White House.

28. (A. Algeria, B. Zimbabwe, C. Rwanda, D. Liberia) : SIERRA LEONE :: ANGOLA : MOZAMBIQUE

The correct answer is (B). Angola and Mozambique were colonies of Portugal before they achieved their independence; Sierra Leone and Zimbabwe were British colonies. Algeria was French; Rwanda was Belgian; Liberia was always independent.

29. FISSION : ENERGY :: (A. fusion, B. inertia, C. mass, D. entropy) : ENERGY

The correct answer is (A). This is a cause-and-effect analogy. Both nuclear fission and nuclear fusion create energy. None of the other choices creates energy.

30. CHRISTIE : (A. Queen, B. Holmes, C. Seaman, D. Gardner) :: POIROT : MASON

The correct answer is (D). In this analogy, there is a relationship between the mystery writer and the character created by the author. Agatha Christie was the creator of Hercule Poirot; Erle Stanley Gardner is the creator of Perry Mason.

31. BACH : HANDEL :: MONET : (A. Brontë, B. Kant, C. Cassatt, D. Sibelius)

The correct answer is (C). Bach and Handel are both well-known Baroque composers. Monet and Cassatt are both well-known Impressionist artists.

32. 9 : 27 :: 4 : (A. 9, B. 8, C. 18, D. 3)

The correct answer is (B). The relationship is based upon a mathematical relationship: 9 is equal to 3^2, whereas 27 is equal to 3^3. 4 is equal to 2^2, whereas 8 is equal to 2^3.

33. (A. C.S.A., B. O.S.S., C. A.C.W., D. O.P.A.) : CIA :: I.W.W. : CIO

The correct answer is (B). This is a sequence analogy. The O.S.S. (Office of Strategic Services) was an intelligence-gathering unit during World War II and was a forerunner of the CIA (Central Intelligence Agency). The I.W.W. (Industrial Workers of the World) was an early labor union and was a forerunner of the CIO (Congress of Industrial Organizations).

34. SUNNITE : SHIITE :: (A. Presbyterian, B. Hindu, C. Catholic, D. Protestant) : EPISCOPALIAN

The correct answer is (A). The Sunnites and the Shiites are all Moslems. The two sects broke apart over a disagreement on succession after the death of Mohammed. Presbyterians and Episcopalians are both Protestant groups.

35. *ANIMAL FARM* : (A. Eric Blair, B. William Blair, C. William Porter, D. Thomas Wolfe) :: *PUDD'NHEAD WILSON* : SAMUEL LANGHORNE CLEMENS

The correct answer is (A). *Pudd'nhead Wilson* is a book written by Samuel Langhorne Clemens, whose pen name was Mark Twain; *Animal Farm* is a book written by Eric Blair, whose pen name was George Orwell.

36. STRIKE : LOCKOUT :: CONTRADICT : (A. appeal, B. repeat, C. agree, D. annul)

The correct answer is (C). This analogy is based upon antonyms. In a strike, management welcomes the workers, but the workers refuse to work. In a lockout, the workers are willing, but management does not allow them to work. Contradict is the antonym of agree.

37. COLLIER : MINER :: (A. diamond, B. remission, C. bracelet, D. talisman) : AMULET

The correct answer is (D). This analogy is based upon synonyms. A collier is a coal miner; a talisman is a good luck charm, as is an amulet.

38. LOBSTER : SPIDER :: (A. arthropod, B. crayfish, C. phylum, D. crustacean) : ARACHNID

The correct answer is (D). A spider is an arachnid, a member of the class Arachnida of the phylum Arthropoda. A lobster is a crustacean, a member of the class Crustacea of the phylum Arthropoda.

39. HOMER : (A. Pindar, B. Ovid, C. Heraclitus, D. Aeneas) :: HERODOTUS : THUCYDIDES

The correct answer is (A). Herodotus and Thucydides were both Greek historians; Homer and Pindar were both Greek poets. Ovid was a Roman poet.

40. HAIL : HALE :: (A. glare, B. pair, C. pear, D. fair) : PARE

The correct answer is (B). This is a nonsemantic relationship. The words of the first pair *hail* and *hale* are homonyms. Both choices (B) and (C) create a pair of homonyms with *pare;* however, choice (B) is the better answer because its spelling is analogous to that of the first member of the initial word pair.

41. MANET : *PROUST* :: GAINSBOROUGH : (A. Goya, B. *La Maja,* C. *Blue Boy,* D. Addison)

The correct answer is (C). The artist Manet painted a portrait of the novelist Marcel Proust; the artist Gainsborough painted a famous portrait of a young man in blue called *Blue Boy.*

42. INFLAMMABLE : COMBUSTIBLE :: INVALUABLE : (A. priceless, B. worthless, C. untrue, D. deteriorating)

The correct answer is (A). Inflammable and combustible are synonyms; invaluable and priceless are synonyms. Often, the prefix "in" means not, but in both these instances, the initial "in" does not mean that the word is negative.

43. 3,280.8 ft. : (A. mile, B. kilometer, C. fathom, D. league) :: 946 ml. : QUART

The correct answer is (B). 946 ml. is equal to one quart; 3,280.8 ft. is equal to one kilometer.

44. OIL : (A. sun, B. gasoline, C. petroleum, D. olive) :: COAL : WIND

The correct answer is (A). Coal is a fossil fuel; wind is a nonfossil power source. Oil is a fossil fuel, while the sun is a nonfossil power source.

45. (A. Brahms, B. Beethoven, C. Debussy, D. Haydn) : TCHAIKOVSKY :: *PASTORALE* : *PATHETIQUE*

The correct answer is (B). Tchaikovsky's sixth symphony is named the *Pathetique;* Beethoven's sixth symphony is named the *Pastorale.*

46. ESTONIA : RUSSIA :: (A. Georgia, B. China, C. Cuba, D. Monaco) : LATVIA

The correct answer is (A). Estonia and Russia were both constituent republics of the now defunct USSR (Union of Soviet Socialist Republics). Georgia and Latvia were also member states of the USSR.

47. FLAMINGO : (A. horned owl, B. flicker, C. catbird, D. heron) :: CHICKEN : TURKEY

The correct answer is (D). The chicken and turkey are both barnyard fowl. The flamingo and heron are both wading birds.

48. 1^2 : 1 :: 5^2 : (A. 3, B. 25, C. 1, D. 10)

The correct answer is (B). This analogy is simply that of the square of a number to the number.

49. SCOTLAND : UNITED KINGDOM :: HOLLAND : (A. The Netherlands, B. Flanders, C. Europe, D. Belgium)

The correct answer is (A). Scotland is a constituent country of the United Kingdom. Holland is one province of the Netherlands.

50. (A. griffin, B. giraffe, C. zebra, D. dinosaur) : DODO :: UNICORN : MASTODON

The correct answer is (A). A unicorn is a mythological animal; a mastodon is an extinct animal. A griffin is a mythological animal; a dodo is an extinct animal.

51. ANOPHELES : MALARIA :: AEDES : (A. cholera, B. dengue, C. bubonic plague, D. typhus)

The correct answer is (B). The anopheles mosquito transmits malaria; the aedes mosquito transmits dengue and yellow fever.

52. OVOLO : CAVETTO :: (A. fertile, B. soprano, C. convex, D. poetic) : CONCAVE

The correct answer is (C). Ovolo and cavetto are moldings. Ovolo is a convex molding; cavetto is a concave molding.

53. CANTERBURY : (A. Chaucer, B. Hemingway, C. Updike, D. Forster) :: CASTERBRIDGE : HARDY

The correct answer is (A). Canterbury is the destination in Chaucer's work *The Canterbury Tales;* Casterbridge is the city in the Thomas Hardy novel *The Mayor of Casterbridge.*

54. (A. laugh, B. squirrels, C. cringe, D. geese) : QUAIL :: GAGGLE : COVEY

The correct answer is (D). A covey is a flock of birds; a gaggle is, specifically, a flock of geese.

55. MANY : RAINDROPS :: MUCH : (A. lightning, B. snowflakes, C. puddle, D. water)

The correct answer is (D). This is a grammatical analogy. The adjective many is used to describe a quantity of an object that can be counted; the adjective much is used to describe a volume that cannot be counted.

56. HEART : STOMACH :: (A. ear, B. arteries, C. intestines, D. capillaries) : DUODENUM

The correct answer is (B). The contents of the stomach empty directly into the duodenum (the top part of the small intestine); blood from the heart goes directly into arteries for distribution.

57. BRISTLES : (A. razor, B. toothbrush, C. monkey, D. flower) :: FEATHERS : DUSTER

The correct answer is (B). Feathers are part of a feather duster; bristles are part of a toothbrush. This is a part-to-whole analogy.

58. CHEETAH : LEOPARD :: WOLF : (A. feline, B. canine, C. hyena, D. lupus)

The correct answer is (C). This is a part-to-part analogy. The cheetah and leopard are both members of the feline family; the wolf and hyena are both members of the canine family.

59. TILES : (A. checkers, B. faucet, C. badminton, D. mah-jongg) :: DICE : BACKGAMMON

The correct answer is (D). This is an analogy of part to whole. Tiles are used in the game of mah-jongg; dice are used in the game of backgammon. Although checkers uses round game pieces, they are not traditionally known as tiles.

60. (A. statehouse, B. battlement, C. church, D. fortress) : CHURCH :: CITADEL : CATHEDRAL

The correct answer is (D). A cathedral is a church; a citadel is a fortress.

61. $5 : \sqrt{36} :: 8 :$ (A. 9, B. $\sqrt{81}$, C. $\sqrt{9}$, D. $\sqrt{64}$)

The correct answer is (B). The relationship is between a number and the expression of a square root. 5 is one less than the square root of 36; 8 is one less than the square root of 81. Therefore, the analogy should read, $5 : \sqrt{36} :: 8 : \sqrt{81}$. Choice (A) makes a correct statement but is not a perfect analogy. If choice (B) were not offered, then choice (A) would suffice. However, you must always choose the answer that creates the most perfect analogy.

62. (A. crime, B. punishment, C. jury, D. verdict) : SENTENCE :: ANTEPENULT : PENULT

The correct answer is (D). This is a sequential analogy. The antepenult is the third syllable from the end of a word; the penult is the next-to-the-last syllable of a word. In the sequence of events from crime to punishment, verdict comes immediately before sentence.

63. PANDA : (A. condor, B. bear, C. goldfish, D. ostrich) :: RACCOON : CROW

The correct answer is (A). The raccoon and crow are both plentiful, common creatures; the panda and condor are both members of endangered species.

64. *LUSITANIA* : BRITAIN :: 007 : (A. Japan, B. Korea, C. USSR, D. James Bond)

The correct answer is (B). The *Lusitania* was a British ship that was sunk by the Germans; flight 007 was a Korean airplane that was shot down by the Soviets over the Sea of Japan. The salient relationship is that between the vessel and the country to which it belonged.

65. YARD : FATHOM :: (A. eclipse, B. new, C. half, D. moon) : FULL

The correct answer is (C). In the parlance of measurement, a yard (3 feet) is half of a fathom (6 feet). In speaking of the moon, a half moon is half of a full moon.

66. LANGSTON HUGHES : DOUGHTRY LONG :: (A. Marianne Moore, B. Gwendolyn Brooks, C. Gertrude Stein, D. Emily Dickinson) : MAYA ANGELOU

The correct answer is (B). Langston Hughes and Doughtry Long are both black male poets; Gwendolyn Brooks and Maya Angelou are both black female poets.

67. SAT : (A. PEP, B. ACT, C. TAT, D. NTE) :: GRE : MAT

The correct answer is (B). The GRE (Graduate Record Exam) and MAT (Miller Analogies Test) are both qualifying examinations for graduate school; the SAT (Scholastic Assessment Test) and ACT Assessment are both qualifying examinations for college admission.

68. TULIP : ASTER :: SPRING : (A. chicken, B. jump, C. fall, D. well)

The correct answer is (C). The nature of the relationship is association. A tulip is a flower associated with spring; an aster is a flower associated with fall.

69. BOLL WEEVIL : GYPSY MOTH :: (A. bee, B. termite, C. cockroach, D. louse) : PRAYING MANTIS

The correct answer is (A). A boll weevil and a gypsy moth are both harmful insects. A bee and a praying mantis are both beneficial insects—the former pollinates plants and makes honey and beeswax; the latter preys upon harmful insects.

70. GHENT : (A. American Revolution, B. World War I, C. War of 1812, D. Hundred Years' War) :: P'ANMUNJOM : KOREAN WAR

The correct answer is (C). P'anmunjom was the site of the signing of the Peace Treaty ending the Korean War; Ghent (in Belgium) was the site of the signing of the Peace Treaty ending the War of 1812.

71. (A. Nymph, B. Syrinx, C. Naiad, D. Chaos) : PAN :: ECHO : NARCISSUS

The correct answer is (B). Echo was a nymph who loved Narcissus; Syrinx was a nymph loved by Pan.

72. (A. terrapin, B. terrestrial, C. teuton, D. termagant) : SYCOPHANT :: VIRAGO : TOADY

The correct answer is (D). On each side of the proportion, the words are synonyms. A virago is a quarrelsome woman, a shrew, or a termagant; a toady is a fawning person, a flatterer, or a sycophant.

73. KNESSET : ISRAEL :: DIET : (A. Kashrut, B. Luther, C. Japan, D. Congress)

The correct answer is (C). The Knesset is the lawmaking body of the government of Israel; the Diet serves as the congressional arm of the government of Japan.

74. *LES MISÉRABLES* : VICTOR HUGO :: (A. *Le Rouge et le Noir*, B. *Notre Dame de Paris*, C. *Les Trois Mousquetaires*, D. *Madame Bovary*) : ALEXANDRE DUMAS

The correct answer is (C). *Les Misérables* is a novel written by Victor Hugo; *Les Trois Mousquetaires* is a novel written by Alexandre Dumas.

75. ITS : IT'S :: (A. their, B. their's, C. there, D. there's) : THEY'RE

The correct answer is (A). This is a grammatical analogy. Simply stated, the relationship on both sides of the proportion is possessive : contraction. Its is the possessive of it, while it's is the contraction for it is; their is the possessive of they, while they're is the contraction for they are.

76. NICTATE : WINK :: (A. oscillate, B. osculate, C. ossify, D. oscultate) : KISS

The correct answer is (B). The analogy is based upon synonyms. To nictate is to wink; to osculate is to kiss.

77. INFLUENZA : VIRUS :: HODGKIN'S DISEASE : (A. schizophrenia, B. pulmonary disease, C. leprosy, D. cancer)

The correct answer is (D). Influenza is one type of virus; Hodgkin's disease is a form of cancer.

78. 28 : 82 :: 56 : (A. 54, B. 30, C. 65, D. 136)

The correct answer is (C). The relationship of the numbers is a nonmathematical one. The second number is merely a mirror image of the first.

79. MAMA LUCIA : (A. *Lucia de Lamermoor,* B. *Cavalleria Rusticana,* C. *Marriage of Figaro,* D. *Tosca*) :: FIGARO : *BARBER OF SEVILLE*

The correct answer is (B). Figaro is a character in the opera *Barber of Seville;* Mama Lucia is a character in the opera *Cavalleria Rusticana.*

80. MINNEAPOLIS : NEW ORLEANS :: ALBANY : (A. Boston, B. Cleveland, C. New York City, D. Louisiana)

The correct answer is (C). The source of the Mississippi River is in Minnesota very close to the city of Minneapolis, while the mouth of the Mississippi River is at New Orleans; the source of the Hudson River is very close to the city of Albany, while the mouth of the Hudson River is at New York City.

81. STAG : BILLY :: DOE : (A. William, B. Hinny, C. Kid, D. Nanny)

The correct answer is (D). This analogy is based upon sex, that is, the relationship of male to female. A stag is a male deer; a doe is a female deer. Billy is the commonly used term referring to a male goat; nanny is the counterpart for a female goat.

82. ROGET : (A. bridge, B. synonyms, C. thesaurus, D. quiz shows) :: WEBSTER : DEFINITIONS

The correct answer is (B). The subject of the book compiled by Webster is definitions; the subject of the book compiled by Roget is synonyms.

83. OCULIST : OPHTHALMOLOGIST :: CHIROPODIST : (A. chiropractor, B. cardiologist, C. osteopath, D. podiatrist)

The correct answer is (D). The analogy is based upon similarity of function. Both an oculist and an ophthalmologist are eye doctors; both a chiropodist and a podiatrist are foot doctors.

84. GNU : GNAT :: (A. koala, B. knight, C. kestrell, D. kangaroo) : KNAVE

The correct answer is (B). This is a nonsemantic analogy. Both a gnu and a gnat are creatures whose names begin with a silent letter "g"; both a knight and a knave are persons whose names begin with a silent letter "k."

85. ALLAH : (A. Islam, B. Mohammed, C. Christianity, D. God) :: HORUS : NEPTUNE

The correct answer is (D). Horus and Neptune are both gods in polytheistic religions; both Allah and God are the deities of monotheistic religions.

86. 15 : 5 :: 23 : (A. 1, B. 2, C. 5, D. 6)

The correct answer is (D). This is a different style of relationship, found by multiplying the two numbers in each double-digit number (15 and 23). $1 \times 5 = 5$; $2 \times 3 = 6$.

87. CYRILLIC : RUSSIAN :: ROMAN : (A. Gypsy, B. English, C. numerals, D. Arabic)

The correct answer is (B). The Russian language is written in the Cyrillic alphabet; the English language is written in the Roman alphabet.

88. PASTERN : (A. flank, B. rural, C. horse, D. church) :: PISTIL : STAMEN

The correct answer is (A). The pistil and stamen are both parts of a flower; the pastern and flank are both parts of a horse. The relationship is that of part to part.

89. @ : & :: 2 : (A. #, B. 5, C. 7, D. $\frac{1}{2}$)

The correct answer is (C). This analogy is based upon the location of certain symbols on the keyboard. The "@" symbol is on the same key as the 2; the "&" symbol shares a key with the 7.

90. SADAT : JERUSALEM :: (A. Mao Tse-tung, B. Nixon, C. Ho Chi Minh, D. Sun Yat Sen) : CHINA

The correct answer is (B). You might call the area of commonality "improbable visits." Anwar Sadat, an Egyptian hard-liner, visited Jerusalem. Richard Nixon, a conservative president, went to China. Mao Tse-tung and Sun Yat Sen were Chinese leaders.

91. (A. Alice, B. Medusa, C. Narcissus, D. Minerva) : ADONIS :: QUASIMODO : SNOW WHITE

The correct answer is (B). The analogy is between hideous ugliness and great beauty. Quasimodo was the hunchback in Victor Hugo's *Hunchback of Notre Dame,* while Snow White was a beautiful fairy tale heroine. Medusa, in Greek mythology, was a Gorgon and very ugly, while Adonis, also from Greek mythology, was the epitome of male beauty.

92. ANTHROPOLOGY : MARGARET MEAD :: (A. archaeology, B. history, C. philosophy, D. psychology) : HOWARD CARTER

The correct answer is (A). Margaret Mead was a famous anthropologist; Howard Carter was an English archaeologist.

93. AMBITION : MACBETH :: JEALOUSY : (A. Caesar, B. Brutus, C. Othello, D. Shylock)

The correct answer is (C). Ambition was the force that drove Macbeth; jealousy was the force that drove Othello.

94. "FAUST" : (A. Mephistopheles, B. Goethe, C. folklore, D. Faulkner) :: "WASTELAND" : ELIOT

The correct answer is (B). The analogy is one of product to its creator. The dramatic poem "Faust" was written by Goethe; the classic poem "The Wasteland" was written by T.S. Eliot.

95. (A. ibid., B. etc., C. asst., D. dz.) : ET AL. :: OP. CIT. : CF.

The correct answer is (A). The analogy is based upon the location in which the abbreviation is likely to be found. Op. cit. (in the work cited) and cf. (compare) are both abbreviations from the Latin commonly used in footnotes. Ibid. (in the same place) and et al. (and others) are also footnote abbreviations.

96. YALTA : ROOSEVELT :: (A. Munich, B. Potsdam, C. Bastogne. D. Corregidor) : TRUMAN

The correct answer is (B). Yalta was the site of a conference of the three major allies of World War II at which President Roosevelt represented the United States; Potsdam was the site of a later conference at which President Truman represented the United States.

97. *THE MAGIC FLUTE* : (A. *Iolanthe*, B. *Turandot*, C. *Il Trovatore*, D. *Don Giovanni*) :: *AIDA : DON CARLOS*

The correct answer is (D). *Aida* and *Don Carlos* are both operas written by Verdi; *The Magic Flute* and *Don Giovanni* are operas written by Mozart.

98. OXYGEN : (A. air, B. hydrogen, C. carbon dioxide, D. carbon monoxide) :: FAUNA : FLORA

The correct answer is (C). The relationship of fauna (animal life) to oxygen is that animals breathe oxygen. The relationship of flora (plant life) to carbon dioxide is that plants breathe carbon dioxide.

99. (A. Sleeping Beauty, B. Cinderella, C. Rapunzel, D. Goldilocks) : PRINCE CHARMING :: FROG : PRINCESS

The correct answer is (A). The frog was under a wicked spell that was broken by the kiss of the princess; Sleeping Beauty was under a wicked spell that was broken by the kiss of Prince Charming.

100. 9 : 104 :: BEETHOVEN : (A. Mozart, B. Sibelius, C. Haydn, D. Casals)

The correct answer is (C). Beethoven wrote 9 symphonies; Haydn was very prolific and wrote 104 symphonies.

101. RUDDER : SHIP :: WHEEL : (A. car, B. truck, C. boat, D. string)

The correct answer is (A). The rudder is used in directing a ship; the steering wheel is used in directing a car.

102. KARATE : FOOT :: FENCING : (A. chop, B. hand, C. foil, D. glove)

The correct answer is (C). In karate, the foot is used as a weapon; in fencing, the foil is the weapon. In boxing, the weapon is a fist. In baseball, the glove is a tool, not a weapon.

103. LEECH : PARASITE :: MUSHROOM : (A. host, B. butcher, C. turner, D. saprophyte)

The correct answer is (D). A leech is a parasite that gains its sustenance by attaching to and drawing from other living things. A mushroom is a saprophyte, an organism (especially a plant) that lives on dead or decaying matter.

104. LEAVENING : FERMENTATION :: ARGUMENT : (A. fight, B. precipitation, C. condensation, D. hail)

The correct answer is (A). Leavening is a process that produces fermentation. An argument can produce a fight. Snow is frozen precipitation.

105. AMUSING : HILARIOUS :: SMART : (A. melancholy, B. genius, C. odd, D. happy)

The correct answer is (B). Something that is hilarious is a more intense form of amusing; genius is a more intense form of smart.

106. LIST : ITEM :: CONSTITUTION : (A. person, B. article, C. disk, D. motion)

The correct answer is (B). Just as an item is an entry or unit on a list, an article is a unit of a constitution.

107. READ : BOOK :: LISTEN : (A. salty, B. movie, C. nose, D. music)

The correct answer is (D). We read a book and listen to music. For choice (B) to be correct, the relationship would have to be changed to WATCH : MOVIE.

108. PREMIERE : MOVIE :: UNVEILING : (A. statue, B. president, C. teenager, D. subject)

The correct answer is (A). The first public showing of a movie is its premiere; similarly, the first public showing of a statue is its unveiling.

109. PARROT : TROPICS :: ROADRUNNER : (A. house, B. India, C. desert, D. zoo)

The correct answer is (C). A parrot is a bird found in the climatic region known as the tropics. Only the habitat of the roadrunner in the warm, arid region known as the desert is parallel to complete this analogy. India and Africa are too large to associate with just one type of habitat.

110. MEDIAN : MIDDLE :: MEAN : (A. radius, B. measurement, C. designer, D. average)

The correct answer is (D). In this analogy of definition, the median is the middle, having an equal number of items above and below it; the mean is the average.

111. BONES : LIGAMENT :: MUSCLE : (A. elasticity, B. tendon, C. cell, D. finger)

The correct answer is (B). Muscles are connected to bones by tendons just as bones are connected to bones by ligaments.

112. DOWN : FLUFFY :: SATIN : (A. fast, B. fluent, C. smooth, D. warm)

The correct answer is (C). Down is fluffy; satin is smooth. The analogy is based upon well-known qualities.

113. BURL : TREE :: PEARL : (A. oyster, B. copper, C. wood, D. sand)

The correct answer is (A). A burl is an outgrowth of a tree that serves no purpose to the tree but that finds utility in its own right when made into a table or craft item. A pearl develops inside an oyster. It serves no useful purpose to the oyster but finds its role in jewelry.

114. YEAST : LEAVEN :: IODINE : (A. bubble, B. antiseptic, C. medicine, D. dough)

The correct answer is (B). Yeast is used as a leaven; iodine is used as an antiseptic. These functions are more specific than aspirin's function as a medicine.

115. LIST : CAPSIZE :: CAREEN : (A. rise, B. crash, C. irk, D. discover)

The correct answer is (B). When a boat lists, or leans to one side, it threatens to capsize. When a car careens out of control, it may crash.

116. PERIMETER : POLYGON :: CIRCUMFERENCE : (A. circle, B. triangle, C. square, D. angle)

The correct answer is (A). The distance around a polygon is its perimeter; the distance around a circle is its circumference.

117. OMEGA : ENDING :: ALPHA : (A. sorority, B. femur, C. beginning, D. ray)

The correct answer is (C). Alpha and omega are the first and last letters of the Greek alphabet.

118. EXPURGATE : PASSAGES :: DEFOLIATE : (A. leaves, B. checks, C. ideas, D. privacy)

The correct answer is (A). Passages can be eliminated from a written work by expurgation; leaves are eliminated from trees by defoliation.

119. GERM : DISEASE :: WAR : (A. treacherous, B. women, C. medicine, D. destruction)

The correct answer is (D). A germ causes disease; war causes destruction.

120. QUASH : MOTION :: QUELL : (A. squeeze, B. destroy, C. riot, D. impel)

The correct answer is (C). To quash a motion (a proposal advanced at a meeting) is to nullify it; to quell a riot is to crush it.

ANSWER SHEET PRACTICE TEST 7

1. Ⓐ Ⓑ Ⓒ Ⓓ
2. Ⓐ Ⓑ Ⓒ Ⓓ
3. Ⓐ Ⓑ Ⓒ Ⓓ
4. Ⓐ Ⓑ Ⓒ Ⓓ
5. Ⓐ Ⓑ Ⓒ Ⓓ
6. Ⓐ Ⓑ Ⓒ Ⓓ
7. Ⓐ Ⓑ Ⓒ Ⓓ
8. Ⓐ Ⓑ Ⓒ Ⓓ
9. Ⓐ Ⓑ Ⓒ Ⓓ
10. Ⓐ Ⓑ Ⓒ Ⓓ
11. Ⓐ Ⓑ Ⓒ Ⓓ
12. Ⓐ Ⓑ Ⓒ Ⓓ
13. Ⓐ Ⓑ Ⓒ Ⓓ
14. Ⓐ Ⓑ Ⓒ Ⓓ
15. Ⓐ Ⓑ Ⓒ Ⓓ
16. Ⓐ Ⓑ Ⓒ Ⓓ
17. Ⓐ Ⓑ Ⓒ Ⓓ
18. Ⓐ Ⓑ Ⓒ Ⓓ
19. Ⓐ Ⓑ Ⓒ Ⓓ
20. Ⓐ Ⓑ Ⓒ Ⓓ
21. Ⓐ Ⓑ Ⓒ Ⓓ
22. Ⓐ Ⓑ Ⓒ Ⓓ
23. Ⓐ Ⓑ Ⓒ Ⓓ
24. Ⓐ Ⓑ Ⓒ Ⓓ
25. Ⓐ Ⓑ Ⓒ Ⓓ
26. Ⓐ Ⓑ Ⓒ Ⓓ
27. Ⓐ Ⓑ Ⓒ Ⓓ
28. Ⓐ Ⓑ Ⓒ Ⓓ
29. Ⓐ Ⓑ Ⓒ Ⓓ
30. Ⓐ Ⓑ Ⓒ Ⓓ

31. Ⓐ Ⓑ Ⓒ Ⓓ
32. Ⓐ Ⓑ Ⓒ Ⓓ
33. Ⓐ Ⓑ Ⓒ Ⓓ
34. Ⓐ Ⓑ Ⓒ Ⓓ
35. Ⓐ Ⓑ Ⓒ Ⓓ
36. Ⓐ Ⓑ Ⓒ Ⓓ
37. Ⓐ Ⓑ Ⓒ Ⓓ
38. Ⓐ Ⓑ Ⓒ Ⓓ
39. Ⓐ Ⓑ Ⓒ Ⓓ
40. Ⓐ Ⓑ Ⓒ Ⓓ
41. Ⓐ Ⓑ Ⓒ Ⓓ
42. Ⓐ Ⓑ Ⓒ Ⓓ
43. Ⓐ Ⓑ Ⓒ Ⓓ
44. Ⓐ Ⓑ Ⓒ Ⓓ
45. Ⓐ Ⓑ Ⓒ Ⓓ
46. Ⓐ Ⓑ Ⓒ Ⓓ
47. Ⓐ Ⓑ Ⓒ Ⓓ
48. Ⓐ Ⓑ Ⓒ Ⓓ
49. Ⓐ Ⓑ Ⓒ Ⓓ
50. Ⓐ Ⓑ Ⓒ Ⓓ
51. Ⓐ Ⓑ Ⓒ Ⓓ
52. Ⓐ Ⓑ Ⓒ Ⓓ
53. Ⓐ Ⓑ Ⓒ Ⓓ
54. Ⓐ Ⓑ Ⓒ Ⓓ
55. Ⓐ Ⓑ Ⓒ Ⓓ
56. Ⓐ Ⓑ Ⓒ Ⓓ
57. Ⓐ Ⓑ Ⓒ Ⓓ
58. Ⓐ Ⓑ Ⓒ Ⓓ
59. Ⓐ Ⓑ Ⓒ Ⓓ
60. Ⓐ Ⓑ Ⓒ Ⓓ

61. Ⓐ Ⓑ Ⓒ Ⓓ
62. Ⓐ Ⓑ Ⓒ Ⓓ
63. Ⓐ Ⓑ Ⓒ Ⓓ
64. Ⓐ Ⓑ Ⓒ Ⓓ
65. Ⓐ Ⓑ Ⓒ Ⓓ
66. Ⓐ Ⓑ Ⓒ Ⓓ
67. Ⓐ Ⓑ Ⓒ Ⓓ
68. Ⓐ Ⓑ Ⓒ Ⓓ
69. Ⓐ Ⓑ Ⓒ Ⓓ
70. Ⓐ Ⓑ Ⓒ Ⓓ
71. Ⓐ Ⓑ Ⓒ Ⓓ
72. Ⓐ Ⓑ Ⓒ Ⓓ
73. Ⓐ Ⓑ Ⓒ Ⓓ
74. Ⓐ Ⓑ Ⓒ Ⓓ
75. Ⓐ Ⓑ Ⓒ Ⓓ
76. Ⓐ Ⓑ Ⓒ Ⓓ
77. Ⓐ Ⓑ Ⓒ Ⓓ
78. Ⓐ Ⓑ Ⓒ Ⓓ
79. Ⓐ Ⓑ Ⓒ Ⓓ
80. Ⓐ Ⓑ Ⓒ Ⓓ
81. Ⓐ Ⓑ Ⓒ Ⓓ
82. Ⓐ Ⓑ Ⓒ Ⓓ
83. Ⓐ Ⓑ Ⓒ Ⓓ
84. Ⓐ Ⓑ Ⓒ Ⓓ
85. Ⓐ Ⓑ Ⓒ Ⓓ
86. Ⓐ Ⓑ Ⓒ Ⓓ
87. Ⓐ Ⓑ Ⓒ Ⓓ
88. Ⓐ Ⓑ Ⓒ Ⓓ
89. Ⓐ Ⓑ Ⓒ Ⓓ
90. Ⓐ Ⓑ Ⓒ Ⓓ

91. Ⓐ Ⓑ Ⓒ Ⓓ
92. Ⓐ Ⓑ Ⓒ Ⓓ
93. Ⓐ Ⓑ Ⓒ Ⓓ
94. Ⓐ Ⓑ Ⓒ Ⓓ
95. Ⓐ Ⓑ Ⓒ Ⓓ
96. Ⓐ Ⓑ Ⓒ Ⓓ
97. Ⓐ Ⓑ Ⓒ Ⓓ
98. Ⓐ Ⓑ Ⓒ Ⓓ
99. Ⓐ Ⓑ Ⓒ Ⓓ
100. Ⓐ Ⓑ Ⓒ Ⓓ
101. Ⓐ Ⓑ Ⓒ Ⓓ
102. Ⓐ Ⓑ Ⓒ Ⓓ
103. Ⓐ Ⓑ Ⓒ Ⓓ
104. Ⓐ Ⓑ Ⓒ Ⓓ
105. Ⓐ Ⓑ Ⓒ Ⓓ
106. Ⓐ Ⓑ Ⓒ Ⓓ
107. Ⓐ Ⓑ Ⓒ Ⓓ
108. Ⓐ Ⓑ Ⓒ Ⓓ
109. Ⓐ Ⓑ Ⓒ Ⓓ
110. Ⓐ Ⓑ Ⓒ Ⓓ
111. Ⓐ Ⓑ Ⓒ Ⓓ
112. Ⓐ Ⓑ Ⓒ Ⓓ
113. Ⓐ Ⓑ Ⓒ Ⓓ
114. Ⓐ Ⓑ Ⓒ Ⓓ
115. Ⓐ Ⓑ Ⓒ Ⓓ
116. Ⓐ Ⓑ Ⓒ Ⓓ
117. Ⓐ Ⓑ Ⓒ Ⓓ
118. Ⓐ Ⓑ Ⓒ Ⓓ
119. Ⓐ Ⓑ Ⓒ Ⓓ
120. Ⓐ Ⓑ Ⓒ Ⓓ

answer sheet

Practice Test 7

120 QUESTIONS • 60 MINUTES

Directions: Each of these test questions consists of three capitalized words and four lettered words enclosed in parentheses. Two of the capitalized words are related in some way. Find the two related words, and establish the nature of the relationship. Then study the four words lettered A, B, C, and D. Select the one lettered word that is related to the remaining capitalized word in the same way that the first two capitalized words are related. Mark the answer sheet for the letter preceding the word you select.

1. TINY : (A. dwarf, B. small, C. infinitesimal, D. huge) :: BIG : ENORMOUS

2. LAMP : LIGHT :: CHAIR : (A. ottoman, B. table, C. back, D. seat)

3. (A. bud, B. spring, C. flower, D. blossom) : BLOOM :: FADE : FALL

4. BLUE : (A. gold, B. gray, C. red, D. green) :: NORTH : SOUTH

5. DOCKET : COURT :: (A. agenda, B. itinerary, C. mileage, D. route) : TRIP

6. NEITHER : WEIRD :: (A. friend, B. yield, C. receipt, D. height) : LEISURE

7. BERING STRAIT : SEWARD PENINSULA :: STRAIT OF MAGELLAN : (A. Trazos-Montes, B. Tierra del Fuego, C. Matan, D. Malay Peninsula)

8. *LORD OF THE FLIES* : *LORD OF THE RINGS* :: GOLDING : (A. Swift, B. King Arthur, C. Tolkien, D. Beckett)

9. ATROPHY : (A. eyes, B. muscles, C. teeth, D. veins) :: INFLAMED : JOINTS

10. ERNEST : RUDYARD :: HEMINGWAY : (A. Proust, B. Lotus, C. Kipling, D. Brecht)

11. $\frac{4}{8} : \frac{8}{4} :: \frac{5}{15} :$ (A. $\frac{1}{3}$, B. $\frac{2}{3}$, C. $\frac{15}{5}$, D. $\frac{3}{1}$)

12. MAY DAY : (A. Labor Day, B. Christmas, C. Bastille Day, D. Tet) :: RAMADAN : LENT

153

13. INGENUOUS : (A. straightforward, B. aloof, C. clever, D. virtuous) :: INIQUITOUS : WICKED

14. PROTRACTOR : ANGLES :: COMPASS : (A. tones, B. area, C. topography, D. direction)

15. TENNESSEE WILLIAMS : *THE GLASS MENAGERIE* :: (A. Thornton Wilder, B. Luigi Pirandello, C. Maxwell Anderson, D. Noel Coward) : *SIX CHARACTERS IN SEARCH OF AN AUTHOR*

16. INJURY : PARAPLEGIA :: STROKE : (A. aphasia, B. quadriplegia, C. fantasia, D. hemiplegia)

17. LIKES : EVERYONE :: (A. indifferent, B. wish, C. loves, D. care) : NOBODY

18. SEPTEMBER : (A. October, B. January, C. Thursday, D. planting) :: HARVEST MOON : HUNTER'S MOON

19. ERATO : THALIA :: (A. movies, B. sleep, C. poetry, D. death) : COMEDY

20. (A. anglophile, B. bibliophile, C. oenophile, D. vines) : WINE :: FRANCOPHILE : FRANCE

21. 6 : −6 :: 31 : (A. −2, B. 3, C. −13, D. 19)

22. RIVE GAUCHE : PARIS :: (A. Philadelphia, B. Albany, C. Riker's Island, D. Brooklyn) : NEW YORK

23. SURINAME : (A. Guyana, B. British Honduras, C. Belize, D. Dutch Guiana) :: ZIMBABWE : RHODESIA

24. BAROQUE : VIVALDI :: (A. Classical, B. Romantic, C. Rococo, D. Impressionist) : SCHUMANN

25. OBSEQUIOUS : OBSTINATE :: DIFFIDENT : (A. indifferent, B. shy, C. distinct, D. defiant)

26. SHIITE : (A. Arab, B. Muslim, C. Sunni, D. Iran) :: ROMAN CATHOLIC : PROTESTANT

27. HONOR : CITATION :: SPEEDING : (A. citation, B. hurry, C. race, D. stop)

28. *HEDDA GABLER* : (A. *The Cherry Orchard,* B. *Riders to the Sea,* C. *An Enemy of the People,* D. *Blood Wedding*) :: *ANNA CHRISTIE* : *MOON FOR THE MISBEGOTTEN*

29. YELLOW : (A. sunflower, B. cornflower, C. rose, D. jacket) :: RED : SALVIA

30. ANODE : CATHODE :: OXIDATION : (A. erosion, B. reduction, C. carbonization, D. hydrogenation)

31. CELLO : VIOLIN :: (A. clarinet, B. French horn, C. accordion, D. rebec) : SAXOPHONE

32. JOAN OF ARC : (A. witch, B. stake, C. king, D. saint) :: GALILEO : SUN

33. (A. Yeats, B. Shakespeare, C. Chaucer, D. Tennyson) : SONNETS :: NASH : LIMERICKS

34. RACQUETBALL : SQUASH :: HOCKEY : (A. badminton, B. rugby, C. volleyball, D. curling)

35. ST. PETERSBURG : HERMITAGE :: (A. Spain, B. Majorca, C. Madrid, D. Seville) : PRADO

36. ABSCISSA : (A. ordinate, B. mantissa, C. coordinate, D. precision) :: X : Y

37. SKINNER : BEHAVIORISM :: (A. Adler, B. Terman, C. Kant, D. Wertheimer) : GESTALT

38. HESTER : INFIDELITY :: (A. Cordelia, B. Goneril, C. Ophelia, D. Cassandra) : DEVOTION

39. CAPILLARIES : CIRCULATION :: VILLI : (A. respiration, B. digestion, C. recreation, D. procreation)

40. SAN MARINO : ITALY :: (A. Ethiopia, B. Capetown, C. Lesotho, D. Swaziland) : SOUTH AFRICA

41. (A. Florida, B. New Mexico, C. Puerto Rico, D. Hawaii) : ALASKA :: SPAIN : RUSSIA

42. KEYNES : ECONOMICS :: DEWEY : (A. zoology, B. electronics, C. medicine, D. education)

43. NEIL ARMSTRONG : YURI GAGARIN :: CHARLES LINDBERGH : (A. George Washington, B. Albert Einstein, C. Orville Wright, D. Guglielmo Marconi)

44. *PILGRIM'S PROGRESS* : (A. *Inferno*, B. *Paradise Lost*, C. *De Monarchia*, D. *Divine Comedy*) :: BUNYAN : DANTE

45. GENGHIS KHAN : MONGOLS :: ATTILA : (A. Roman Empire, B. Germany, C. Huns, D. Trojans)

46. HARE : (A. rabbit, B. tortoise, C. terrapin, D. berries) :: FOX : GRAPES

47. 4 : 6 :: (A. 10, B. 6, C. 9, D. 16) : 36

48. THOMAS MANN : *BUDDENBROOKS* :: THOMAS WOLFE : (A. *Death in Venice*, B. *Look Homeward, Angel*, C. *The Magic Mountain*, D. *Joseph and His Brothers*)

49. (A. Earth, B. moon, C. Russia, D. Stalin) : SPUTNIK :: JUPITER : IO

50. FREYA : ASGARD :: (A. Hera, B. Venus, C. Minerva, D. Aphrodite) : OLYMPUS

51. (A. isosceles, B. scalene, C. right, D. obtuse) : EQUILATERAL :: DUPLE : TRIPLE

52. ELWAY : JORDAN :: (A. football, B. baseball, C. hockey, D. horseracing) : BASKETBALL

53. OBVERSE : (A. coin, B. sweater, C. reverse, D. crochet) :: STARBOARD : PORT

54. PASTEL : MUTED :: LIGHT : (A. sound, B. voice, C. trumpet, D. wheel)

55. (A. one, B. two, C. three, D. nine) : BETWEEN :: SIX : AMONG

56. XENOPHOBIA : PREJUDICE :: PECCATOPHOBIA : (A. tantrums, B. bad habits, C. clumsiness, D. virtue)

57. HARPSICHORD : VIRGINAL :: (A. piccolo, B. saxophone, C. sousaphone, D. oboe) : CLARINET

58. LEAGUE : YARD :: MILES : (A. inches, B. feet, C. yards, D. furlongs)

59. ATOM : MOLECULE :: GENE : (A. heredity, B. genetics, C. DNA, D. chromosome)

60. FIRE : SMOKE :: (A. pipe, B. hose, C. leak, D. break) : STAIN

61. BUTTER : MARGARINE :: SUGAR : (A. salt, B. strychnine, C. aspartame, D. vinegar)

62. TOM SAWYER : (A. Mark Twain, B. Samuel Langhorne Clemens, C. Becky Thatcher, D. David Copperfield) :: PORTHOS : ATHOS

63. (A. white, B. bluing, C. blanch, D. yellow) : BLEACH :: HENNA : ANIL

64. CHECKERS : RICHARD NIXON :: TRAVELER : (A. Robert E. Lee, B. Franklin Roosevelt, C. Dwight Eisenhower, D. Aristotle Onassis)

65. BRUTE : SQUIRE :: TUBER : (A. leaves, B. yams, C. quires, D. sterns)

66. $\frac{1}{8}$: 12.5% :: (A. $\frac{1}{6}$, B. $\frac{3}{11}$, C. $\frac{2}{7}$, D. $\frac{3}{8}$) : 37.5%

67. CRETACEOUS : DINOSAURS :: TERTIARY : (A. vampires, B. fish, C. reptiles, D. mammals)

68. MAPLE : (A. syrup, B. oak, C. cyanide, D. leaf) :: PRIVET : HEMLOCK

69. (A. Washington, B. Jefferson, C. Franklin, D. Lincoln) : MADISON :: DECLARATION OF INDEPENDENCE : CONSTITUTION

70. ALZHEIMER'S DISEASE : HANSEN'S DISEASE :: (A. cerebral palsy, B. copper deficiency, C. dementia, D. lymphatic cancer) : LEPROSY

71. SALVADOR DALI : RENE MAGRITTE :: (A. e.e. cummings, B. William Wordsworth, C. Jack London, D. Leo Tolstoy) : DON MARQUIS

72. INDEPENDENCE : COOPERATION :: PHOTOSYNTHESIS : (A. parasitism, B. parthenogenesis, C. symbiosis, D. carbohydrates)

73. (A. stars, B. restaurants, C. tires, D. highways) : MICHELIN :: GASOLINE : EXXON

74. SWIFT : (A. Barrie, B. Kipling, C. Dorothy, D. Baum) :: LILLIPUT : OZ

75. FOUR : BASEBALL :: (A. ten, B. eleven, C. fifty, D. one hundred twenty) : FOOTBALL

76. (A. remuneration, B. stipend, C. pay, D. overtime) : SALARY :: COMMISSION : ROYALTY

77. LAWYER : BARRISTER :: ATTORNEY : (A. judge, B. juror, C. advocate, D. appellant)

78. KOALA : (A. eucalyptus, B. wallaby, C. bamboo, D. mulberry) :: WHALE : PLANKTON

79. DEER : (A. deer, B. moose, C. dear, D. swan) :: GOOSE : GEESE

80. 27 : (A. 3, B. 9, C. 5.19, D. 729) :: 125 : 5

81. EGG : CHICKEN :: CHICKEN : (A. rooster, B. capon, C. egg, D. hen)

82. PARIS : FRANCE :: (A. Tripoli, B. Rabat, C. Marseilles, D. Dakar) : SENEGAL

83. CCC : TVA :: FDIC : (A. OPA, B. WMC, C. OSS, D. FHA)

84. ELABORATE : (A. streamlined, B. boring, C. oblique, D. obligatory) :: SERIF : SANS SERIF

85. BULL RUN : MANASSAS :: STREAM : (A. battle, B. town, C. war, D. tribe)

86. GREENWICH VILLAGE : (A. London, B. Kensington, C. New York, D. Piccadilly Circus) :: MONTMARTRE : PARIS

87. UNITED STATES : DOW JONES :: JAPAN : (A. Hang Seng, B. Nikkei, C. Tokyo, D. Kyoto)

88. ZOLA : *NANA* :: (A. Humbert Humbert, B. Don Juan, C. Don Quixote, D. Nabokov) : *LOLITA*

89. KANT : CATEGORICAL IMPERATIVE :: (A. Descartes, B. Nietzsche, C. Sartre, D. Mill) : UTILITY

90. NOON : EVENING :: (A. snack, B. lunch, C. brunch, D. afternoon) : DINNER

91. MENTICIDE : BRAINWASHING :: OPPROBRIUM : (A. commendation, B. reproach, C. indoctrination, D. repression)

92. CALPURNIA : (A. Oedipus, B. Caesar, C. King Lear, D. Cicero) :: CRESSIDA : TROILUS

93. BLIND : DEAF :: (A. Milton, B. Scott, C. Mozart, D. Justice) : BEETHOVEN

94. REMUS : (A. Brer Rabbit, B. Aquarius, C. Quisling, D. Romulus) :: CASTOR : POLLUX

95. DOG : FLEA :: HORSE : (A. rider, B. fly, C. mane, D. shoe)

96. 10 : (A. decimal, B. common, C. unnatural, D. metric) :: e : NATURAL

97. BROUGHAM : CARRIAGE :: HOME : (A. horse, B. town, C. domicile, D. family)

98. EURO : (A. Brazil, B. Nigeria, C. Greece, D. India) :: REAL : BRAZIL

99. (A. Shangri-La, B. Lilliput, C. Atlantis, D. Ilium) : BRIGADOON :: FOUNTAIN OF YOUTH : NEVER-NEVER LAND

100. PARTHENON : PANTHEON :: (A. Taj Mahal, B. St. Paul's, C. Angkor Wat, D. Erechtheum) : SISTINE CHAPEL

101. QUEUE : PEOPLE :: STRING : (A. geese, B. pails, C. hay, D. pearls)

102. RECRUIT : ENLIST :: EMPLOYEE : (A. putrefy, B. apply, C. disinherit, D. leave)

103. CONTROL : ORDER :: ANARCHY : (A. clown, B. pupil, C. climax, D. chaos)

104. REMORSE : RUE :: PLEASURE : (A. pain, B. enjoy, C. commiserate, D. age)

105. RETARDANT : FIRE :: REPELLENT : (A. infestation, B. fertilizer, C. vaccination, D. accelerant)

106. SEWER : SEAM :: ELECTRICIAN : (A. thimble, B. scalpel, C. splice, D. spore)

107. APOLOGY : ACCEPT :: FORGIVENESS : (A. feature, B. beg, C. promise, D. force)

108. WOOD : CARVE :: CLAY : (A. sway, B. burn, C. mold, D. blow)

109. SPIRE : TOWER :: CREST : (A. mountain, B. pond, C. state, D. hat)

110. SOLECISM : GRAMMAR :: FOUL : (A. marriage, B. game, C. incest, D. stumble)

111. GRAVEL : CONCRETE :: EGGS: (A. soufflé, B. stones, C. mixer, D. truck)

112. APOGEE : ORBIT :: APEX : (A. pedigree, B. detergent, C. mountain, D. radius)

113. WHEELBARROW : TRANSPORT :: LEVER : (A. pull, B. handle, C. hone, D. lift)

114. ASYLUM : REFUGEE :: DESTINATION : (A. escape, B. traveler, C. lunatic, D. injury)

115. WORRIED : HYSTERICAL :: HAPPY : (A. hot, B. ecstatic, C. lonely, D. serious)

116. VALANCE : ROD :: PENDANT : (A. chain, B. curtain, C. pleat, D. cravat)

117. TELEMETRY : DISTANT :: MICROMETRY : (A. earthshaking. B. real, C. tiny, D. vision)

118. NATION : BORDER GUARDS :: PROPERTY : (A. state, B. fence, C. hollow, D. satellite)

119. TOLERATE : PREJUDICE :: SURVIVE : (A. food, B. cramps, C. kill, D. estimate)

120. SOLDIER : REGIMENT :: STAR : (A. navy, B. river, C. constellation, D. amphibian)

ANSWER KEY AND EXPLANATIONS

1. **C**		25. **D**		49. **A**		73. **C**		97. **C**
2. **D**		26. **C**		50. **D**		74. **D**		98. **C**
3. **A**		27. **A**		51. **A**		75. **A**		99. **A**
4. **B**		28. **C**		52. **A**		76. **B**		100. **D**
5. **B**		29. **A**		53. **C**		77. **C**		101. **D**
6. **D**		30. **B**		54. **A**		78. **A**		102. **B**
7. **B**		31. **A**		55. **B**		79. **A**		103. **D**
8. **C**		32. **C**		56. **D**		80. **A**		104. **B**
9. **B**		33. **B**		57. **D**		81. **C**		105. **A**
10. **C**		34. **D**		58. **B**		82. **D**		106. **C**
11. **C**		35. **C**		59. **D**		83. **D**		107. **B**
12. **A**		36. **A**		60. **C**		84. **A**		108. **C**
13. **A**		37. **D**		61. **C**		85. **B**		109. **A**
14. **D**		38. **A**		62. **C**		86. **C**		110. **B**
15. **B**		39. **B**		63. **B**		87. **B**		111. **A**
16. **D**		40. **C**		64. **A**		88. **D**		112. **C**
17. **C**		41. **A**		65. **C**		89. **D**		113. **D**
18. **A**		42. **D**		66. **D**		90. **B**		114. **B**
19. **C**		43. **C**		67. **D**		91. **B**		115. **B**
20. **C**		44. **D**		68. **B**		92. **B**		116. **A**
21. **D**		45. **C**		69. **B**		93. **A**		117. **C**
22. **D**		46. **B**		70. **C**		94. **D**		118. **B**
23. **D**		47. **D**		71. **A**		95. **B**		119. **B**
24. **B**		48. **B**		72. **C**		96. **B**		120. **C**

1. TINY : (A. dwarf, B. small, C. infinitesimal, D. huge) :: BIG : ENORMOUS

   The correct answer is (C). This is an analogy of degree. Enormous is an intense degree of big; infinitesimal is an intense degree of tiny.

2. LAMP : LIGHT :: CHAIR : (A. ottoman, B. table, C. back, D. seat)

   The correct answer is (D). This is an analogy not of true synonyms but of synonyms as used in common parlance. Thus, "turn on a light" is used interchangeably with "turn on a lamp," and "have a seat" is used interchangeably with "have a chair."

3. (A. bud, B. spring, C. flower, D. blossom) : BLOOM :: FADE : FALL

   The correct answer is (A). This analogy is based upon sequence. A flower must fade before it falls. The same flower must bud before it can bloom. The sequence is bud, bloom, fade, and fall.

4. BLUE : (A. gold, B. gray, C. red, D. green) :: NORTH : SOUTH

   The correct answer is (B). During the Civil War, the uniforms of the North were blue, and the uniforms of the South were gray. This is an analogy of association.

5. DOCKET : COURT :: (A. agenda, B. itinerary, C. mileage, D. route) : TRIP

The correct answer is (B). The court docket is the official register of cases to be tried; the trip itinerary is the step-by-step schedule for a trip, including the route to be traveled, sights to be seen, and stops to be made.

6. NEITHER : WEIRD :: (A. friend, B. yield, C. receipt, D. height) : LEISURE

The correct answer is (D). This is a grammatical analogy. It is based upon the fact that the related words are all exceptions to the "i before e except after c" spelling rule. Neither and weird are both exceptions to this rule; so are height and leisure.

7. BERING STRAIT : SEWARD PENINSULA :: STRAIT OF MAGELLAN : (A. Trazos-Montes, B. Tierra del Fuego, C. Matan, D. Malay Peninsula)

The correct answer is (B). The Bering Strait separates the Seward Peninsula from Russia; the Strait of Magellan separates Tierra del Fuego from mainland South America.

8. *LORD OF THE FLIES* : *LORD OF THE RINGS* :: GOLDING : (A. Swift, B. King Arthur, C. Tolkien, D. Beckett)

The correct answer is (C). Golding is the author of *Lord of the Flies;* Tolkien is the author of *Lord of the Rings*.

9. ATROPHY : (A. eyes, B. muscles, C. teeth, D. veins) :: INFLAMED : JOINTS

The correct answer is (B). The analogy is based upon the association of body part to malady. Joints can become inflamed; muscles can atrophy or waste away.

10. ERNEST : RUDYARD :: HEMINGWAY : (A. Proust, B. Lotus, C. Kipling, D. Brecht)

The correct answer is (C). In this literary analogy, the relationship is based upon association of first and last names. Ernest Hemingway was an author, as was Rudyard Kipling.

11. $\frac{4}{8} : \frac{8}{4} :: \frac{5}{15} :$ (A. $\frac{1}{3}$, B. $\frac{2}{3}$, C. $\frac{15}{5}$, D. $\frac{3}{1}$)

The correct answer is (C). This is a simple relationship. The second term is the reciprocal of the first. $\frac{8}{4}$ is the reciprocal of $\frac{4}{8}$; $\frac{15}{5}$ is the reciprocal of $\frac{5}{15}$.

12. MAY DAY : (A. Labor Day, B. Christmas, C. Bastille Day, D. Tet) :: RAMADAN : LENT

The correct answer is (A). Ramadan and Lent are both prolonged periods of fasting and prayer—Ramadan for the Moslems and Lent for Christians. May Day and Labor Day are both secular holidays in celebration of labor.

13. INGENUOUS : (A. straightforward, B. aloof, C. clever, D. virtuous) :: INIQUITOUS : WICKED

The correct answer is (A). This is an analogy of synonyms. Iniquitous means wicked; ingenuous means straightforward or sincere.

14. PROTRACTOR : ANGLES :: COMPASS : (A. tones, B. area, C. topography, D. direction)

The correct answer is (D). This analogy is based upon function. The function of a protractor is to measure angles; the function of a compass is to measure direction.

15. TENNESSEE WILLIAMS : *THE GLASS MENAGERIE* :: (A. Thornton Wilder, B. Luigi Pirandello, C. Maxwell Anderson, D. Noel Coward) : *SIX CHARACTERS IN SEARCH OF AN AUTHOR*

The correct answer is (B). Tennessee Williams is the author of *The Glass Menagerie*; Luigi Pirandello is the author of *Six Characters in Search of an Author*.

16. INJURY : PARAPLEGIA :: STROKE : (A. aphasia, B. quadriplegia, C. fantasia, D. hemiplegia)

The correct answer is (D). An injury to the spinal column may cause paralysis of the lower half of the body—paraplegia; a stroke may cause paralysis of either the right or left half of the body—hemiplegia.

17. LIKES : EVERYONE :: (A. indifferent, B. wish, C. loves, D. care) : NOBODY

The correct answer is (C). This analogy is a grammatical one. Everyone is a singular pronoun that takes the singular form of the verb likes; nobody is a singular pronoun that takes the singular form of the verb loves.

18. SEPTEMBER : (A. October, B. January, C. Thursday, D. planting) :: HARVEST MOON : HUNTER'S MOON

The correct answer is (A). The Harvest Moon, the full moon following the autumnal equinox, generally falls in September; the Hunter's Moon, the next full moon following the Harvest Moon, generally falls in October.

19. ERATO : THALIA :: (A. movies, B. sleep, C. poetry, D. death) : COMEDY

The correct answer is (C). Erato and Thalia are both muses. Erato is the muse of poetry; Thalia is the muse of comedy.

20. (A. anglophile, B. bibliophile, C. oenophile, D. vines) : WINE :: FRANCOPHILE : FRANCE

The correct answer is (C). A francophile loves France. An oenophile loves wine.

21. 6 : −6 :: 31 : (A. −2, B. 3, C. −13, D. 19)

The correct answer is (D). The only feasible mathematical relationship is that of subtraction. $6 − 12 = −6$; $31 − 12 = 19$. The analogy is correct because on both sides of the proportion, 12 was subtracted from the first number to yield the second number.

22. RIVE GAUCHE : PARIS :: (A. Philadelphia, B. Albany, C. Riker's Island, D. Brooklyn) : NEW YORK

The correct answer is (D). The Rive Gauche is a part of Paris located across the river from the main business part of the city; Brooklyn is a part of New York City located across the river from the main business section.

23. SURINAME : (A. Guyana, B. British Honduras, C. Belize, D. Dutch Guiana) :: ZIMBABWE : RHODESIA

The correct answer is (D). Zimbabwe is the current name for that African country that used to be called Rhodesia; Suriname is the name taken when that South American country gained its independence and ceased being Dutch Guiana. Belize was formerly known as British Honduras.

answers practice test 7

24. BAROQUE : VIVALDI :: (A. Classical, B. Romantic, C. Rococo, D. Impressionist) : SCHUMANN

The correct answer is (B). The music composed by Vivaldi was of the Baroque style; Schumann was strictly a Romantic composer.

25. OBSEQUIOUS : OBSTINATE :: DIFFIDENT : (A. indifferent, B. shy, C. distinct, D. defiant)

The correct answer is (D). This is an analogy of antonyms. The obsequious person is spineless and overly agreeable, whereas the obstinate person is stubborn and stands his or her ground. The diffident person is shy and lacking in self-confidence, while the defiant person is confident and bold.

26. SHIITE : (A. Arab, B. Muslim, C. Sunni, D. Iran) :: ROMAN CATHOLIC : PROTESTANT

The correct answer is (C). Roman Catholic and Protestant are two leading branches of Christianity. Shiite and Sunni are two leading branches of Islam.

27. HONOR : CITATION :: SPEEDING : (A. citation, B. hurry, C. race, D. stop)

The correct answer is (A). The relationship in the analogy is one of cause and effect. When you are to be honored, you receive a citation, which is a formal document describing your achievements. When you are stopped for speeding, you receive a citation, which is an official summons to appear in court. Citation is a word with two very different meanings.

28. *HEDDA GABLER* : (A. *The Cherry Orchard,* B. *Riders to the Sea,* C. *An Enemy of the People,* D. *Blood Wedding*) :: *ANNA CHRISTIE : MOON FOR THE MISBEGOTTEN*

The correct answer is (C). *Anna Christie* and *Moon for the Misbegotten* are both plays written by Eugene O'Neill; *Hedda Gabler* and *An Enemy of the People* are both plays written by Henrik Ibsen.

29. YELLOW : (A. sunflower, B. cornflower, C. rose, D. jacket) :: RED : SALVIA

The correct answer is (A). This analogy is one of characteristic. The characteristic color of salvia is flaming red; the characteristic color of a sunflower is yellow. A cornflower is blue.

30. ANODE : CATHODE :: OXIDATION : (A. erosion, B. reduction, C. carbonization, D. hydrogenation)

The correct answer is (B). The anode is the site of oxidation in an electrical cell; the cathode is the site of reduction in that same electrical cell.

31. CELLO : VIOLIN :: (A. clarinet, B. French horn, C. accordion, D. rebec) : SAXOPHONE

The correct answer is (A). The cello and violin are both stringed instruments; the clarinet and saxophone are both woodwinds with sounds produced by reeds. A rebec is an ancient stringed instrument.

32. JOAN OF ARC : (A. witch, B. stake, C. king, D. saint) :: GALILEO : SUN

The correct answer is (C). Galileo fell out of favor with the church because of his insistence that the sun was the center of the universe; Joan of Arc fell out of favor with the church because of her defense of the king as the ruler on Earth.

33. (A. Yeats, B. Shakespeare, C. Chaucer, D. Tennyson) : SONNETS :: NASH : LIMERICKS

    The correct answer is (B). Ogden Nash is well known as a writer of limericks; Shakespeare is well known for his sonnets as well as for his plays.

34. RACQUETBALL : SQUASH :: HOCKEY : (A. badminton, B. rugby, C. volleyball, D. curling)

    The correct answer is (D). Racquetball and squash are both racquet sports played within an enclosed court; hockey and curling both take place on the ice.

35. ST. PETERSBURG : HERMITAGE :: (A. Spain, B. Majorca, C. Madrid, D. Seville) : PRADO

    The correct answer is (C). The Hermitage is a famous art gallery in the city of St. Petersburg; the Prado is a famous art gallery in the city of Madrid.

36. ABSCISSA : (A. ordinate, B. mantissa, C. coordinate, D. precision) :: X : Y

    The correct answer is (A). In coordinate geometry, an abscissa is the horizontal coordinate of a point in a plane obtained by measuring parallel to the x-axis; an ordinate is obtained by measuring parallel to the y-axis.

37. SKINNER : BEHAVIORISM :: (A. Adler, B. Terman, C. Kant, D. Wertheimer) : GESTALT

    The correct answer is (D). B.F. Skinner was a psychologist closely associated with the school of psychology called behaviorism; Max Wertheimer was the founder of the Gestalt school of psychology.

38. HESTER : INFIDELITY :: (A. Cordelia, B. Goneril, C. Ophelia, D. Cassandra) : DEVOTION

    The correct answer is (A). This analogy is based upon characteristics. Hester Prynne in Hawthorne's *Scarlet Letter* was an adulteress; therefore, infidelity was one of her characteristics. Cordelia in Shakespeare's *King Lear* was known for her devotion.

39. CAPILLARIES : CIRCULATION :: VILLI : (A. respiration, B. digestion, C. recreation, D. procreation)

    The correct answer is (B). Capillaries, the smallest blood vessels, are part of the circulatory system; villi, fingerlike projections in the small intestine that help absorb nutrients, are part of the digestive system.

40. SAN MARINO : ITALY :: (A. Ethiopia, B. Capetown, C. Lesotho, D. Swaziland) : SOUTH AFRICA

    The correct answer is (C). San Marino is a tiny independent country that exists entirely within the boundaries of Italy; Lesotho is a small independent country entirely bordered by South Africa.

41. (A. Florida, B. New Mexico, C. Puerto Rico, D. Hawaii) : ALASKA :: SPAIN : RUSSIA

    The correct answer is (A). Alaska was purchased from Russia; Florida was purchased from Spain.

42. KEYNES : ECONOMICS :: DEWEY : (A. zoology, B. electronics, C. medicine, D. education)

The correct answer is (D). John Maynard Keynes formulated and published controversial and influential theories in economics; John Dewey was equally influential for his novel theories in education.

43. NEIL ARMSTRONG : YURI GAGARIN :: CHARLES LINDBERGH : (A. George Washington, B. Albert Einstein, C. Orville Wright, D. Guglielmo Marconi)

The correct answer is (C). The four analogous people were all pioneers in flight. Neil Armstrong was the first person to walk on the moon; Yuri Gagarin, a Soviet, was the first person to go into outer space; Charles Lindbergh was the first aviator to cross the Atlantic alone; and Orville Wright was the first person to fly in an airplane.

44. *PILGRIM'S PROGRESS* : (A. *Inferno*, B. *Paradise Lost*, C. *De Monarchia*, D. *Divine Comedy*) :: BUNYAN : DANTE

The correct answer is (D). *Pilgrim's Progress* is a religious allegory written by John Bunyan; *Divine Comedy* is an allegorical autobiography heavily religious in content, written by Dante.

45. GENGHIS KHAN : MONGOLS :: ATTILA : (A. Roman Empire, B. Germany, C. Huns, D. Trojans)

The correct answer is (C). Genghis Khan was leader of the Mongols, conquerors of the thirteenth century; Attila was leader of the Huns, who conquered most of the Roman Empire in the middle of the fifth century.

46. HARE : (A. rabbit, B. tortoise, C. terrapin, D. berries) :: FOX : GRAPES

The correct answer is (B). The analogy is based upon the association of significant elements in two of *Aesop's Fables*. The fox attempts to reach the grapes; the hare attempts to win a race with the tortoise.

47. 4 : 6 :: (A. 10, B. 6, C. 9, D. 16) : 36

The correct answer is (D). This is an A : C :: B : D correspondence. 6 squared is 36; 4 squared is 16. On one side of the proportion are the square roots; on the other side, in the same order, are the squares.

48. THOMAS MANN : *BUDDENBROOKS* :: THOMAS WOLFE : (A. *Death in Venice*, B. *Look Homeward, Angel*, C. *The Magic Mountain*, D. *Joseph and His Brothers*)

The correct answer is (B). Thomas Mann is the author of *Buddenbrooks*; Thomas Wolfe is the author of *Look Homeward, Angel*.

49. (A. Earth, B. moon, C. Russia, D. Stalin) : SPUTNIK :: JUPITER : IO

The correct answer is (A). Io is one of the four large moons of Jupiter. A moon is a satellite. Sputnik was the first man-made satellite of Earth.

50. FREYA : ASGARD :: (A. Hera, B. Venus, C. Minerva, D. Aphrodite) : OLYMPUS

The correct answer is (D). The Norse gods live at Asgard; the Norse goddess of love and beauty is Freya. The Greek gods live at Olympus; the Greek goddess of love and beauty is Aphrodite.

51. (A. isosceles, B. scalene, C. right, D. obtuse) : EQUILATERAL :: DUPLE : TRIPLE

    The correct answer is (A). In music, duple time is time that is divisible by 2; triple time is time that is divisible by 3 (into equal segments). An isosceles triangle is one in which two sides are equal; all three sides of an equilateral triangle are of equal length.

52. ELWAY : JORDAN :: (A. football, B. baseball, C, hockey, D. horseracing) : BASKETBALL

    The correct answer is (A). This analogy is based upon the association between the athlete and the sport in which he excels. John Elway played football, and Michael Jordan played basketball. Both led their teams to victory in multiple championship games.

53. OBVERSE : (A. coin, B. sweater, C. reverse, D. crochet) :: STARBOARD : PORT

    The correct answer is (C). Starboard and port are basically opposite sides of a ship; obverse and reverse are the opposite sides of a coin.

54. PASTEL : MUTED :: LIGHT : (A. sound, B. voice, C. trumpet, D. wheel)

    The correct answer is (A). Color is created by light waves. A pastel color is one that has been softened. Thus, pastel color is softened light waves. When a sound has been softened, we say that it has been muted.

55. (A. one, B. two, C. three, D. nine) : BETWEEN :: SIX : AMONG

    The correct answer is (B). This is a grammatical analogy. The preposition among is used for comparison of more than two persons or things; the preposition between is used for comparisons between only two persons or things.

56. XENOPHOBIA : PREJUDICE :: PECCATOPHOBIA : (A. tantrums, B. bad habits, C. clumsiness, D. virtue)

    The correct answer is (D). This is a cause-and-effect relationship. Xenophobia (fear of strangers) leads to prejudice; peccatophobia (fear of sinning) leads to virtue.

57. HARPSICHORD : VIRGINAL :: (A. piccolo, B. saxophone, C. sousaphone, D. oboe) : CLARINET

    The correct answer is (D). A harpsichord is a manual double-keyboard instrument, while a virginal is a single-keyboard instrument closely related to the harpsichord; the oboe is a double-reed wind instrument, while the clarinet is a single-reed woodwind.

58. LEAGUE : YARD :: MILES : (A. inches, B. feet, C. yards, D. furlongs)

    The correct answer is (B). The analogy is based on a proportional part-to-whole relationship. A league is composed of 3 miles, and a yard is composed of 3 feet.

59. ATOM : MOLECULE :: GENE : (A. heredity, B. genetics, C. DNA, D. chromosome)

    The correct answer is (D). This analogy is based upon a part-to-whole relationship. An atom is a constituent part of a molecule; a gene is a constituent part of a chromosome.

60. FIRE : SMOKE :: (A. pipe, B. hose, C. leak, D. break) : STAIN

    The correct answer is (C). Smoke is presumptive evidence of fire; a stain is presumptive evidence of a leak.

61. BUTTER : MARGARINE :: SUGAR : (A. salt, B. strychnine, C. aspartame, D. vinegar)

The correct answer is (C). Margarine is a synthetic shortening used in place of butter that closely resembles butter in taste and color; aspartame is a synthetic sweetener used in place of sugar. Strychnine is a poison.

62. TOM SAWYER : (A. Mark Twain, B. Samuel Langhorne Clemens, C. Becky Thatcher, D. David Copperfield) :: PORTHOS : ATHOS

The correct answer is (C). The analogy is based upon the friendship of two characters in the same novel. Athos and Porthos are two major characters in Alexandre Dumas's novel *The Three Musketeers;* Tom Sawyer and Becky Thatcher are two major characters in Mark Twain's novel *The Adventures of Tom Sawyer.*

63. (A. white, B. bluing, C. blanch, D. yellow) : BLEACH :: HENNA : ANIL

The correct answer is (B). Henna and anil are both plants that yield dyeing agents. Bluing and bleach are both agents that serve to whiten or remove dye.

64. CHECKERS : RICHARD NIXON :: TRAVELER : (A. Robert E. Lee, B. Franklin Roosevelt, C. Dwight Eisenhower, D. Aristotle Onassis)

The correct answer is (A). This analogy is based upon animals and the famous people with whom their names are closely associated. Checkers was Richard Nixon's dog. Traveler was Robert E. Lee's horse.

65. BRUTE : SQUIRE :: TUBER : (A. leaves, B. yams, C. quires, D. stems)

The correct answer is (C). This nonsemantic analogy is based upon anagrams. Tuber is an anagram of brute; quires is an anagram of squire. The fact that there is absolutely no meaningful relationship between any two of the capitalized words should immediately alert you to a nonsemantic analogy. All the words are nouns, although brute could be an adjective and squire a verb, so no grammatical analogy is feasible. The qu in squire leads you directly to the correct answer.

66. $\frac{1}{8}$: 12.5% :: (A. $\frac{1}{6}$, B. $\frac{3}{11}$, C. $\frac{2}{7}$, D. $\frac{3}{8}$) : 37.5%

The correct answer is (D). The relationship here is between the fraction and its percent equivalent. $\frac{1}{8}$ is equivalent to 12.5%; $\frac{3}{8}$ is equivalent to 37.5%.

67. CRETACEOUS : DINOSAURS :: TERTIARY : (A. vampires, B. fish, C. reptiles, D. mammals)

The correct answer is (D). This analogy refers to geologic periods. During the Cretaceous period, dinosaurs were the predominant animal form; during the Tertiary period, mammals were predominant.

68. MAPLE : (A. syrup, B. oak, C. cyanide, D. leaf) :: PRIVET : HEMLOCK

The correct answer is (B). The analogy is based upon function. Privet and hemlock serve as hedges on or between properties; maple and oak serve as shade trees.

69. (A. Washington, B. Jefferson, C. Franklin, D. Lincoln) : MADISON :: DECLARATION OF INDEPENDENCE : CONSTITUTION

The correct answer is (B). The relationship in this analogy is between the author and the document. Although both documents were the products of many men's thinking, the acknowledged author of the Constitution is Madison, and the authorship of the Declaration of Independence is attributed to Jefferson.

70. ALZHEIMER'S DISEASE : HANSEN'S DISEASE :: (A. cerebral palsy, B. copper deficiency, C. dementia, D. lymphatic cancer) : LEPROSY

The correct answer is (C). This analogy is based upon alternative names for the same disease. Hansen's disease is leprosy; Alzheimer's disease is a form of dementia.

71. SALVADOR DALI : RENE MAGRITTE :: (A. e.e. cummings, B. William Wordsworth, C. Jack London, D. Leo Tolstoy) : DON MARQUIS

The correct answer is (A). Salvador Dali and Rene Magritte are both famous Surrealist painters; e.e. cummings and Don Marquis are both writers who are famous for writing only in lowercase.

72. INDEPENDENCE : COOPERATION :: PHOTOSYNTHESIS : (A. parasitism, B. parthenogenesis, C. symbiosis, D. carbohydrates)

The correct answer is (C). Photosynthesis is the independent creation of food (carbohydrates) by chlorophyll-bearing plants; symbiosis is the cooperative arrangement by which two plants, two animals, or an animal and a plant live together and mutually supply each other's needs.

73. (A. stars, B. restaurants, C. tires, D. highways) : MICHELIN :: GASOLINE : EXXON

The correct answer is (C). Gasoline is the chief product of Exxon; tires are the chief product of Michelin.

74. SWIFT : (A. Barrie, B. Kipling, C. Dorothy, D. Baum) :: LILLIPUT : OZ

The correct answer is (D). In this analogy, fictional countries are paired with their creators. Jonathan Swift was the creator of Lilliput in his social novel *Gulliver's Travels;* L. Frank Baum created the land of Oz in *The Wizard of Oz.*

75. FOUR : BASEBALL :: (A. ten, B. eleven, C. fifty, D. one hundred twenty) : FOOTBALL

The correct answer is (A). Four balls in baseball entitle the batter to walk to first base; the game then continues without the teams changing positions. Ten yards in football constitute a first down; the game continues with the same team in possession of the ball.

76. (A. remuneration, B. stipend, C. pay, D. overtime) : SALARY :: COMMISSION : ROYALTY

The correct answer is (B). Commission and royalty are both forms of payment that are based upon a percentage of the money brought in; salary and stipend are both fixed rates of payment.

77. LAWYER : BARRISTER :: ATTORNEY : (A. judge, B. juror, C. advocate, D. appellant)

The correct answer is (C). All four words are synonyms or near synonyms. Lawyer and attorney are terms most often used in the United States, while barrister and advocate are more often used in England.

78. KOALA : (A. eucalyptus, B. wallaby, C. bamboo, D. mulberry) :: WHALE : PLANKTON

The correct answer is (A). The chief food of the whale is plankton; the sole food of the koala is leaves of the eucalyptus tree.

79. DEER : (A. deer, B. moose, C. dear, D. swan) :: GOOSE : GEESE

   The correct answer is (A). This is a grammatical analogy. On both sides of the proportion are words that form their plurals in an irregular manner. The plural of goose is geese; the plural of deer is deer.

80. 27 : (A. 3, B. 9, C. 5.19, D. 729) :: 125 : 5

   The correct answer is (A). 125 is the cube of 5; 27 is the cube of 3. Conversely, 5 is the cube root of 125; 3 is the cube root of 27.

81. EGG : CHICKEN :: CHICKEN : (A. rooster, B. capon, C. egg, D. hen)

   The correct answer is (C). The relationship in this analogy is not only sequential, but it also is circular. There is a conundrum, "Which came first, the chicken or the egg?" The answer is that the chicken comes from an egg, and an egg comes from a chicken. The sequence is analogous on both sides of the proportion.

82. PARIS : FRANCE :: (A. Tripoli, B. Rabat, C. Marseilles, D. Dakar) : SENEGAL

   The correct answer is (D). The relationship is that of the capital city to the country of which it is the capital. Paris is the capital of France; Dakar is the capital of Senegal.

83. CCC : TVA :: FDIC : (A. OPA, B. WMC, C. OSS, D. FHA)

   The correct answer is (D). All four related terms are agencies that were set up early in the Franklin D. Roosevelt administration to help the nation to recover from the Depression. CCC is the Civilian Conservation Corps; TVA is the Tennessee Valley Authority; FDIC is the Federal Deposit Insurance Corporation; and FHA is the Federal Housing Administration. OPA (Office of Price Administration) and OSS (Office of Security Services) were World War II agencies. WMC is the Women's Marine Corps.

84. ELABORATE : (A. streamlined, B. boring, C. oblique, D. obligatory) :: SERIF : SANS SERIF

   The correct answer is (A). Serif and sans serif refer to typefaces. Serif type has elaborate little cross strokes at the tops and bottoms of capital letters. Sans serif type has no such embellishments; hence, it is streamlined.

85. BULL RUN : MANASSAS :: STREAM : (A. battle, B. town, C. war, D. tribe)

   The correct answer is (B). In Civil War histories, the labels First Battle of Bull Run and Battle of Manassas are used interchangeably to refer to the same battle. Northerners named battles for streams; Southerners called the battles by the names of the towns they were in or near.

86. GREENWICH VILLAGE : (A. London, B. Kensington, C. New York, D. Piccadilly Circus) :: MONTMARTRE : PARIS

   The correct answer is (C). Montmartre is traditionally known as the artists' district of Paris; Greenwich Village is traditionally known as the artists' district of New York City.

87. UNITED STATES : DOW JONES :: JAPAN : (A. Hang Seng, B. Nikkei, C. Tokyo, D. Kyoto)

   The correct answer is (B). The analogy is one of country to major stock market index. The Dow Jones average is the major index of the U.S. stock market and is widely quoted as an indicator of market performance; the Nikkei average is the major index of Japan's market performance. The Hang Seng is the index of Hong Kong.

88. ZOLA : *NANA* :: (A. Humbert Humbert, B. Don Juan, C. Don Quixote, D. Nabokov) : *LOLITA*

    The correct answer is (D). Emile Zola is the author of the novel *Nana;* Vladimir Nabokov is the author of the novel *Lolita.*

89. KANT : CATEGORICAL IMPERATIVE :: (A. Descartes, B. Nietzsche, C. Sartre, D. Mill) : UTILITY

    The correct answer is (D). Kant's test of the morality of an action was the categorical imperative, the test of whether the action would be pleasing to another person in a particular situation; Mill's test of the morality of an action was its utility—that is, whether it would be pleasing to the greatest number of people.

90. NOON : EVENING :: (A. snack, B. lunch, C. brunch, D. afternoon) : DINNER

    The correct answer is (B). This is a sequential relationship. Noon comes before evening; lunch comes before dinner. Or, you may see the relationship as being one of characteristic. At noon, one will have lunch; in the evening, one will have dinner. A snack can be eaten at any time. Brunch is a combination of breakfast and lunch.

91. MENTICIDE : BRAINWASHING :: OPPROBRIUM : (A. commendation, B. reproach, C. indoctrination, D. repression)

    The correct answer is (B). This is an analogy based on synonyms. Menticide is brainwashing; opprobrium is reproach.

92. CALPURNIA : (A. Oedipus, B. Caesar, C. King Lear, D. Cicero) :: CRESSIDA : TROILUS

    The correct answer is (B). On both sides of this analogy, we find women who warned their men of impending danger. In Shakespeare's *Troilus and Cressida,* Cressida warns her brother, Troilus, of the perils of fighting the Greeks. In Shakespeare's *Julius Caesar,* Calpurnia warns her husband, Caesar, of the dangers of going to the Senate.

93. BLIND : DEAF :: (A. Milton, B. Scott, C. Mozart, D. Justice) : BEETHOVEN

    The correct answer is (A). This is an analogy of characteristic. The composer Beethoven was deaf; the poet Milton was blind.

94. REMUS : (A. Brer Rabbit, B. Aquarius, C. Quisling, D. Romulus) :: CASTOR : POLLUX

    The correct answer is (D). Castor and Pollux are mythological twins and are the astronomical constellations that make up the zodiac sign Gemini; Remus and Romulus were mythological twins who founded the city of Rome. The analogy is based upon the fact that both pairs are twins.

95. DOG : FLEA :: HORSE : (A. rider, B. fly, C. mane, D. shoe)

    The correct answer is (B). This analogy is based upon the relationship of object to actor, with a very special relationship between the two. The actor acts as irritant to the object. Thus, a flea irritates a dog; a fly irritates a horse. The rider may at times irritate the horse, though not as consistently as the fly.

96. 10 : (A. decimal, B. common, C. unnatural, D. metric) :: e : NATURAL

    The correct answer is (B). A logarithm to the base e is a natural logarithm; a logarithm to the base 10 is a common logarithm.

97. BROUGHAM : CARRIAGE :: HOME : (A. horse, B. town, C. domicile, D. family)

The correct answer is (C). The terms in this analogy are synonyms. A brougham is a carriage; a home is a domicile.

98. EURO : (A. Brazil, B. Nigeria, C. Greece, D. India) :: REAL : BRAZIL

The correct answer is (C). This analogy is based upon country to currency. The national currency of Brazil is the real; the national currency of Greece is the euro.

99. (A. Shangri-La, B. Lilliput, C. Atlantis, D. Ilium) : BRIGADOON :: FOUNTAIN OF YOUTH : NEVER-NEVER LAND

The correct answer is (A). The four related terms are all places in which time stands still and people never age.

100. PARTHENON : PANTHEON :: (A. Taj Mahal, B. St. Paul's, C. Angkor Wat, D. Erechtheum) : SISTINE CHAPEL

The correct answer is (D). In this analogy, the association is one of place and function. The Pantheon and the Sistine Chapel are both famous places of worship in Rome; the Parthenon and the Erechtheum are both famous temples in Athens.

101. QUEUE : PEOPLE :: STRING : (A. geese, B. pails, C. hay, D. pearls)

The correct answer is (D). People form in a queue like pearls on a string.

102. RECRUIT : ENLIST :: EMPLOYEE : (A. putrefy, B. apply, C. disinherit, D. leave)

The correct answer is (B). To join the military, one can enlist to become a recruit. To join the work force, one can apply to become an employee.

103. CONTROL : ORDER :: ANARCHY : (A. clown, B. pupil, C. climax, D. chaos)

The correct answer is (D). Control results in order; anarchy results in chaos.

104. REMORSE : RUE :: PLEASURE : (A. pain, B. enjoy, C. commiserate, D. age)

The correct answer is (B). To rue is to feel remorse; to enjoy is to feel pleasure. To cogitate does not necessarily result in rationality.

105. RETARDANT : FIRE :: REPELLENT : (A. infestation, B. fertilizer, C. vaccination, D. accelerant)

The correct answer is (A). A retardant protects from fire, as a repellant protects from infestation by insects.

106. SEWER : SEAM :: ELECTRICIAN : (A. thimble, B. scalpel, C. splice, D. spore)

The correct answer is (C). A sewer uses a seam to connect pieces of fabric. An electrician uses a splice to connect pieces of wire.

107. APOLOGY : ACCEPT :: FORGIVENESS : (A. feature, B. beg, C. promise, D. force)

The correct answer is (B). You can accept someone else's apology; you can beg someone else's forgiveness. You cannot break someone else's promise.

108. WOOD : CARVE :: CLAY : (A. sway, B. burn, C. mold, D. blow)

The correct answer is (C). One can create something by carving wood; one can also create something by molding clay.

109. SPIRE : TOWER :: CREST : (A. mountain, B. pond, C. state, D. hat)

The correct answer is (A). A spire surmounts a tower; a crest is the highest point of a mountain.

110. SOLECISM : GRAMMAR :: FOUL : (A. marriage, B. game, C. incest, D. stumble)

The correct answer is (B). A solecism is a violation of the rules of grammar; a foul is a violation of the rules of a game.

111. GRAVEL : CONCRETE :: EGGS: (A. soufflé, B. stones, C. mixer, D. truck)

The correct answer is (A). Gravel is an ingredient of concrete; eggs are an ingredient of a soufflé.

112. APOGEE : ORBIT :: APEX : (A. pedigree, B. detergent, C. mountain, D. radius)

The correct answer is (C). The apogee is the outer limit of an orbit; the apex is the upper limit of a mountain.

113. WHEELBARROW : TRANSPORT :: LEVER : (A. pull, B. handle, C. hone, D. lift)

The correct answer is (D). A lever helps you lift objects; a wheelbarrow helps you transport them easily.

114. ASYLUM : REFUGEE :: DESTINATION : (A. escape, B. traveler, C. lunatic, D. injury)

The correct answer is (B). A refugee seeks asylum; a traveler seeks a destination.

115. WORRIED : HYSTERICAL :: HAPPY : (A. hot, B. ecstatic, C. lonely, D. serious)

The correct answer is (B). One who is extremely worried may be hysterical; one who is extremely happy may be ecstatic.

116. VALANCE : ROD :: PENDANT : (A. chain, B. curtain, C. pleat, D. cravat)

The correct answer is (A). A valance (a short, decorative drapery) hangs from a curtain rod. A pendant hangs from a chain around a person's neck.

117. TELEMETRY : DISTANT :: MICROMETRY : (A. earthshaking. B. real, C. tiny, D. vision)

The correct answer is (C). Telemetry is concerned with the distant, and micrometry is concerned with the tiny.

118. NATION : BORDER GUARDS :: PROPERTY : (A. state, B. fence, C. hollow, D. satellite)

The correct answer is (B). Border guards protect the boundaries of a nation; a fence protects the boundaries of a property.

119. TOLERATE : PREJUDICE :: SURVIVE : (A. food, B. cramps, C. kill, D. estimate)

The correct answer is (B). Prejudice can interfere with one's ability to tolerate; cramps can interfere with one's ability to swim and thereby survive.

120. SOLDIER : REGIMENT :: STAR : (A. navy, B. river, C. constellation, D. amphibian)

The correct answer is (C). A soldier is part of a regiment; a star is part of a constellation. This is a simple part-to-whole analogy.

ANSWER SHEET PRACTICE TEST 8

1. Ⓐ Ⓑ Ⓒ Ⓓ	31. Ⓐ Ⓑ Ⓒ Ⓓ	61. Ⓐ Ⓑ Ⓒ Ⓓ	91. Ⓐ Ⓑ Ⓒ Ⓓ
2. Ⓐ Ⓑ Ⓒ Ⓓ	32. Ⓐ Ⓑ Ⓒ Ⓓ	62. Ⓐ Ⓑ Ⓒ Ⓓ	92. Ⓐ Ⓑ Ⓒ Ⓓ
3. Ⓐ Ⓑ Ⓒ Ⓓ	33. Ⓐ Ⓑ Ⓒ Ⓓ	63. Ⓐ Ⓑ Ⓒ Ⓓ	93. Ⓐ Ⓑ Ⓒ Ⓓ
4. Ⓐ Ⓑ Ⓒ Ⓓ	34. Ⓐ Ⓑ Ⓒ Ⓓ	64. Ⓐ Ⓑ Ⓒ Ⓓ	94. Ⓐ Ⓑ Ⓒ Ⓓ
5. Ⓐ Ⓑ Ⓒ Ⓓ	35. Ⓐ Ⓑ Ⓒ Ⓓ	65. Ⓐ Ⓑ Ⓒ Ⓓ	95. Ⓐ Ⓑ Ⓒ Ⓓ
6. Ⓐ Ⓑ Ⓒ Ⓓ	36. Ⓐ Ⓑ Ⓒ Ⓓ	66. Ⓐ Ⓑ Ⓒ Ⓓ	96. Ⓐ Ⓑ Ⓒ Ⓓ
7. Ⓐ Ⓑ Ⓒ Ⓓ	37. Ⓐ Ⓑ Ⓒ Ⓓ	67. Ⓐ Ⓑ Ⓒ Ⓓ	97. Ⓐ Ⓑ Ⓒ Ⓓ
8. Ⓐ Ⓑ Ⓒ Ⓓ	38. Ⓐ Ⓑ Ⓒ Ⓓ	68. Ⓐ Ⓑ Ⓒ Ⓓ	98. Ⓐ Ⓑ Ⓒ Ⓓ
9. Ⓐ Ⓑ Ⓒ Ⓓ	39. Ⓐ Ⓑ Ⓒ Ⓓ	69. Ⓐ Ⓑ Ⓒ Ⓓ	99. Ⓐ Ⓑ Ⓒ Ⓓ
10. Ⓐ Ⓑ Ⓒ Ⓓ	40. Ⓐ Ⓑ Ⓒ Ⓓ	70. Ⓐ Ⓑ Ⓒ Ⓓ	100. Ⓐ Ⓑ Ⓒ Ⓓ
11. Ⓐ Ⓑ Ⓒ Ⓓ	41. Ⓐ Ⓑ Ⓒ Ⓓ	71. Ⓐ Ⓑ Ⓒ Ⓓ	101. Ⓐ Ⓑ Ⓒ Ⓓ
12. Ⓐ Ⓑ Ⓒ Ⓓ	42. Ⓐ Ⓑ Ⓒ Ⓓ	72. Ⓐ Ⓑ Ⓒ Ⓓ	102. Ⓐ Ⓑ Ⓒ Ⓓ
13. Ⓐ Ⓑ Ⓒ Ⓓ	43. Ⓐ Ⓑ Ⓒ Ⓓ	73. Ⓐ Ⓑ Ⓒ Ⓓ	103. Ⓐ Ⓑ Ⓒ Ⓓ
14. Ⓐ Ⓑ Ⓒ Ⓓ	44. Ⓐ Ⓑ Ⓒ Ⓓ	74. Ⓐ Ⓑ Ⓒ Ⓓ	104. Ⓐ Ⓑ Ⓒ Ⓓ
15. Ⓐ Ⓑ Ⓒ Ⓓ	45. Ⓐ Ⓑ Ⓒ Ⓓ	75. Ⓐ Ⓑ Ⓒ Ⓓ	105. Ⓐ Ⓑ Ⓒ Ⓓ
16. Ⓐ Ⓑ Ⓒ Ⓓ	46. Ⓐ Ⓑ Ⓒ Ⓓ	76. Ⓐ Ⓑ Ⓒ Ⓓ	106. Ⓐ Ⓑ Ⓒ Ⓓ
17. Ⓐ Ⓑ Ⓒ Ⓓ	47. Ⓐ Ⓑ Ⓒ Ⓓ	77. Ⓐ Ⓑ Ⓒ Ⓓ	107. Ⓐ Ⓑ Ⓒ Ⓓ
18. Ⓐ Ⓑ Ⓒ Ⓓ	48. Ⓐ Ⓑ Ⓒ Ⓓ	78. Ⓐ Ⓑ Ⓒ Ⓓ	108. Ⓐ Ⓑ Ⓒ Ⓓ
19. Ⓐ Ⓑ Ⓒ Ⓓ	49. Ⓐ Ⓑ Ⓒ Ⓓ	79. Ⓐ Ⓑ Ⓒ Ⓓ	109. Ⓐ Ⓑ Ⓒ Ⓓ
20. Ⓐ Ⓑ Ⓒ Ⓓ	50. Ⓐ Ⓑ Ⓒ Ⓓ	80. Ⓐ Ⓑ Ⓒ Ⓓ	110. Ⓐ Ⓑ Ⓒ Ⓓ
21. Ⓐ Ⓑ Ⓒ Ⓓ	51. Ⓐ Ⓑ Ⓒ Ⓓ	81. Ⓐ Ⓑ Ⓒ Ⓓ	111. Ⓐ Ⓑ Ⓒ Ⓓ
22. Ⓐ Ⓑ Ⓒ Ⓓ	52. Ⓐ Ⓑ Ⓒ Ⓓ	82. Ⓐ Ⓑ Ⓒ Ⓓ	112. Ⓐ Ⓑ Ⓒ Ⓓ
23. Ⓐ Ⓑ Ⓒ Ⓓ	53. Ⓐ Ⓑ Ⓒ Ⓓ	83. Ⓐ Ⓑ Ⓒ Ⓓ	113. Ⓐ Ⓑ Ⓒ Ⓓ
24. Ⓐ Ⓑ Ⓒ Ⓓ	54. Ⓐ Ⓑ Ⓒ Ⓓ	84. Ⓐ Ⓑ Ⓒ Ⓓ	114. Ⓐ Ⓑ Ⓒ Ⓓ
25. Ⓐ Ⓑ Ⓒ Ⓓ	55. Ⓐ Ⓑ Ⓒ Ⓓ	85. Ⓐ Ⓑ Ⓒ Ⓓ	115. Ⓐ Ⓑ Ⓒ Ⓓ
26. Ⓐ Ⓑ Ⓒ Ⓓ	56. Ⓐ Ⓑ Ⓒ Ⓓ	86. Ⓐ Ⓑ Ⓒ Ⓓ	116. Ⓐ Ⓑ Ⓒ Ⓓ
27. Ⓐ Ⓑ Ⓒ Ⓓ	57. Ⓐ Ⓑ Ⓒ Ⓓ	87. Ⓐ Ⓑ Ⓒ Ⓓ	117. Ⓐ Ⓑ Ⓒ Ⓓ
28. Ⓐ Ⓑ Ⓒ Ⓓ	58. Ⓐ Ⓑ Ⓒ Ⓓ	88. Ⓐ Ⓑ Ⓒ Ⓓ	118. Ⓐ Ⓑ Ⓒ Ⓓ
29. Ⓐ Ⓑ Ⓒ Ⓓ	59. Ⓐ Ⓑ Ⓒ Ⓓ	89. Ⓐ Ⓑ Ⓒ Ⓓ	119. Ⓐ Ⓑ Ⓒ Ⓓ
30. Ⓐ Ⓑ Ⓒ Ⓓ	60. Ⓐ Ⓑ Ⓒ Ⓓ	90. Ⓐ Ⓑ Ⓒ Ⓓ	120. Ⓐ Ⓑ Ⓒ Ⓓ

answer sheet

Practice Test 8

120 QUESTIONS • 60 MINUTES

Directions: Each of these test questions consists of three capitalized words and four lettered words enclosed in parentheses. Two of the capitalized words are related in some way. Find the two related words, and establish the nature of the relationship. Then study the four words lettered A, B, C, and D. Select the one lettered word that is related to the remaining capitalized word in the same way that the other two capitalized words are related. Mark the answer sheet for the letter preceding the word you select.

1. TROT : GALLOP :: LOPE : (A. walk, B. scurry, C. row, D. step)

2. TRELLIS : PROP :: PILLAR : (A. climb, B. buttress, C. plant, D. sow)

3. (A. gun, B. cola, C. crown, D. wrap) : ROYAL :: CRUCIFIX : RELIGIOUS

4. ISLAND : OCEAN :: (A. hill, B. forest, C. oasis, D. tree) : DESERT

5. MATHEMATICS : NUMEROLOGY :: ASTRONOMY : (A. botany, B. physiology, C. medicine, D. astrology)

6. BUCOLIC : URBAN :: (A. dense, B. ephemeral, C. plastic, D. mist) : SMOG

7. (A. trustworthy, B. dislikable, C. silly, D. tender) : ABHORRENT :: DIFFICULT : ARDUOUS

8. WOOD : CORD :: MILK : (A. pasture, B. industry, C. quart, D. cow)

9. PLAUSIBLE : (A. deception, B. watertight, C. attractive, D. explanation) :: DEFENSIBLE : THEORY

10. MINARET : MOSQUE :: (A. religion, B. steeple, C. dainty, D. classic) : CHURCH

11. (A. wheat, B. bread, C. raillery, D. oat) : CHAFF :: WINE : DREGS

12. DEVIOUS : SPY :: (A. productive, B. orthodox, C. balanced, D. normal) : FARMER

13. EBB : WAX :: SLACKEN : (A. fall, B. spring, C. recede, D. grow)

175

14. DRAMA : (A. class, B. director, C. playwright, D. producer) :: MAGAZINE : EDITOR

15. COMMONPLACE : CLICHÉ :: TERSE : (A. play, B. pun, C. gift, D. maxim)

16. PLEASED : THRILLED :: (A. tipsy, B. lively, C. dumb, D. liberal) : DRUNK

17. (A. stack, B. shrub, C. pine, D. grove) : WILLOW :: THICKET : BLACKBERRY

18. MORAL : (A. civil, B. law, C. sin, D. priest) :: LEGAL : CRIME

19. ELLIPSE : CURVE :: SQUARE : (A. triangle, B. base, C. distance, D. polygon)

20. SILK : RAYON :: (A. cake, B. sugar, C. cane, D. spice) : ASPARTAME

21. REQUEST : (A. respond, B. require, C. inquire, D. demand) :: WISH : CRAVE

22. (A. music, B. CD, C. photograph, D. present) : ALBUM :: MONEY : WALLET

23. WATER : FAUCET :: FUEL : (A. throttle, B. gasoline, C. race, D. speed)

24. HOLOCAUST : FIRE :: (A. murder, B. hanging, C. rope, D. tree) : NOOSE

25. OSCILLATE : (A. fan, B. turn, C. unsure, D. pendulum) :: SPIN : GYROSCOPE

26. HERB : DILL :: CONIFER : (A. berry, B. legume, C. fir, D. fruit)

27. (A. food, B. cerebellum, C. intestine, D. trapezium) : DIGESTIVE :: PORES : EXCRETORY

28. FLASK : BOTTLE :: (A. novel, B. author, C. pamphlet, D. page) : BOOK

29. MONEY : (A. greed, B. finance, C. capitalism, D. avarice) :: FOOD : VORACITY

30. HAIR : BALDNESS :: RAIN : (A. umbrella, B. wet, C. drought, D. spring)

31. (A. boat, B. canoe, C. water, D. cruise) : SHIP :: BOOK : TOME

32. SCYTHE : DEATH :: HEART : (A. blood, B. organ, C. love, D. February)

33. (A. leash, B. kennel, C. cat, D. bone) : DOG :: STALL : HORSE

34. CARNIVORE : ANIMALS :: (A. omnivore, B. vegetarian, C. health, D. minerals) : VEGETABLES

35. LIBEL : SLANDER :: OAK : (A. leaf, B. spruce, C. chair, D. plant)

36. (A. definition, B. etymology, C. entry, D. binding) : DICTIONARY :: NOTE : SCORE

37. MAUVE : (A. color, B. art, C. tan, D. brown) :: BASIL : SPICE

38. MUFFLE : SILENCE :: STYMIE : (A. cover, B. lose, C. loud, D. defeat)

39. WHALE : FISH :: (A. wing, B. fly, C. bat, D. cage) : BIRD

40. (A. word, B. discourse, C. move, D. verb) : ACTION :: PRONOUN : PERSON

41. PLUTOCRAT : WEALTH :: THEOCRAT : (A. industry, B. religion, C. autocrat, D. ruler)

42. NEWS REPORT : (A. editorial, B. newsworthy, C. unpredictable, D. descriptive) :: SECURITY GUARD : PROTECTIVE

43. PROPHYLACTIC : PREVENT :: THERAPEUTIC : (A. clean, B. aspirin, C. cure, D. surgery)

44. RIGGING : ROPE :: SAILS : (A. hewn, B. boat, C. canvas, D. mate)

45. MATRICULATE : GRADUATION :: (A. endow, B. enlist, C. bestowal, D. harvest) : DISCHARGE

46. (A. energy, B. power, C. water, D. electric) : HYDRAULIC :: AIR : PNEUMATIC

47. RABIES : HYDROPHOBIA :: MEASLES : (A. pneumonia, B. rhinitis, C. influenza, D. rubeola)

48. STABLE : (A. hen, B. horse, C. barn, D. coop) :: STY : HOG

49. PETAL : BLOSSOM :: (A. spin, B. vane, C. wind, D. Holland) : WINDMILL

50. ROLE : ACTOR :: POSITION : (A. soldier, B. singer, C. composition, D. ballplayer)

51. (A. *Iliad*, B. *Cinderella*, C. prosody, D. Dickens) : EPIC :: *HAMLET* : TRAGEDY

52. SILO : FODDER :: CASK : (A. corn, B. crops, C. tractor, D. wine)

53. KILT : SARI :: (A. gown, B. tartan, C. man, D. fakir) : WOMAN

54. PROW : (A. train, B. ship, C. wheel, D. beak) :: NOSE : AIRPLANE

55. TRESS : HAIR :: SKEIN : (A. butter, B. wool, C. geese, D. cotton)

56. EPOXY : AFFIX :: (A. crowbar, B. tongs, C. secure, D. proxy) : PRY

57. (A. military, B. authority, C. parent, D. discipline) : ORDER :: TRAINING : PREPARATION

58. SUFFICIENT : OVERABUNDANT :: SCARCE : (A. empty, B. absent, C. abundant, D. few)

59. WATERMARK : (A. stamp, B. paper, C. signal, D. buoy) :: BIRTHMARK : PERSON

60. BRIGHT : BRILLIANT :: (A. sparkly, B. light, C. happy, D. angry) : OVERJOYED

61. XYLOPHONE : PERCUSSION :: BASSOON : (A. wood, B. string, C. wind, D. brass)

62. (A. mare, B. filly, C. deer, D. stallion) : GELDING :: BULL : STEER

63. GRIPPING : PLIERS :: ELEVATING : (A. chisel, B. hammer, C. jack, D. knife)

64. (A. tire, B. radius, C. circumference, D. Earth) : CIRCLE :: SPOKE : WHEEL

65. ZODIAC : (A. Virgo, B. sign, C. day, D. astrology) :: YEAR : MONTH

66. AXIOM : TRANSITIVITY :: THEOREM : (A. sensitivity, B. Pythagorean, C. commutativity, D. geometry)

67. ALLAY : FEARS :: (A. bandage, B. feed, C. pacify, D. carry) : INFANT

68. (A. house, B. door, C. ceiling, D. alcove) : ROOM :: CAVE : MOUNTAIN

69. DINOSAUR : CROCODILE :: WOOLLY MAMMOTH : (A. horse, B. elephant, C. fur, D. exotic)

70. MISDEMEANOR : FELONY :: CRACKED : (A. code, B. safe, C. thief, D. smashed)

71. EROSION : (A. explosion, B. corrosion, C. die, D. flooding) :: CONTAMINATION : POLLUTION

72. (A. hygrometer, B. barometer, C. weather, D. pressure) : HUMIDITY :: THERMOMETER : TEMPERATURE

73. MEAL : REPAST :: DRINK : (A. beverage, B. glass, C. prior, D. later)

74. CULL : INFERIOR :: (A. reject, B. select, C. affect, D. superior) : CHOICE

75. BALLAD : SONG :: BROADLOOM : (A. wreath, B. oil, C. major, D. carpet)

76. (A. herd, B. pride, C. den, D. pod) : WHALES :: BRACE : DUCKS

77. HIGHWAY : (A. chart, B. avenue, C. road map, D. construction) :: HALLWAY : BLUEPRINT

78. MONARCH : REGAL :: SERF : (A. lord, B. lowly, C. courtly, D. royalty)

79. BOLD : COWED :: (A. daring, B. demanding, C. intrepid, D. good) : SATISFIED

80. GALLON : MILK :: YARD : (A. foot, B. bushel, C. fabric, D. stick)

81. (A. epistolary, B. news, C. expository, D. column) : ARTICLE :: NARRATIVE : STORY

82. GOLD : (A. metal, B. silver, C. valuable, D. prospector) :: CLUES : DETECTIVE

83. (A. sucrose, B. sweetener, C. dextrose, D. enzyme) : SUGAR :: FAT : LIPID

84. SWARM : APIARY :: FLOCK : (A. aerie, B. field, C. eagles, D. aviary)

85. LATCH : GATE :: BUCKLE : (A. hasp, B. lock, C. key, D. belt)

86. STYLUS : INCISE :: (A. stiletto, B. penknife, C. sword, D. knead) : WHITTLE

87. COCKPIT : (A. interior, B. propeller, C. tail, D. supportive) :: AILERON : EXTERIOR

88. VICAR : CLERGY :: DRAGOON : (A. Catholic, B. military, C. Protestant, D. rabbi)

89. (A. steal, B. embezzle, C. garner, D. money) : WEALTH :: COLLATE : PAGES

90. (A. street, B. pedestrian, C. downtown, D. walk) : SIDEWALK :: BEACH : BOARDWALK

91. GLUTTON : UNDISCRIMINATING :: GOURMET : (A. epicurean, B. edible, C. selective, D. plenty)

92. COUPLET : POEM :: (A. page, B. sentence, C. epic, D. alphabet) : PARAGRAPH

93. CLIMBER : PEAK :: HUNTER : (A. game, B. rifle, C. bull's-eye, D. camouflage)

94. OIL : (A. water, B. ore, C. well, D. truck) :: SILVER : MINE

95. (A. chalkboard, B. pigments, C. easel, D. canvas) : PALETTE :: TREES : NURSERY

96. SIEVE : FILTER :: COLANDER : (A. drain, B. water, C. drip, D. food)

97. INDUBITABLE : (A. unhappy, B. contradict, C. unlikely, D. false) :: IMMOVABLE : BUDGE

98. (A. doe, B. stallion, C. calf, D. foal) : ROOSTER :: MARE : HEN

99. JUDO : WEAPONS :: SOCCER : (A. football, B. helmets, C. hands, D. clubs)

100. JUDICIAL : ENFORCE :: LEGISLATIVE : (A. veto, B. pass, C. appoint, D. elected)

101. MOTORCYCLE : BICYCLE :: AUTOMOBILE : (A. bus, B. airplane, C. transportation, D. wagon)

102. SAGE : FOX :: (A. brains, B. student, C. school, D. wisdom) : CUNNING

103. (A. guess, B. value, C. calculate, D. worth) : RECOMMEND :: ESTIMATE : SUGGEST

104. ETYMOLOGY : WORDS :: HAGIOLOGY : (A. saints, B. senility, C. selling, D. writing)

105. BRING : BROUGHT :: WRITE : (A. wrought, B. writer, C. writing, D. wrote)

106. (A. eat, B. money, C. dough, D. yeast) : COAL :: BREAD : COKE

107. RAIN : DROP :: SNOW : (A. ice, B. skid, C. icicle, D. flake)

108. ANTWERP : (A. Russia, B. France, C. Belgium, D. Sicily) :: LIMA : PERU

109. BLADE : (A. razor, B. grass, C. knife, D. skate) :: WHEEL : BIKE

110. PEDIATRICS : GERIATRICS :: OBSTETRICS : (A. anthropology, B. medicine, C. biology, D. thanatology)

111. (A. stockbroker, B. finance, C. senator, D. bookkeeper) : ACCOUNTANT :: TYPIST : SECRETARY

112. LAWYER : JUDGE :: (A. messenger, B. typist, C. article, D. reporter) : EDITOR

113. RAISIN : GRAPE :: PRUNE : (A. juice, B. kumquat, C. plum, D. molasses)

114. STARVATION : (A. feed, B. poor, C. energy, D. famine) :: DISEASE : EPIDEMIC

115. (A. counselor, B. court, C. fair, D. scales) : JUSTICE :: HOSPITAL : HEALTH

116. RUNG : LADDER :: STEP : (A. rise, B. run, C. stairway, D. banister)

117. AFTERNOON : DUSK :: (A. evening, B. 2 p.m., C. dark, D. morning) : 5 p.m.

118. VIBRATION : (A. sound, B. lyrics, C. physics, D. music) :: GRAVITY : PULL

119. (A. breathe, B. water, C. hydrogen, D. Saturn) : GAS :: MERCURY : LIQUID

120. BOMB : TARGET :: TRAIN : (A. conductor, B. station, C. passengers, D. track)

ANSWER KEY AND EXPLANATIONS

1. **B**	25. **D**	49. **B**	73. **A**	97. **B**
2. **B**	26. **C**	50. **D**	74. **B**	98. **B**
3. **C**	27. **C**	51. **A**	75. **D**	99. **C**
4. **C**	28. **C**	52. **D**	76. **D**	100. **B**
5. **D**	29. **D**	53. **C**	77. **C**	101. **D**
6. **D**	30. **C**	54. **B**	78. **B**	102. **D**
7. **B**	31. **A**	55. **B**	79. **B**	103. **C**
8. **C**	32. **C**	56. **A**	80. **C**	104. **A**
9. **D**	33. **B**	57. **D**	81. **C**	105. **D**
10. **B**	34. **B**	58. **B**	82. **D**	106. **C**
11. **A**	35. **B**	59. **B**	83. **C**	107. **D**
12. **A**	36. **C**	60. **C**	84. **D**	108. **C**
13. **D**	37. **A**	61. **C**	85. **D**	109. **D**
14. **B**	38. **D**	62. **D**	86. **B**	110. **D**
15. **D**	39. **C**	63. **C**	87. **A**	111. **D**
16. **A**	40. **D**	64. **B**	88. **B**	112. **D**
17. **D**	41. **B**	65. **B**	89. **C**	113. **C**
18. **C**	42. **D**	66. **B**	90. **A**	114. **D**
19. **D**	43. **C**	67. **C**	91. **C**	115. **B**
20. **B**	44. **C**	68. **D**	92. **B**	116. **C**
21. **D**	45. **B**	69. **B**	93. **A**	117. **B**
22. **C**	46. **C**	70. **D**	94. **C**	118. **A**
23. **A**	47. **D**	71. **D**	95. **B**	119. **C**
24. **B**	48. **B**	72. **A**	96. **A**	120. **B**

1. TROT : GALLOP :: LOPE : (A. walk, B. scurry, C. row, D. step)

   The correct answer is (B). A gallop is faster than a trot. Only scurry and lope have a similar speed differential.

2. TRELLIS : PROP :: PILLAR : (A. climb, B. buttress, C. plant, D. sow)

   The correct answer is (B). A trellis may be used to prop a rosebush, as a pillar is used to buttress a structure.

3. (A. gun, B. cola, C. crown, D. wrap) : ROYAL :: CRUCIFIX : RELIGIOUS

   The correct answer is (C). A crown is a royal symbol; a crucifix is a religious symbol.

4. ISLAND : OCEAN :: (A. hill, B. forest, C. oasis, D. tree) : DESERT

   The correct answer is (C). An island is surrounded by the ocean, as an oasis is surrounded by the desert.

5. MATHEMATICS : NUMEROLOGY :: ASTRONOMY : (A. botany, B. physiology, C. medicine, D. astrology)

   The correct answer is (D). Mathematics is the science of numbers, while numerology is the occult study of numbers. Astronomy is the science of celestial bodies, while astrology is the occult study of celestial bodies.

6. BUCOLIC : URBAN :: (A. dense, B. ephemeral, C. plastic, D. mist) : SMOG

   The correct answer is (D). Bucolic relates to rural life and suggests the natural; urban implies the manufactured. Mist is a natural occurrence; smog is fog made foul by smoke and chemical fumes.

7. (A. trustworthy, B. dislikable, C. silly, D. tender) : ABHORRENT :: DIFFICULT : ARDUOUS

   The correct answer is (B). To be abhorrent is to be extremely dislikable; to be arduous is to be extremely difficult.

8. WOOD : CORD :: MILK : (A. pasture, B. industry, C. quart, D. cow)

   The correct answer is (C). Wood may be measured by the cord; milk may be measured by the quart.

9. PLAUSIBLE : (A. deception, B. watertight, C. attractive, D. explanation) :: DEFENSIBLE : THEORY

   The correct answer is (D). An explanation that is plausible is one that is possible or believable—it may or may not be true, but at least it doesn't fly in the face of logic. Similarly, a theory that is defensible is one that knowledgeable people can advocate—it may or may not be true, but at least it makes basic sense.

10. MINARET : MOSQUE :: (A. religion, B. steeple, C. dainty, D. classic) : CHURCH
    The correct answer is (B). A minaret is a high tower attached to a mosque; a steeple is a high structure rising above a church.

11. (A. wheat, B. bread, C. raillery, D. oat) : CHAFF :: WINE : DREGS

    The correct answer is (A). Chaff is the worthless husks of grain left after the threshing of wheat; dregs are the worthless residue created by the process of making wine.

12. DEVIOUS : SPY :: (A. productive, B. orthodox, C. balanced, D. normal) : FARMER

    The correct answer is (A). A spy must be devious in order to succeed; a farmer, to succeed, must be productive.

13. EBB : WAX :: SLACKEN : (A. fall, B. spring, C. recede, D. grow)

    The correct answer is (D). Ebb and wax are opposite motions, as are slacken and grown. Ebb and slacken connote recession, while wax and grown connote expansion. Choices (A) and (B) reverse the order of the analogy.

14. DRAMA : (A. class, B. director, C. playwright, D. producer) :: MAGAZINE : EDITOR

    The correct answer is (B). The director is responsible for the production of a drama; the editor is responsible for the production of a magazine.

15. COMMONPLACE : CLICHÉ :: TERSE : (A. play, B. pun, C. gift, D. maxim)

    The correct answer is (D). A cliché is commonplace; a maxim is terse. The analogy is based on inherent characteristics. A pun may be annoying, but it does not have to be.

16. PLEASED : THRILLED :: (A. tipsy, B. lively, C. dumb, D. liberal) : DRUNK

    The correct answer is (A). To be thrilled is to be extremely pleased; to be drunk is to be extremely tipsy.

17. (A. stack, B. shrub, C. pine, D. grove) : WILLOW :: THICKET : BLACKBERRY

    The correct answer is (D). A collection of willow trees may make up a grove; a collection of blackberry bushes is a type of thicket.

18. MORAL : (A. civil, B. law, C. sin, D. priest) :: LEGAL : CRIME

    The correct answer is (C). A sin is not moral; a crime is not legal.

19. ELLIPSE : CURVE :: SQUARE : (A. triangle, B. base, C. distance, D. polygon)

    The correct answer is (D). An ellipse is a kind of curve; a square is a kind of polygon.

20. SILK : RAYON :: (A. cake, B. sugar, C. cane, D. spice) : ASPARTAME

    The correct answer is (B). Rayon is a manufactured substitute for silk; aspartame is a substitute for sugar.

21. REQUEST : (A. respond, B. require, C. inquire, D. demand) :: WISH : CRAVE

    The correct answer is (D). To demand is to request in a very strong manner; to crave is to wish in a very strong manner.

22. (A. music, B. CD, C. photograph, D. present) : ALBUM :: MONEY : WALLET

    The correct answer is (C). An album holds photographs; a wallet holds money.

23. WATER : FAUCET :: FUEL : (A. throttle, B. gasoline, C. race, D. speed)

    The correct answer is (A). A faucet controls the flow of water; a throttle controls the flow of fuel.

24. HOLOCAUST : FIRE :: (A. murder, B. hanging, C. rope, D. tree) : NOOSE

    The correct answer is (B). A holocaust is death and destruction caused by fire; hanging is death caused by a noose about the neck.

25. OSCILLATE : (A. fan, B. turn, C. unsure, D. pendulum) :: SPIN : GYROSCOPE

    The correct answer is (D). A pendulum oscillates—that is, swings backward and forward; a gyroscope spins.

26. HERB : DILL :: CONIFER : (A. berry, B. legume, C. fir, D. fruit)

    The correct answer is (C). Dill is one kind of herb; fir is one kind of conifer, or cone-producing tree.

27. (A. food, B. cerebellum, C. intestine, D. trapezium) : DIGESTIVE :: PORES : EXCRETORY

    The correct answer is (C). The intestine is part of the digestive system; pores are part of the excretory system.

28. FLASK : BOTTLE :: (A. novel, B. author, C. pamphlet, D. page) : BOOK

    The correct answer is (C). A flask is a small bottle; a pamphlet is a small book.

29. MONEY : (A. greed, B. finance, C. capitalism, D. avarice) :: FOOD : VORACITY

    The correct answer is (D). Avarice is extreme desire, even greed, for money; voracity is extreme desire, even greed, for food.

30. HAIR : BALDNESS :: RAIN : (A. umbrella, B. wet, C. drought, D. spring)

   The correct answer is (C). A lack of hair is baldness; a lack of rain is drought.

31. (A. boat, B. canoe, C. water, D. cruise) : SHIP :: BOOK : TOME

   The correct answer is (A). A ship is a large boat; a tome is a large book.

32. SCYTHE : DEATH :: HEART : (A. blood, B. organ, C. love, D. February)

   The correct answer is (C). A scythe symbolizes death; a heart symbolizes love.

33. (A. leash, B. kennel, C. cat, D. bone) : DOG :: STALL : HORSE

   The correct answer is (B). A kennel is a man-made shelter for dogs; a stall, also man-made, is usually employed to house a horse.

34. CARNIVORE : ANIMALS :: (A. omnivore, B. vegetarian, C. health, D. minerals) : VEGETABLES

   The correct answer is (B). A carnivore eats meat; a vegetarian eats vegetables.

35. LIBEL : SLANDER :: OAK : (A. leaf, B. spruce, C. chair, D. plant)

   The correct answer is (B). Libel is a written defamation of character; slander is a false and defamatory oral statement about a person. Both are forms of defamation. An oak is a deciduous tree; a spruce is a coniferous tree. Both are types of trees.

36. (A. definition, B. etymology, C. entry, D. binding) : DICTIONARY :: NOTE : SCORE

   The correct answer is (C). An entry is the smallest unit in a dictionary; a note is the smallest unit in a musical score.

37. MAUVE : (A. color, B. art, C. tan, D. brown) :: BASIL : SPICE

   The correct answer is (A). Mauve is a color; basil is a spice. This is a simple part-to-whole analogy.

38. MUFFLE : SILENCE :: STYMIE : (A. cover, B. lose, C. loud, D. defeat)

   The correct answer is (D). To muffle something is almost to silence it; to stymie something is almost to defeat it.

39. WHALE : FISH :: (A. wing, B. fly, C. bat, D. cage) : BIRD

   The correct answer is (C). A whale is an aquatic mammal that superficially resembles a fish; a bat is a nocturnal flying mammal that resembles a bird.

40. (A. word, B. discourse, C. move, D. verb) : ACTION :: PRONOUN : PERSON

   The correct answer is (D). A verb can name an action just as a pronoun can name a person.

41. PLUTOCRAT : WEALTH :: THEOCRAT : (A. industry, B. religion, C. autocrat, D. ruler)

   The correct answer is (B). A plutocrat is a ruler distinguished by wealth; a theocrat rules on the basis of religion.

42. NEWS REPORT : (A. editorial, B. newsworthy, C. unpredictable, D. descriptive) :: SECURITY GUARD : PROTECTIVE

   The correct answer is (D). A news report is descriptive of an event; a security guard is protective of an area or person.

43. PROPHYLACTIC : PREVENT :: THERAPEUTIC : (A. clean, B. aspirin, C. cure, D. surgery)

The correct answer is (C). Prophylactic means tending to prevent; therapeutic means tending to cure.

44. RIGGING : ROPE :: SAILS : (A. hewn, B. boat, C. canvas, D. mate)

The correct answer is (C). The rigging on a ship consists mainly of rope; the sails are traditionally made of canvas.

45. MATRICULATE : GRADUATION :: (A. endow, B. enlist, C. bestowal, D. harvest) : DISCHARGE

The correct answer is (B). Matriculation, or enrollment, is the beginning of a process that is meant to end with graduation. Enlistment and discharge are a similar beginning and ending, referring to military service.

46. (A. energy, B. power, C. water, D. electric) : HYDRAULIC :: AIR : PNEUMATIC

The correct answer is (C). The hydraulic system is operated by means of water; the pneumatic system is operated by means of air pressure.

47. RABIES : HYDROPHOBIA :: MEASLES : (A. pneumonia, B. rhinitis, C. influenza, D. rubeola)

The correct answer is (D). Hydrophobia is another name for rabies; rubeola is another name for measles.

48. STABLE : (A. hen, B. horse, C. barn, D. coop) :: STY : HOG

The correct answer is (B). A horse is usually kept and fed in a stable; a hog is usually kept and fed in a sty.

49. PETAL : BLOSSOM :: (A. spin, B. vane, C. wind, D. Holland) : WINDMILL

The correct answer is (B). A blossom is made up of petals, as a windmill is made up of vanes (also called arms), which catch the wind.

50. ROLE : ACTOR :: POSITION : (A. soldier, B. singer, C. composition, D. ballplayer)

The correct answer is (D). An actor plays a role; a ballplayer plays a position.

51. (A. *Iliad*, B. *Cinderella*, C. prosody, D. Dickens) : EPIC :: *HAMLET* : TRAGEDY

The correct answer is (A). *Hamlet* is an example of a tragedy, as the *Iliad* is an example of an epic.

52. SILO : FODDER :: CASK : (A. corn, B. crops, C. tractor, D. wine)

The correct answer is (D). Fodder or silage for animals is stored in a silo; wine is stored in a cask.

53. KILT : SARI :: (A. gown, B. tartan, C. man, D. fakir) : WOMAN

The correct answer is (C). A kilt is a traditional skirt-like garment worn by a man in the Scottish highlands; a sari is a traditional garment worn by a woman in India.

54. PROW : (A. train, B. ship, C. wheel, D. beak) :: NOSE : AIRPLANE

The correct answer is (B). The prow is the forward part of a ship; the nose is the forward part of an airplane.

55. TRESS : HAIR :: SKEIN : (A. butter, B. wool, C. geese, D. cotton)

    The correct answer is (B). A tress is a lock of hair, especially the long unbound hair of a woman; a skein is a loosely coiled length of wool or cotton yarn.

56. EPOXY : AFFIX :: (A. crowbar, B. tongs, C. secure, D. proxy) : PRY

    The correct answer is (A). As epoxy may be used to affix or attach objects, a crowbar may be used to pry them apart. The analogy is based upon function or purpose.

57. (A. military, B. authority, C. parent, D. discipline) : ORDER :: TRAINING : PREPARATION

    The correct answer is (D). Discipline leads to order; training leads to preparation.

58. SUFFICIENT : OVERABUNDANT :: SCARCE : (A. empty, B. absent, C. abundant, D. few)

    The correct answer is (B). Something that is overabundant is more than sufficient; something that is absent is more than scarce. The analogy is one of degree.

59. WATERMARK : (A. stamp, B. paper, C. signal, D. buoy) :: BIRTHMARK : PERSON

    The correct answer is (B). Paper, especially fine stationery, may be identified by a watermark; a person may be identified by a birthmark.

60. BRIGHT : BRILLIANT :: (A. sparkly, B. light, C. happy, D. angry) : OVERJOYED

    The correct answer is (C). Something that is brilliant is extremely bright; someone who is overjoyed is extremely happy.

61. XYLOPHONE : PERCUSSION :: BASSOON : (A. wood, B. string, C. wind, D. brass)

    The correct answer is (C). A xylophone is a percussion instrument; a bassoon is a wind instrument.

62. (A. mare, B. filly, C. deer, D. stallion) : GELDING :: BULL : STEER

    The correct answer is (D). A stallion is an adult male horse, while a gelding is a castrated horse. Similarly, a bull is an adult male bovine, while a steer is a bovine animal castrated before sexual maturity.

63. GRIPPING : PLIERS :: ELEVATING : (A. chisel, B. hammer, C. jack, D. knife)

    The correct answer is (C). Pliers are tools designed specifically for gripping; a jack is a tool specially designed for elevating.

64. (A. tire, B. radius, C. circumference, D. Earth) : CIRCLE :: SPOKE : WHEEL

    The correct answer is (B). A radius extends from the center of a circle to its edge; a spoke extends from the center of a wheel to its edge.

65. ZODIAC : (A. Virgo, B. sign, C. day, D. astrology) :: YEAR : MONTH

    The correct answer is (B). The zodiac has 12 signs; the year has 12 months.

66. AXIOM : TRANSITIVITY :: THEOREM : (A. sensitivity, B. Pythagorean, C. commutativity, D. geometry)

    The correct answer is (B). Transitivity is an axiom; the Pythagorean theorem is a theorem in geometry.

answers practice test 8

67. ALLAY : FEARS :: (A. bandage, B. feed, C. pacify, D. carry) : INFANT

    The correct answer is (C). To allay fears is to alleviate or subdue them; to pacify an infant is to calm the infant.

68. (A. house, B. door, C. ceiling, D. alcove) : ROOM :: CAVE : MOUNTAIN

    The correct answer is (D). An alcove is a small, recessed section of a room; a cave is a chamber in a mountain.

69. DINOSAUR : CROCODILE :: WOOLLY MAMMOTH : (A. horse, B. elephant, C. fur, D. exotic)

    The correct answer is (B). The dinosaur is an extinct relative of the crocodile; the woolly mammoth is an extinct relative of the elephant.

70. MISDEMEANOR : FELONY :: CRACKED : (A. code, B. safe. C. thief, D. smashed)

    The correct answer is (D). A misdemeanor, though illegal, is not so serious a crime as is a felony. Though something that is cracked is damaged, it is not so seriously damaged as a smashed object.

71. EROSION : (A. explosion, B. corrosion, C. die, D. flooding) :: CONTAMINATION : POLLUTION

    The correct answer is (D). Flooding can cause erosion. Pollution can cause contamination.

72. (A. hygrometer, B. barometer, C. weather, D. pressure) : HUMIDITY :: THERMOMETER : TEMPERATURE

    The correct answer is (A). A hygrometer is used to measure humidity; a thermometer is used to measure temperature.

73. MEAL : REPAST :: DRINK : (A. beverage, B. glass, C. prior, D. later)

    The correct answer is (A). A meal can also be called a repast. A drink can also be called a beverage.

74. CULL : INFERIOR :: (A. reject, B. select, C. affect, D. superior) : CHOICE

    The correct answer is (B). To cull is to remove what is inferior, or worthless; to select is to pick out the choice, the best.

75. BALLAD : SONG :: BROADLOOM : (A. wreath, B. oil, C. major, D. carpet)

    The correct answer is (D). A ballad is a type of song; broadloom is a kind of carpet.

76. (A. herd, B. pride, C. den, D. pod) : WHALES :: BRACE : DUCKS

    The correct answer is (D). A group of whales is a pod; a group of ducks is a brace.

77. HIGHWAY : (A. chart, B. avenue, C. road map, D. construction) :: HALLWAY : BLUEPRINT

    The correct answer is (C). An architect's blueprint would show the location of a hallway, much as a road map shows the location of a highway.

78. MONARCH : REGAL :: SERF : (A. lord, B. lowly, C. courtly, D. royalty)

    The correct answer is (B). A monarch is a ruler; a serf is a peasant. Only regal and lowly repeat this contrast.

79. BOLD : COWED :: (A. daring, B. demanding, C. intrepid, D. good) : SATISFIED

The correct answer is (B). Someone who is bold is not easily cowed; someone who is demanding is not easily satisfied.

80. GALLON : MILK :: YARD : (A. foot, B. bushel, C. fabric, D. stick)

The correct answer is (C). Milk may be sold by the gallon. The other combinations of goods and measurements are unlikely except for fabric, which tends to be sold by the yard.

81. (A. epistolary, B. news, C. expository, D. column) : ARTICLE :: NARRATIVE : STORY

The correct answer is (C). An article is a form of expository writing; a story is a form of narrative writing.

82. GOLD : (A. metal, B. silver, C. valuable, D. prospector) :: CLUES : DETECTIVE

The correct answer is (D). A prospector looks for gold; a detective looks for clues.

83. (A. sucrose, B. sweetener, C. dextrose, D. enzyme) : SUGAR :: FAT : LIPID

The correct answer is (C). Dextrose is a kind of sugar; fat is a kind of lipid.

84. SWARM : APIARY :: FLOCK : (A. aerie, B. field, C. eagles, D. aviary)

The correct answer is (D). You would expect to see a swarm of bees in an apiary, or collection of hives. You would expect to see a flock of birds in an aviary.

85. LATCH : GATE :: BUCKLE : (A. hasp, B. lock, C. key, D. belt)

The correct answer is (D). A latch may fasten a gate, as a buckle fastens a belt.

86. STYLUS : INCISE :: (A. stiletto, B. penknife, C. sword, D. knead) : WHITTLE

The correct answer is (B). Cutting motions have different names depending on the tool used. A stylus is used to incise, but a penknife may be used to whittle.

87. COCKPIT : (A. interior, B. propeller, C. tail, D. supportive) :: AILERON : EXTERIOR

The correct answer is (A). The cockpit is an interior section of an airplane; an aileron is on an airplane's exterior, on its wings.

88. VICAR : CLERGY :: DRAGOON : (A. Catholic, B. military, C. Protestant, D. rabbi)

The correct answer is (B). A vicar is a member of the clergy; a dragoon is a member of the military.

89. (A. steal, B. embezzle, C. garner, D. money) : WEALTH :: COLLATE : PAGES

The correct answer is (C). One would garner (gather) wealth; one would collate (assemble) pages.

90. (A. street, B. pedestrian, C. downtown, D. walk) : SIDEWALK :: BEACH : BOARDWALK

The correct answer is (A). A street is paralleled by a sidewalk, a walkway for pedestrians. A beach is paralleled by a boardwalk, also a walkway for pedestrians.

91. GLUTTON : UNDISCRIMINATING :: GOURMET : (A. epicurean, B. edible, C. selective, D. plenty)

The correct answer is (C). A glutton is undiscriminating in his or her love of food; a gourmet is highly selective in choice of food.

92. COUPLET : POEM :: (A. page, B. sentence, C. epic, D. alphabet) : PARAGRAPH

The correct answer is (B). A couplet may be part of a poem; a sentence may be part of a paragraph.

93. CLIMBER : PEAK :: HUNTER : (A. game, B. rifle, C. bull's-eye, D. camouflage)

The correct answer is (A). A climber seeks to reach the peak; a hunter seeks game.

94. OIL : (A. water, B. ore, C. well, D. truck) :: SILVER : MINE

The correct answer is (C). Oil is extracted from the earth by means of a well; silver is extracted by means of a mine.

95. (A. chalkboard, B. pigments, C. easel, D. canvas) : PALETTE :: TREES : NURSERY

The correct answer is (B). A palette holds a variety of pigments; a nursery contains a variety of trees.

96. SIEVE : FILTER :: COLANDER : (A. drain, B. water, C. drip, D. food)

The correct answer is (A). A colander is used to drain food; a sieve is used to filter.

97. INDUBITABLE : (A. unhappy, B. contradict, C. unlikely, D. false) :: IMMOVABLE : BUDGE

The correct answer is (B). If something is indubitable, you cannot contradict it; if something is immovable, you cannot budge it.

98. (A. doe, B. stallion, C. calf, D. foal) : ROOSTER :: MARE : HEN

The correct answer is (B). A stallion and a rooster are two different animals of the same sex, as are a mare and a hen.

99. JUDO : WEAPONS :: SOCCER : (A. football, B. helmets, C. hands, D. clubs)

The correct answer is (C). In judo, participants use no weapons; in soccer, players (with the exception of the goalie) may not use their hands.

100. JUDICIAL : ENFORCE :: LEGISLATIVE : (A. veto, B. pass, C. appoint, D. elected)

The correct answer is (B). A judicial function is to enforce laws; a legislative function is to pass laws.

101. MOTORCYCLE : BICYCLE :: AUTOMOBILE : (A. bus, B. airplane, C. transportation, D. wagon)

The correct answer is (D). A motorcycle is a technologically sophisticated bicycle; an automobile is similarly related to a wagon.

102. SAGE : FOX :: (A. brains, B. student, C. school, D. wisdom) : CUNNING

The correct answer is (D). A fox is known for its cunning; a sage is known for his or her wisdom.

103. (A. guess, B. value, C. calculate, D. worth) : RECOMMEND :: ESTIMATE : SUGGEST

The correct answer is (C). To recommend is stronger and more compelling than to suggest; to calculate is much more accurate and specific than to estimate.

104. ETYMOLOGY : WORDS :: HAGIOLOGY : (A. saints, B. senility, C. selling, D. writing)

The correct answer is (A). It is hard to get away from definition or at least association. Etymology is the study of words; hagiology is the study of saints.

105. BRING : BROUGHT :: WRITE : (A. wrought, B. writer, C. writing, D. wrote)

The correct answer is (D). BRING : BROUGHT :: WRITE : WROTE :: present : past. Avoid the temptation to choose a relationship based only upon sound before looking for meaningful relationships.

106. (A. eat, B. money, C. dough, D. yeast) : COAL :: BREAD : COKE

The correct answer is (C). Coke is a byproduct that follows coal; bread is the product that follows dough. The relationship is strictly sequential. The dough and coal are related only insofar as they precede bread and coke.

107. RAIN : DROP :: SNOW : (A. ice, B. skid, C. icicle, D. flake)

The correct answer is (D). Rain falls in drops; snow falls in flakes. The relationship is whole to part.

108. ANTWERP : (A. Russia, B. France, C. Belgium, D. Sicily) :: LIMA : PERU

The correct answer is (C). Antwerp is a city in Belgium; Lima is a city in Peru.

109. BLADE : (A. razor, B. grass, C. knife, D. skate) :: WHEEL : BIKE

The correct answer is (D). A blade on a skate touches the ground; a wheel on a bike touches the ground.

110. PEDIATRICS : GERIATRICS :: OBSTETRICS : (A. anthropology, B. medicine, C. biology, D. thanatology)

The correct answer is (D). Pediatrics deals with children; geriatrics deals with the aged. Similarly, obstetrics deals with birth, and thanatology deals with death.

111. (A. stockbroker, B. finance, C. senator, D. bookkeeper) : ACCOUNTANT :: TYPIST : SECRETARY

The correct answer is (D). A bookkeeper is a novice accountant as a typist is a novice secretary. The relationship is cause and effect.

112. LAWYER : JUDGE :: (A. messenger, B. typist, C. article, D. reporter) : EDITOR

The correct answer is (D). A lawyer may become a judge; a reporter may become an editor. The relationship is the ultimate of accomplishments for the professional.

113. RAISIN : GRAPE :: PRUNE : (A. juice, B. kumquat, C. plum, D. molasses)

The correct answer is (C). A raisin is a dried grape; a prune is a dried plum. The relationship is object to outcome.

114. STARVATION : (A. feed, B. poor, C. energy, D. famine) :: DISEASE : EPIDEMIC

The correct answer is (D). Starvation is associated with famine as disease is associated with an epidemic. The relationship is object to outcome.

115. (A. counselor, B. court, C. fair, D. scales) : JUSTICE :: HOSPITAL : HEALTH

The correct answer is (B). One seeks justice in court and health in a hospital. The relationship is cause and effect.

116. RUNG : LADDER :: STEP : (A. rise, B. run, C. stairway, D. banister)

The correct answer is (C). A rung is part of a ladder as a step is part of a stairway. They are both used to go up and down.

117. AFTERNOON : DUSK :: (A. evening, B. 2 p.m., C. dark, D. morning) : 5 p.m.

The correct answer is (B). Afternoon is to dusk as 2 p.m. is to 5 p.m. 2 p.m. is usually afternoon; 5 p.m. can be dusk. The relationship is synonymous.

118. VIBRATION : (A. sound, B. lyrics, C. physics, D. music) :: GRAVITY : PULL

The correct answer is (A). A vibration causes sound; gravity causes a pull. The relationship is object to effect.

119. (A. breathe, B. water, C. hydrogen, D. Saturn) : GAS :: MERCURY : LIQUID

The correct answer is (C). Hydrogen is a gas; mercury is a liquid. Both hydrogen and mercury are elements. The relationship is part to whole.

120. BOMB : TARGET :: TRAIN : (A. conductor, B. station, C. passengers, D. track)

The correct answer is (B). A bomb travels to a target as a train travels to a station. The relationship is object to outcome.

APPENDIXES

Mythology

The Greeks had the most highly developed mythology, in terms of genealogy, personalities, and lifestyles of the gods. Roman mythology closely parallels Greek mythology; many of the gods and goddesses are counterparts of Greek gods. The other highly developed European mythology is Norse mythology, which developed independently from the Greeks and Romans but, because mythology existed to explain the same phenomena in each society, has many similarities.

The Greek gods lived on Mt. Olympus. Roman gods had no comparable dwelling place. The home of the Norse gods was at Asgard, where the dining hall of the heroes was Valhalla and the private dining room of the gods was Gimli.

Kronos and Rhea were parents of the six original Greek gods; their Roman counterparts are Saturn and Ops. The original Greek gods were:

Zeus—King of the gods; comparable to the Roman Jupiter and the Norse Odin.

Hera—Both sister and wife of Zeus and queen of the gods; comparable to the Roman Juno, wife of Jupiter, and the Norse Frigg or Frigga, wife of Odin.

Poseidon—Ruler of the sea and of earthquakes; comparable to the Roman Neptune and to the Norse Njord.

Hades—Ruler of the dead and god of wealth; comparable to the Roman Pluto.

Demeter—Goddess of agriculture; comparable to the Roman Ceres.

Hestia—Goddess of the hearth; comparable to the Roman Vesta.

appendix a

Parentage of some of the "younger" Greek gods is consistent from myth to myth. Some of the most important gods of consistently acknowledged parentage are these:

Athene or Athena—Goddess who "sprung full-blown from the head of Zeus"; goddess of wisdom, cities, heroes in war, and handicrafts. Her Roman counterpart, Minerva, had the same miraculous birth.

Persephone—Daughter of Zeus and Demeter; goddess of agriculture (like her mother) and queen of the dead; wife of Hades; comparable to the Roman Proserpina.

Apollo and Artemis—Twin children of Zeus and Leto. Apollo, god of prophesy, music, and medicine, is a god of purification and giver of oracles. Apollo's name carries over into Roman mythology, where his twin sister is Diana. Apollo's Norse counterpart is Freyr, twin brother of Freya. Artemis is goddess of the moon and of the hunt as well as of woods, meadows, wild animals, and fertility. Artemis has a Roman counterpart in Diana. Freya, goddess of love and beauty, though Freyr's twin sister, is more comparable to Aphrodite.

Hermes—Son of Zeus and Maia; herald of the gods and leader of men, god of trade and eloquence. Hermes's Roman counterpart is Mercury.

Ares—Son of Zeus and Hera; god of war, with a Roman counterpart, Mars.

Dionysus—Son of Zeus and Semele; god of wine and joy; comparable to Roman Bacchus.

Some gods and goddesses of disputed or unknown parentage include these:

Aphrodite—Goddess of sexual love; comparable to the Roman Venus and to the Norse Freya.

Hephaistos—God of fire and thunderbolts, the divine smith and craftsman; comparable to the Roman Vulcan.

Adonis—God of male beauty, vegetation, and rebirth.

Phoebus Apollos—Driver of the sun's chariot in its daily journey across the sky.

Eos—Goddess of the dawn; comparable to the Roman Aurora.

Hebe—God of youth; comparable to the Roman Juventas.

Hypnos—God of sleep; comparable to the Roman Somnus.

Pan—God of woods and fields; comparable to the Roman Faunus.

Thanatos—God of death; comparable to the Roman Mors.

Nike—Goddess of victory; comparable to the Roman Victoria.

Mythology, especially Greek mythology, often makes references to personifications in groups. In some groups, the individuals have distinctive names. Some of the most common are these:

Muses:

Calliope—Muse of epic poetry

Clio—Muse of history

Erato—Muse of love songs and love poetry

Euterpe—Muse of lyric poetry and flute playing

Melpomene—Muse of music, song, and tragedy

Polyhymnia—Muse of serious poetry and hymns, of mime, and of geometry

Terpischore—Muse of choral dancing and choral singing

Thalia—Muse of comedy

Urania—Muse of astronomy and astrology

Fates:

Atropos—Cutter of the thread; comparable to the Roman Morta

Clotho—Spinner of the thread of life; comparable to the Roman Nona

Lachesis—Determiner of the length; comparable to the Roman Decuma

Furies:

Alecto—Unending

Tisiphone—Retaliation

Megaera—Envy

Graces:

Aglaia—Brilliance

Euphrosyne—Joy

Thalia—Bloom

Winds:

Aeolus—Keeper of the winds

Boreas—The north wind

Eurus—The east wind

Notus—The south wind

Zephyrus—The west wind

Half-people, half-animals:

Centaur—Head and torso of a man, lower half of a horse

Harpy—Head of a woman, body of a bird

Minotaur—Head of a man, body of a bull

Satyr—Head and torso of a man, lower half of a goat

Minor deities of nature:

Dryads—Tree nymphs

Naiads—Water, stream, and fountain nymphs

Napaeae—Wood nymphs

Nereids—Sea nymphs

Oceanids—Ocean nymphs

Oreads—Mountain nymphs

Rivers of the Underworld:

Acheron—Woe

Cocytus—Wailing

Lethe—Forgetfulness

Phlegethon—Fire

Styx—The last river that souls must cross

Mathematics

Some mathematical analogy questions draw upon specific knowledge of algebra, geometry, trigonometry, and calculus. In order to answer these questions, you must have real understanding of the various branches of mathematics. Other mathematical analogies rest upon a more generalized or superficial understanding of the mathematics, with perhaps more complex reasoning required. The following tables compile in one easy reference the general mathematical information you are most likely to find useful.

ROMAN NUMERALS

I = 1	D = 500	$\overline{C}$ = 100,000
V = 5	M = 1,000	$\overline{D}$ = 500,000
X = 10	$\overline{V}$ = 5,000	$\overline{M}$ = 1,000,000
L = 50	$\overline{X}$ = 10,000	
C = 100	$\overline{L}$ = 50,000	

RULES

1. A letter repeated once or twice repeats its value that many times. (XXX = 30; MM = 2,000)

2. One or more letters placed after another letter of greater value increases the greater value by the amount of the smaller. (XII = 12; DCX = 610)

3. A letter placed before another letter of greater value decreases the greater value by the amount of the smaller. (IX = 9; CD = 400)

General Measures

Time	Angles and Arcs	Counting
1 minute (min) = 60 seconds (sec)	1 minute (′) = 60 seconds (″)	1 dozen (doz) = 12 units
1 hour (hr) = 60 minutes	1 degree (°) = 60 minutes	1 gross (gr) = 12 dozen
1 day = 24 hours	1 circle = 360°	1 gross = 144 units
1 week = 7 days		
1 year = 52 weeks		
1 calendar year = 365 days		

THE METRIC SYSTEM

Length

Unit	Abbreviation	Number of Meters
myriameter	mym	10,000
kilometer	km	1,000
hectometer	hm	100
dekameter	dam	10
meter	m	1
decimeter	dm	0.1
centimeter	cm	0.01
millimeter	mm	0.001

Area

Unit	Abbreviation	Number of Square Meters
square kilometer	sq km or km^2	1,000,000
hectare	ha	10,000
are	a	100
centare	ca	1
square centimeter	sq cm or cm^2	0.0001

Volume

Unit	Abbreviation	Number of Cubic Meters
dekastere	das	10
stere	s	1
decistere	ds	0.10
cubic centimeter	cu cm *or* cm³ *or* cc	0.000001

Capacity

Unit	Abbreviation	Number of Liters
kiloliter	kl	1,000
hectoliter	hl	100
dekaliter	dal	10
liter	l	1
deciliter	dl	0.10
centiliter	cl	0.01
milliliter	ml	0.001

Mass and Weight

Unit	Abbreviation	Number of Grams
metric ton	MT *or* t	1,000,000
quintal	q	100,000
kilogram	kg	1,000
hectogram	hg	100
dekagram	dag	10
gram	g *or* gm	1
decigram	dg	0.10
centigram	cg	0.01
milligram	mg	0.001

Temperature

Scale	Abbreviation	Degrees
Celsius *or* Centigrade	°C	Freezing Point 0°C
		Boiling Point 100°C

U.S. MEASURES

Length

1 foot (ft *or* ') = 12 inches (in *or* ")
1 yard (yd) = 36 inches
1 yard = 3 feet
1 rod (rd) = 16 feet
1 mile (mi) = 5,280 feet
1 mile = 1,760 yards
1 mile = 320 rods

Weight

1 pound (lb) = 16 ounces (oz)
1 hundredweight (cwt) = 100 pounds
1 ton (T) = 2,000 pounds

Area

1 square foot (ft^2) = 144 square inches (in^2)
1 square yard (yd^2) = 9 feet

Temperature

Scale	Abbreviation	Degrees
Fahrenheit	°F	Freezing Point 32°F Boiling Point 212°F

Capacity (Liquid)

1 cup (c) = 8 fluid ounces (fl oz)
1 pint (pt) = 2 cups
1 pint = 4 gills (gi)
1 quart (qt) = 2 pints
1 gallon (gal) = 4 quarts
1 barrel (bbl) = 31 gallons

Capacity (Dry)

1 quart (qt) = 2 pints (pt)

1 peck (pk) = 8 quarts

1 bushel (bu) = 4 pecks

Volume

1 cubic foot (ft^3 or cu ft) = 1,728 cubic inches

1 cubic yard (yd^3 or cu yd) = 27 cubic feet

1 gallon = 231 cubic inches

Table of U.S./Metric Conversions (Approximate)

U.S. to Metric	Metric to U.S.	Table of Metric Conversions*
1 inch = 2.54 centimeters	1 centimeter = .39 inch	1 liter = 1,000 cubic centimeters (cm^3)
1 yard = .9 meter	1 meter = 1.1 yards	1 milliliter = 1 cubic centimeter
1 mile = 1.6 kilometers	1 kilometer = .6 mile	
1 ounce = 28 grams	1 kilogram = 2.2 pounds	1 liter of water weighs 1 kilogram
1 pound = 454 grams	1 liter = 1.06 liquid quart	1 milliliter of water weighs 1 gram
1 fluid ounce = 30 milliliters	Celsius to Fahrenheit =	
1 liquid quart = .95 liters	$(°C \times \frac{9}{5}) + 32°$	
32°F = 0°C	100°C = 212°F	
212°F = 100°C		
Fahrenheit to Celsius =		
$(°F - 32°) \times \frac{5}{9}$		

* These conversions are exact only under specific conditions. If the conditions are not met, the conversions are approximate.

Nations of the World

Over the course of history, many nations of the world have changed identities and alliances as well as borders and governments. A brief course in world history and geography is a logical impossibility, but this selective list of some of today's nations and their previous identities and affiliations might prove helpful for the sequential and the language-spoken types of analogy questions.

Current Name	Previous Name or Names
Algeria	Ancient Numidia (French)
Angola	Portuguese West Africa
Armenia	Armenian S.S.R. . . . Transcaucasian S.S.R. . . . Transcaucasian Federation . . . Armenia . . . Persia
Azerbaijan	Azerbaijan S.S.R. . . . Transcaucasian S.R.R. . . . Transcaucasian Federation . . . Persia . . . ancient Albania
Bangladesh	East Pakistan . . . British India
Belarus	Byelorussia . . . White Russia
Belize	British Honduras
Benin	Dahomey (French)
Bosnia-Herzegovina	Yugoslavia . . . Serbia
Botswana	Bechuanaland (English)
Burkina Faso	Upper Volta (French)
Burundi	Ruanda-Urundi . . . Belgian Congo . . . German East Africa
Cambodia	Kampuchea . . . Khmer Republic . . . French Indo-China
Central African Republic	Central African Empire . . . French Equatorial Africa . . . Ubangi-Shari
Chad	French Equatorial Africa
Congo (capital: Brazzaville)	Middle Congo (French)

Current Name	Previous Name or Names
Congo (capital: Kinshasa).........	Zaire . . . Belgian Congo . . . Congo Free State
Croatia........................	Yugoslavia
Czech Republic	Czechoslovakia . . . Czechoslovak Austria-Hungary
Djibouti.......................	Afars and Issas . . . French Somaliland
East Timor.....................	Portuguese Timor . . . Indonesia
England........................	Ancient Albion
Equatorial Guinea...............	Spanish Guinea
Estonia........................	Estonian S.S.R. . . . Estonia . . . Sweden . . . Germany
Ethiopia.......................	Ancient Abyssinia . . . Italian East Africa
France.........................	Ancient Gaul
Gabon..........................	French Equatorial Africa
Georgia........................	Georgian S.S.R. . . . Transcaucasian S.S.R. . . . Transcaucasian Federation
Germany........................	Prussia and many independent kingdoms
Ghana..........................	Gold Coast (English)
Greece.........................	Ancient Hellas . . . Ottoman Empire
Guinea.........................	French Guinea
Guinea-Bissau..................	Portuguese Guinea
Guyana.........................	British Guiana
Indonesia......................	Netherlands East Indies . . . Dutch East Indies
Iran...........................	Persia
Iraq...........................	Ancient Babylonia and Assyria . . . ancient Mesopotamia . . . Ottoman Empire
Israel.........................	Palestine . . . ancient Canaan
Jordan.........................	Palestine . . . Transjordan . . . ancient Edom and Moab
Kazakhstan	Kazakh S.S.R.
Kiribati.......................	Gilbert Islands (English)
Kyrgyzstan.....................	Kirghiz S.S.R.
Lao People's Democratic Republic..	French Indo-China
Latvia.........................	Latvian S.S.R. . . . Latvia . . . Russia . . . Poland
Lesotho........................	Basutoland (English)
Lithuania......................	Lithuanian S.S.R. . . . Lithuania . . . Russia . . . Poland
Macedonia......................	Yugoslavia . . . Bulgaria . . . Greece
Madagascar	Malagasy Republic (French)

Current Name	Previous Name or Names
Malawi	Nyasaland (English)
Malaysia	Malaya and Sabah (North Borneo) and Sarawak (English)
Mali	French Sudan
Moldova	Moldovan S.S.R. . . . Moldavia . . . Turkey . . . Romania . . . Bessarabia
Mongolia	Outer Mongolia
Mozambique	Portuguese East Africa
Myanmar	Burma . . . British India
Namibia	Southwest Africa . . . German Southwest Africa (English and Afrikaans)
Niger	French West Africa
Oman	Muscat and Oman (Portuguese)
Pakistan	West Pakistan . . . British India
Papua New Guinea	Territory of Papua and New Guinea (English, German)
Portugal	Part of Spain
Russian Federation	Leader of the Union of Soviet Socialist Republics (U.S.S.R.), a.k.a. Soviet Union, which at one time included a large number of states such as Estonia, Georgia, Kazakhstan, Kyrgyzstan, Latvia, Lithuania, and the Ukraine
Rwanda	Ruanda-Urundi . . . Belgian Congo . . . German East Africa
Senegal	French West Africa
Slovakia	Czechoslovakia . . . Austria-Hungary
Slovenia	Yugoslavia
Somalia	Somaliland (English)
Spain	Ancient Iberia
Sri Lanka	Ceylon (English)
Sudan	Anglo-Egyptian Sudan . . . ancient Nubia
Suriname	Dutch Guiana
Switzerland	Ancient Helvetia
Taiwan	Formosa
Tajikistan	Tajik S.S.R. . . . Afghanistan . . . Persia
Thailand	Siam
Togo	Togoland (French)
Tunisia	Ancient Carthage (French)

Current Name	Previous Name or Names
Turkmenistan	Turkmen S.S.R. . . . Turkmenia . . . ancient Persia
Tuvalu	Ellice Islands (English)
Ukraine	Ukrainian S.S.R. . . . Ukrainian National Republic . . . Russia
United Arab Emirates	Trucial Oman, Trucial States, which were: Abu Dhabi, Ash Shariqah, Ras al Khaymah, Dubayy, Ajman, al Fujayrah, and Umm al Qaywayn
United Republic of Tanzania	Tanganyika and Zanzibar (English)
Uzbekistan	Uzbekistan S.S.R. . . . Uzbek Republic . . . ancient Persia
Vanuatu	New Hebrides (French and English)
Vietnam	French Indo-China
Yemen	(English) . . . Ottoman Empire
Yugoslavia (includes Serbia and Montenegro)	Yugoslavia including Croatia, Bosnia-Herzegovina, Slovenia, and Macedonia
Zambia	Northern Rhodesia (English)
Zimbabwe	Rhodesia (English)

Vocabulary

A

abbreviate (verb) To make briefer, to shorten. *Because time was running out, the speaker was forced to abbreviate his remarks.* abbreviation (noun).

aberration (noun) A deviation from what is normal or natural, an abnormality. *Jack's extravagant lunch at Lutece was an aberration from his usual meal, a peanut butter sandwich and a diet soda.* aberrant (adjective).

abeyance (noun) A temporary lapse in activity; suspension. *In the aftermath of the bombing, all normal activities were held in abeyance.*

abjure (verb) To renounce or reject; to officially disclaim. *While being tried by the inquisition in 1633, Galileo abjured all his writings holding that the Earth and other planets revolved around the sun.*

abrade (verb) To irritate by rubbing; to wear down in spirit. *Olga's "conditioning facial" abraded Sabrina's skin so severely that she vowed never to let anyone's hands touch her face again.* abrasion (noun).

abridge (verb) To shorten, to reduce. The Bill of Rights *is designed to prevent Congress from abridging the rights of Americans.* abridgment (noun).

abrogate (verb) To nullify, to abolish. *During World WarII, the United States abrogated the rights of Japanese Americans by detaining them in internment camps.* abrogation (noun).

abscond (verb) To make a secret departure, to elope. *Theresa will never forgive her daughter, Elena, for absconding to Miami with Philip when they were only 17.*

accretion (noun) A gradual build-up or enlargement. *My mother's house is a mess due to her steady accretion of bric-a-brac and her inability to throw anything away.*

adjunct (noun) Something added to another thing, but not a part of it; an associate or assistant. *While Felix and Fritz were adjuncts to Professor Himmelman during his experiments in electrodynamics, they did not receive credit when the results were published.*

adroit (adjective) Skillful, adept. *The writer Laurie Colwin was particularly adroit at concocting love stories involving admirable and quirky female heroines and men who deserve them.*

adulterate (verb) To corrupt, to make impure. *Unlike the chickens from the large poultry companies, Murray's free-roaming chickens have not been adulterated with hormones and other additives.*

adversary (noun) An enemy or opponent. *When the former Soviet Union became an American ally, the United States lost its last major international adversary.* adverse (adjective).

aesthete (noun) Someone devoted to beauty and to beautiful things. *A renowned aesthete, Oscar Wilde was the center of a group that glorified beauty and adopted the slogan "art for art's sake."* aesthetic (adjective).

affability (noun) The quality of being easy to talk to and gracious. *Affability is a much-desired trait in any profession that involves dealing with many people on a daily basis.* affable (adjective).

affected (adjective) False, artificial. *At one time, Japanese women were taught to speak in an affected high-pitched voice, which was thought girlishly attractive.* affect (verb), affectation (noun).

affinity (noun) A feeling of shared attraction, kinship; a similarity. *When they first fell in love, Andrew and Tanya marveled over their affinity for bluegrass music, obscure French poetry, and beer taken with a squirt of lemon juice. People often say there is a striking affinity between dogs and their owners (but please don't tell Clara that she and her bassett hound are starting to resemble each other).*

aggrandize (verb) To make bigger or greater; to inflate. *When he was mayor of New York City, Ed Koch was renowned for aggrandizing his accomplishments and strolling through city events shouting, "How'm I doing?"* aggrandizement (noun).

agitation (noun) A disturbance; a disturbing feeling of upheaval and excitement. *After the CEO announced the coming layoffs, the employees' agitation was evident as they remained in the auditorium talking excitedly among themselves.* agitated (adjective), agitate (verb).

alias (noun) An assumed name. *Determined not to reveal his upper-class roots, Harold Steerforth Hetherington III went under the alias of "Hound Dog" when playing trumpet in his blues band.*

allegiance (noun) Loyalty or devotion shown to one's government or to a person, group, or cause. *At the moving naturalization ceremony, forty-three new Americans from twenty-five lands swore allegiance to the United States.*

allocate (verb) To apportion for a specific purpose; to distribute. *The president talked about the importance of education and health care in his State of the Union address, but, in the end, the administration did not allocate enough resources for these pressing concerns.* allocation (noun).

amalgamate (verb) To blend thoroughly. *The tendency of grains to sort when they should mix makes it difficult for manufacturers to create powders that are amalgamated.* amalgamation (noun).

ameliorate (verb) To make something better or more tolerable. *The living conditions of the tenants were certainly ameliorated when the landlord finally installed washing machines and dryers in the basement.* amelioration (noun).

amortize (verb) To pay off or reduce a debt gradually through periodic payments. *If you don't need to take a lump sum tax deduction, it's best to amortize large business expenditures by spreading the cost out over several years.*

amplify (verb) To enlarge, expand, or increase. *Uncertain as to whether they understood, the students asked the teacher to amplify his explanation.* amplification (noun).

anachronistic (adjective) Out of the proper time. *The reference, in Shakespeare's* Julius Caesar, *to "the clock striking twelve" is anachronistic, since there were no striking timepieces in ancient Rome.* anachronism (noun).

anarchy (noun) Absence of law or order. *For several months after the Nazi government was destroyed, there was no effective government in parts of Germany, and anarchy ruled.* anarchic (adjective).

animosity (noun) Hostility, resentment. *During the last debate, the candidates could no longer disguise their animosity and began to trade accusations and insults.*

anomaly (noun) Something different or irregular. *The tiny planet Pluto, orbiting next to the giants Jupiter, Saturn, and Neptune, has long appeared to be an anomaly.* anomalous (adjective).

antagonism (noun) Hostility, conflict, opposition. *As more and more reporters investigated the Watergate scandal, antagonism between the Nixon administration and the press increased.* antagonistic (adjective), antagonize (verb).

WORD ORIGIN

Greek *chronos* = time. Also found in English *chronic*, *chronicle*, *chronograph*, *chronology*, and *synchronize*.

WORD ORIGIN

Greek *pathos* = suffering. Also found in English *apathy, empathy, pathetic, pathos,* and *sympathy*.

antipathy (noun) A long-held feeling of dislike or aversion. *When asked why he didn't call for help immediately after his wife fell into a coma, the defendant emphasized his wife's utter antipathy to doctors.*

apprehension (noun) A feeling of fear or foreboding; an arrest. *The peculiar feeling of apprehension that Harold Pinter creates in his plays derives as much from the long silences between speeches as from the speeches themselves. The police officer's dramatic apprehension of the gunman took place in full view of the midtown lunch crowd.* apprehend (verb).

arabesque (noun) Intricate decorative patterns involving intertwining lines and sometimes incorporating flowers, animals, and fruits. *Borders of gold and fanciful arabesques surround the Arabic script on every page of this ancient edition of the Koran.*

WORD ORIGIN

Latin *arbiter* = judge. Also found in English *arbiter, arbitrage,* and *arbitrate*.

arbitrary (adjective) Based on random or merely personal preference. *Both computers cost the same and had the same features, so in the end I made an arbitrary decision about which one to buy.*

archaic (adjective) Old-fashioned, obsolete. *Those who believe in "open marriage" often declare that they will not be bound by archaic laws and religious rituals, but state instead that love alone should bring two people together.* archaism (noun).

ardor (noun) A strong feeling of passion, energy, or zeal. *The young revolutionary proclaimed his convictions with an ardor that excited the crowd.* ardent (adjective).

arid (adjective) Very dry; boring and meaningless. *The arid climate of Arizona makes farming difficult. Some find the law a fascinating topic, but for me it is an arid discipline.* aridity (noun).

WORD ORIGIN

Latin *articulus* = joint, division. Also found in English *arthritis, article,* and *inarticulate*.

articulate (adjective) To express oneself clearly and effectively. *Compared to the elder George Bush, with his stammering and his frequently incomplete sentences, Bill Clinton was considered a highly articulate president.*

asperity (noun) Harshness, severity. *Total silence at the dinner table, baths in icy water, prayers five times a day—these practices all contributed to the asperity of life in the monastery.*

assail (verb) To attack with blows or words. *When the president's cabinet members rose to justify the case for military intervention in Iraq, they were assailed by many audience members who were critical of U.S. policy.* assailant (noun).

assay (verb) To analyze for particular components; to determine weight, quality, etc. *The jeweler assayed the stone pendant Gwyneth inherited from her mother and found it to contain a topaz of high quality.*

assimilate (verb) To absorb into a system or culture. *New York City has assimilated one group of immigrants after another, from the Jewish, German, and Irish immigrants who arrived at the turn of the last century to the waves of Mexican and Latin American immigrants who arrived in the 1980s.* assimilated (adjective).

assuage (verb) To ease, to pacify. *Knowing that the pilot's record was perfect did little to assuage Linnet's fear of flying in the two-seater airplane.*

audacious (adjective) Bold, daring, adventurous. *Her plan to cross the Atlantic single-handed in a twelve-foot sailboat was an audacious, if not reckless one.* audacity (noun).

authoritarian (adjective) Favoring or demanding blind obedience to leaders. *Despite most Americans' strong belief in democracy, the American government has sometimes supported authoritarian regimes in other countries.* authoritarianism (noun).

authoritative (adjective) Official, conclusive. *For more than five decades, American parents regarded Doctor Benjamin Spock as the most authoritative voice on baby and child care.* authority (noun), authorize (verb).

avenge (verb) To exact a punishment for or on behalf of someone. *In Shakespeare's tragedy Hamlet, the ghost of the dead king of Denmark visits his son, Prince Hamlet, and urges him to avenge his murder.*

aver (verb) To claim to be true; to avouch. *The fact that the key witness averred the defendant's innocence is what ultimately swayed the jury to deliver a "not guilty" verdict.*

avow (verb) To declare boldly. *Immediately after Cyrus avowed his atheism at our church fund-raiser, there was a long, uncomfortable silence.* avowal (noun), avowed (adjective).

B

barren (adjective) Desolate; infertile. *The subarctic tundra is a barren wasteland inhabited only by lichens and mosses. Women who try to conceive in their 40s are often barren and must turn to artificial means of producing a child.*

belligerent (adjective) Quarrelsome, combative. *Mrs. Juniper was so belligerent toward the clerks at the local stores that they cringed when they saw her coming.*

belligerent (noun) An opposing army, a party waging war. *The Union and Confederate forces were the belligerents in the American Civil War.*

WORD ORIGIN

Latin *bene* = well. Also found in English *benediction*, *benefactor*, *beneficent*, *beneficial*, *benefit*, and *benign*.

benevolent (adjective) Wishing or doing good. *In old age, Carnegie used his wealth for benevolent purposes, donating large sums to found libraries and schools around the country.* benevolence (noun).

berate (verb) To scold or criticize harshly. *The judge angrily berated the two lawyers for their childish and unprofessional behavior.*

boggle (verb) To overwhelm with amazement. *The ability of physicists to isolate the most infinitesimal particles of matter truly boggles the mind.*

bogus (adjective) Phony, a sham. *Senior citizens are often the target of telemarketing scams pushing bogus investment opportunities.*

bombastic (adjective) Inflated or pompous in style. *Old-fashioned bombastic political speeches don't work on television, which demands a more intimate, personal style of communication.* bombast (noun).

boor (noun) Crude, insensitive and overbearing. *Harold was well-known to be a boor; at parties he horrified people with stories of his past sexual exploits and old, off-color jokes.* boorish (adjective).

brazenly (adverb) Acting with disrespectful boldness. *Some say that the former White House intern brazenly threw herself at the president, but the American public will probably never know the full truth.* brazen (adjective).

broach (verb) To bring up an issue for discussion, to propose. *Knowing my father's strictness about adhering to a budget, I just can't seem to broach the subject of my massive credit-card debt.*

burgeon (verb) To bloom, literally or figuratively. *Due to the extremely mild winter, the forsythia burgeoned as early as March. The story of two prison inmates in Manuel Puig's play* The Kiss of the Spiderwoman *is testimony that tenderness can burgeon in the most unlikely places.*

burnish (verb) To shine by polishing, literally or figuratively. *After stripping seven layers of old paint off the antique door, the carpenter stained the wood and burnished it to a rich hue. When Bill Gates, the wealthiest man in the country, decided to endorse the Big Bertha line of golf cubs, many suggested that he was trying to burnish his image as a "regular guy."*

buttress (noun) Something that supports or strengthens. *The endorsement of the American Medical Association is a powerful buttress for the claims made on behalf of this new medicine.* buttress (verb).

C

cacophony (noun) Discordant sounds; dissonance. *In the minutes before classes start, the high school's halls are filled with a cacophony of shrieks, shouts, banging locker doors, and pounding feet.* cacophonous (adjective).

cadge (verb) To beg for, to sponge. *Few in our crowd want to go out on the town with Piper, since he routinely cadges cigarettes, subway tokens, and drinks.*

calibrate (verb) To determine or mark graduations (of a measuring instrument); to adjust or finely tune. *We tried to calibrate the heating to Rufus's liking, but he still ended up shivering in our living room.* calibration (noun).

castigate (verb) To chastise; to punish severely. *The editor castigated Bob for repeatedly failing to meet his deadlines.* castigation (noun).

catalytic (adjective) Bringing about, causing, or producing some result. *The conditions for revolution existed in America by 1765; the disputes about taxation that arose during the following decade were the catalytic events that sparked the rebellion.* catalyze (verb).

caustic (adjective) Burning, corrosive. *No pretensions were safe when the famous satirist H.L. Mencken unleashed his caustic wit.*

chaos (noun) Disorder, confusion, chance. *The first few moments after the explosion were pure chaos: no one was sure what had happened, and the area was filled with people running and yelling.* chaotic (adjective).

charisma (noun) Dynamic charm or appeal. *Eva Peron was such a fiery orator and had so much charisma that she commanded an enormous political following.* charismatic (adjective).

chary (adjective) Slow to accept, cautious. *Yuan was chary about going out with Xinhua, since she had been badly hurt in her previous relationship.*

chronology (noun) An arrangement of events by order of occurrence, a list of dates; the science of time. *If you ask Susan about her 2-year-old son, she will give you a chronology of his accomplishments and childhood illnesses, from the day he was born to the present. The village of Copan was where Mayan astronomical learning, as applied to chronology, achieved its most accurate expression in the famous Mayan calendar.* chronological (adjective).

churlish (adjective) Coarse and ill-mannered. *Few journalists were eager to interview the aging film star, since he was reputed to be a churlish, uncooperative subject.* churl (noun).

WORD ORIGIN

Greek *kaustikos* = burning. Also found in English *holocaust.*

WORD
ORIGIN

Latin *circus* =
circle. Also found
in English
circumference,
circumnavigate,
circumscribe, and
circumvent.

circumspect (adjective) Prudent, cautious. *After he had been acquitted of the sexual harassment charge, the sergeant realized he would have to be more circumspect in his dealings with the female cadets.* circumspection (noun).

cleave (verb) NOTE: A tricky verb that can mean either to stick closely together or to split apart. (Pay attention to context.) *The more abusive his father became, the more Timothy cleaved to his mother and refused to let her out of his sight. Sometimes a few words carelessly spoken are enough to cleave a married couple and leave the relationship in shambles.* cleavage (noun).

coagulant (noun) Any material that causes another to thicken or clot. *Hemophilia is characterized by excessive bleeding from even the slightest cut, and is caused by a lack of one of the coagulants necessary for blood clotting.* coagulate (verb).

coalesce (verb) To fuse, to unite. *The music we know as jazz coalesced from diverse elements from many musical cultures, including those of West Africa, America, and Europe.* coalescence (noun).

coerce (verb) To force someone either to do something or to refrain from doing something. *The Miranda ruling prevents police from coercing a confession by forcing them to read criminals their rights.* coercion (noun).

cogent (adjective) Forceful and convincing. *The committee members were won over to the project by the cogent arguments of the chairman.* cogency (noun).

WORD
ORIGIN

Latin *mensura* =
to measure. Also
found in English
measure,
immeasurable,
immense, and
mensuration.

commensurate (adjective) Aligned with, proportional. *Many Ph.D.'s in the humanities do not feel their paltry salaries are commensurate with their abilities, their experience, or the heavy workload they are asked to bear.*

commingle (verb) To blend, to mix. *Just as he had when he was only five years old, Elmer did not allow any of the foods on his plate to commingle: the beans must not merge with the rice nor the chicken rub shoulders with the broccoli!*

complaisant (adjective) Tending to bow to others' wishes; amiable. *Of the two Dashwood sisters, Elinor was the more complaisant, often putting the strictures of society and family above her own desires.* complaisance (noun).

compound (verb) To intensify, to exacerbate. *When you make a faux pas, my father advised me, don't compound the problem by apologizing profusely; just say you're sorry and get on with life!*

conceivable (adjective) Possible, imaginable. *It's possible to find people with every conceivable interest by surfing the World Wide Web—from fans of minor film stars to those who study the mating habits of crustaceans.* conception (noun).

concur (verb) To agree, to approve. *We concur that a toddler functions best on a fairly reliable schedule; however, my husband tends to be a bit more rigid than I am.* concurrence (noun).

condensation (noun) A reduction to a denser form (from steam to water); an abridgment of a literary work. *The condensation of humidity on the car's windshield made it difficult for me to see the road. It seems as though every beach house I've ever rented features a shelf full of* Reader's Digest *condensations of B-grade novels.* condense (verb).

condescending (adjective) Having an attitude of superiority toward another; patronizing. *"What a cute little car!" she remarked in a condescending fashion. "I suppose it's the nicest one someone like you could afford!"* condescension (noun).

condone (verb) To overlook, to permit to happen. *Schools with Zero Tolerance policies do not condone alcohol, drugs, vandalism, or violence on school grounds.*

congruent (adjective) Coinciding; harmonious. *Fortunately, the two employees who had been asked to organize the department had congruent views on the budget.* congruence (noun).

conjunction (noun) The occurrence of two or more events together in time or space; in astronomy, the point at which two celestial bodies have the least separation. *Low inflation, occurring in conjunction with low unemployment and relatively low interest rates, has enabled the United States to enjoy a long period of sustained economic growth. The moon is in conjunction with the sun when it is new; if the conjunction is perfect, an eclipse of the sun will occur.* conjoin (verb).

consolation (noun) Relief or comfort in sorrow or suffering. *Although we miss our dog very much, it is a consolation to know that she died quickly, without much suffering.* console (verb).

consternation (noun) Shock, amazement, dismay. *When a voice in the back of the church shouted out "I know why they should not be married!" the entire gathering was thrown into consternation.*

convergence (noun) The act of coming together in unity or similarity. *A remarkable example of evolutionary convergence can be seen in the shark and the dolphin, two sea creatures that developed from different origins to become very similar in form and appearance.* converge (verb).

conviviality (noun) Fond of good company and eating and drinking. *The conviviality of my fellow employees seemed to turn every staff meeting into a party, complete with snacks, drinks, and lots of hearty laughter.* convivial (adjective).

WORD ORIGIN

Latin *jungere* = to join. Also found in English in*junction, junction,* and *juncture.*

WORD ORIGIN

Latin *vivere* = to live. Also found in English *revive, vital, vivid,* and *vivisection.*

WORD
ORIGIN

Latin *volvere* = to
roll. Also found in
English *devolve*,
involve,
revolution,
revolve, and
voluble.

convoluted (adjective) Twisting, complicated, intricate. *Income tax law has become so convoluted that it's easy for people to violate it completely by accident.* convolute (verb), convolution (noun).

cordon (verb) To form a protective or restrictive barrier. *Well before the Academy Awards® ceremony began, the police cordoned off the hordes of fans who were desperate to ogle the arriving stars.* cordon (noun).

corral (verb) To enclose, to collect, to gather. *Tyrone couldn't enjoy the wedding at all, since he spent most of his time corralling his two children into the reception room and preventing them from running amok through the Potters' mansion.* corral (noun).

corroborating (adjective) Supporting with evidence; confirming. *A passerby who had witnessed the crime gave corroborating testimony about the presence of the accused person.* corroborate (verb), corroboration (noun).

corrosive (adjective) Eating away, gnawing, or destroying. *Years of poverty and hard work had a corrosive effect on her strength and beauty.* corrode (verb), corrosion (noun).

cosmopolitanism (noun) International sophistication; worldliness. *Budapest is known for its cosmopolitanism, perhaps because it was the first Eastern European city to be more open to capitalism and influences from the West.* cosmopolitan (adjective).

covert (adjective) Secret, clandestine. *The CIA has often been criticized for its covert operations in the domestic policies of foreign countries, such as the failed Bay of Pigs operation in Cuba.*

covetous (adjective) Envious, particularly of another's possessions. *Benita would never admit to being covetous of my new sable jacket, but I found it odd that she couldn't refrain from trying it on each time we met.* covet (verb).

craven (adjective) Cowardly. *Local firefighters were outraged by the craven behavior of a police officer who refused to come to the aid of a hepatitis C-positive accident victim.*

credulous (adjective) Ready to believe; gullible. *Elaine was not very credulous of the explanation Serge gave for his acquisition of the Matisse lithograph.* credulity (noun).

cryptic (adjective) Puzzling, ambiguous. *I was puzzled by the cryptic message left on my answering machine about the arrival of "a shipment of pomegranates from an anonymous donor."*

culmination (noun) The climax. *The Los Angeles riots, in the aftermath of the Rodney King verdict, were the culmination of long-standing racial tensions between the residents of South Central LA and the police.* culminate (verb).

culpable (adjective) Deserving blame, guilty. *Although he committed the crime, because he was mentally ill he should not be considered culpable for his actions.* culpability (noun).

curmudgeon (noun) A crusty, ill-tempered person. *Todd hated to drive with his Uncle Jasper, a notorious curmudgeon, who complained nonstop about the air-conditioning and Todd's driving.* curmudgeonly (adjective).

cursory (adjective) Hasty and superficial. *Detective Martinez was rebuked by his superior officer for drawing conclusions about the murder after only a cursory examination of the crime scene.*

D

debilitating (adjective) Weakening; sapping the strength of. *One can't help but marvel at the courage Steven Hawking displays in the face of such a debilitating disease as ALS.* debilitate (verb).

decelerate (verb) To slow down. *Randall didn't decelerate enough on the winding roads, and he ended up smashing his new sports utility vehicle into a guard rail.* deceleration (noun).

decimation (noun) Almost complete destruction. *Michael Moore's documentary* Roger and Me *chronicles the decimation of the economy of Flint, Michigan, after the closing of a General Motors factory.* decimate (verb).

decry (verb) To criticize or condemn. *Cigarette ads aimed at youngsters have led many to decry the unfair marketing tactics of the tobacco industry.*

defamation (noun) Act of harming someone by libel or slander. *When the article in* The National Enquirer *implied that she was somehow responsible for her husband's untimely death, Renata instructed her lawyer to sue the paper for defamation of character.* defame (verb).

defer (verb) To graciously submit to another's will; to delegate. *In all matters relating to the children's religious education, Joy deferred to her husband, since he clearly cared more about giving them a solid grounding in Judaism.* deference (noun).

deliberate (verb) To think about an issue before reaching a decision. *The legal pundits covering the O.J. Simpson trial were shocked by the short time the jury took to deliberate after a trial that lasted months.* deliberation (noun).

WORD ORIGIN

Latin *celer* = swift. Also found in English *accelerate* and *celerity*.

WORD
ORIGIN
Greek *demos* =
people. Also
found in English
democracy,
demographic,
and *endemic.*

demagogue (noun) A leader who plays dishonestly on the prejudices and emotions of his followers. *Senator Joseph McCarthy was a demagogue who used the paranoia and biases of the anti-Communist 1950s as a way of seizing fame and considerable power in Washington.* demagoguery (noun).

demographic (adjective) Relating to the statistical study of population. *Three demographic groups have been the intense focus of marketing strategy: baby boomers, born between 1946 and 1964; baby busters, or the youth market, born between 1965 and 1976; and a group referred to as tweens, those born between 1977 and 1983.* demography (noun), demographics (noun).

demonstratively (adverb) Openly displaying feeling. *The young congressman demonstratively campaigned for reelection, kissing every baby and hugging every senior citizen at the Saugerties Chrysanthemum festival.* demonstrative (adjective).

derisive (adjective) Expressing ridicule or scorn. *Many women's groups were derisive of Avon's choice of a male CEO, since the company derives its $5.1 billion in sales from an army of female salespeople.* derision (noun).

derivative (adjective) Imitating or borrowed from a particular source. *When a person first writes poetry, her poems are apt to be derivative of whatever poetry she most enjoys reading.* derivation (noun), derive (verb).

desiccate (verb) To dry out, to wither; to drain of vitality. *The long drought thoroughly desiccated our garden; what was once a glorious Eden was now a scorched and hellish wasteland. A recent spate of books has debunked the myth that menopause desiccates women and affirmed, instead, that women often reach heights of creativity in their later years.* desiccant (noun), desiccation (noun).

despotic (adjective) Oppressive and tyrannical. *During the despotic reign of Idi Amin in the 1970s, an estimated 200,000 Ugandans were killed.* despot (noun).

desultory (adjective) Disconnected, aimless. *Tina's few desultory stabs at conversation fell flat as Guy just sat there, stone-faced; it was a disastrous first date.*

deviate (verb) To depart from a standard or norm. *Having agreed upon a spending budget for the company, we mustn't deviate from it; if we do, we may run out of money before the year ends.* deviation (noun).

diatribe (noun) Abusive or bitter speech or writing. *While angry conservatives dismissed Susan Faludi's* Backlash *as a feminist diatribe, it is actually a meticulously researched book.*

diffident (adjective) Hesitant, reserved, shy. *Someone with a diffident personality is most likely to succeed in a career that involves very little public contact.* diffidence (noun).

digress (verb) To wander from the main path or the main topic. *My high school biology teacher loved to digress from science into personal anecdotes about his college adventures.* digression (noun), digressive (adjective).

dirge (noun) Song or hymn of grief. *When Princess Diana was killed in a car crash, Elton John resurrected his hit song "Candle in the Wind," rewrote it as "Good-bye England's Rose," and created one of the most widely heard funeral dirges of all time.*

disabuse (verb) To correct a fallacy, to clarify. *I hated to disabuse Filbert, who is a passionate collector of musical trivia, but I had to tell him that the Monkees had hardly sung a note and had lip-synched their way through almost all of their albums.*

disburse (verb) To pay out or distribute (funds or property). *Jaime was flabbergasted when his father's will disbursed all of the old man's financial assets to Raymundo and left him with only a few sticks of furniture.* disbursement (noun).

discern (verb) To detect, notice, or observe. *With difficulty, I could discern the shape of a whale off the starboard bow, but it was too far away to determine its size or species.* discernment (noun).

discordant (adjective) Characterized by conflict. *Stories and films about discordant relationships that resolve themselves happily are always more interesting than stories about content couples who simply stay content.* discordance (noun).

discourse (noun) Formal and orderly exchange of ideas, a discussion. *In the late twentieth century, cloning and other feats of genetic engineering became popular topics of public discourse.* discursive (adjective).

discredit (verb) To cause disbelief in the accuracy of some statement or the reliability of a person. *Although many people still believe in UFOs, among scientists the reports of "alien encounters" have been thoroughly discredited.*

discreet (adjective) Showing good judgment in speech and behavior. *Be discreet when discussing confidential business matters—don't talk among strangers on the elevator, for example.* discretion (noun).

discrete (adjective) Separate, unconnected. *Canadians get peeved when people can't seem to distinguish between Canada and the United States, forgetting that Canada has its own discrete heritage and culture.*

disparity (noun) Difference in quality or kind. *There is often a disparity between the kind of serious, high-quality television people say they want and the low-brow programs they actually watch.* disparate (adjective).

WORD ORIGIN

Latin *credere* = to believe. Also found in English *credential, credible, credit, credo, credulous,* and *incredible.*

WORD ORIGIN

Latin *simulare* = to resemble. Also found in English *semblance*, *similarity*, *simulacrum*, *simultaneous*, and *verisimilitude*.

dissemble (verb) To pretend, to simulate. *When the police asked whether Nancy knew anything about the crime, she dissembled innocence.*

dissipate (verb) To spread out or scatter. *The windows and doors were opened, allowing the smoke that had filled the room to dissipate.* dissipation (noun).

dissonance (noun) Lack of music harmony; lack of agreement between ideas. *Most modern music is characterized by dissonance, which many listeners find hard to enjoy. There is a noticeable dissonance between two common beliefs of most conservatives: their faith in unfettered free markets and their preference for traditional social values.* dissonant (adjective).

distillation (noun) Something distilled, an essence or extract. In chemistry, a process that drives gas or vapor from liquids or solids. *Sharon Olds's poems are powerful distillations of motherhood and other primal experiences. In Mrs. Hornmeister's chemistry class, our first experiment was to create a distillation of carbon gas from wood.* distill (verb).

diverge (verb) To move in different directions. *Frost's poem "The Road Not Taken" tells of the choice he made when "Two roads diverged in a yellow wood."* divergence (noun), divergent (adjective).

diversify (verb) To balance by adding variety. *Any financial manager will recommend that you diversify your stock portfolio by holding some less-volatile blue-chip stocks along with more growth-oriented technology issues.* diversification (noun), diversified (adjective).

divest (verb) To rid (oneself) or be freed of property, authority, or title. *In order to turn around its ailing company and concentrate on imaging, Eastman Kodak divested itself of peripheral businesses in the areas of household products, clinical diagnostics, and pharmaceuticals.* divestiture (noun).

divulge (verb) To reveal. *The people who count the votes for the Oscar® awards are under strict orders not to divulge the names of the winners.*

dogmatic (adjective) Holding firmly to a particular set of beliefs with little or no basis. *Believers in Marxist doctrine tend to be dogmatic, ignoring evidence that contradicts their beliefs or explaining it away.* dogma (noun), dogmatism (noun).

dolt (noun) A stupid or foolish person. *Due to his frequent verbal blunders, politician Dan Quayle was widely considered to be a dolt.*

dormant (adjective) Temporarily inactive, as if asleep. *An eruption of Mt. Rainier, a dormant volcano in Washington state, would cause massive, life-threatening mud slides in the surrounding area. Bill preferred to think that his math skills were dormant rather than extinct.* dormancy (noun).

dross (noun) Something that is trivial or inferior; an impurity. *As a reader for the* Paris Review, *Julia spent most of her time sifting through piles of manuscripts to separate the extraordinary poems from the dross.*

dubious (adjective) Doubtful, uncertain. *Despite the chairman's attempts to convince the committee members that his plan would succeed, most of them remained dubious.* dubiety (noun).

dupe (noun) Someone who is easily cheated. *My cousin Ravi is such a dupe; he actually gets excited when he receives those envelopes saying "Ravi Murtugudde, you may have won a million dollars," and he even goes so far as to try claiming his prize.*

E

eccentricity (noun) Odd or whimsical behavior. *Rock star Michael Jackson is now better known for his offstage eccentricities—such as sleeping in an oxygen tank, wearing a surgical mask, and building his own theme park—than for his on-stage performances.* eccentric (adjective).

edifying (adjective) Instructive, enlightening. *Ariel would never admit it to her high-brow friends, but she found the latest self-help bestseller edifying and actually helpful.* edification (noun), edify (verb).

efficacy (noun) The power to produce the desired effect. *While teams have been enormously popular in the workplace, there are some who now question their efficacy and say that "one head is better than ten."* efficacious (noun).

effrontery (noun) Shameless boldness. *The sports world was shocked when a pro basketball player had the effrontery to choke the head coach of his team during a practice session.*

elaborate (verb) To expand upon something; develop. *One characteristics of the best essayists is their ability to elaborate ideas through examples, lists, similes, small variations, and even exaggerations.* elaborate (adjective), elaboration (noun).

elegy (noun) A song or poem expressing sorrow. *Thomas Gray's "Elegy Written in a Country Churchyard," one of the most famous elegies in Western literature, mourns the unsung, inglorious lives of the souls buried in an obscure, rustic graveyard.* elegaic (adjective).

embellish (verb) To enhance or exaggerate; to decorate. *The long-married couple told their stories in tandem, with the husband outlining the plot and the wife embellishing it with colorful details.*

WORD ORIGIN

Latin *dormire* = to sleep. Also found in English *dormitory*.

WORD ORIGIN

Latin *facere* = to do. Also found in English *facility, factor, facsimile,* and *faculty*.

embellished (adjective). *Both Salman Rushdie, of India, and Patrick Chamoiseau, of Martinique, emerged from colonized countries and created embellished versions of their colonizers' languages in their novels.*

embezzle (verb) To steal money or property that has been entrusted to your care. *The church treasurer was found to have embezzled thousands of dollars by writing phony checks on the church bank account.* embezzlement (noun).

emollient (noun) Something that softens or soothes. *She used a hand cream as an emollient on her dry, work-roughened hands.* emollient (adjective).

empirical (adjective) Based on experience or personal observation. *Although many people believe in ESP, scientists have found no empirical evidence of its existence.* empiricism (noun).

emulate (verb) To imitate or copy. *The British band Oasis is quite open about their desire to emulate their idols, the Beatles.* emulation (noun).

encomium (noun) A formal expression of praise. *For many filmmakers, winning the Palm d'Or at the Cannes Film Festival is considered the highest encomium.*

enervate (verb) To reduce the energy or strength of someone or something. *The stress of the operation left her feeling enervated for about two weeks.* enervation (noun).

engender (verb) To produce, to cause. *Countless disagreements over the proper use of national forests and parklands have engendered feelings of hostility between ranchers and environmentalists.*

enhance (verb) To improve in value or quality. *New kitchen appliances will enhance your house and increase the amount of money you'll make when you sell it.* enhancement (noun).

enigmatic (adjective) Puzzling, mysterious. *Alain Resnais' enigmatic film* Last Year at Marienbad *sets up a puzzle that is never resolved: a man meets a woman at a hotel and believes he once had an affair with her—or did he?* enigma (noun).

enmity (noun) Hatred, hostility, ill will. *Long-standing enmity, like that between the Protestants and Catholics in Northern Ireland, is difficult to overcome.*

ensure (verb) To make certain; to guarantee. *In order to ensure a sufficient crop of programmers and engineers for the future, the United States needs to raise the quality of its math and science schooling.*

epicure (noun) Someone who appreciates fine wine and fine food, a gourmand. *M.F.K. Fisher, a famous epicure, begins her book* The Gastronomical Me *by saying, "There is a communion of more than bodies when bread is broken and wine is drunk."* epicurean (adjective).

epithet (noun) Term or words used to characterize a person or thing, often in a disparaging way. *In her recorded phone conversations with Linda Tripp, Monica Lewinsky is said to have referred to President Clinton by a number of epithets, including "The Creep" and "The Big He."* epithetical (adjective).

equable (adjective) Steady, uniform. *While many people can't see how Helena could possibly be attracted to "Boring Bruno," his equable nature is the perfect complement to her volatile personality.*

equivocate (verb) To use misleading or intentionally confusing language. *When Pedro pressed Renee for an answer to his marriage proposal, she equivocated by saying, "I've just got to know when your Mercedes will be out of the shop!"* equivocal (adjective), equivocation (noun).

eradicate (verb) To destroy completely. *American society has failed to eradicate racism, although some of its worst effects have been reduced.* eradication (noun).

erudition (noun) Extensive knowledge, usually acquired from books. *When Dorothea first saw Mr. Casaubon's voluminous library she was awed, but after their marriage she quickly realized that erudition is no substitute for originality.* erudite (adjective).

esoterica (noun) Items of interest to a select group. *The fish symposium at St. Antony's College in Oxford explored all manner of esoterica relating to fish, as is evidenced in presentations such as "The Buoyant Slippery Lipids of the Escolar and Orange Roughy," or "Food on Board Whale Shipsùfrom the Inedible to the Incredible."* esoteric (adjective).

espouse (verb) To take up as a cause; to adopt. *No politician in American today will openly espouse racism, although some behave and speak in racially prejudiced ways.*

estimable (adjective) Worthy of esteem and admiration. *After a tragic fire raged through Malden Mills, the estimable mill owner, Aaron Feuerstein, restarted operations and rebuilt the company within just one month.* esteem (noun).

eulogy (noun) A formal tribute usually delivered at a funeral. *Most people in Britain applauded Lord Earl Spencer's eulogy for Princess Diana, not only as a warm tribute to his sister Diana, but also as a biting indictment of the Royal Family.* eulogize (verb).

euphemism (noun) An agreeable expression that is substituted for an offensive one. *Some of the more creative euphemisms for "layoffs" in current use are: "release of resources," "involuntary severance," "strengthening global effectiveness," and "career transition program."* euphemistic (adjective).

WORD ORIGIN

Latin *aequus* = equal. Also found in English *equality*, *equanimity*, and *equation*.

WORD ORIGIN

Latin *radix* = root. Also found in English *radical*.

exacerbate (verb) To make worse or more severe. *The roads in our town already have too much traffic; building a new shopping mall will exacerbate the problem.*

excoriation (noun) The act of condemning someone with harsh words. *In the small office we shared, it was painful to hear my boss's constant excoriation of his assistant for the smallest faults—a misdirected letter, an unclear phone message, or even a tepid cup of coffee.* excoriate (verb).

exculpate (verb) To free from blame or guilt. *When someone else confessed to the crime, the previous suspect was exculpated.* exculpation (noun), exculpatory (adjective) .

executor (noun) The person appointed to execute someone's will. *As the executor of his aunt Ida's will, Phil must deal with squabbling relatives, conniving lawyers, and the ruinous state of Ida's house.*

exigent (adjective) Urgent, requiring immediate attention. *A 2-year-old is likely to behave as if her every demand is exigent, even if it involves simply retrieving a beloved stuffed hedgehog from under the couch.* exigency (noun).

expedient (adjective) Providing an immediate advantage or serving one's immediate self-interest. *When the passenger next to her was hit by a bullet, Sharon chose the most expedient means to stop the bleeding; she whipped off her pantyhose and made an impromptu, but effective, tourniquet.* expediency (noun).

extant (adjective) Currently in existence. *Of the seven ancient "Wonders of the World," only the pyramids of Egypt are still extant.*

extenuate (verb) To make less serious. *Karen's guilt is extenuated by the fact that she was only 12 when she committed the theft.* extenuating (adjective), extenuation (noun).

extol (verb) To greatly praise. *At the party convention, one speaker after another took to the podium to extol the virtues of their candidate for the presidency.*

extraneous (adjective) Irrelevant, nonessential. *One review of the new Chekhov biography said the author had bogged down the book with far too many extraneous details, such as the dates of Chekhov's bouts of diarrhea.*

extrapolate (verb) To deduce from something known, to infer. *Meteorologists were able to use old weather records to extrapolate backward and compile lists of El Niño years and their effects over the last century.* extrapolation (noun).

extricate (verb) To free from a difficult or complicated situation. *Much of the humor in the TV show "I Love Lucy" comes in watching Lucy try to extricate herself from the problems she creates by fibbing or trickery.* extricable (adjective).

F

facetious (adjective) Humorous in a mocking way; not serious. *French composer Erik Satie often concealed his serious artistic intent by giving his works facetious titles such as "Three Pieces in the Shape of a Pear."*

facilitate (verb) To make easier or to moderate. *When the issue of racism reared its ugly head, the company brought in a consultant to facilitate a discussion of diversity in the workplace.* facile (adjective), facility (noun).

fallacy (noun) An error in fact or logic. *It's a fallacy to think that "natural" means "healthful"; after all, the deadly poison arsenic is completely natural.* fallacious (adjective).

fatuous (adjective) Inanely foolish; silly. *Once backstage, Elizabeth showered the opera singer with fatuous praise and embarrassing confessions, which he clearly had no interest in hearing.*

fawn (verb) To flatter in a particularly subservient manner. *Mildly disgusted, Pedro stood alone at the bar and watched Renee fawn over the heir to the Fabco Surgical Appliances fortune.*

feckless (adjective) Weak and ineffective; irresponsible. *Our co-op board president is a feckless fellow who has let much-needed repairs go unattended while our maintenance fees continue to rise.*

feint (noun) A bluff; a mock blow. *It didn't take us long to realize that Gaby's tears and stomachaches were all a feint, since they appeared so regularly at her bedtime.*

ferret (verb) To bring to light by an extensive search. *With his repeated probing and questions, Fritz was able to ferret out the location of Myrna's safe deposit box.*

finesse (noun) Skillful maneuvering; delicate workmanship. *With her usual finesse, Charmaine gently persuaded the Duncans not to install a motorized Santa and sleigh on their front lawn.*

florid (adjective) Flowery, fancy; reddish. *The grand ballroom was decorated in a florid style. Years of heavy drinking had given him a florid complexion.*

flourish (noun) An extraneous embellishment; a dramatic gesture. *The napkin rings made out of intertwined ferns and flowers were just the kind of flourish one would expect from Carol, a slavish follower of the home and garden TV show.*

WORD ORIGIN

Latin *fluere* = to flow. Also found in English *affluent*, *effluvia*, *fluid*, and *influx*.

fluctuation (noun) A shifting back and forth. *Investment analysts predict fluctuations in the Dow Jones Industrial Average due to the instability of the value of the dollar.* fluctuate (verb).

foil (verb) To thwart or frustrate. *I was certain that Jerry's tendency to insert himself into everyone's conversations would foil my chances to have a private word with Helen.*

foment (verb) To rouse or incite. *The petty tyrannies and indignities inflicted on the workers by upper management helped foment the walkout at the meat-processing plant.*

forestall (verb) To hinder or prevent by taking action in advance. *The pilot's calm, levelheaded demeanor during the turbulence forestalled any hysteria among the passengers of Flight 268.*

fortuitous (adjective) Lucky, fortunate. *Although the mayor claimed credit for the falling crime rate, it was really caused by a series of fortuitous accidents.*

foster (verb) To nurture or encourage. *The white-water rafting trip was supposed to foster creative problem-solving and teamwork between the account executives and the creative staff at Apex Advertising Agency.*

fracas (noun) A noisy fight; a brawl. *As Bill approached the stadium ticket window, he was alarmed to see the fracas that had broken out between a group of Giants fans and a man wearing a Cowboys jersey and helmet.*

functionary (noun) Someone holding office in a political party or government. *The man shaking hands with the governor was a low-ranking Democratic Party functionary who had worked to garner the Hispanic vote.*

G

gainsay (verb) To contradict or oppose; deny, dispute. *Dot would gainsay her married sister's efforts to introduce her to eligible men by refusing to either leave her ailing canary or give up her thrice-weekly bingo nights.*

garble (verb) To distort or slur. *No matter how much money the Metropolitan Transit Authority spends on improving the subway trains, the public address system in almost every station seems to garble each announcement.* garbled (adjective).

garrulous (adjective) Annoyingly talkative. *Claude pretended to be asleep so he could avoid his garrulous seatmate, a self-proclaimed expert on bonsai cultivation.*

generic (adjective) General; having no brand name. *Connie tried to reduce her grocery bills by religiously clipping coupons and buying generic brands of most products.*

gist (noun) The main point, the essence. *Although they felt sympathy for the victim's family, the jurors were won over by the gist of the defense's argument: there was insufficient evidence to convict.*

gouge (verb) To cut out, to scoop out with one's thumbs or a sharp instrument; to overcharge, to cheat. *Instead of picking the lock with a credit card, the clumsy thieves gouged a hole in my door. The consumer watchdog group accused the clothing stores of gouging customers with high prices.*

guile (noun) Deceit, duplicity. *In Margaret Mitchell's* Gone With the Wind, *Scarlett O'Hara uses her guile to manipulate two men and then is matched for wits by a third: Rhett Butler.* guileful (adjective).

gullible (adjective) Easily fooled. *Terry was so gullible she actually believed Robert's stories of his connections to the Czar and Czarina.* gullibility (noun).

WORD ORIGIN

Latin *genus* = type or kind; birth. Also found in English *congenital, genetic, genital, genre, genuine,* and *genus.*

H

hackneyed (adjective) Without originality, trite. *When someone invented the phrase "No pain, no gain," it was clever and witty, but now it is so commonly heard that it seems hackneyed.*

harrow (verb) To cultivate with a harrow; to torment or vex. *During grade school, my sister was harrowed mercilessly for being overweight.*

harrowing (adjective) Nerve-wracking, traumatic. *Jon Krakauer's best-selling book* Into Thin Air *chronicles the tragic consequences of leading groups of untrained climbers up Mt. Everest.*

haughty (adjective) Overly proud. *The fashion model strode down the runway, her hips thrust forward and a haughty expression, something like a sneer, on her face.* haughtiness (noun).

hierarchy (noun) A ranking of people, things, or ideas from highest to lowest. *A cabinet secretary ranks just below the president and vice president in the hierarchy of the government's executive branch.* hierarchical (adjective).

homogeneous (adjective) Uniform, made entirely of one thing. *It's hard to think of a more homogenous group than those eerie children in* Village of the Damned, *who all had perfect features, white-blond hair, and silver, penetrating eyes.*

WORD ORIGIN

Greek *homos* = same. Also found in English *homologous, homonym,* and *homosexual.*

hone (verb) To improve and make more acute or affective. *While she was a receptionist, Norma honed her skills as a stand-up comic by trying out jokes on the tense crowd in the waiting room.*

hoodwink (verb) To deceive by trickery or false appearances; to dupe. *That was my cousin Ravi calling to say that he's been hoodwinked again, this time by some outfit offering time shares in a desolate tract of land in central Florida.*

I

iconoclast (noun) Someone who attacks traditional beliefs or institutions. *Comedian Dennis Miller relishes his reputation as an iconoclast, though people in power often resent his satirical jabs.* iconoclasm (noun), iconoclastic (adjective).

idolatry (noun) The worship of a person, thing, or institution as a god. *In communist China, admiration for Mao resembled idolatry; his picture was displayed everywhere, and millions of Chinese memorized his sayings and repeated them endlessly.* idolatrous (adjective).

idyll (noun) A rustic, romantic interlude; poetry or prose that celebrates simple pastoral life. *Her picnic with Max at Fahnstock Lake was not the serene idyll she had envisioned; instead, they were surrounded by hundreds of other picnickers blaring music from their boom boxes and cracking open soda cans.* idyllic (adjective).

illicit (adjective) Illegal, wrongful. *When Janet caught her 13-year-old son and his friend downloading illicit pornographic photos from the World Wide Web, she promptly pulled the plug on his computer.*

illuminate (verb) To brighten with light; to enlighten or elucidate; to decorate (a manuscript). *The frosted-glass sconces in the dressing rooms at Le Cirque not only illuminate the rooms but make everyone look like a movie star. Alice Munro is a writer who can illuminate an entire character with a few deft sentences.*

immaculate (adjective) Totally unblemished, spotlessly clean. *The cream-colored upholstery in my new Porsche was immaculate—that is, until a raccoon came in through the window and tracked mud across the seats.*

immaterial (adjective) Of no consequence, unimportant. *"The fact that your travel agent is your best friend's son should be immaterial," I told Rosa, "so, if he keeps putting you on hold and acting nasty, just take your business elsewhere."*

immutable (adjective) Incapable of change. *Does there ever come an age when we realize that our parents' personalities are immutable, when we can relax and stop trying to make them change?*

impartial (adjective) Fair, equal, unbiased. *If a judge is not impartial, then all of her rulings are questionable.* impartiality (noun).

impassivity (noun) Apathy, unresponsiveness. *Dot truly thinks that Mr. Right will magically show up on her doorstep, and her utter impassivity regarding her social life makes me want to shake her!* impassive (adjective).

imperceptible (adjective) Impossible to perceive, inaudible or incomprehensible. *The sound of footsteps was almost imperceptible, but Donald's paranoia had reached such a pitch that he immediately assumed he was being followed.*

imperturbable (adjective) Cannot be disconcerted, disturbed, or excited. *The proper English butler in Kazuo Ishiguro's novel* Remains of the Day *appears completely imperturbable, even when his father dies or when his own heart is breaking.*

impetuous (adjective) Acting hastily or impulsively. *Ben's resignation was an impetuous act; he did it without thinking, and he soon regretted it.* impetuosity (noun).

implacable (adjective) Unbending, resolute. *The state of Israel is implacable in its policy of never negotiating with criminals.*

implosion (noun) To collapse inward from outside pressure. *While it is difficult to know what is going on in North Korea, no one can rule out a violent implosion of the North Korean regime and a subsequent flood of refugees across its borders.* implode (verb).

incessant (adjective) Unceasing. *The incessant blaring of the neighbor's car alarm made it impossible for me to concentrate on my upcoming Bar exam.*

inchoate (adjective) Only partly formed or formulated. *At editorial meetings, Nancy had a habit of presenting her inchoate book ideas before she had a chance to fully determine their feasibility.*

incise (verb) To carve into, to engrave. *My wife felt nostalgic about the old elm tree since we had incised our initials in it when we were both in high school.*

incisive (adjective) Admirably direct and decisive. *Ted Koppel's incisive questions have made many politicians squirm and stammer.*

incongruous (adjective) Unlikely. *Art makes incongruous alliances, as when punk-rockers, Tibetan folk musicians, gospel singers, and beat poets shared the stage at the Tibet House benefit concert.* incongruity (noun).

WORD ORIGIN
Latin *mutare* = to change. Also found in English *immutable*, *mutant*, and *mutation*.

WORD ORIGIN
Latin *placare* = to please. Also found in English *complacent*, *placate*, and *placid*.

WORD ORIGIN
Latin *caedere* = to cut. Also found in English *concise*, *decide*, *excise*, *incision*, and *precise*.

incorrigible (adjective) Impossible to manage or reform. *Lou is an incorrigible trickster, constantly playing practical jokes no matter how much his friends complain.*

incursion (noun) A hostile entrance into a territory; a foray into an activity or venture. *It is a little-known fact that the Central Intelligence Agency organized military incursions into China during the 1950s. The comic* Peanuts *was Barbara's first incursion into the world of comic strip artists.*

indefatigable (adjective) Tireless. *Eleanor Roosevelt's indefatigable dedication to the cause of human welfare won her affection and honor throughout the world.* indefatigability (noun).

indelicate (adjective) Blunt, undisguised. *No sooner had we sat down to eat than Mark made an indelicate remark about my high salary.*

inevitable (adjective) Unable to be avoided. *Once the Japanese attacked Pearl Harbor, U.S. involvement in World WarII was inevitable.* inevitability (noun).

infer (verb) To conclude, to deduce. *Can I infer from your hostile tone of voice that you are still angry about yesterday's incident?* inference (noun).

inimical (adjective) Unfriendly, hostile; adverse or difficult. *Relations between Greece and Turkey have been inimical for centuries.*

inimitable (adjective) Incapable of being imitated, matchless. *John F. Kennedy's administration dazzled the public, partly because of the inimitable style and elegance of his wife, Jacqueline.*

inopportune (adjective) Awkward, untimely. *When Gus heard raised voices and the crash of breaking china behind the kitchen door, he realized that he'd picked an inopportune moment to visit the Fairlights.*

inscrutability (noun) Quality of being extremely difficult to interpret or understand, mysteriousness. *I am still puzzling over the inscrutability of the package I received yesterday, which contained twenty pomegranates and a note that said simply "Yours."* inscrutable (adjective).

insensible (adjective) Unaware, incognizant; unconscious, out cold. *It's a good thing that Marty was insensible to the titters and laughter that greeted his arrival in the ballroom. In the latest episode of gang brutality, an innocent young man was beaten insensible after two gang members stormed his apartment.*

insinuate (verb) Hint or intimate; to creep in. *During an extremely unusual broadcast, the newscaster insinuated that the Washington bureau chief was having a nervous breakdown. Marla managed to insinuate herself into the Duchess' conversation during the charity event.* insinuation (noun).

insipid (adjective) Flavorless, uninteresting. *Most TV shows are so insipid that you can watch them while reading or chatting without missing a thing.* insipidity (noun).

insolence (noun) An attitude or behavior that is bold and disrespectful. *Some feel that news reporters who shout accusatory questions at the president are behaving with insolence toward his high office.* insolent (adjective).

insoluble (adjective) Unable to be solved, irresolvable; indissoluble. *Fermat's last theorum remained insoluble for over 300 years until a young mathematician from Princeton solved it in 1995. If you are a gum chewer, you probably wouldn't like to know that insoluble plastics are a common ingredient of most popular gums.*

insular (adjective) Narrow or isolated in attitude or viewpoint. *New Yorkers are famous for their insular attitudes; they seem to think that nothing important has ever happened outside of their city.* insularity (noun).

intercede (verb) To step in, to moderate; to mediate or negotiate on behalf of someone else. *After their rejection by the co-op board, Kevin and Sol asked Rachel, another tenant, to intercede for them at the next board meeting.* intercession (noun).

interim (noun) A break or interlude. *In the interim between figure-skating programs, the exhausted skaters retreat to the "kiss and cry" room to wait for their scores.*

interpolate (verb) To interject. *The director's decision to interpolate topical political jokes into his production of Shakespeare's* Twelfth Night *was not viewed kindly by the critics.* interpolation (noun).

intransigent (adjective) Unwilling to compromise. *Despite the mediator's attempts to suggest a fair solution to the disagreement, the two parties were intransigent, forcing a showdown.* intransigence (noun).

intrinsically (adverb) Essentially, inherently. *There is nothing intrinsically difficult about upgrading a computer's microprocessor, yet Al was afraid to even open up the computer's case.* intrinsic (adjective).

inundate (verb) To overwhelm; to flood. *When AOL first announced its flat-rate pricing, the company was inundated with new customers, and thus began the annoying delays in service.* inundation (noun).

invective (noun) Insulting, abusive language. *I remained unscathed by his blistering invective because in my heart I knew I had done the right thing.*

invigorate (verb) To give energy to, to stimulate. *As her car climbed the mountain road, Lucinda felt herself invigorated by the clear air and the cool breezes.* invigoration (noun).

WORD ORIGIN

Latin *unda* = wave. Also found in English *undulate*.

irascible (adjective) Easily provoked into anger, hot-headed. *Soup chef Al Yeganah, the model for Seinfeld's "Soup Nazi," is an irascible man who flies into a temper tantrum if his customers don't follow his rigid procedure for purchasing soup.* irascibility (noun).

J

jeopardize (verb) To put in danger. *Terrorist attacks on civilians jeopardize the fragile peace in the Middle East.* jeopardy (noun).

jocular (adjective) Humorous, amusing. *Listening to the CEO launch into yet another uproarious anecdote, Ted was frankly surprised by the jocular nature of the "emergency" board meeting.* jocularity (noun).

L

labyrinthine (adjective) Extremely intricate or involved; circuitous. *Was I the only one who couldn't follow the labyrinthine plot of the movie* L.A. Confidential? *I was so confused I had to watch it twice to see "who did it."*

laconic (adjective) Concise to the point of terseness; taciturn. *Tall, handsome and laconic, the actor Gary Cooper came to personify the strong, silent American, a man of action and few words.*

lambaste (verb) To give someone a dressing-down; to attack someone verbally; to whip. *Once inside the locker room, the coach thoroughly lambasted the team for their incompetent performance on the football field.*

laudable (adjective) Commendable, praiseworthy. *The Hunt's Point nonprofit organization has embarked on a series of laudable ventures pairing businesses and disadvantaged youth.*

WORD ORIGIN

Latin *laus* = praise. Also found in English *applaud, laud, laudatory,* and *plaudit.*

lethargic (adjective) Lacking energy; sluggish. *Visitors to the zoo are surprised that the lions appear so lethargic, but, in the wild, lions sleep up to 18 hours a day.* lethargy (noun).

levy (verb) To demand payment or collection of a tax or fee. *The environmental activists pushed Congress to levy higher taxes on gasoline, but the auto makers' lobbyists quashed their plans.*

lien (noun) A claim against a property for the satisfaction of a debt. *Nat was in such financial straits when he died that his Fishkill property had several liens against it, and all of his furniture was being repossessed.*

limn (verb) To outline in distinct detail; to delineate. *Like many of her novels, Edith Wharton's* The Age of Innocence *expertly limns the tyranny of New York's upper class society in the 1800s.*

loquacity (noun) Talkativeness, wordiness. *While some people deride his loquacity and his tendency to use outrageous rhymes, no one can doubt that Jesse Jackson is a powerful orator.* loquacious (adjective).

lucid (adjective) Clear and understandable. *Hawking's* A Short History of the Universe *is a lucid explanation of a difficult topic, modern scientific theories of the origin of the universe.* lucidity (noun).

M

magnanimous (adjective) Noble, generous. *When media titan Ted Turner pledged a gift of $1 billion to the United Nations, he challenged other wealthy people to be equally magnanimous.* magnanimity (noun).

maladroit (adjective) Inept, awkward. *It was painful to watch the young congressman's maladroit delivery of the nominating speech.*

malinger (verb) To pretend illness to avoid work. *During the labor dispute, hundreds of employees malingered, forcing the company to slow production and costing it millions in profits.*

malleable (adjective) Able to be changed, shaped, or formed by outside pressures. *Gold is a very useful metal because it is so malleable. A child's personality is malleable, and is often deeply influenced by things her parents say and do.* malleability (noun).

mandate (noun) Order, command. *The new policy on gays in the military went into effect as soon as the president issued his mandate about it.* mandate (verb), mandatory (adjective).

marginal (adjective) At the outer edge or fringe; of minimal quality or acceptability. *In spite of the trend toward greater paternal involvement in child-rearing, most fathers still have a marginal role in their children's lives. Jerry's GRE scores were so marginal that he didn't get accepted into the graduate school of his choice.*

marginalize (verb) To push toward the fringes; to make less consequential. *Hannah argued that the designation of a certain month as "Black History Month" or "Gay and Lesbian Book Month" actually does a disservice to minorities by marginalizing them.*

martial (adjective) Of, relating to, or suited to military life. *My old teacher, Miss Woody, had such a martial demeanor that you'd think she was running a boot camp instead of teaching fifth grade. The military seized control of Myanmar in 1988, and this embattled country has been ruled by martial law since then.*

WORD ORIGIN

Latin *lux* = light. Also found in English *elucidate*, *pellucid*, and *translucent*.

WORD ORIGIN

Latin *mandare* = entrust, order. Also found in English *command*, *demand*, and *remand*.

WORD
ORIGIN
Latin *medius* =
middle. Also
found in English
intermediate,
media, and
medium.

mediate (verb) To reconcile differences between two parties. *During the baseball strike, both the players and the club owners expressed willingness to have the president mediate the dispute.* mediation (noun).

mercenary (adjective) Doing something only for pay or for personal advantage. *People had criticized the U.S. motives in the Persian Gulf War as mercenary, pointing out that the U.S. would not have come to Kuwait's defense had it grown carrots rather than produced oil.* mercenary (noun).

mercurial (adjective) Changing quickly and unpredictably. *The mercurial personality of Robin Williams, with his many voices and styles, made him a natural choice to play the part of the ever-changing genie in* Aladdin.

metamorphose (verb) To undergo a striking transformation. *In just a century, book publishers have metamorphosed from independent, exclusively literary businesses to minor divisions in multimedia entertainment conglomerates.* metamorphosis (noun).

meticulous (adjective) Very careful with details. *Watch repair calls for a craftsperson who is patient and meticulous.*

mettle (noun) Strength of spirit; stamina. *Linda's mettle was severely tested while she served as the only female attorney at Smith, Futterweitt, Houghton, and Dobbs.* mettlesome (adjective).

mimicry (noun) Imitation, aping. *The continued popularity of Elvis Presley has given rise to a class of entertainers who make a living through mimicry of "The King."* mimic (noun and verb).

minatory (adjective) Menacing, threatening. *As soon as she met Mrs. Danforth, the head housemaid at Manderlay, the young bride was cowed by her minatory manner and quickly retreated to the morning room.*

mince (verb) To chop into small pieces; to speak with decorum and restraint. *Malaysia's prime minister Mahathir Mohamad was not a man known to mince words; he had accused satellite TV of poisoning Asia and had denounced the Australian press as "congenital liars."*

WORD
ORIGIN
Greek *anthropos*
= human. Also
found in English
anthropology,
anthropoid,
anthropomorphic,
and *philanthropy*.

misanthrope (noun) Someone who hates or distrusts all people. *In the beloved Christmas classic,* It's a Wonderful Life, *Lionel Barrymore plays Potter, the wealthy misanthrope who is determined to make life miserable for everyone, and particularly for the young, idealistic George Bailey.* misanthropic (adjective), misanthropy (noun).

miscreant (adjective) Unbelieving, heretical; evil, villainous. *After a one-year run playing Iago in* Othello, *and then two years playing Bill Sikes in* Oliver, *Sean was tired of being typecast in miscreant roles.* miscreant (noun).

mitigate (verb) To make less severe; to relieve. *There's no doubt that Wallace committed the assault, but the verbal abuse Wallace had received helps to explain his behavior and somewhat mitigates his guilt.* mitigation (noun).

monopoly (noun) A condition in which there is only one seller of a certain commodity. *Wary of Microsoft's seeming monopoly of the computer operating-system business, rivals are asking for government intervention.* **monopolistic** (adjective) *Renowned consumer advocate Ralph Nader once quipped, "The only difference between John D. Rockefeller and Bill Gates is that Gates recognizes no boundaries to his monopolistic drive."*

monotonous (adjective) Tediously uniform, unchanging. *Brian Eno's "Music for Airports" is characterized by minimal melodies, subtle textures, and variable repetition, which I find rather bland and monotonous.* monotony (noun).

morose (adjective) Gloomy, sullen. *After Chuck's girlfriend dumped him, he lay around the house for a couple of days, refusing to come to the phone and feeling morose.*

mutation (noun) A significant change; in biology, a permanent change in hereditary material. *Most genetic mutations are not beneficial, since any change in the delicate balance of an organism tends to be disruptive.* mutate (verb).

N

nadir (noun) Lowest point. *Pedro and Renee's marriage reached a new nadir last Christmas Eve when Pedro locked Renee out of the house upon her return from the supposed "business trip."*

nascent (adjective) Newly born, just beginning. *While her artistry is still nascent, it was 15-year-old Tara Lipinski's technical wizardry that enabled her to win a gold medal in the 1998 Winter Olympics.* nascence (noun).

noisome (adjective) Putrid, fetid, noxious. *We were convinced that the noisome odor infiltrating every corner of our building was evidence of a mouldering corpse.*

notorious (adjective) Famous, especially for evil actions or qualities. *Warner Brothers produced a series of movies about notorious gangsters such as John Dillinger and Al Capone.* notoriety (noun).

O

WORD
ORIGIN
Latin *durus* =
hard. Also found
in English *durable*
and *endure*.

obdurate (adjective) Unwilling to change; stubborn, inflexible. *Despite the many pleas he received, the governor was obdurate in his refusal to grant clemency to the convicted murderer.*

oblivious (adjective) Unaware, unconscious. *Karen practiced her oboe solo with complete concentration, oblivious to the noise and activity around her.* oblivion (noun), obliviousness (noun).

obscure (adjective) Little known; hard to understand. *Mendel was an obscure monk until decades after his death, when his scientific work was finally discovered. Most people find the writings of James Joyce obscure; hence the popularity of books that explain the many odd references and tricks of language in his work.* obscure (verb), obscurity (noun).

obsolete (adjective) No longer current; old-fashioned. *W.H. Auden said that his ideal landscape would contain water wheels, grain mills, and other forms of obsolete machinery.* obsolescence (noun).

obstinate (adjective) Stubborn, unyielding. *Despite years of government effort, the problem of drug abuse remains obstinate.* obstinacy (noun).

obtuse (adjective) Dull-witted, insensitive; incomprehensible, unclear, or imprecise. *Amy was so obtuse she didn't realize that Alexi had proposed marriage to her. French psychoanalyst Jacques Lacan's collection of papers, Ecrits, is notoriously obtuse, yet it has still been highly influential in linguistics, film theory, and literary criticism.*

obviate (verb) Preclude, make unnecessary. *Truman Capote's meticulous accuracy and total recall obviated the need for note-taking when he wrote his account of a 1959 murder, In Cold Blood.*

odium (noun) Intense feeling of hatred, abhorrence. *When the neighbors learned that a convicted sex offender was now living in their midst, they could not restrain their odium and began harassing the man whenever he left his house.* odious (adjective).

opprobrium (noun) Dishonor, disapproval. *Switzerland came under public opprobrium when it was revealed that Swiss bankers had hoarded the gold the Nazis had confiscated from their victims.* opprobrious (adjective).

orthodox (adjective) In religion, conforming to a certain doctrine; conventional. *George Eliot's relationship with George Lewes, a married journalist, offended the sensibilities of her more orthodox peers.* orthodoxy (noun).

ossified (adjective) In biology, to turn into bone; to become rigidly conventional and opposed to change. *His harsh view of co-education had ossified over the years, so that he was now the only teacher who sought to bar girls from the venerable boys' school.* ossification (noun).

ostentatious (adjective) Overly showy, pretentious. *To show off his new wealth, the financier threw an ostentatious party featuring a full orchestra, a famous singer, and tens of thousands of dollars' worth of food.* ostentation (noun).

ostracize (verb) To exclude from a group. *In Biblical times, those who suffered from the disease of leprosy were ostracized and forced to live alone.* ostracism (noun).

P

paean (adjective) A joyous expression of praise, gratitude, or triumph. *Choreographer Paul Taylor's dance "Eventide" is a sublime paean to remembered love, with couple after loving couple looking back as they embrace an unknown future.*

parody (noun) An imitation created for comic effect; a caricature. *While the creators of the 1970s comedy series* All in the Family *intended Archie Bunker to be a parody of closed-mindedness in Americans, large numbers of people adopted Bunker as a working-class hero.*

parse (verb) To break a sentence down into grammatical components; to analyze bit by bit. *In the wake of the sex scandal, journalists parsed every utterance by administration officials regarding the president's alleged promiscuity. At $1.25 million a day,* Titanic *is the most expensive movie ever made, but director James Cameron refused to parse the film's enormous budget for inquisitive reporters.*

partisan (adjective) Reflecting strong allegiance to a particular party or cause. *The vote on the president's budget was strictly partisan: every member of the president's party voted yes, and all others voted no.* partisan (noun).

pastoral (adjective) Simple and rustic, bucolic, rural. *While industry grew and the country expanded westward, the Hudson River School of painters depicted the landscape as a pastoral setting where humans and nature could coexist.*

patron (noun) A special guardian or protector; a wealthy or influential supporter of the arts. *Dominique de Menil used her considerable wealth to become a well-known patron of the arts; she and her husband owned a collection of more than 10,000 pieces ranging from cubist paintings to tribal artifacts.* patronize (verb).

peccadillo (noun) A minor offense, a lapse. *What Dr. Sykes saw as a major offense—being addressed as Marge rather than Doctor—Tina saw as a mere peccadillo and one that certainly should not have lost her the job.*

pedantic (adjective) Academic, bookish. *The men Hillary met through personal ads in the New York Review of Books were invariably pasty-skinned pedantic types who dropped the names of nineteenth-century writers in every sentence.* pedantry (noun).

pedestrian (adjective) Unimaginative, ordinary. *The new Italian restaurant received a bad review due to its reliance on pedestrian dishes such as pasta with marinara sauce or chicken parmigiana.*

perfidious (adjective) Disloyal, treacherous. *Although he was one of the most talented generals of the American Revolution, Benedict Arnold is remembered today as a perfidious betrayer of the patriot cause.* perfidy (noun).

WORD ORIGIN

Latin *fides* = faith. Also found in English *confide, confidence, fidelity,* and *infidel.*

peripatetic (adjective) Moving or traveling from place to place; always on the go. *In Barbara Wilson's* Trouble in Transylvania, *peripatetic translator Cassandra Reilly is on the road again, this time to China by way of Budapest, where she plans to catch the TransMongolian Express.*

permeate (verb) To spread through or penetrate. *Little by little, the smell of gas from the broken pipe permeated the house.*

personification (noun) The embodiment of a thing or an abstract idea in human form. *Many people view Theodore Kaczynski, the killer known as the Unabomber, as the very personification of evil.* personify (verb).

pervasive (adjective) Spreading throughout. *As news of the disaster reached the town, a pervasive sense of gloom could be felt everywhere.* pervade (verb).

philistine (noun) Someone who is smugly ignorant and uncultured. *A true philistine, Meg claimed she didn't read any book that wasn't either recommended by Oprah Winfrey or on the best-seller list.* philistine (adjective).

pith (noun) The core, the essential part; in biology, the central strand of tissue in the stems of most vascular plants. *After spending seventeen years in psychoanalysis, Frieda had finally come face to face with the pith of her deep-seated anxiety.* pithy (adjective).

placate (verb) To soothe or appease. *The waiter tried to placate the angry customer with the offer of a free dessert.* placatory (adjective).

placid (adjective) Unmarked by disturbance; complacent. *Dr. Kahn was convinced that the placid exterior presented by Frieda in her early analysis sessions masked a deeply disturbed psyche.* placidity (noun).

plaintive (adjective) Expressing suffering or melancholy. *In the beloved children's book* The Secret Garden, *Mary is disturbed by plaintive cries echoing in the corridors of gloomy Misselthwaite Manor.*

plastic (adjective) Able to be molded or reshaped. *Because it is highly plastic, clay is an easy material for beginning sculptors to use.* plasticity (noun).

platitude (noun) A trite remark or saying; a cliché. *How typical of June to send a sympathy card filled with mindless platitudes like "One day at a time," rather than calling the grieving widow.* platitudinous (adjective).

plausible (adjective) Apparently believable. *The idea that a widespread conspiracy to kill the president has been kept secret by all the participants for more than thirty years hardly seems plausible.* plausibility (noun).

plummet (verb) To dive or plunge. *On October 27, 1997, the stock market plummeted by 554 points and left us all wondering if the bull market was finally over.*

polarize (adjective) To separate into opposing groups or forces. *For years, the abortion debate polarized the American people, with many people voicing views at either extreme and few people trying to find a middle ground.* polarization (noun).

ponderous (adjective) Unwieldy and bulky; oppressively dull. *Unfortunately, the film director weighed the movie down with a ponderous voice-over narrated by the protagonist as an old man.*

poseur (noun) Someone who pretends to be what he isn't. *Gerald had pretensions for literary stardom with his book proposal on an obscure World WarII battle, yet most agents soon realized that the book would never be written and categorized him as a poseur.*

positivism (noun) A philosophy that denies speculation and assumes that the only knowledge is scientific knowledge. *David Hume carried his positivism to an extreme when he argued that our expectation that the sun will rise tomorrow has no basis in reason and is purely a matter of belief.* positivistic (adjective).

pragmatism (noun) A belief in approaching problems through practical rather than theoretical means. *Roosevelt's attitude toward the economic troubles of the Depression was based on pragmatism: "Try something," he said. "If it doesn't work, try something else."* pragmatic (adjective).

precedent (noun) An earlier occurrence that serves as an example for a decision. *In a legal system that reveres precedent, even defining the nature of a completely new type of dispute can seem impossible.* precede (verb).

precept (noun) A general principle or law. *One of the central precepts of Tai Chi Ch'uan is the necessity of allowing ki (cosmic energy) to flow through one's body in slow, graceful movements.*

precipitate (verb) To spur or activate. *In the summer of 1997, the selling off of the Thai baht precipitated a currency crisis that spread throughout Asia.*

WORD ORIGIN

Latin *claudere* = to close. Also found in English *conclude*, *include*, *recluse*, and *seclude*.

preclude (verb) To prevent, to hinder. *Unfortunately, Jasmine's appointment at the New Age Expo precluded her attendance at our weekend Workshop for Shamans and Psychics.* preclusive (adjective), preclusion (noun).

precursor (noun) A forerunner, a predecessor. *The Kodak Brownie camera, a small boxy camera made of jute board and wood, was the precursor to today's sleek digital cameras.* precursory (adjective).

preponderance (noun) A superiority in weight, size, or quantity; a majority. *In Seattle, there is a great preponderance of seasonal affective disorder, or SAD, a malady brought on by light starvation during the dark Northwest winter.* preponderate (verb).

presage (verb) To foretell, to anticipate. *According to folklore, a red sky at dawn presages a day of stormy weather.*

prescience (noun) Foreknowledge or foresight. *When she saw the characteristic eerie yellowish-black light in the sky, Dorothy had the prescience to seek shelter in the storm cellar.* prescient (adjective).

presumptuous (adjective) Going beyond the limits of courtesy or appropriateness. *The senator winced when the presumptuous young staffer addressed him as "Ted."* presume (verb), presumption (noun).

prevaricate (verb) To lie, to equivocate. *When it became clear to the FBI that the mobster had threatened the 12-year-old witness, they could well understand why the youngster had prevaricated during the hearing.*

primacy (noun) State of being the utmost in importance; preeminence. *The anthropologist Ruth Benedict was an inspiration to Margaret Mead for her emphasis on the primacy of culture in the formation of an individual's personality.* primal (adjective).

pristine (adjective) Pure, undefiled. *As climbers who have scaled Mt. Everest can attest, the trails to the summit are hardly in pristine condition and are actually strewn with trash.*

probity (noun) Goodness, integrity. *The vicious editorial attacked the moral probity of the senatorial candidate, saying he had profited handsomely from his pet project, the senior-citizen housing project.*

procure (verb) To obtain by using particular care and effort. *Through partnerships with a large number of specialty wholesalers, W.W. Grainger is able to procure a startling array of products for its customers, from bear repellent for Alaska pipeline workers to fork-lift trucks and toilet paper.* procurement (noun).

prodigality (noun) The condition of being wastefully extravagant. *Richard was ashamed of the prodigality of his bride's parents when he realized that the cost of the wedding reception alone was more than his father earned in one year.* prodigal (adjective).

proliferate (verb) To increase or multiply. *For about fifteen years, high-tech companies had proliferated in northern California, Massachusetts, and other regions.* proliferation (noun).

prolixity (noun) A diffuseness; a rambling and verbose quality. *The prolixity of Sarah's dissertation on Ottoman history defied even her advisor's attempts to read it.* prolix (adjective).

propagate (verb) To cause to grow; to foster. *John Smithson's will left his fortune for the founding of an institution to propagate knowledge, leaving open whether that meant a university, a library, or a museum.* propagation (noun).

prophetic (adjective) Auspicious, predictive of what's to come. *We often look at every event leading up to a new love affair as prophetic—the flat tire that caused us to be late for work, the chance meeting in the elevator, the horoscope that augured "a new beginning."* prophecy (noun), prophesy (verb).

propitiating (adjective) Conciliatory, mollifying or appeasing. *Management's offer of a 5 percent raise was meant as a propitiating gesture, yet the striking workers were unimpressed.* propitiate (verb).

propriety (noun) Appropriateness. *Some people expressed doubts about the propriety of the president discussing his underwear on MTV.*

proximity (noun) Closeness, nearness. *Neighborhood residents were angry over the proximity of the proposed sewage plant to the local elementary school.* proximate (adjective).

pundit (noun) Someone who offers opinions in an authoritative style. *The Sunday morning talk shows are filled with pundits, each with his or her own theory about this week's political news.*

pungency (noun) Marked by having a sharp, biting quality. *Unfortunately, the pungency of the fresh cilantro overwhelmed the delicate flavor of the poached turbot.* pungent (adjective).

purify (verb) To make pure, clean, or perfect. *The new water-treatment plant is supposed to purify the drinking water provided to everyone in the nearby towns.* purification (noun).

Q

quiescent (adjective) In a state of rest or inactivity; latent. *Polly's ulcer has been quiescent ever since her mother-in-law moved out of the condo, which was well over a year ago.* quiescence (noun).

WORD ORIGIN

Latin *poena* = pain. Also found in English *impunity, penal, penalty,* and *punishment.*

quixotic (adjective) Foolishly romantic, idealistic to an impractical degree. *In the novel Shoeless Joe, Ray Kinsella carries out a quixotic plan to build a baseball field in the hopes that past baseball greats will come to play there.*

quotidian (adjective) Occurring every day; commonplace and ordinary. *Most of the time, we long to escape from quotidian concerns, but in the midst of a crisis we want nothing more than to be plagued by such simple problems as a leaky faucet or a whining child.*

R

raconteur (noun) An excellent storyteller. *A member of the Algonquin Roundtable, Robert Benchley was a natural raconteur with a seemingly endless ability to turn daily life and its irritations into entertaining commentary.*

rancorous (adjective) Marked by deeply embedded bitterness or animosity. *While Ralph and Kishu have been separated for three years, their relationship is so rancorous that they had to hire a professional mediator just to discuss divorce arrangements.* rancor (noun).

rapacious (adjective) Excessively grasping or greedy. *Some see global currency speculators like George Soros as rapacious parasites who destroy economies and then line their pockets with the profits.* rapacity (noun).

rarefied (adjective) Of interest or relating to a small, refined circle; less dense, thinner. *Those whose names dot the society pages live in a rarefied world where it's entirely normal to dine on caviar for breakfast or order a $2,000 bottle of wine at Le Cirque. When she reached the summit of Mt. McKinley, Deborah could hardly breathe in the rarefied air.*

raucous (adjective) Boisterous, unruly, and wild. *Sounds of shouts and raucous laughter drifted out of the hotel room where Felipe's bachelor party was being held.*

reactionary (adjective) Ultra conservative. *Every day, more than twenty million listeners used to tune in to hear Rush Limbaugh spew his reactionary opinions about "Feminazis" and environmental "fanatics."* reactionary (noun).

recede (verb) To draw back, to ebb, to abate. *Once his hairline began to recede, Hap took to wearing bizarre accessories, like velvet ascots, to divert attention from it.* recession (noun).

reclusive (adjective) Withdrawn from society. *During the last years of her life, Garbo led a reclusive existence, rarely appearing in public.* recluse (noun).

recompense (noun) Compensation for a service rendered or to pay for damages. *The 5 percent of the estate, which Phil received as executor of his aunt Ida's will, is small recompense for the headaches he endured in settling her affairs.* recompense (verb).

reconcile (verb) To make consistent or harmonious. *Franklin D. Roosevelt's greatness as a leader can be seen in his ability to reconcile the differing demands and values of the varied groups that supported him.* reconciliation (noun).

recondite (adjective) Profound, deep, abstruse. *Professor Miyaki's recondite knowledge of seventeenth-century Flemish painters made him a prized—if barely understood—member of the art history department.*

redemptive (adjective) Liberating and reforming. *While she doesn't attend formal church services, Carrie is a firm believer in the redemptive power of prayer.* redeem (verb), redemption (noun).

refractory (adjective) Stubbornly resisting control or authority. *Like a refractory child, Jill stomped out of the car, slammed the door, and said she would walk home, even though her house was 10 miles away.*

relevance (noun) Connection to the matter at hand; pertinence. *Testimony in a criminal trial may only be admitted to the extent that it has clear relevance to the question of guilt or innocence.* relevant (adjective).

reparation (noun) The act of making amends; payment of damages by a defeated nation to the victors. *The Treaty of Versailles, signed in 1919, formally asserted Germany's war guilt and ordered it to pay reparations to the allies.*

reproof (noun) A reprimand, a reproach, or castigation. *Joe thought being grounded for one month was a harsh reproof for coming home late only once.* reprove (verb).

repudiate (verb) To reject, to renounce. *After it became known that the politician had been a leader of the Ku Klux Klan, most Republican leaders repudiated him.* repudiation (noun).

repugnant (adjective) Causing dislike or disgust. *After the news broke about Mad Cow Disease, much of the beef-loving British public began to find the thought of a Sunday roast repugnant.*

requiem (noun) A musical composition or poem written to honor the dead. *Many financial analysts think that the ailing typewriter company should simply say a requiem for itself and shut down; however, the CEO has other plans.*

resilient (adjective) Able to recover from difficulty. *A pro athlete must be mentally resilient, able to lose a game one day and come back the next with renewed enthusiasm and confidence.* resilience (noun).

resonant (adjective) Full of special import or meaning. *I found the speaker's words particularly resonant because I, too, had served in Vietnam and felt the same mixture of shame and pride.* resonance (noun).

WORD ORIGIN

Latin *frangere* = to break. Also found in English *fraction, fractious, fracture, frangible, infraction,* and *refract.*

resplendent (adjective) Glowing, shining. *In late December, midtown New York is resplendent with holiday lights and decorations.* resplendence (noun).

rite (noun) Ceremony. *From October to May, the Patwin Indians of California's Sacramento Valley held a series of rites and dances designed to bring the tribe health and prosperity.*

rogue (noun) A mischievously dishonest person; a scamp. *In Jane Austen's* Pride and Prejudice, *Wickham, a charming rogue, seduces Darcy's young sister Georgiana and later does the same thing with Kitty Bennett.*

ruffian (noun) A brute, roughneck, or bully. *In Dickens's* Oliver Twist, *Fagin instructs his gang of orphaned ruffians on the arts of picking pockets and shoplifting.*

rumination (noun) The act of engaging in contemplation. *Marcel Proust's semi-autobiographical novel cycle* Remembrance of Things Past *is less a narrative than an extended rumination on the nature of memory.* ruminate (verb).

S

sage (noun) A person of great wisdom, a knowing philosopher. *It was the Chinese sage Confucius who first taught what is now known the world over as "The Golden Rule."* sagacious (adjective), sagacity (noun).

salutary (adjective) Restorative, healthful. *I find a short dip in an icy stream to be extremely salutary, although the health benefits of my bracing swims are, as yet, unclear.*

sanction (verb) Support or authorize. *Even after a bomb exploded on the front porch of his home, the Reverend Martin Luther King Jr. refused to sanction any violent response and urged his angry followers to love their enemies.* sanctify (verb), sanction (noun).

WORD ORIGIN

Latin *salus* = health. Also found in English *salubrious*, *salutation*, and *salute*.

sap (verb) To exhaust, to deplete. *The exhaustive twelve-city reading tour so sapped the novelist's strength that she told her publicist that she hoped her next book would be a flop! While the African nation was making enormous economic strides under its new president, rebel fighting had sapped much of the country's resources.*

satiate (verb) To fulfill to or beyond capacity. *Judging by the current crop of films featuring serial killers, rape, ritual murder, gun-slinging, and plain old-fashioned slugfests, the public appetite for violence has not yet been satiated.* satiation (noun), satiety (noun).

saturate (verb) To drench or suffuse with liquid or anything that permeates or invades. *The hostess's furious dabbing at the tablecloth was in vain, since the spilt wine had already saturated the damask cloth.* saturation (noun), saturated (adjective).

scrutinize (verb) To study closely. *The lawyer scrutinized the contract, searching for any detail that could pose a risk for her client.* scrutiny (noun).

scurvy (adjective) Shabby, low. *I couldn't believe that Farouk was so scurvy as to open up my computer files and read my e-mail.*

sedulous (adjective) Diligent, industrious. *Those who are most sedulous about studying this vocabulary list are likely to breeze through the antonyms sections of their GRE exam.*

sequential (adjective) Arranged in an order or series. *The courses required for the chemistry major are sequential; you must take them in the prescribed order, since each course builds on the previous ones.* sequence (noun).

sidereal (adjective) Relating to the stars or the constellations. *Jacqueline was interested in matters sidereal, and was always begging my father to take the dusty old telescope out of our garage.*

signatory (noun) Someone who signs an official document or petition along with others. *Alex urged me to join the other signatories and add my name to the petition against toxic sludge in organic foods, but I simply did not care enough about the issue. The signatories of the Declaration of Independence included John Adams, Benjamin Franklin, John Hancock, and Thomas Jefferson.*

sinuous (noun) Winding, circuitous, serpentine. *Frank Gehry's sinuous design for the Guggenheim Museum in Bilbao, Spain, has led people to hail the museum as the first great building of the twenty-first century.* sinuosity (noun).

specious (adjective) Deceptively plausible or attractive. *The infomercial for "Fat-Away" offered mainly specious arguments for a product that is, essentially, a heavy-duty girdle.*

splice (verb) To unite by interweaving separate strands or parts. *Amateur filmmaker Duddy Kravitz shocked and angered his clients by splicing footage of tribal rituals into his films of their weddings and bar mitzvahs.*

spontaneous (adjective) Happening without plan or outside cause. *When the news of John F. Kennedy's assassination hit the airwaves, people everywhere gathered in a spontaneous effort to express their shock and grief.* spontaneity (noun).

spurious (adjective) False, fake. *The so-called Piltdown Man, supposed to be the fossil of a primitive human, turned out to be spurious, though who created the hoax is still uncertain.*

squander (verb) To use up carelessly, to waste. *Those who had made donations to the charity were outraged to learn that its director had squandered millions on fancy dinners, first-class travel, and an expensive apartment for entertaining.*

stanch (verb) To stop the flow. *When the patient began to bleed profusely, the doctor stanched the blood flow by applying direct pressure to the wound.*

WORD ORIGIN

Latin *sequi* = to follow. Also found in English *consequence*, *sequel,* and *subsequent.*

stint (verb) To limit, to restrain. *The British bed and breakfast certainly did not stint on the breakfast part of the equation; they provided us with fried tomatoes, fried sausages, fried eggs, smoked kippers, fried bread, fried mushrooms, and bowls of a cereal called "Wheatabix" (which tasted like cardboard).* stinting (adjective).

stolid (adjective) Impassive, unemotional. *The popular animated television series* King of the Hill *chronicles the woes of a stolid, conservative Texan confronting changing times.* stolidity (noun).

subordination (noun) The state of being subservient or treated as less valuable. *Heather left the naval academy because she could no longer stand the subordination of every personal whim or desire to the rigorous demands of military life.* subordinate (verb).

subpoena (noun) An order of a court, legislation, or grand jury that compels a witness to be present at a trial or hearing. *The young man's lawyer asked the judge to subpoena a boa constrictor into court on the grounds that the police had used the snake as an "instrument of terror" to coerce his confession.*

subside (verb) To settle or die down. *The celebrated lecturer had to wait ten minutes for the applause to subside before he began his speech.*

subsidization (noun) The state of being financed by a grant from a government or other agency. *Without subsidization, the nation's passenger rail system would probably go bankrupt.* subsidize (verb).

substantiated (adjective) Verified or supported by evidence. *The charge that Nixon had helped to cover up crimes was substantiated by his comments about it on a series of audio tapes.* substantiate (verb), substantiation (noun).

subsume (verb) To encompass or engulf within something larger. *In Alan Dershowitz's* Reversal of Fortune, *he makes it clear that his work as a lawyer subsumes his personal life.*

subterranean (adjective) Under the surface of the earth. *Subterranean testing of nuclear weapons was permitted under the Nuclear Test Ban Treaty of 1963.*

summarily (adverb) Quickly and concisely. *No sooner had I voiced my concerns about the new ad campaign than my boss put her hand on my elbow and summarily ushered me out of her office.*

superficial (adjective) On the surface only; without depth or substance. *Her wound was only superficial and required no treatment except a light bandage. His superficial attractiveness hides the fact that his personality is lifeless and his mind is dull.* superficiality (noun).

superimpose (verb) To place or lay over or above something. *The artist stirred controversy by superimposing portraits of certain contemporary politicians over images of such reviled historical figures as Hitler and Stalin.*

supersede (verb) To displace, to substitute or supplant. *"I'm sorry," the principal announced, "but today's afternoon classes will be superseded by an assembly on drug and alcohol abuse."*

supine (adjective) Prone. *One always feels rather vulnerable when wearing a flimsy paper gown and lying supine on a doctor's examining table.*

supposition (noun) Assumption, conjecture. *While most climate researchers believe that increasing levels of greenhouse gases will warm the planet, skeptics claim that this theory is mere supposition.* suppose (verb).

surge (noun) A gush; a swelling or sweeping forward. *When Mattel gave the Barbie doll a makeover in the late 1980s, by manufacturing dolls like doctor Barbie and astronaut Barbie, the company experienced a surge in sales.*

T

tangential (adjective) Touching lightly; only slightly connected or related. *Having enrolled in a class on African-American history, the students found the teacher's stories about his travels in South America only of tangential interest.* tangent (noun).

tedium (noun) Boredom. *For most people, watching even a 15-minute broadcast of the earth as seen from space would be an exercise in sheer tedium.* tedious (adjective).

temperance (noun) Moderation or restraint in feelings and behavior. *Most professional athletes practice temperance in their personal habits; too much eating or drinking and too many late nights, they know, can harm their performance.*

temperate (adjective) Moderate, calm. *The warm gulf streams are largely responsible for the temperate climate of the British Isles.*

tenuous (adjective) Lacking in substance; weak, flimsy, very thin. *His tenuous grasp of the Spanish language was evident when he addressed Señor Chavez as "Señora."*

terrestrial (adjective) Of the earth. *The movie* Close Encounters of the Third Kind *tells the story of the first contact between beings from outer space and terrestrial creatures.*

throwback (noun) A reversion to an earlier type; an atavism. *The late-model Volkswagen Beetle, with its familiar bubble shape, looked like a throwback to the 1960s, but it was actually packed with modern high-tech equipment.*

WORD ORIGIN

Latin *tangere* = to touch. Also found in English *contact*, *contiguous*, *tactile*, *tangent*, and *tangible*.

tiff (noun) A small, almost inconsequential quarrel or disagreement. *Megan and Bruce got into a tiff when Bruce criticized her smoking.*

tirade (noun) A long, harshly critical speech. *Reformed smokers, like Bruce, are prone to delivering tirades on the evils of smoking.*

torpor (noun) Apathy, sluggishness. *Stranded in an airless hotel room in Madras after a 27-hour train ride, I felt such overwhelming torpor that I doubted I would make it to Bangalore, the next destination in my journey.* torpid (adjective).

tout (verb) To praise highly, to brag publicly. *A much happier Eileen is now touting the benefits of Prozac, but, to tell you the truth, I miss her witty, self-lacerating commentaries.*

tractable (adjective) Obedient, manageable. *When he turned 3, Harrison suddenly became a tractable, well-mannered little boy after being, quite frankly, an unruly little monster!*

tranquillity (noun) Freedom from disturbance or turmoil; calm. *She moved from New York City to rural Vermont seeking the tranquillity of country life.* tranquil (adjective).

transgress (verb) To go past limits; to violate. *If Iraq has developed biological weapons, then it has transgressed the UN's rules against manufacturing weapons of mass destruction.* transgression (noun).

transmute (verb) To change in form or substance. *Practitioners of alchemy, a forebearer of modern chemistry, tried to discover ways to transmute metals such as iron into gold.* transmutation (noun).

treacherous (adjective) Untrustworthy or disloyal; dangerous or unreliable. *Nazi Germany proved to be a treacherous ally, first signing a peace pact with the Soviet Union, then invading. Be careful crossing the rope bridge; parts of the span are badly frayed and treacherous.* treachery (noun).

tremor (noun) An involuntary shaking or trembling. *Brooke felt the first tremors of the 1989 San Francisco earthquake while she was sitting in Candlestick Park watching a Giants baseball game.*

trenchant (adjective) Caustic and incisive. *Essayist H.L. Mencken was known for his trenchant wit and was famed for mercilessly puncturing the American middle class (which he called the "booboisie").*

trepidation (noun) Fear and anxiety. *After the tragedy of TWA flight 800, many previously fearless flyers were filled with trepidation whenever they stepped into an airplane.*

turbulent (adjective) Agitated or disturbed. *The night before the championship match, Martina was unable to sleep, her mind turbulent with fears and hopes.* turbulence (noun).

WORD ORIGIN

Latin *tractare* = to handle. Also found in English *intractable, tractate,* and *traction.*

WORD ORIGIN

Latin *trepidus* = alarmed. Also found in English *intrepid.*

turpitude (noun) Depravity, wickedness. *Radical feminists who contrast women's essential goodness with men's moral turpitude can be likened to religious fundamentalists who make a clear distinction between the saved and the damned.*

tyro (noun) Novice, amateur. *For an absolute tyro on the ski slopes, Gina was surprisingly agile at taking the moguls.*

U

unalloyed (adjective) Unqualified, pure. *Holding his newborn son for the first time, Malik felt an unalloyed happiness that was unlike anything else he had ever experienced in his 45 years.*

undermine (verb) To excavate beneath; to subvert, to weaken. *Dot continued to undermine my efforts to find her a date by showing up at our dinner parties in her ratty old sweat suit.*

unfeigned (adjective) Genuine, sincere. *Lashawn responded with such unfeigned astonishment when we all leapt out of the kitchen that I think she had had no inkling of the surprise party.*

univocal (adjective) With a single voice. *While they came from different backgrounds and classes, the employees were univocal in their demands that the corrupt CEO resign immediately.*

unstinting (adjective) Giving with unrestrained generosity. *Few people will be able to match the unstinting dedication and care which Mother Teresa had lavished on the poor people of Calcutta.*

urbanity (noun) Sophistication, suaveness, and polish. *Part of the fun in a Cary Grant movie lies in seeing whether the star can be made to lose his urbanity and elegance in the midst of chaotic or kooky situations.* urbane (adjective).

usurious (adjective) Lending money at an unconscionably high interest rate. *Some people feel that Shakespeare's portrayal of the Jew, Shylock, the usurious money lender in* The Merchant of Venice, *has enflamed prejudice against the Jews.* usury (adjective).

WORD ORIGIN

Latin *urbs* = city. Also found in English *suburb* and *urban*.

V

WORD ORIGIN

Latin *validus* = strong. Also found in English *invalid, invaluable, prevail,* and *value*.

validate (verb) To officially approve or confirm. *The election of the president is formally validated when the members of the Electoral College meet to confirm the verdict of the voters.* valid (adjective), validity (noun).

vapid (adjective) Flat, flavorless. *Whenever I have insomnia, I just tune the clock radio to Lite FM, and soon those vapid songs from the 1970s have me floating away to dreamland.* vapidity (noun).

venal (adjective) Corrupt, mercenary. *Sese Seko Mobuto was the venal dictator of Zaire who reportedly diverted millions of dollars in foreign aid to his own personal fortune.* venality (noun).

veneer (noun) A superficial or deceptive covering. *Beneath her folksy veneer, Samantha is a shrewd and calculating businessperson just waiting for the right moment to pounce.*

venerate (verb) To admire or honor. *In Communist China, Mao Tse-Tung is venerated as an almost god-like figure.* venerable (adjective), veneration (noun).

veracious (adjective) Truthful, earnest. *Many people still feel that Anita Hill was entirely veracious in her allegations of sexual harassment during the Clarence Thomas confirmation hearings.* veracity (noun).

WORD ORIGIN

Latin *verus* = true. Also found in English *verisimilitude, veritable,* and *verity*.

verify (verb) To prove to be true. *The contents of Robert L. Ripley's syndicated "Believe it or Not" cartoons could not be verified, yet the public still thrilled to reports of "the man with two pupils in each eye," "the human unicorn," and other amazing oddities.* verification (noun).

veritable (adjective) Authentic. *A French antiques dealer recently claimed that a fifteenth-century child-sized suit of armor that he purchased in 1994 is the veritable suit of armor worn by heroine Joan of Arc.*

vindictive (adjective) Spiteful. *Paula embarked on a string of petty, vindictive acts against her philandering boyfriend, such as mixing dry cat food with his cereal and snipping the blooms off his prize African violets.*

viscid (adjective) Sticky. *The 3M company's "Post-It," a simple piece of paper with one viscid side, has become as commonplace—and as indispensable—as the paper clip.*

viscous (adjective) Having a gelatinous or gooey quality. *I put too much liquid in the batter, and so my Black Forest cake turned out to be a viscous, inedible mass.*

vitiate (verb) To pollute, to impair. *When they voted to ban smoking from all bars in California, the public affirmed their belief that smoking vitiates the health of all people, not just smokers.*

vituperative (adjective) Verbally abusive, insulting. *Elizabeth Taylor should have won an award for her harrowing portrayal of Martha, the bitter, vituperative wife of a college professor in Edward Albee's* Who's Afraid of Virginia Woolf? vituperate (verb).

volatile (adjective) Quickly changing; fleeting, transitory; prone to violence. *Public opinion is notoriously volatile; a politician who is very popular one month may be voted out of office the next.* volatility (noun).

volubility (noun) Quality of being overly talkative, glib. *As Lorraine's anxiety increased, her volubility increased in direct proportion, so during her job interview the poor interviewer couldn't get a word in edgewise.* voluble (adjective).

voracious (adjective) Gluttonous, ravenous. *"Are all your appetites so voracious?" Wesley asked Nina as he watched her finish off seven miniature sandwiches and two lamb kabob skewers in a matter of minutes.* voracity (noun).

W

wag (noun) Wit, joker. *Tom was getting tired of his role as the comical wag who injected life into Kathy's otherwise tedious parties.* waggish (adjective).

whimsical (adjective) Based on a capricious, carefree, or sudden impulse or idea; fanciful, playful. *Dave Barry's* Book of Bad Songs *is filled with the kind of goofy jokes that are typical of his whimsical sense of humor.* whim (noun).

X

xenophobia (noun) Fear of foreigners or outsiders. *Slobodan Milosevic's nationalistic talk played on the deep xenophobia of the Serbs, who after 500 years of brutal Ottoman occupation had come to distrust all outsiders.*

Z

zenith (noun) Highest point. *Compiling this vocabulary list was the zenith of my literary career: after this, there was nowhere to go but downhill.*

WORD ORIGIN

Latin *vorare* = to eat. Also found in English *carnivorous, devour,* and *omnivorous.*

Controlled Testing Centers

Please refer to the MAT Web site, www.milleranalogies.com, for the most up-to-date list of test centers.

UNITED STATES
(includes Armed Forces and Territories)

ALABAMA

Alabama State University; phone: (334) 229-4308

Athens State University; phone: (256) 233-8285

Auburn University; phone: (334) 244-3306

Birmingham Southern College; phone: (205) 226-4803

Jacksonville State University; phone: (256) 782-5475

Miles College; phone: (205) 929-1695

Spring Hill College; phone: (251) 380-3468

Troy State University–Dothan; phone: (334) 983-6556

Troy State University–Montgomery; phone: (334) 670-3221

Troy State University–Phenix City; phone: (334) 448-5120

Troy State University–Troy; phone: (334) 670-3379

United States Sports Academy; phone: (251) 626-3303

University of Alabama–Birmingham; phone: (205) 934-3704

University of Alabama–Gadsden; phone: (256) 546-2886

University of Alabama–Huntsville; phone: (256) 824-6725

University of Alabama–Tuscaloosa; phone: (205) 348-6760

University of Montevallo; phone: (205) 665-6350

University of North Alabama; phone: (256) 765-4252

University of South Alabama; phone: (251) 460-6271

University of West Alabama; phone: (205) 652-3439

ALASKA

Kenai Peninsula College; phone: (907) 262-0328

University of Alaska–Anchorage; phone: (907) 786-4500

University of Alaska–Fairbanks; phone: (907) 474-5277

University of Alaska–Fairbanks/N.W.; phone: (907) 443-2201

ARKANSAS

Arkansas State University; phone: (870) 972-2038

Arkansas Tech University; phone: (479) 968-0302

Harding University; phone: (501) 279-4415

Henderson State University; phone: (870) 230-5470

Southern Arkansas University; phone: (870) 235-4145

University of Arkansas–Fayetteville; phone: (479) 575-3948

University of Arkansas–Little Rock; phone: (501) 569-3198

University of Arkansas–Monticello; phone: (870) 460-1453

ARIZONA

Arizona State University–Tempe; phone: (480) 965-7146

Arizona State University West; phone: (602) 543-8136

Northern Arizona University; phone: (928) 523-2261

Troy State University–Davis-Monthan AFB; phone: (520) 748-2625

University of Arizona; phone: (520) 621-7589

CALIFORNIA

California Polytechnic State University; phone: (805) 756-1551

California State University–Bakersfield; phone: (805) 664-3373

California State University–East Bay; phone: (510) 885-3661

California State University–Fresno; phone: (559) 278-2457

California State University–Los Angeles; phone: (323) 343-3160

California State University–Stanislaus; phone: (209) 667-3157

Chapman University–Fairfield; phone: (707) 438-0108

Chapman University–Palm Desert; phone: (760) 341-8051

Chapman University–Palmdale; phone: (661) 267-2001

Chapman University–Sacramento; phone: (916) 922-0119

Fresno Pacific College; phone: (559) 453-2213

Humboldt State University; phone: (707) 826-3611

La Sierra University; phone: (951) 785-2453

Loma Linda University; phone: (909) 558-4547

San Francisco State University; phone: (415) 338-2271

University of California–Riverside; phone: (951) 827-5531

University of California–Santa Barbara; phone: (805) 893-4411

University of La Verne; phone: (909) 593-3511

University of San Diego; phone: (619) 260-4585

University of the Pacific; phone: (209) 946-2521

Vanguard University; phone: (714) 556-3610 Ext. 348

Whittier College; phone: (562) 907-4847

COLORADO

Adams State College; phone: (719) 587-7958

Colorado State University–Pueblo; phone: (719) 549-2663

Mesa State College; phone: (970) 255-2750

Regis University; phone: (303) 458-3575

University of Colorado–Boulder; phone: (303) 492-5854

University of Colorado–Colorado Springs; phone: (719) 262-3265

University of Denver; phone: (303) 871-2150

University of Northern Colorado; phone: (970) 351-2790

CONNECTICUT

Connecticut College; phone: (860) 439-2330

Southern Connecticut State University; phone: (203) 392-5906

Trinity College; phone: (860) 297-2415

University of Connecticut; phone: (860) 486-0174

University of Hartford; phone: (860) 768-5447

Western Connecticut State University; phone: (203) 837-8690

DELAWARE

University of Delaware; phone: (302) 831-6717

DISTRICT OF COLUMBIA

Catholic University of America; phone: (202) 319-5765

Gallaudet University; phone: (202) 651-5355

FLORIDA

Barry University–Miami Shores; phone: (305) 899-3950

Barry University–Orlando; phone: (321) 235-8400

Florida Atlantic University; phone: (561) 297-3160

Florida Gulf Coast University; phone: (239) 590-7952

Florida Southern College; phone: (863) 680-4299

Jacksonville University; phone: (904) 256-7193

Lynn University; phone: (561) 237-7841

Nova Southeastern University; phone: (561) 622-8041 Ext. 19

Saint Thomas University; phone: (305) 474-6838

Stetson University; phone: (904) 822-8909

Troy State University–Florida Region; phone: (407) 599-6993

Troy State University–Ft. Walton Beach; phone: (850) 244-7414

University of Florida; phone: (352) 392-1575

GEORGIA

Albany State University; phone: (912) 430-4667

Armstrong Atlantic State University; phone: (912) 927-5269

Augusta State University; phone: (706) 737-1471

Berry College; phone: (706) 290-2660

Brenau University; phone: (912) 882-7125

Brenau University–Gainesville; phone: (770) 534-6220

Columbus State University; phone: (706) 568-2226

Georgia College & State University; phone: (478) 445-5016

Georgia Perimeter College; phone: (678) 407-5322

Georgia Southern University; phone: (912) 681-5415

Georgia State University; phone: (404) 651-2217

Mercer University; phone: (478) 301-2863

North Georgia College & State University; phone: (706) 864-1799

Piedmont College; phone: (706) 778-0118

Shorter College; phone: (770) 951-8382

Troy State University; phone: (912) 264-9268

Troy University; phone: (770) 385-8315

Valdosta State University; phone: (229) 245-3878

HAWAII

Brigham Young University–Hawaii Campus; phone: (808) 293-3536

University of Hawaii–Manoa; phone: (808) 956-3455

IDAHO

Boise State University; phone: (208) 426-1583

Idaho State University; phone: (208) 236-2130

University of Idaho; phone: (208) 885-6716

ILLINOIS

Bradley University; phone: (309) 677-3181

Eastern Illinois University; phone: (217) 581-5986

Greenville College; phone: (618) 664-2800

Illinois Institute of Technology; phone: (312) 808-7132

Illinois State University; phone: (309) 438-2100

National-Louis University; phone: (847) 947-5548

Northern Illinois University; phone: (815) 753-1204

Quad-Cities Graduate Study Center; phone: (309) 794-7376

Quincy University; phone: (217) 228-5316

Saint Xavier University; phone: (773) 298-3053

Southern Illinois University–Carbondale; phone: (618) 453-6003

Southern Illinois University–Edwardsville; phone: (618) 650-3717

Trinity International University; phone: (847) 317-4067

University of Illinois–Chicago; phone: (312) 996-0919

University of Illinois–Urbana-Champaign; phone: (217) 333-3706

Western Illinois University; phone: (309) 298-2453

INDIANA

Ball State University; phone: (765) 677-1290

Bureau of Evaluative Studies & Testing; phone: (812) 855-1595

Butler University; phone: (317) 940-9266

Indiana *(continued)*

Indiana-Purdue University–Ft. Wayne; phone: (260) 481-6599

Indiana-Purdue University–Indianapolis; phone: (317) 274-2620

Indiana Wesleyan University; phone: (765) 677-2257

Oakland City University; phone: (812) 749-1509

Purdue University–West Lafayette; phone: (765) 494-1145

IOWA

Buena Vista College; phone: (712) 749-2218

Clarke College; phone: (563) 588-6331

Drake University; phone: (515) 271-2182

Indian Hills Community College; phone: (641) 683-5233

Iowa State University; phone: (515) 294-5058

Morningside College; phone: (712) 274-5375

University of Northern Iowa; phone: (319) 273-6024

Viterbo College; phone: (515) 224-4811

KANSAS

Benedictine College; phone: (913) 360-7578

Emporia State University; phone: (620) 341-5103

Fort Hays State University; phone: (785) 628-4401

Friends University; phone: (316) 295-5824

Kansas State University; phone: (785) 532-6492

Pittsburg State University; phone: (620) 235-4267

University of Kansas; phone: (785) 864-2768

Washburn University; phone: (785) 231-1010

Wichita State University; phone: (316) 978-5339

KENTUCKY

Eastern Kentucky University; phone: (859) 622-1281

Morehead State University; phone: (606) 783-2526

Murray State University; phone: (270) 762-6851

University of Louisville; phone: (502) 852-6606

Western Kentucky University; phone: (270) 745-3159

LOUISIANA

Louisiana Tech. University; phone: (318) 257-2488

Loyola University; phone: (504) 864-7840

McNeese State University; phone: (337) 475-5140

Our Lady of Holy Cross College; phone: (504) 394-7744

University of Louisiana–Lafayette; phone: (337) 482-6480

University of New Orleans; phone: (504) 280-7219

Xavier University of Louisiana; phone: (504) 483-7487

MAINE

Colby College; phone: (207) 872-3343

University of Maine–Farmington; phone: (207) 778-7034

University of Maine–Machias; phone: (207) 255-1228

University of Maine–Orono; phone: (207) 581-1410

University of Maine–Presque Isle; phone: (207) 768-9589

University of Southern Maine; phone: (207) 780-4383

MARYLAND

College of Southern Maryland; phone: (301) 934-7862

Frostburg State University; phone: (301) 687-4193

Johns Hopkins University; phone: (410) 516-7819

Montgomery College; phone: (301) 279-5086

University of Maryland–College Park; phone: (301) 314-7688

Western Maryland College; phone: (410) 857-2500

MASSACHUSETTS

American International College; phone: (413) 747-6269

Bridgewater State College; phone: (508) 531-1780

Fitchburg State College; phone: (978) 665-4472

Massachusetts College of Liberal Arts; phone: (413) 662-5332

Northeastern University; phone: (617) 373-2331

Salem State College; phone: (978) 542-7044

Springfield College; phone: (413) 748-3345

Tufts University; phone: (617) 627-3360

Westfield State College; phone: (413) 572-8020

Massachusetts (continued)

Worcester State College; phone: (508) 929-8072

MICHIGAN

Central Michigan University; phone: (989) 774-1092

Ferris State University; phone: (231) 591-3628

Gogebic Community College; phone: (906) 932-4231

Lake Superior State University; phone: (906) 635-2452

Michigan State University; phone: (517) 355-8385

Oakland University; phone: (248) 370-3229

University of Michigan; phone: (734) 764-8312

Wayne State University; phone: (313) 577-3400

Western Michigan University; phone: (616) 387-1850

MINNESOTA

Bemidji State University; phone: (218) 755-2075

Carleton College; phone: (507) 646-4293

College of St. Scholastica; phone: (218) 723-6085

Minnesota State University–Mankato; phone: (507) 389-1455

Minnesota State University–Moorhead; phone: (218) 477-2227

St. Cloud State University; phone: (320) 308-3112

University of Minnesota–Duluth; phone: (218) 726-7985

University of Minnesota–Minneapolis; phone: (612) 624-9853

University of Minnesota–Morris; phone: (320) 589-6060

University of St. Thomas; phone: (651) 962-6781

MISSISSIPPI

Alcorn State University; phone: (601) 877-6230

Delta State University; phone: (662) 846-4690

Jackson State University; phone: (601) 979-2484

Mississippi State University; phone: (662) 325-2091

Mississippi State University–Meridian Branch; phone: (601) 484-0178

Mississippi University for Women; phone: (662) 329-7349

University of Southern Mississippi; phone: (601) 266-4602

MISSOURI

Drury University–St. Robert Annex; phone: (573) 451-2400

Drury University–Springfield; phone: (417) 873-7419

Lincoln University; phone: (573) 681-5167

Missouri Southern State College; phone: (417) 625-9529

Northwest Missouri State University; phone: (660) 562-1220

Saint Louis University; phone: (314) 977-2963

Southeast Missouri State University; phone: (573) 651-2837

Southwest Missouri State University; phone: (417) 836-5116

Truman State University; phone: (660) 785-4140

University of Missouri–Columbia; phone: (573) 882-4801

University of Missouri–Kansas City; phone: (816) 235-1635

University of Missouri–Rolla; phone: (573) 341-4222

Washington University; phone: (314) 935-6777

MONTANA

Montana State University–Bozeman; phone: (406) 994-6984

Montana State University–Northern; phone: (406) 265-3745

Troy State University–Malmstrom AFB; phone: (406) 727-5451

University of Great Falls; phone: (406) 791-5308

University of Montana; phone: (406) 243-2175

NEBRASKA

Bellevue University; phone: (402) 293-3731

Concordia University; phone: (402) 643-7464

Peru State College; phone: (402) 872-2222

University of Nebraska–Kearney; phone: (308) 865-8235

University of Nebraska–Omaha; phone: (402) 554-4800

NEVADA

University of Nevada–Las Vegas; phone: (702) 895-3627

University of Nevada–Reno; phone: (775) 784-4648

NEW HAMPSHIRE

Plymouth State College; phone: (603) 535-2636

Rivier College; phone: (603) 897-8282

University of New Hampshire; phone: (603) 862-2009

NEW JERSEY

Brookdale College; phone: (732) 224-2584

Drew University; phone: (973) 408-3398

Fairleigh Dickinson University–Hackensack; phone: (201) 692-2645

Kean University; phone: (908) 737-3930

Rowan University; phone: (856) 256-4042

Rutgers–State University of New Jersey; phone: (732) 932-9742

Seton Hall University; phone: (973) 761-9355

St. Peter's College; phone: (201) 915-9254

William Paterson University; phone: (973) 720-2274

NEW MEXICO

Eastern New Mexico University; phone: (505) 562-2280

New Mexico State University–Carlsbad; phone: (505) 234-9322

New Mexico State University–Las Cruces; phone: (505) 646-1921

San Juan College; phone: (505) 566-3299

University of New Mexico; phone: (505) 277-5346

NEW YORK

Buffalo State College; phone: (716) 878-5601

Cornell University; phone: (607) 255-6927

Dowling College; phone: (631) 244-1301

Fordham University; phone: (718) 817-3775

Hofstra University; phone: (516) 463-5624

Niagara University; phone: (716) 286-8536

Plattsburgh Extension Center; phone: (518) 792-5425

Plattsburgh State University; phone: (518) 792-5425

Skidmore College; phone: (888) 845-2890

St. Bonaventure University; phone: (716) 375-2310

State University of New York–Buffalo; phone: (716) 645-6854

State University of New York–New Paltz; phone: (845) 257-2803

State University of New York–Plattsburgh; phone: (518) 564-2164

University of Rochester; phone: (716) 275-2354

NORTH CAROLINA

Appalachian State University; phone: (828) 262-6801

Catawba College; phone: (704) 637-4101

East Carolina University; phone: (252) 328-6811

Fayetteville State University; phone: (910) 486-1814

Gardner-Webb University; phone: (704) 406-4242

North Carolina State University; phone: (919) 515-2251

Pfeiffer University; phone: (704) 463-1360

University of North Carolina–Charlotte; phone: (704) 687-2105

University of North Carolina–Greensboro; phone: (336) 334-5874

University of North Carolina–Pembroke; phone: (910) 521-6202

University of North Carolina–Wilmington; phone: (910) 962-3746

Western Carolina University; phone: (828) 227-3264

Wingate University; phone: (704) 233-8075

NORTH DAKOTA

Dickinson State University; phone: (701) 483-2999

Minot State University; phone: (701) 858-3371

North Dakota State University; phone: (701) 231-7671

University of North Dakota; phone: (701) 777-2127

OHIO

Ashland University; phone: (419) 289-5390

Bowling Green State University; phone: (419) 372-7533

Case Western Reserve University; phone: (216) 368-5230

Cleveland State University; phone: (216) 687-2272

Franciscan University–Steubenville; phone: (740) 283-3771

Kent State University; phone: (330) 672-2360

Marietta College; phone: (740) 376-4794

Miami University; phone: (513) 529-4634

Mount Union College; phone: (330) 823-2494

Muskingum College; phone: (740) 826-8091

Ohio *(continued)*

Oberlin College; phone: (440) 775-8355

Ohio State University; phone: (614) 292-2241

Ohio University–Athens; phone: (740) 593-1616

Ohio University–Zanesville; phone: (740) 588-1510

Ohio Wesleyan University; phone: (740) 368-3145

University of Akron; phone: (330) 972-7084

University of Cincinnati; phone: (513) 556-7173

University of Dayton; phone: (937) 229-3277

University of Toledo; phone: (419) 530-2011

Walsh University; phone: (330) 490-7312

Wright State University–Celina; phone: (419) 586-0315

Wright State University–Dayton; phone: (937) 775-5750

Xavier University–Cincinnati; phone: (513) 745-3531

Youngstown State University; phone: (330) 941-3175

OKLAHOMA

Cameron University; phone: (580) 581-2503

East Central University; phone: (580) 310-5319

Northeastern State University; phone: (918) 456-5511

Northwestern Oklahoma State University; phone: (580) 327-8149

Oklahoma State University–Stillwater; phone: (405) 744-5958

Oklahoma State University–Tulsa; phone: (918) 594-8354

Oral Roberts University; phone: (918) 495-6084

Southern Nazarene University; phone: (405) 491-6323

University of Central Oklahoma; phone: (405) 974-2388

University of Oklahoma; phone: (405) 325-2911

OREGON

Eastern Oregon State College; phone: (541) 962-3833

Lewis and Clark College; phone: (503) 768-7160

Oregon Institute of Technology; phone: (541) 885-1015

Oregon State University; phone: (541) 737-2131

Portland State University; phone: (503) 725-4428

University of Oregon; phone: (541) 346-3230

University of Portland; phone: (503) 943-7135

Western Oregon State University; phone: (503) 838-8483

PENNSYLVANIA

Albright College; phone: (610) 921-7630

Arcadia University; phone: (215) 572-2938

Bloomsburg University of Pennsylvania; phone: (570) 389-4269

Bucknell University; phone: (570) 577-1604

Chestnut Hill College; phone: (215) 248-7077

Duquesne University; phone: (412) 396-6204

East Stroudsburg University; phone: (570) 422-3277

Edinboro University of Pennsylvania; phone: (888) 845-2890

Franklin & Marshall College; phone: (717) 291-4083

Gannon University; phone: (814) 871-7680

Grove City College; phone: (724) 458-3352

Immaculata College; phone: (610) 647-4400

Indiana University of Pennsylvania; phone: (724) 357-2235

La Salle University; phone: (215) 991-3590

Mansfield University of Pennsylvania; phone: (570) 662-4133

Marywood University; phone: (570) 876-5817

Millersville University; phone: (717) 872-3710

Pennsylvania State–Harrisburg; phone: (717) 948-6025

Shippensburg University of Pennsylvania; phone: (717) 477-1123 Ext. 3158

Slippery Rock University of Pennsylvania; phone: (724) 738-2123

Temple University–Harrisburg; phone: (717) 232-6400

Temple University–Philadelphia; phone: (215) 204-8611

The Pennsylvania State University; phone: (814) 865-2191

University of Pittsburgh; phone: (412) 624-6440

University of Pittsburgh–Bradford; phone: (814) 362-7657

Villanova University; phone: (610) 519-4050

Widener University; phone: (610) 499-4176

PUERTO RICO

University of Puerto Rico; phone: (787) 764-0000 Ext. 5683

RHODE ISLAND

Providence College; phone: (401) 865-2247

Rhode Island College; phone: (401) 456-8003

Salve Regina College; phone: (401) 341-2913

SOUTH CAROLINA

Clemson University; phone: (864) 656-0515

Coastal Carolina University; phone: (843) 913-7887

Frances Marion University; phone: (843) 673-9707

Furman University; phone: (864) 294-3031

Morris College; phone: (803) 934-3259

South Carolina State University; phone: (803) 536-7024

Southern Wesleyan University; phone: (864) 639-2453

The Citadel; phone: (803) 953-6799

University of South Carolina–Aiken; phone: (803) 641-3579

University of South Carolina–Beaufort; phone: (843) 208-8029

University of South Carolina–Columbia; phone: (803) 777-2780

University of South Carolina–Salkehatchie; phone: (800) 922-5500

University of South Carolina–Spartanburg; phone: (864) 503-5195

Winthrop University; phone: (803) 323-2233

SOUTH DAKOTA

Augustana College; phone: (605) 274-4127

Northern State University; phone: (605) 626-2530

South Dakota State University; phone: (605) 688-4217

University of South Dakota; phone: (605) 677-5611

TENNESSEE

Austin Peay State University; phone: (931) 221-6269

Church of God Theological Seminary; phone: (423) 478-7036

Cumberland University; phone: (615) 444-2562

Freed-Hardeman University; phone: (901) 989-6060

Lambuth University; phone: (731) 425-3297

Lee University; phone: (423) 614-8415

Middle Tennessee State University; phone: (615) 898-2863

Milligan College; phone: (423) 461-8415

Tennessee State University; phone: (615) 963-7111

Trevecca Nazarene University; phone: (615) 248-1346

Union University; phone: (731) 661-5040

University of Memphis; phone: (901) 678-2428

University of Tennessee–Chattanooga; phone: (423) 425-4288

University of Tennessee–Knoxville; phone: (865) 974-6622

TEXAS

Abilene Christian University; phone: (325) 674-2451

Baylor University; phone: (254) 710-2061

Lamar University; phone: (409) 880-8444

Midwestern State University; phone: (940) 397-4676

Our Lady of the Lake University; phone: (210) 431-3998

Sam Houston State University; phone: (409) 294-1721

Southern Methodist University; phone: (214) 768-2269

Southwestern Baptist Theology Seminary; phone: (817) 923-1921 Ext. 2570

St. Mary's University; phone: (210) 436-3135

Stephen F. Austin State University; phone: (936) 468-2401

Texas A&M University–College Station; phone: (979) 845-4427

Texas A&M University–Kingsville; phone: (361) 593-3303

Texas Christian University; phone: (817) 257-7863

Texas Tech University; phone: (806) 742-3671

University of Houston; phone: (713) 743-5444

University of Houston–Clear Lake; phone: (281) 283-2600

University of Texas–Arlington; phone: (817) 272-2362

University of Texas–Austin; phone: (512) 232-2662

University of Texas–Brownsville; phone: (956) 544-8875

University of Texas–El Paso; phone: (915) 747-5009

University of Texas–Pan American; phone: (956) 316-2457

University of Texas–Tyler; phone: (903) 566-7079

UTAH

Brigham Young University; phone: (801) 422-6147

College of Eastern Utah; phone: (435) 613-5325

Utah *(continued)*

College of Eastern Utah–San Juan; phone: (435) 678-2201 Ext. 171

Dixie College; phone: (435) 652-7696

Southern Utah University; phone: (435) 586-5419

University of Utah; phone: (801) 581-8733

Utah State University–Logan; phone: (801) 797-1004

Weber State University; phone: (801) 626-6803

VERMONT

Castleton State College; phone: (802) 468-1346

Lyndon State College; phone: (802) 626-6497

VIRGINIA

Army Education Center–Fort Belvoir; phone: (703) 805-9270

Averett College/Counseling Center; phone: (804) 791-5624

College of William & Mary; phone: (757) 221-2317

Eastern Mennonite University; phone: (540) 432-4131

Jefferson College of Health Sciences; phone: (540) 985-6971

Liberty University; phone: (434) 582-2385

Lynchburg College; phone: (434) 544-8673

Mary Washington College; phone: (540) 654-1010

Marymount University–Arlington; phone: (703) 284-5960

Marymount University–Sterling; phone: (703) 430-7122

Old Dominion University; phone: (757) 683-3697

Radford University; phone: (540) 831-5214

Regent University; phone: (757) 226-4103

Troy State University–Atlantic Region; phone: (757) 451-8202

Troy State University–Langley AFB; phone: (757) 451-8202

Troy State University–Oceana; phone: (757) 451-8202

Virginia Commonwealth University; phone: (804) 828-6277

Virginia Polytechnic & State University; phone: (540) 231-6557

VIRGIN ISLANDS

University of the Virgin Islands; phone: (340) 692-4156

WASHINGTON

Gonzaga University; phone: (509) 323-4054

Troy State University; phone: (253) 964-0545

University of Washington; phone: (206) 543-1170

Walla Walla College; phone: (509) 527-2147

Western Washington University; phone: (360) 650-3080

WEST VIRGINIA

Marshall University; phone: (304) 696-2777

Marshall University Graduate College; phone: (304) 746-1937

Mountain State University; phone: (304) 929-1333

West Liberty State College; phone: (304) 336-8215

West Virginia University–Carruth Center; phone: (304) 293-3807

West Virginia University–Counseling; phone: (304) 293-4431

West Virginia Wesleyan College; phone: (304) 473-8430

WISCONSIN

Beloit College; phone: (608) 363-2675

Carthage College; phone: (262) 551-5959

Marquette University; phone: (414) 288-7172

Nova Southeastern University; phone: (920) 563-2961

University of Wisconsin–Eau Claire; phone: (715) 836-5522

University of Wisconsin–Green Bay; phone: (920) 465-2163

University of Wisconsin–La Crosse; phone: (608) 785-8073

University of Wisconsin–Milwaukee; phone: (414) 229-4689

University of Wisconsin–Oshkosh; phone: (920) 424-0068

University of Wisconsin–Platteville; phone: (608) 342-1865

University of Wisconsin–Stevens Point; phone: (715) 346-4472

University of Wisconsin–Stout; phone: (715) 232-1211

University of Wisconsin–Superior; phone: (715) 394-8308

University of Wisconsin–Whitewater; phone: (414) 472-5613

UNITED STATES ARMED FORCES

Troy State University–Pacific Region; phone: (732) 793-3000

CANADA

ALBERTA

University of Alberta; phone: (780) 492-7773

University of Calgary; phone: (403) 220-5524

University of Lethbridge; phone: (403) 329-2192

BRITISH COLUMBIA

University of British Columbia; phone: (604) 822-3180

University of Victoria; phone: (250) 721-8341

MANITOBA

University of Manitoba; phone: (204) 474-8593

NEW BRUNSWICK

St. Thomas University; phone: (506) 452-0418

NEWFOUNDLAND

Memorial University–Newfoundland; phone: (709) 737-8874

NOVA SCOTIA

Dalhousie University; phone: (902) 494-2081

ONTARIO

Lakehead University; phone: (807) 343-8498

McMaster University; phone: (905) 525-9140

Queen's University; phone: (613) 533-6004

University of Ottawa; phone: (613) 562-5201

University of Western Ontario; phone: (519) 661-3559

QUEBEC

Concordia University–SGW Campus; phone: (514) 848-3545

SASKATCHEWAN

St. Thomas More College; phone: (306) 244-3821

NOTES

NOTES

Thomson Peterson's
Book Satisfaction Survey

Give Us Your Feedback

Thank you for choosing Thomson Peterson's as your source for personalized solutions for your education and career achievement. Please take a few minutes to answer the following questions. Your answers will go a long way in helping us to produce the most user-friendly and comprehensive resources to meet your individual needs.

When completed, please tear out this page and mail it to us at:

> Editorial Department
> Thomson Peterson's
> 2000 Lenox Drive
> Lawrenceville, NJ 08648

You can also complete this survey online at **www.petersons.com/booksurvey.**

1. **What is the ISBN of the book you have purchased? (The ISBN can be found on the book's back cover in the lower right-hand corner.)** _____

2. **Where did you purchase this book?**
   - ❑ Retailer, such as Barnes & Noble
   - ❑ Online reseller, such as Amazon.com
   - ❑ Petersons.com or Thomson Learning Bookstore
   - ❑ Other (please specify) _____

3. **If you purchased this book on Petersons.com or through the Thomson Learning Bookstore, please rate the following aspects of your online purchasing experience on a scale of 4 to 1 (4 = Excellent and 1 = Poor).**

	4	3	2	1
Comprehensiveness of Peterson's Online Bookstore page	❑	❑	❑	❑
Overall online customer experience	❑	❑	❑	❑

4. **Which category best describes you?**
   - ❑ High school student
   - ❑ Parent of high school student
   - ❑ College student
   - ❑ Graduate/professional student
   - ❑ Returning adult student
   - ❑ Teacher
   - ❑ Counselor
   - ❑ Working professional/military
   - ❑ Other (please specify) _____

5. **Rate your overall satisfaction with this book.**

Extremely Satisfied	Satisfied	Not Satisfied
❑	❑	❑

6. Rate each of the following aspects of this book on a scale of 4 to 1 (4 = Excellent and 1 = Poor).

	4	3	2	1
Comprehensiveness of the information	❑	❑	❑	❑
Accuracy of the information	❑	❑	❑	❑
Usability	❑	❑	❑	❑
Cover design	❑	❑	❑	❑
Book layout	❑	❑	❑	❑
Special features (e.g., CD, flashcards, charts, etc.)	❑	❑	❑	❑
Value for the money	❑	❑	❑	❑

7. This book was recommended by:
❑ Guidance counselor
❑ Parent/guardian
❑ Family member/relative
❑ Friend
❑ Teacher
❑ Not recommended by anyone—I found the book on my own
❑ Other (please specify) _____

8. Would you recommend this book to others?

Yes	Not Sure	No
❑	❑	❑

9. Please provide any additional comments.

_____

_____

_____

_____

_____

Remember, you can tear out this page and mail it to us at:

Editorial Department
Thomson Peterson's
2000 Lenox Drive
Lawrenceville, NJ 08648

or you can complete the survey online at **www.petersons.com/booksurvey.**

Your feedback is important to us at Thomson Peterson's, and we thank you for your time!

If you would like us to keep in touch with you about new products and services, please include your e-mail here: _____